Music Therapy Supervision

Edited by
Michele Forinash

Barcelona
PUBLISHERS

This original book is published and distributed by Barcelona Publishers, 4 White Brook Road, Lower Village, Gilsum, NH 03448

ISBN: 1891278-11-8

First Barcelona Publishers printing February 2001

10 9 7 8 6 5 4 3 2 1

Copyeditor: Cynthia Cloutier
Cover design and layout copyright © 2001 Frank McShane
Cover photograph by Jenny Zatzkin

Printed in the U.S.A.

To my daughters
Adele Forinash Aziz,
Kylene Forinash Aziz,
and
Mariele Forinash Aziz.
You are the light and music of my life.

Acknowledgments

There are many people who have been part of the process of the development of this book. I especially want to thank:

Kenneth Bruscia, for his friendship and encouragement. His mentoring has greatly influenced my continuing professional growth. I am most grateful for his vision, support, and wit.

The authors, for the time and energy they put into this work. Their words are defining supervision in our field. I have learned so much from all of them and without them this book wouldn't exist.

My husband, Mike Aziz, for his support and editorial advice. I am especially grateful for his perseverance and his love of a challenge, both of which turned out to be crucial when faced with some of the technical difficulties.

My mother, Ruth Forinash, and my children, Adele, Kylene, and Mariele, for their support during what must have seemed like a never-ending project.

Lisa Summer, in whose company I first became excited about supervision. Many of the ideas I have about supervision came from hours of brainstorming with her.

Lisa Kynvi, Jenny Zatzkin, and Aaron Lightstone for technical help in the final moments.

My family and friends have supported me over the years. With a thoughtful word or passing idea, many have helped me in sometimes subtle but important ways, thanks to: Joan and George Aziz; Jenny, John, Neall, Alex, and Abigail Caughman; Kyle Forinash; Miriam, Matt, and Jillian Griffith; Caryl-Beth Thomas; Ann Marie Testarmata; John, Lin, Nick, and Marina Zoeller Richie; Kenneth Aigen; Rick, Leslie, Derrick, and Amelia Amodei; Karen Wacks; Colin Lee; Kimberly Khare; Dorit Amir; Laurie Farnan; Barbara Hesser; Christine Routhier; Alan, Ann, and Max Turry; John and Rose Richie; Lisa, Andey, and Joa Kynvi; Barbara, Patrick, and Ethan Calhoun; my colleagues in the Massachusetts Music Therapy Alliance, the American Music Therapy Association and the Expressive Therapies Division of Lesley University; and especially "Chief."

I also want to thank the many children in my life, especially those mentioned above, for always reminding me—even when I didn't feel like it—to play, draw, dance, sing, and dream.

Contents

Part One
Literature, Ethics, and Multicultural Approaches

Part Two
Preprofessional Supervision

Part Three
Professional Supervision

Part Four
Institute Supervision

Contributors

Dorit Amir, DA, ACMT, has been the head of the music therapy program at Bar Ilan University in Ramat-Gan, Israel, since 1982. She has worked with a rich variety of populations, and has supervised both students and professional music therapists on all levels both in Israel and in the U.S. Amir is the author of the new book *Meeting the Sounds: Music Therapy Practice, Theory and Research,* published in 1999 in Israel, in the Hebrew language. Address: Bar Ilan University, Ramat-Gan, Israel. E-mail: amir@mail.biu.ac.il.

Diane Austin, MA, ACMT, is an analytically-oriented music therapist with a private practice in Brooklyn Heights, New York. She teaches vocal improvisation, leads music therapy groups, and supervises students in the music therapy department at New York University. She is director of the music therapy program for adolescents in foster care at Turtle Bay Music School in Manhattan. She is a member of the Clinical Practice Commission for the Music Therapy World Federation. She has authored numerous articles and chapters on music psychotherapy, and has lectured and conducted workshops throughout the world. Austin is currently completing her doctorate in music therapy at New York University. Address: 28 Willow Street, Brooklyn, NY 11201. Telephone: 718-722-7910. E-mail: music@themystery.com.

Elizabeth Baratta, MA, is an expressive therapist working with adults with mental illness at Crossroads, a program of May Behavioral Health in Cambridge, Massachusetts. Since starting at Crossroads as an intern in 1998, Baratta has incorporated music, art, and movement into her work helping others stabilize their illnesses and reach their personal goals. Address: The May Institute, Inc., Behavioral Health Services, 780 American Legion Highway, Boston, MA 02131.

Michael Bertolami, MA, MT-BC, is a music therapist at Perkins School for the Blind in Watertown, Massachusetts. In addition to his work with multihandicapped, visually impaired children, Bertolami also provides music therapy services to developmentally disabled adults at several day treatment programs and group homes in the Boston area. Address: Perkins School for the Blind, 175 No. Beacon St., Watertown, MA 02472. E-mail: Mbert@gis.net.

Kenneth Bruscia, PhD, MT-BC, is professor of music therapy at Temple University in Philadelphia, Pennsylvania, where he has taught for twenty-five years. He is certified to practice Guided Imagery and Music (GIM), and is endorsed as a primary trainer. He has several years of clinical experience with a wide range of clienteles and has authored several books and articles. Address: Temple University, Esther Boyer College of Music, Philadelphia, PA 19122. Telephone: 215-204-8542.

Cheryl Dileo, PhD, MT-BC, is professor of music therapy at Temple University in Philadelphia, Pennsylvania. She is the immediate past president of the World Federation of Music Therapy, past president of the National Association for Music

Therapy, and has served in many leadership positions for these and other organizations during the past twenty-five years. She is the author/editor of nine books and over seventy chapters and articles on music therapy; her specialties include medical music therapy, professional ethics, and music therapy education and training. Dileo is a consulting editor for the *Journal of Music Therapy, The International Journal of Arts Medicine,* and *The Arts in Psychotherapy.* She is a frequent international lecturer, having taught in seventeen countries on five continents. Address: Temple University, Esther Boyer College of Music, Philadelphia, PA 19122. Telephone: 215-204-8542.

Janice M. Dvorkin, PsyD, ACMT, is assistant professor and the coordinator of music therapy at the University of the Incarnate Word in San Antonio, Texas. She has a practice in music psychotherapy, and provides clinical services as a music therapist and licensed psychologist. Dvorkin is currently serving on the Assembly of Delegates of the AMTA and is the vice president of the Southwestern region. She has practiced as a music therapist for over twenty years and has provided clinical supervision for twelve years. She has published her work in numerous books and journals, and has presented her work to music therapists and other health professionals nationally and internationally. Dvorkin has presented workshops describing her work as therapist and supervisor using her theoretical model of "Object Relations Music Therapy." She is presently writing two books addressing the use of this theory of music psychotherapy. Address: University of the Incarnate Word, San Antonio, TX 78209. E-mail: dvorkin@universe.uiwtx.edu.

Karen Estrella, MA, MT-BC, ATR-BC, LMHC, is assistant professor of expressive therapies at Lesley University in Cambridge, Massachusetts. She is completing her doctoral work in clinical psychology at The Fielding Institute. She has over fifteen years' experience practicing music therapy, expressive therapies, and mental health counseling, primarily in community-based mental health programs with a variety of people from a multiplicity of cultural backgrounds. Estrella's interest in multiculturalism and supervision comes directly from her clinical experiences in urban settings, and from her current practice as therapist and supervisor in private practice. Address: Lesley University, Division of Expressive Therapies, 29 Everett Street, Cambridge, MA 02143. E-mail: kestrella@mail.lesley.edu.

Laurie A. Farnan, MMT, MT-BC, has coordinated the music therapy program at the Central Wisconsin Center for the Developmentally Disabled in Madison, Wisconsin, since 1975 and the clinical training program for music therapy interns since 1980. She is the co-author of *Music Is for Everyone*, and *Everyone Can Move.* She authored a column on "Issues in Clinical Training" for *Music Therapy Perspectives* for seven years as well as served on the editorial board. She has authored numerous chapters and articles on clinical techniques with people with profound mental retardation and complex developmental disabilities. She has served on state, regional, and national levels in NAMT and AMTA, including the Clinical Training Committee, the Assembly of Delegates, and the AMTA Commission on Education and Clinical

Training. Address: Central Wisconsin Center for the Developmentally Disabled, Madison, WI 53704. Telephone: 608-243-2295. E-mail: farnala@DHFS.state.wi.us.

Susan Feiner, MA, MT-BC, CSW is the associate director of the music therapy program at New York University in New York City. She has over twenty years of experience in clinical music therapy and supervision. In addition to her work at New York University, she maintains a private practice in music psychotherapy, supervision and guided imagery and music. Feiner has presented at numerous conferences and teaches workshops on music therapy supervision. Address: New York University, Music Therapy Program, Department of Music and Performing Arts Professions, 35 West Fourth Street, New York, NY 10012. Telephone: 212-998-5452. E-mail: sf24@nyu.edu.

Michele Forinash, DA, MT-BC, LMHC, is assistant professor and coordinator of the music therapy specialization in the Division of Expressive Therapies at Lesley University in Cambridge, Massachusetts. She is currently vice president of the American Music Therapy Association. Forinash has published several articles and chapters on qualitative research in music therapy. Address: Lesley University, Division of Expressive Therapies, 29 Everett Street, Cambridge, MA 02143. E-mail: mforinas@mail.lesley.edu.

Isabelle Frohne-Hagemann, PhD, was born in Hamburg, Germany, and has lived in Berlin since 1992. She has studied in various fields including education, music, medicine, psychotherapy, and supervision. Since 1984 she has been the head of the postgraduate training course "Integrative Music Therapy" at the European Academy for Psychosocial Health, Fritz Perls Institute in Hückeswagen, Germany. She is a qualified integrative music therapist, psychotherapist and supervisor. She worked as an assistant professor from 1975 to 1990 at the Academy of Music in Hamburg. Frohne-Hagemann has contributed to over seventy-five publications dealing with theoretical and practical themes in music therapy. At present she is studying Guided Imagery and Music at the Mid-Atlantic Training Institute. Address: Rathenower Str. 29, D-12305 Berlin, Germany. E-mail: ifrone@aol.com.

Suzanne B. Hanser, EdD, MT-BC, chairs the music therapy department at Berklee College of Music in Boston, Massachusetts, and is a lecturer in the Department of Social Medicine at Harvard Medical School. She is past president of the National Association for Music Therapy. Hanser received a National Research Service Award from the National Institute on Aging and was a senior postdoctoral fellow at Stanford University School of Medicine. Hanser is the author of *The New Music Therapist's Handbook* along with numerous book chapters and articles. She has served on the Scientific Advisory Board of the World Congress for Music Therapy and has presented at many international conferences. Address: Berklee College of Music, Boston, MA 02215. Telephone: 617-747-2639. E-mail: shanser@berklee.edu.

Andrew Hubbard, MA, CMT, has been a music therapist for over ten years and recently completed his graduate education in expressive therapies. He works with an adult psychiatric population in day treatment. Address: Riverside Community Care/Blackstone Valley Day Treatment and Outpatient Center, 206 Milford Street, Upton, MA 01568. Telephone: 508-529-7000.

Mechtild Jahn-Langenberg, PhD, Dipl.-Musiktherapeutin has been the director of the music therapy department at the University of the Arts, Berlin, Seminar Musiktherapie (postgraduate program, master's degree) since 1995. She has specialized in analytical music therapy with psychosomatic patients (children and adults), qualitative research, and has initiated international symposia since 1994 with this focus. In addition to teaching and training she has a private practice as an analytical music therapist and supervisor. Address: Hochschule der Künste, Berlin Fakultät Musik/Seminar Musiktherapie Mierendorffstr. 30 10589 Berlin, Germany. Telephone: 030-3185-2552 (2553). E-mail: langenmu@hdk-berlin.de.

Kimberly Khare, MA, CMT, NRMT, is director of music therapy at the Community Music Center of Boston and adjunct faculty at Lesley University in Cambridge, Massachusetts. She completed her music therapy training at New York University and her Nordoff-Robbins certification at the Nordoff-Robbins Center at New York University. Address: Community Music Center of Boston, 34 Warren Ave., Boston, MA, 02116. E-mail: therapists@cmcb.org.

Colin Lee, PhD, RMTh, MTA, is the director of the music therapy program at Wilfrid Laurier University in Waterloo, Canada. He has extensive clinical and supervisory experience and is an active researcher in the areas of palliative care, the analysis of clinical improvisation, and autism. He has authored *Art and Music: Therapy and Research, Lonely Waters,* and *Music at the Edge: The music therapy experiences of a musician with AIDS* along with numerous articles on music therapy. He has developed a theory of Aesthetic Music Therapy which will be published in 2002. Address: Wilfrid Laurier University Music Therapy Program, Waterloo, Canada. E-mail clee@wlu.ca.

Frances J. McClain, PhD, MT-BC, is the director of music therapy at Queens College in Charlotte, North Carolina. Throughout her career, she has worked with various clinical populations, ranging from young children with special needs to the elderly. She has written articles, served as a consultant, and presented workshops throughout the Southeast and in Taiwan. She has received outstanding teaching awards from Queens College and an award for outstanding achievements in professional practice from the Southeastern Region of the National Association for Music Therapy. Address: Queens College, Charlotte, NC 28274. Telephone: 704-337-2301.

Mary-Carla MacDonald, MA, MT-BC, is assistant professor in the music therapy department at Anna Maria College in Paxton, Massachusetts. Originally from Prince Edward Island, Canada she moved to the Boston area several years ago to pursue graduate training. MacDonald has worked at a variety of facilitates including the Massachusetts Hospital School and McLean Psychiatric Hospital. Address: Music

Therapy Department, Anna Maria College, Box 45 Paxton, MA 01612. Telephone: 508-849-3464. E-mail: mmacdonald@annamaria.edu.

Benedikte B. Scheiby, MA, MMEd, DPMtp, CMT, was born in Denmark. She studied with Mary Priestley and in 1980, together with Inge N. Pedersen, established a music therapy training program at Aalborg University. Since 1991 she has been working as an adjunct faculty member in the music therapy program at New York University and in the art therapy program at Pratt Institute, Brooklyn, New York. Since 1996 she has been working as a Music Therapy Supervisor at Beth Abraham Hospital in New York. Scheiby maintains a private practice, a supervision practice, and has developed a postgraduate Analytical Music Therapy Institute. She has written and presented extensively on AMT. Address: 50 Hudson St., Hastings-on-Hudson, NY 10706. Telephone: 914-478-5362.

Trudy Shulman-Fagen, MA, MT-BC, LMHC, is adjunct faculty at Lesley University in Cambridge, Massachusetts, and maintains a private practice. She has been working over the past twenty years with a focus on anxiety disorders, trauma, and serious physical illness as well as in student training and supervision. She integrates hypnosis and archetypal imagery into her music therapy practice as well as additional forms of arts modality and meditation. Shulman-Fagen continues to raise her three daughters while exploring new avenues of music, spiritual practice, and arts therapies to facilitate healing and growth. Address: 30 Lincoln St., Newton Highlands, MA 02461. Telephone: 617-964-2551. E-mail: Tshulfagen@aol.com.

Deborah Spragg, MA, returned to graduate school to study expressive arts therapies after having completed her PhD in music composition. She is currently a group therapist at Wild Acre Inns, a system of residential treatment facilities in Boston, Massachusetts. She works with both chronically mentally ill clients and those who are transitioning back to their communities. Address: Lincoln, Massachusetts E-mail: dspragg@worldnet.att.net.

Gillian Stephens Langdon, MA, is the director of creative arts therapies at the Bronx Psychiatric Center where she has been a music therapist and intern supervisor for over twenty-eight years. She has written various articles and chapters on music therapy and music therapy supervision. She was active in the American Association for Music Therapy as a member of the board of directors and founder and chair of the Publications Committee. She has presented at conferences on music therapy supervision built from her experience as a music therapist with adult inpatient psychiatric clients, young adult in- and outpatient programs, and from her experience in individual and group supervision and private practice. Address: Bronx Psychiatric Center, Department of Creative Arts Therapies, 1500 Waters Place, Bronx, NY 10461. Telephone: 718-931-0600 x2813.

Brynjulf Stige, is associate professor in music therapy at Sogn og Fjordane College in Sandane, Norway and at the University of Oslo, Norway. He has worked for five years as a music therapist with a cultural, socioecological, and community-based approach before he, in 1988 became the first coordinator of the music therapy training in western Norway. Stige has published articles and books on music education and music therapy. He is currently a research fellow at the University of Oslo, studying meaning making in individual music therapy with psychiatric clients. He is also the editor-in-chief of the *Nordic Journal of Music Therapy*. Address: Sogn og Fjordane College, Studiesenter Sandane, 6823 Sandane, Norway. Telephone: +47 57 86 68 12. E-mail: brynjulf.stige@hisf.no.

Lisa Summer, MCAT, MT-BC has taught at Anna Maria College for five years where she serves as associate professor/director of music therapy and chair of the Division of Human Behavior and Human Services. She has chronicled her clinical use of classical music and imagery in group and individual music psychotherapy in a monograph, *Guided Imagery and Music (GIM) in the Institutional Setting*, as well as several textbook chapters and articles. She is author of a critical survey of music healers, *Music: The New Age Elixir*, with her opera composer, husband. Address: Anna Maria College, Box, 45 Paxton, MA 01612. E-mail: Lsummer@annamaria.edu.

Caryl-Beth Thomas, MA, ACMT, LMHC, is adjunct faculty at Lesley University in Cambridge, Massachusetts, and at Northeastern University in Boston, Massachusetts. She is clinical training director and a staff music therapist for the Community Music Center of Boston, working with a variety of populations and age groups. Serving the professional community of music therapy for many years, she is currently vice president of the New England Region of AMTA, and was a member of the Education and Clinical Training Commission of AMTA. Address: 27 Weston St., Hyde Park, MA 02136. E-mail: Cbethomas@aol.com

Alan Turry, MA, MT-BC, NRMT, is co-director of the Nordoff-Robbins Center for Music Therapy at New York University. A certified instructor in Nordoff-Robbins music therapy, he coordinates the training program and is director of clinical services. Active as a music therapist since 1981, he has taught both nationally and internationally. Turry teaches clinical improvisation in the New York University master's program and is currently a doctoral student at the university. Address: Nordoff-Robbins Center for Music Therapy, New York University, New York, NY 10003. E-mail: at8@is6.nyu.edu.

Madelaine Ventre, MS, MT-BC, FAMI, is director of the Creative Therapies Institute, an AMI (Association for Music and Imagery) fellow and primary trainer, and an ATMA (Association for Teachers of Mandala Assessment) approved instructor. She has been a clinician for over thirty years and in private practice in GIM for over twenty years. Ventre has been a visiting specialist at Montclair State University since 1978 and an adjunct faculty member at New York University since 1981, when she instituted the first university training in GIM. She has trained GIM students nationally and internationally. Ventre has published in professional journals and books and presented at national and international conferences. Address: Center for Creative Therapies and the Arts, 1107 Plank Rd. Forestburgh, NY 12777. Telephone: 845 796-2554. E-mail: mv7@is9.nyu.edu.

Chapter 1

Overview

Michele Forinash, DA, MT-BC, LMHC
Assistant Professor, Coordinator of Music Therapy
Lesley University
Cambridge, MA

Introduction

When I accepted the first music therapy intern at my clinical site in 1985, I began my journey as a music therapy supervisor and began thinking about supervision and working on my skills and identity as a supervisor. I frequently felt at a loss as a supervisor and often struggled to find the "best" way to supervise any given student. In more recent years I have begun supervising supervisors and helping them in their process of development. Once again I was facing new territory that I didn't fully understand. My inquiry into supervision took a more determined tone in 1996, as my colleague Lisa Summer and I began meeting together to discuss teaching and supervision and began to formulate basic assumptions and questions about supervision. It was no surprise then, that when asked by my colleague Ken Bruscia in the winter of 1998 what topic I felt needed to be addressed in the music therapy literature, my answer was immediate—supervision.

What is supervision anyway? For some, supervision simply means the process of addressing management issues such as how to create schedules, how to organize staff or interns, or how to build employee morale. While that is part of what supervisors do, there are many more layers to supervision.

The focus of the supervision relationship is to address the complexities involved in helping supervisees in their ongoing (and never-ending) development as competent and compassionate professionals. Supervision is a relationship, one in which both supervisor and supervisee actively participate and interact. It is a process of unfolding—not simply following a recipe, but engaging in a rich and dynamic relationship. Supervision then is also a journey, or odyssey of sorts, in which supervisor and supervisee learn and grow and from which both will very likely leave transformed in some way. While personal growth is not the focus of supervision, it is a common by-product for both participants. Supervisors are not expert, all-knowing, omnipotent beings, and likewise supervisees are not simply blank slates upon which to download the correct manner of working as music therapists. Both are complex individuals who bring their unique perspectives and multiple levels of experience to the relationship and to the understanding of music therapy. As no two supervisors are identical or supervise in the same way, no two interns develop in exactly the same way. Rather than having a map with specific directions to guide us as supervisors, we have signposts that give us some indication of the direction we are heading without necessarily predicting the bumps and turns we might encounter. Supervision, then, is also a challenge—of learning how and when to use our various tools to aid in the development of each supervisee, whether they are new students, practicing professionals, or those pursuing advanced institute training.

As part of our continuing development as supervisors, Lisa and I began presenting on supervision at regional and national music therapy conferences and at my university as part of a series on supervision. We didn't see ourselves as experts on music therapy supervision; instead we came to the topic with shared philosophical questions about supervision. We called these shared questions *dilemmas,* for we were driven to study and further understand supervision because we were faced with supervision situations for which we had only questions, not answers. As music therapy educators, our interest in supervision made sense: we function as overall supervisors for our students, we oversee students' onsite supervisors and students' university academic supervisors. We know that their successes as music therapists and their longevity in the field are directly impacted by supervision experiences both as students and as professionals.

The dilemmas about supervision that Lisa and I first shared have continued to be a driving force in my exploration of this topic. As an academician involved in preprofessional supervision, I have thought a lot about how best to supervise and oversee the development of those seeking their first credential. As a music therapist for twenty years, I have thought about the importance of articulating supervision strategies and approaches so professionals continue their growth and development in the field, as well as become supervisors themselves.

An initial dilemma Lisa and I faced was the realization that many people, whether supervising students or professionals, begin their supervisory experience from a reactive stance. Given that few supervisors have had specific training in supervision, this first stance is often a reaction to what one has previously experienced as supervisee. Supervision that one received as a preprofessional that was useful or helpful most likely led to a supervision approach where one attempted to emulate his/her previous supervisor. In the same vein, initial supervision that was felt to be ineffectual tended to create a supervision approach that was opposite or dramatically different to one's initial supervision experience.

A dilemma that became apparent in our reflections on student supervision was of the concept of, as Lisa stated, the "music therapy child." Borrowing directly from the Nordoff-Robbins concept of the "music child" (1977, p. iv), the music therapy child is the competent music therapist that we believe our students can become. As therapists, we are drawn to nurture this not-yet-actualized being. We long to provide opportunities for the natural growth and development of our students as clinicians. However, we are confronted with the reality of the academic year in which we live. We can't always wait for the natural unfolding of this music therapy child and are often unable to let students blossom at their own pace. Our on-site and off-site supervisors share this dilemma and our task becomes one of reconciling these two contradictory impulses that we embody.

Another dilemma we discussed was whether we, as supervisors, should attempt to clone ourselves in our supervisees. Is supervision simply teaching our supervisees how to emulate us as music therapists? Do we expect them to become copies of us with our attitudes and biases, or conversely are we there to help supervisees find their own unique "voices" as therapists, much as a garden trellis supports the growing and blooming flowers?

Lisa and I also discussed how we choose our interventions in supervision. If a student has skill areas that need to be addressed, do we use an action-oriented approach and teach the necessary skills? If the supervision issue is based on the student's unconscious processes do we use an insight-oriented approach? What factors enter into our decisions about how to intervene?

Building on the previous dilemma we were faced with the question of how to deal with the supervisee's personal issues in supervision. At some point, personal issues will surface for those in supervision. How do we determine whether, when and how to address such issues? If we choose to address them, how is it best to do so? Where do we draw the line between supervision and therapy? Are there different issues to consider depending on whether the supervisee is a student, a new professional, or a professional seeking advanced training?

Given that we are an arts-based therapy, a dilemma arises around how to integrate music and the arts into the practice of supervision. As in therapy practice, how do we find the balance between words and music? How do the arts work for us in supervision? In using the arts in supervision, are we modeling for our supervisees our belief in the power of arts processes? Is it important to do this? What are the unique perspectives that an arts-based supervision approach can bring?

Having articulated some of the dilemmas, one might expect to find the answers to these questions in this text. But this text does not contain exact recipes for how to supervise, nor does it give absolute answers to many of the questions that have been raised. It does, however, provide ideas, frameworks, structures, and techniques one can use in supervision. The reader is encouraged to approach this text as a resource for ideas about supervision.

Throughout the book the reader will find supervision approaches and strategies that are very different from each other and may, in fact, at times seem contradictory to each other. As the field is comprised of different theoretical and philosophical approaches to practicing music therapy, there are as many diverse ways to supervise. Readers will likely find supervision strategies with which they resonate and would feel comfortable implementing, as well as approaches that may seem quite new and different from their current approach. It is my hope that readers will use this text to inform their own philosophies about supervision, generate their own questions, and determine whether and how the ideas presented might apply to their own experience and development as music therapy supervisors.

Outline

Part One
Literature, Ethics, and Multicultural Issues

Part One provides an overview of issues that exist across all types of music therapy supervision. McClain's provides a literature review (Chapter 2), which addresses what has been written about both preprofessional and professional supervision. The review of the preprofessional supervision is largely limited to music therapy training in the United States.

Supervisory relationships, like therapy relationships, are often complex and intricate, and Dileo (Chapter 3) discusses the role of ethics in the supervisory relationship and offers clear guidelines for maintaining appropriate relationships and ethical standards. Estrella (Chapter 4) examines the impact of multiculturalism on our field. She clearly articulates the significance of the issues involved, and also offers competencies in multicultural counseling that must be integrated into our profession.

Part Two
Preprofessional Supervision

There is great diversity in music therapy training worldwide–in the U.S. alone entry-level training can be pursued on the undergraduate or graduate level. Thus, determining how best to describe the person who is seeking their credential in music therapy was no easy task. In fact, an entire book could be devoted to the various approaches to training throughout the world, not to mention on the specifics of supervising in each of the approaches! The term preprofessional was chose to refer to those who do not yet have a credential in music therapy and it was chosen over student, intern, or practicum student to more fully encompass the diversity.

Preprofessional supervisors are the backbone of our profession. They are the ones who provide our students with hands-on clinical experience that has been shown to be so beneficial and necessary for one's professional development. Consequently, this part of the book provides specific frameworks for understanding the supervisory relationship and the developmental processes that occur in clinical placements, and provides diverse strategies for supervising the preprofessional.

Summer (Chapter 5) and Hanser (Chapter 6) present different approaches to practicum supervision. As Summer points out, the practicum is often the crucible for a music therapy student: it is when a student's potential in the field is determined. These chapters define the specific beginning tasks of the practicum student and supervision strategies for working with these initial issues.

Feiner (Chapter 7), Farnan (Chapter 8), and Thomas (Chapter 9) are devoted to individual internship supervision. The authors provide different descriptions of the developmental stages of internship and a delineation of how the competencies currently used in the field can be addressed during the course of internship. The authors include vignettes that demonstrate their different theoretical approaches as supervisors. Shulman-Fagen (Chapter 10) presents off-site, group internship supervision and how the arts can be integrated into this. Stige (Chapter 11) writing about his experiences as a preprofessional supervisor in Norway, focuses on how to nurture the development of the supervisory personality in the preprofessional. This chapter provides ideas for those trying to develop music therapy training programs in areas where there may not be many music therapy supervisors available.

Part Three
Professional Supervision

Years ago most music therapists finished their internships and never again received supervision. Some felt that after receiving their entry-level credential, they had learned all there was to know about music therapy. In recent years this attitude has begun to change. As the breadth and depth of our field continues to develop, professionals are realizing the critical need to continue their development as clinicians. Rather than seeking supervision from professionals outside of the field of music therapy, they are continuing their ongoing development by working with supervisors who are music therapists—those who intimately understand the transformative experience of creative exploration though music and the arts. What this implies, though is the critical importance of training competent music therapy supervisors.

Part Three, consequently, addresses many of the varied supervision needs of music therapy professionals. We begin to see the specialization of types of professional supervision. Baratta, Bertolami, Hubbard, MacDonald, and Spragg (Chapter 12) discuss peer supervision and the role it can play in the transition from student to professional. Amir (Chapter 13) discusses supervision of new music therapy professionals working in educational settings in Israel. Stephens Langdon (Chapter 14) discusses the music based, experiential group supervision format. Austin and Dvorkin (Chapter 15) discuss the role of peer supervision for advanced professionals. Specific approaches to supervision such as Frohne-Hagemann's integrative approach (Chapter 16), Lee and Khare's music-centered approach, (Chapter 17), and Jahn-Langenberg's psychodynamic perspective (Chapter 18) are also addressed.

As there are now growing numbers of doctoral programs in music and expressive therapies, there are consequently more opportunities for an examination of the parallel process of supervising doctoral students who are supervising preprofessionals (Bruscia, Chapter 19).

Part Four
Supervision in Institute Training

In recent years there has been a growing trend to articulate and define specific approaches to advanced training in music therapy. This is defined here as Institute Training, and refers to advanced and specialized study in music therapy that usually occurs after the completion of a graduate (master's) degree and leads toward an advanced professional designation.

Three models of music therapy are included in this section. Scheiby (Chapter 20) discusses supervision in Analytical Music Therapy as developed by Mary Priestley, which leads to the Analytical Music Therapist (AMT) designation. Ventre (Chapter 21) illustrates supervision in the Bonny Method of Guided Imagery and Music, which leads to the Fellow of the Association of Music and Imagery (FAMI) designation. Turry (Chapter 22) articulates supervision in Nordoff-Robbins Music Therapy, which leads to the Nordoff-Robbins Music Therapist (NRMT) designation.

Conclusion

The further investigation of supervision, the appropriate training of supervisors, and the understanding of the role of supervision in preprofessional training, in continuing professional development, and in institute training are critical for the continued development of the field of music therapy. By beginning the process of formally articulating and sharing our philosophies of supervision, we can expand the breadth and depth of knowledge in our field and greatly impact our growing profession.

Reference

Nordoff, P., and Robbins, C. (1977). *Creative Music Therapy.* New York: John Day Company.

Part One

**Literature, Ethics,
and
Multicultural Approaches**

Chapter 2

Music Therapy Supervision:
A Review of the Literature

Frances J. McClain, PhD, MT-BC
Director of Music Therapy
Queens College, Charlotte, NC

This review of the literature is divided into two sections. The first is supervision in preprofessional training. This addresses training that leads to the entry-level credential in the field. The second section is supervision in professional training and includes those pursuing clinical supervision as a professional.

Preprofessional Supervision

In the United States preprofessional training includes preinternship and internship experiences which provide a continuum of training during and sometimes after coursework. Throughout the literature, several terms are used synonymously for preinternship, including practicum, fieldwork, or practical experience. In this discussion, the term preinternship will be used to refer to any series of clinical placements which occur throughout academic coursework and before the internship. While the structure and experiences of preinternship and internship have important distinctions, both seek to integrate academic theory and clinical practice (Bruscia, 1987; Hanser, 1987). From the first preinternship experience to the completion of the internship, supervision is a critical component.

Throughout the literature, supervision is a comprehensive term for a concept that includes teaching, modeling, observing, shaping, coaching, and evaluating the skills and behaviors of students. Supervision is integral to both preinternship and internship, although the methods and amount of time vary in each. While internships are generally clearly defined and structured, this may not always be true for preinternships. Early and on-going concerns of educators, clinicians, and students have been the lack of adequate preinternship training and supervision (Alley, 1978; Braswell, Decuir, and Brooks, 1985; Braswell, Maranto and Decuir, 1979 and 1980; Galloway, 1966; Gault, 1978; Graham, 1971; Madsen, 1965; Maranto, 1987 and 1989; Steele, 1989; Tims, 1989). Certainly in preinternship training, students want to be observed, but equally important, they also want to observe music therapists (McClain, 1993). While it has not always been possible in the past to have a music therapist as supervisor, two alternatives have been considered. One involves supervision and experiential learning through practicum classes and seminars (Bruscia, 1987; Hanser, 1980; Krout, 1982; Tims, 1989). Another method uses advanced undergraduate students as supervisors/proctors and coaches (Hanser, 1978; Prickett, 1987).

As with preinternship, there is also a need to improve supervision during the internship. This and other related topics were discussed by supervisors, students, and clinicians in the column "Issues in Clinical Training" in *Music Therapy Perspectives*. As author of the column, Farnan called for greater utilization of different management styles (1994) and closer coordination and communication between intern and supervisor (1996).

Within the unified American Music Therapy Association (AMTA), the former National Association for Music Therapy (NAMT) and the former American Association for Music Therapy (AAMT) models specify guidelines for supervision, although implementation varies. The AAMT model stipulates daily supervision by a qualified professional at the clinical site and continual supervision by music therapy faculty. Each degree program establishes its own minimum qualification requirements for clinical supervisors (AAMT Educational Guidelines). The NAMT model stipulates that each intern is entitled to one hour of individual consultation per week with the supervisor and an average of four hours per week of observation and constructive feedback with the supervisor. While group supervision is encouraged, it cannot substitute for individual consultation (NAMT Clinical Training Guidelines). Neither model is limited to just the supervision cited. Rather, supervision extends to all phases of the internship, in both formal and informal ways.

Primary roles of a supervisor involve modeling, facilitating, and evaluating certain skills and abilities known as competencies. The topic of professional competencies has been the focus of much research and has served as one of the driving forces to replace curriculum-based with competency-based education. Throughout the literature, competencies can generally be grouped into four categories: 1) academic/theoretical; 2) clinical/music therapy; 3) music; and 4) personal. The latter three are more frequently associated with preinternship and internship experiences. Studies involving clinical training have dealt with competencies best learned in preinternship, those most needed for successful internship, those acquired during internship, and those needed by entry-level professionals (Alley, 1978; Boyle and Krout, 1988; Braswell, Decuir, and Brooks, 1985; Braswell, Decuir, and Maranto, 1980; Brookins, 1984; Bruscia and Maranto, 1988; Bruscia, Hesser, and Boxill 1981; Cassity, 1987; Darrow and Gibbons, 1987; Decuir and Jacobs, 1990; Hanser and Furman, 1980; Jensen and McKinney, 1990; Kim, 1990; Maranto, 1988; Petrie, 1989; Standley, 1985; Taylor, 1987; Ten Eyck, 1985; Wright, 1992).

While it is true that certain settings may be more appropriate to gain certain types of competencies, it is also important to view competencies as a continuum of skills. For in reality, a competency may be introduced in the classroom, practiced in a preinternship setting, and refined during the internship.

Whether in preinternship training or clinical internship, supervision can involve a variety of methods and techniques. Bruscia and Maranto (1988) found that supervisors preferred observation and feedback most, followed by supervisory conferences or discussions, modeling, and written or form evaluations. In addition, videotaping has been examined as a method of feedback. Throughout the literature, studies have investigated self-analysis versus instructor analysis (Greenfield, 1978), subjective versus objective analysis (Alley, 1980; Madsen and Alley, 1979) immediate or live feedback versus videotape analysis (Anderson, 1982; Hanser and Furman, 1980), and visual feedback (Greenfield, 1980) versus audio-cueing (Adamek, 1994; Furman, Adamek and Furman, 1992). All of these studies validate the importance of some type of feedback and perhaps concur with Killian (1981) that it is the presence, rather than the type of feedback, that is most significant.

As methods of feedback vary, so do approaches to supervision. There are several theoretical models of supervision from other disciplines that are applicable to music therapy. Some of them are based on a developmental model because students are seen as going through various stages or levels of growth. The supervisor is aware that his/her role will change as the needs, preferences, and competencies of interns change (Memory, Unkefer, and Smeltekop, 1987; Stephens, 1987). A developmental progression extends beyond growth in academic, clinical, and music competencies; it also relates to personal growth as well. Feelings of students, including distress and burnout, have been examined (Glider, 1987). Madsen and Kaiser (1999) examined fears of preintern students while Grant and McCarty (1990) studied the emotional stages of interns during each month of internship. Interestingly, some of the fears of the preinterns were similar to those expressed by interns in the early months of the internship. By understanding these feelings, supervisors can help interns make a smoother transition into their new setting.

Clinical training is an interactional process that involves the professional rights and responsibilities of students and supervisors. In order for students to demonstrate ethical behavior in relating to supervisors, clients, and staff, more emphasis must be placed on teaching ethics in classroom and clinical settings (Maranto and Wheeler, 1986). Chapter 3 of this book provides a thorough discussion of ethical issues. Equally important, educators and supervisors must demonstrate ethical behavior through cooperative efforts, competent supervision, fair grading and input, and safeguards in videotaping (Hadsell and Jones, 1988; Maranto, 1987c). In addition, students have the right to clearly defined expectations, a good role model, regular feedback, clearly defined problem areas and ways for remediation, and respect from the staff. Likewise, students also have the responsibilities to appear, act, and communicate as professionals, have a good attitude, accept and give feedback, be on time, honor deadlines, and report concerns and problems (Beck, MacLean, and Pinson, 1986).

Discussion advocating change and flexibility in internships have been ongoing (Boone, 1989; Briggs, 1987; Bruscia, 1987; Gaston, 1964; Graham, 1971; Maranto, 1989; Standley, 1989). With unification and growth of the music therapy profession, the call has intensified. The NAMT and AAMT models of internship represent but two of several types in related therapies. In examining the models for art, dance, occupational, physical therapies, and therapeutic recreation, Farnan (1998) suggests the need to be more flexible in the way music therapy internship sites are set up, approved, and maintained. The Experimental Internship model, designed as a onetime clinical program for a single intern, is an example of such flexibility (Niles, 1996). It can allow an intern to work under multiple supervisors in multiple facilities. Other approaches emphasize the need to expand beyond traditional Western models. In order to establish a global perspective, Marks (1992) advocates providing international internships. To accommodate national diversity, Moreno (1988) and Troppozada (1995) cite the need for more multicultural training to work with clients of different ethnic and cultural backgrounds. Since many music therapy curricula do not offer such training, the internship may be the first time students are exposed to ethnically diverse clients and music (see Chapter 4 for a complete discussion of multicultural issues). Clinical supervisors, therefore, may have a unique opportunity to add yet another dimension to the training of interns.

Once an intern has completed clinical training and entered the profession, the therapist may have a greater appreciation and need for advanced supervision.

Professional Supervision

The phenomenal growth of music therapy necessitates more advanced clinical training. Music therapists want and need professional supervision because more clinicians are: 1) seeking graduate degrees, continuing education, or postgraduate institute training; 2) exploring new areas and models of specialization; 3) experiencing greater opportunities for administrative roles and professional responsibilities; 4) working in more diverse clinical settings and practice; 5) advocating for greater quality of care and treatment; and 6) seeking opportunities for personal exploration and rejuvenation. Just as the needs for advanced supervision are complex, so are the variables impacting the process of supervision. Both the supervisor and supervisee come into the process with their own training, background, preferred therapy and supervision model, and level of professional development (Brown, 1997). These variables and others certainly add to the depth and breadth of professional supervision.

What then are some of the advanced knowledge and skills expected in professional supervision? Some of the clinical competencies Bruscia (1986) has identified include knowledge and understanding of major theories, literature, roles and responsibilities, stages of growth and development, group and interpersonal dynamics, types of interventions, appropriate goal-setting, feedback, and evaluation. Hesser (1985) sees the attainment of advanced competencies occurring in a developmental progression involving three stages. In the first stage, supervisees concentrate on gaining or strengthening entry-level competencies. In the second stage, supervisees identify their area of specialization. As they start to specialize, they begin to build their own theoretical framework. It is a time of personal questioning and reflections. The third stage focuses on developing the supervisee's own personal style as a therapist. The supervisor assists the supervisee in applying his/her own framework and methods to the therapeutic process.

Training in professional supervision offers therapists opportunities to become acquainted with, experience, and/or specialize in various models and theoretical perspectives. One such model is psychoanalytical. Within the psychoanalytical framework, Dvorkin (1999) sees the supervisor assuming two roles in her work with the supervisee-therapist and teacher.

When it is too difficult for the supervisee to verbalize feelings about any aspect of his/her professional or personal life, s/he is asked to express it musically. Within that context, the supervisor becomes a therapist who listens and interacts with the supervisee. As a teacher, the supervisor helps the supervisee learn how to make choices of interactions that will enhance his/her effectiveness as a therapist.

Similar to Dvorkin, Frohne-Hagemann also sees the supervisor as a counselor. In her integrative model of supervision (1999), helping supervisees learn to understand, explain, and improve their therapeutic work involves four phases: 1) perceiving and relating; 2) working through and understanding; 3) gaining a multi-perspective awareness; and 4) integration and training.

Advanced supervision can be diverse, complex, and rewarding to the supervisor and supervisee. It can be greatly enhanced when therapists can work with other supervising therapists who can model objectivity, sensitivity, knowledge, and professionalism.

References

Adamek, M. S. (1994). Audio-cueing and immediate feedback to improve group leadership skills: A live supervision model. *Journal of Music Therapy*, 31, 135–160.

Alley, J. M. (1978). Competency based evaluation of a music therapy curriculum. *Journal of Music Therapy*, 15, 9–14.

Alley, J. M. (1980). The effect of self-analysis of videotapes on selected competencies of music therapy majors. *Journal of Music Therapy*, 17, 113–132.

Alley, J. M. (1982). The effect of videotape analysis on music therapy competencies: An observation of simulated and clinical activities. *Journal of Music Therapy*, 19, 141–160.

American Association for Music Therapy (AAMT) (1989). *Education and Training Manual on AAMT Approval of Educational Programs in Music Therapy.* Philadelphia, PA: Author.

Andersen, J. F. (1982). The effect of feedback versus no feedback on music therapy competencies. *Journal of Music Therapy*, 19, 130–140.

Beck, J. B., MacLean, B. and Pinson, J. (1986). The clinical training committee speaks out. *Music Therapy Perspectives*, 3, 47–49.

Boone, P. M. (1989). Future trends and new models for clinical training. *Music Thearpy Perspectives*, 7, 96–99.

Boyle, M. E, and Krout, R. (1988). *Music Therapy Clinical Training Manual.* St. Louis, MO: MMB Music Inc.

Braswell, C., Decuir, A., and Brooks, D. (1985). A survey of clinical training in music therapy: Degree of compliance with NAMT guidelines. *Journal of Music Therapy*, 22, 73–86.

Braswell, C., Decuir, A., and Maranto, C. D. (1980). Ratings of entry level skills by music therapy clinicians, educators and interns. *Journal of Music Therapy*, 17, 133–147.

Braswell, C., Maranto, C. D., and Decuir, A. (1979). A survey of clinical practice in music therapy, Part II: Clinical practice, education and clinical training. *Journal of Music Therapy,* 16, 65–69.

Briggs, C. (1987). A creative arts therapy model for education and clinical training in music therapy. In C. D. Maranto and K. Bruscia (eds.), *Perspectives on Music Therapy Education and Training.* Philadelphia, PA: Temple University, Esther Boyer College of Music.

Brookins, L. M. (1984). The music therapy clinical intern: Performance skills, academic knowledge, personal qualities and interpersonal skills necessary for a student seeking clinical training. *Journal of Music Therapy,* 21, 193–201.

Brown, S. (1997). Supervision in context: A balancing act. *British Journal of Music Therapy,* 11, 4–12.

Bruscia, K. (1986). Advanced competencies in music therapy. *Music Therapy,* 6, 57–67.

Bruscia, K. (1987). Variations in clinical training: AAMT and NAMT. In C. D. Maranto and K. Bruscia (eds.), *Perspectives on Music Therapy Education and Training.* Philadelphia, PA: Temple University, Esther Boyer College of Music.

Bruscia, K. (1989). The content of music therapy education at undergraduate and graduate levels. *Music Therapy Perspectives,* 7, 83–87.

Bruscia, K. and Maranto, C. D. (1988). Academic and clinical training programs. In C.D. Maranto and K. Bruscia (eds.), *Methods of Teaching and Training the Music Therapist.* Philadelphia, PA: Temple University, Esther Boyer College of Music.

Bruscia, K., Hesser, B., and Boxill, E. (1981). Essential competencies for the practice of music therapy. *Music Therapy* 1, 4–49.

Cassity, M. (1987). Functional piano skills for music therapy interns. In C. D. Maranto and K. Brusica (eds.), *Perspectives on Music Therapy Education and Training.* Philadelphia, PA: Temple University, Esther Boyer College of Music.

Darrow, A., and Gibbons, A. (1987). Organization and administration of music therapy practica: A procedural guide. In C. D. Maranto and K. Bruscia (eds.), *Perspectives of Music Therapy Education and Training.* Philadelphia, PA: Temple University, Esther Boyer College of Music.

Decuir, A., and Jacobs, K. (1990). A comparison of clinical evaluations and student self-evaluations of undergraduate practicum experiences in music therapy. *Music Therapy Perspectives,* 8, 20–22.

Dvorkin, J. (1999). Psychoanalytically oriented music therapy supervision in T. Wigram and J. De Backer (eds.), *Clinical Applications of Music Therapy in Developmental Disability, Paediatrics and Neurology.* London: Jessica Kingsley Publishers.

Farnan, L. (1994). Issues in clinical training. *Music Therapy Perspectives,* 12, 70–71.

Farnan, L. (1996). Issues in clinical training. *Music Therapy Perspectives,* 14, 70–71.

Farnan, L. (1998). Issues in clinical training: Comparison of internship models. *Music Therapy Perspectives,* 16(1), 7–8.

Frohne-Hagemann, I. (1999). Integrative approaches to supervision for music therapists. In T. Wigram and J. De Backer (eds.), *Clinical Applications of Music Therapy in Developmental Disabilities.* London: Jessica Kingsley Publishers.

Furman, C., Adamek, M., and Furman, A. (1992). The use of an auditory device to transmit feedback to student therapists. *Journal of Music Therapy,* 19, 40–53.

Galloway, H. P. (1966). Articulation problems in the academic and clinical training of music therapists. Unpublished master's thesis, Florida State University. In C. D. Maranto and K. Bruscia (eds.), *Master's Theses Index and Abstracts* (1988). Philadelphia, PA: Temple University, Esther Boyer College of Music.

Gaston, E. T. (1964). Developments in the training of music therapists. *Journal of Music Therapy,* 1, 148–150.

Gault, A. W. (1978). An assessment of the effectiveness of clinical training in collegiate music therapy curricula. *Journal of Music Therapy,* 15, 36–39.

Gibbons, A., and Darrow, A. (1987). College/university music therapy clinics: Financial considerations. In C. D. Maranto and K. Bruscia (eds.), *Perspectives on Music Therapy Education and Training.* Philadelphia, PA: Temple University, Esther Boyer College of Music.

Glider, A. S. (1987). Trainee distress and burn-out: Threats for music therapy. In C. D. Maranto and K. Bruscia (eds.), *Perspectives of Music Therapy Education and Training.* Philadelphia, PA: Temple University, Esther Boyer College of Music.

Graham, M. (1971). A new approach to student affiliation in music therapy. *Journal of Music Therapy,* 8, 43–52.

Grant R., and McCarty, B. (1980). Emotional stages in music therapy internship. *Journal of Music Therapy,* 17, 102–118.

Greenfield, D. G. (1978). Evaluation of music therapy practicum competencies: Comparison of self- and instructor ratings of videotapes. *Journal of Music Therapy,* 15, 13–20.

Greenfield D. G. (1980). The use of visual feedback in training music therapy competencies. *Journal of Music Therapy,* 17, 94–110.

Hadsell, A., and Jones, J. L. (1988). Music therapy practicum: A cooperative effort. *Music Therapy Perspectives,* 5, 57–59.

Hanser, S. B. (1978). A systems analysis model for teaching practicum skills. *Journal of Music Therapy,* 15, 21–35.

Hanser, S. B. (1980). *Music Therapy Practicum: A Manual for Behavior Change Through Music.* Stockton, CA: University of the Pacific.

Hanser, S. B. (1987). Observation and feedback techniques for student practica. In C. D. Maranto and K. Bruscia (eds.), *Perspectives on Music Therapy Education and Training.* Philadelphia, PA: Temple University, Esther Boyer College of Music.

Hanser, S. B., and Furman, C. E. (1980). The effect of videotape-based feedback vs. field-based feedback on the development on applied clinical skills. *Journal of Music Therapy,* 17, 103–111.

Hesser, B. (1985). Advanced clinical training in music therapy. *Music Therapy,* 5, 66–73.

Jensen, K., and McKinney, C. (1990). Undergraduate music therapy education and training: Current Status and proposals for the future. *Journal of Music Therapy,* 27, 158–177.

Killian, N. (1981). Effect of instructions and feedback on music teaching skills. *Journal of Music Therapy,* 18, 166–173.

Kim, S. K. (1990). Competency ratings in applications to the American Association for Music Therapy for Certification. 1981–1987. *Music Therapy, 9*, 82–102.

Krout, R. E. (1982). Supervision of music therapy practicum within a classroom setting. *Music Therapy Perspectives, 1*, 21–24.

Madsen, C. (1965). A new music therapy curriculum *Journal of Music Therapy, 2*, 83–85.

Madsen, C. M., and Alley, J. M. (1979). The effect of reinforcement on attentiveness comparison of behaviorally trained music therapist and other professionals with implications for competency-based academic preparation. *Journal of Music Therapy, 16*, 70–82.

Madsen, C., and Kaiser, D. A. (1999). Pre-internship fears of music therapists. *Journal of Music Therapy, 26*, 17–25.

Maranto, C. D. (1987a). The California Symposium: Summary and recommendations. *Music Therapy Perspectives, 6*, 82–84.

Maranto, C. D. (1987b). Continuing themes in the literature on music therapy education and training. In C. D. Maranto and K. Bruscia (eds.), *Perspectives on Music Therapy Education and Training*. Philadelphia, PA: Temple University, Esther Boyer College of Music.

Maranto C. D. (1987c). Ethical issues in music therapy education. In C. D. Maranto and K. Bruscia (eds.), *Perspectives on Music Therapy Education and Training*. Philadelphia, PA: Temple University, Esther Boyer College of Music.

Maranto, C. D. (1988). Practica and internship. In C. D. Maranto and K Bruscia (eds.), *Methods of Teaching and Training the Music Therapist*. Philadelphia, PA: Temple University, Esther Boyer College of Music.

Maranto, C. D. (1989). California symposium on music therapy education and training: Summary and recommendations. *Music Therapy Perspectives, 7*, 108–109.

Maranto, C. D., and Wheeler, B. (1986). Teaching ethics in music therapy. *Music Therapy Perspectives, 3*, 17–19.

Marks, D. (1992). Music therapy clinical internship training in Canada: Profiles and perspectives. *Music Therapy Perspectives, 10*, 99–104.

McClain, F. (1993). *Student evaluations of practicum training in music therapy.* Unpublished doctoral dissertation, Temple University, Esther Boyer College of Music.

Memory, B. C., Unkefer, R., and Smeltekop, R. (1987). Supervision in music therapy: Theoretical models. In C. D. Maranto and K. Bruscia (eds.), *Perspectives on Music Therapy Education and Training*. Philadelphia, PA: Temple University, Esther Boyer College of Music.

Moreno, J. (1988) Multicultural Music Therapy: The world music connection. *Journal of Music Therapy, 25*, 17–27.

National Association for Music Therapy (NAMT) (1997). *Clinical Training Guidelines*. Silver Spring MD: Author.

Niles, S. (1996). Experimental internships. *Music Therapy Perspectives, 14*, 12–13.

Petrie, C. F (1989). The identification of a contemporary hierarchy of intended learning outcomes for music therapy students entering internship. *Journal of Music Therapy, 26*, 125–129.

Prickett, C. A. (1987). The effects of self-monitoring on positive comments given by music therapy students' coaching peers *Journal of Music Therapy, 24*, 54-75.

Standley, J. M. (1985). An investigation of the relationship between selected characteristics, education values and teaching competencies of freshmen music education/ therapy majors. *Journal of Music Therapy, 22*, 2–11.

Standley, J. M. (1989). A prospectus for the future of music therapy education standards, requirements and professional designations. *Music Therapy Perspectives, 7*, 103–107.

Steele, A. L. (1989). Clinical practice: One operational format. *Music Therapy Perspectives, 6*, 16–17.

Stephens, G. (1987). The experiential music therapy group as a method of training and supervision. In C. D. Maranto and K. Bruscia (eds.), *Perspectives of Music Therapy Education and Training.* Philadelphia, PA: Temple University, Esther Boyer College of Music.

Taylor, D. B. (1987). A survey of professional music therapists concerning entry level competencies. *Journal of Music Therapy, 24*, 114–145.

Ten Eyck, S. G. (1985). The effect of simulation and observation training on the music therapy behaviors of undergraduate music therapy/music education majors in a field teaching experience. *Journal of Music Therapy, 22*, 160–182.

Tims, F. (1989). Experiential learning in the music therapy curriculum. *Music Therapy Perspectives, 7*, 91–92.

Troppozado, M. (1995). Multicultural training for music therapists: An examination of current issues based on a national survey of professional music therapists. *Journal of Music Therapy, 32*, 65–90.

Wright, L. (1992). A levels systems approach to structuring and sequencing pre-practica musical and clinical competencies in a university music therapy clinic. *Music Therapy Perspectives, 10*, 36–44.

Acknowledgments

The author gratefully acknowledges the mentorship of Dr. Kenneth Bruscia for serving as my doctoral adviser during the initial period of this research.

Chapter 3

Ethical Issues in Supervision

Cheryl Dileo, PhD, MT-BC
Professor of Music Therapy
Temple University
Philadelphia, PA

Introduction

Supervision is at the foundation of promoting professional growth in music therapy in the following ways: 1) it is one of the fundamental methods through which students learn to acquire the skills necessary to practice music therapy competently and ethically; 2) it is one of the primary means to enhance and improve the skills of music therapists already working in the field; and 3) it is essential to those music therapists acquiring advanced training in various specialized methods of music therapy.

The topic of ethics in music therapy supervision has not been extensively discussed in the literature (Maranto, 1987), but is nevertheless critical for two main reasons: 1) the supervisory process itself implies a number of important ethical issues, as will be described in this chapter, and 2) a main purpose of supervision is to teach ethical behavior to preprofessionals and to monitor this behavior in professional-level supervisees. Thus, ethics is fundamental to the supervisory process itself, and is also an important content area that must be conveyed during supervision. The responsibility of the supervisor then is to serve both as a teacher and a model for ethical behavior: "the content, skills, and modeling that a supervisor imparts are all key aspects of promoting ethical practice" (Vasquez, 1992, p. 196).

Roles in Supervision

Supervision implicitly involves a triad, including music therapy supervisor, supervisee, and client, rather than simply a supervisor-supervisee dyad. All three parties take a risk in entering the supervisory relationship. Both the supervisee and client(s) involved are consumers and recipients of the supervisor's clinical knowledge and skills as well as ethical standards (Kurpius, Gibson, Lewis, and Corbet, 1991; Upchurch, 1985), and can be affected if these are inadequate.

The nature of the supervisor's role in music therapy involves a number of sometimes conflicting and enhanced responsibilities, and as such is difficult to define precisely. The conflicts between these roles require competent ethical decision making. Supervisors are expected to serve as teachers, administrators, and evaluators. At the same time, an additional role is to facilitate self-awareness in the supervisee, a role which is "therapy-like" (Kurpius, et al., 1991; Newman, 1981). To make things even more complicated, because of the power inherent in all of these roles, the supervisor's tasks are often viewed as "parent-like."

Music therapy supervisors are vulnerable ethically for several reasons: 1) the power differences between his or her role and that of the supervisee; 2) the "therapeutic" aspects inherent in the relationship; and 3) the role conflicts between the two participants. These multiple supervisory roles include safeguarding the welfare of: 1) the clients (which always comes first); 2) the supervisee (which comes second); 3) the public; and 4) the profession. In addition, because of the "therapy-like" qualities of supervision, both clients and supervisees may be harmed if the supervisor is not objective, if he or she utilizes bad judgment or exploits his or her power (Sherry, 1991).

Responsibilities of Supervisors - Rights of Supervisees

No matter what the context of music therapy supervision or the roles assumed, however, the ethical imperative of the supervisor is to provide training and to facilitate growth in three essential areas: ethical functioning, professional competence, and personal functioning (Vasquez, 1992). Corey, Corey, and Callanan (1998, pp. 292–293) enumerate some of the specific responsibilities of supervisors to those they supervise. These responsibilities fall into several categories: 1) competence in supervision; 2) providing adequate information regarding supervision; 3) shared decision making regarding supervision needs; 4) selecting the appropriate role as supervisor (consultant, instructor, etc.) and clarifying this with the supervisee; 5) fostering clinical and ethical competence; 6) utilizing an informed style of supervision consistent with one's own style; 7) holding regular meetings and providing timely feedback; 8) providing supervisory interventions in a way that enhances personal awareness, clinical decision making, and self-confidence; 9) advancing abilities to work with culturally diverse groups; 10) helping supervisees identify the boundaries of their abilities; 11) monitoring the clients involved assuring that clients are not at risk and maintaining confidentiality in record keeping; 12) instructing and demonstrating appropriate professional and ethical standards; and 13) monitoring techniques and methods used in treatment.

Tyler and Tyler (1997) suggest that the same ethical standards used in clinical work apply also to the supervisor relationship, i.e., the rights of supervisees should be enumerated within supervision so that they may be empowered to identify expectations, implement decisions, and take an active role in the process. These authors further identify a bill of rights for supervisees which includes: 1) sessions free from distractions and interruptions; 2) awareness of the supervisory approaches used; 3) confidentiality of material related to the supervisee and client involved, except as required by law; 4) free access to records maintained during supervision; 5) provision of feedback to supervisors regarding the quality of supervision; and 6) consultation with other professionals, if needed.

Specific Ethical Issues in Supervision

A list of specific ethical issues in supervision is included in Table 1. A number of these issues will be discussed later in the chapter.

Table 1

Ethical Issues in Supervision

I. Supervisor Competence
- Personal Functioning
- Qualifications/Training
- Competence in Specific Clinical Areas
- Competence to Work with Various Types of Supervisce's Needs

II. Adequacy of Supervision
- Fulfillment of Duties/Responsibilities
  - Preparation for Supervision
  - Appropriate and Mutual Goal-Setting for Supervision: Adequate Discussion of Expectations and Details of Supervision
  - Consideration for Supervisee's Needs and Interests
  - Appropriate Supervisory Methods (Safeguards for Experiential Methods)
- Awareness of Limits
- Role Modeling
- Sensitivity to Multicultural and Gender Issues
- Confidentiality of Client(s) and Supervisee Maintained
- Adequacy of Supervision Evaluated

III. Supervisor's Behaviors
- Gender and Other Role Stereotyping
- Gender Discrimination
- Negative Countertransference (Creation of Overdependence)
- Establishment of Dual Relationships
- Ethical Role Modeling

IV. Misuse of Supervisor's Power/Authority
- Supervisee Abuse
- Sexual Harassment
- Imposition of Beliefs

V. Informed Consent
- From Client
- From Supervisee

VI. Evaluation
- Criteria for Evaluation Clarified
- Timely, Relevant, Objective Feedback
- Chance for Supervisee to Remediate Problems
- Information on How and With Whom Supervisory Information is Shared

VII. Supervisee's Behaviors (Negative Transference)

Confidentiality of Information

As supervision involves a triad, instead of a dyad, clients whose treatment is being supervised must be informed of and consent to this fact in advance of supervision. Specific information and details about how their clinical information will be shared and their identity protected should be disclosed as part of this informed consent procedure.

Similarly, supervisees should be informed regarding if and how the information obtained in the supervisory process will be shared and with whom, including information concerning their skills and abilities, personal functioning, and ethical behavior. Measures to maintain and protect confidentiality should be implemented, but the limits of those measures need to be acknowledged.

Competence of Supervisors

Competence in music therapy supervision goes beyond clinical or educational competence, and includes "a unique combination of psychotherapeutic, educational and evaluative skills. In addition, it entails specific personal attributes, such as conveying positive attitudes about the profession" (Newman, 1981, p. 691).

To become competent as supervisors, education in supervisory methods is required, as well as training in various methods of supervision and in working with difficult and multiculturally diverse individuals (Corey, Corey, and Callanan, 1998). Supervisors also need to be competent in and have in-depth knowledge of particular clinical areas.

Supervisors should be aware of various developmental stages of professional growth and use supervisory methods based on supervisees' needs at these stages. This may involve a delicate balance between directing and allowing, between providing answers and facilitating problem solving, between challenging and accepting, and between controlling and letting go.

Supervisors must also have a comprehensive understanding of the supervisory process, of the dynamics of supervision, and of their own supervisory styles. Styles of supervision are manifest in the types of questions explored, such as: What is going on with you? How are you reacting to your clients? How is your behavior affecting them? Which clients bring out your own resistances? How are your values manifested by the way you interact with your clients? How might our relationship, in these supervisory sessions, mirror your relationships with your clients? Are you feeling free enough to bring into these supervisory sessions any difficulties you are having with your clients (Corey, Corey, and Callanan, 1998, p. 294)? Supervisors should be aware of the limits of their own styles according to the needs of their supervisees.

Although supervision is not therapy, it is intended to facilitate both personal and professional growth. As such, the supervisor facilitates self-awareness in the supervisee both in relationship to the client and in relationship to the supervisor.

At the most basic level, however, "the most important element in the supervisory process is the kind of person the supervisor is. The methods and techniques supervisors used are less important than their ability to establish an effective and collaborative working relationship with supervisees" (Corey, Corey, and Callanan, 1998, p. 293).

When a music therapy supervisor is/becomes emotionally unstable, the supervisee is at an even greater risk than a client would be. Whereas the client can terminate services relatively easily, the preprofessional supervisee may not be able to do so for fear of grade recrimination or long-term career implications (Keith-Spiegel and Koocher, 1985).

Several researchers have studied what "good" and "bad" supervision implies to preprofessional supervisees. Allen, Szollos, and Williams (1986) surveyed doctoral psychology students' best and worst experiences in psychotherapy supervision according to its context, personal qualities of the supervisor, and various interactional components. It was found that earmarks of quality supervision were most often associated with the expertise and trustworthiness of the supervisor, length of the supervision experience, and the focus on personal issues rather than on technical skills. Highly esteemed supervisors were psychodynamic rather than behavioral in orientation, were able to develop supportive relationships with supervisees, and to provide clear expectations and feedback. The worst supervisory experiences were characterized by supervisors' authoritarian and sexist behavior.

Rosenblatt and Mayer (1975), through preprofessionals' autobiographical accounts, identified various supervisory styles judged stressful, dissatisfying, and/or objectionable by supervisees. Among the types of styles identified were the following: 1) constrictive supervision (inadequate autonomy given to preprofessionals in making clinical decisions and/or overintense supervision); 2) amorphous supervision (too little supervision offered); 3) unsupportive supervision (the exacerbation of preprofessionals' insecurities through cold, aloof, or hostile interactions); and 4) therapeutic supervision (the attribution of all or most of the preprofessionals' clinical inadequacies to personality deficiencies which are subsequently explored). Of the four supervisory styles identified, therapeutic supervision elicited the most distress from supervisees in that it stimulated fears about the capability to work clinically, as these deficiencies are not easily or quickly remedied. In addition, any objections to these "accusations" could be interpreted as resistance, further confirming the supervisor's position. Thus, recipients of "therapeutic" supervision felt vulnerable and defenseless.

Power in the Supervisory Relationship

To some extent, the role of the music therapy supervisor with preprofessional therapists can be likened to that of "professional parent" (Alonso, 1985; Jacobs, 1991): supervisors nurture, guide, and support individuals in their professional formation. This role is inherently hierarchical, and the supervisor assumes a position of power and responsibility with regard to the vulnerable preprofessional. As therapist/clinicians, supervisors may experience anxiety with the full extent of the power necessary in evaluating and judging preprofessionals' capabilities (which is qualitatively different from their role as therapists) (Alonso, 1985). As the perception of power in life is something critical to all, supervisors may be prone to misusing this power to meet their own needs (Jacobs, 1991). This misuse of power in supervision is at the root of many ethical problems. Moreover, in situations where the supervisor "feels unsupported, uncherished or underpaid by the institution, there is serious potential for these conflicts to spill over into the supervisory hour" (Alonso, 1985, p. 103).

Pinderhughes (1989) discusses the potential tendency for supervisors to use the vertical relationship of supervision, i.e., "keeping subordinates in a one-down position" (p. 111) to enhance their own feelings of self-worth and competence. Indeed, the supervisee may present a threat to the supervisor who may feel placed in competition with him or her. Preprofessionals provide a captive audience for the misuse of power and may even imitate this behavior in relationships with their clients (Jacobs, 1991).

The inherent power of the supervisor's role can create issues of dependency for supervisees. For the most part, this power is magnified by differences in status, expertise, and age, and the supervisee almost inevitably must assume a subordinate position. This dependency can stimulate both positive and negative feelings in the supervisee, for example, admiration, respect, and awe for the supervisor's abilities, but also fear, jealousy, and anger for this disparity in abilities. Dependency on the supervisor can also evoke parent/authority issues for the supervisee.

Both professional and preprofessional supervisees who are the recipients of supervisory power abuse in any number of ways are unlikely to react for fear of recrimination, for fear of losing support, for fear of being "pathologized" by the supervisor, or for fear of having their complaints ignored or dismissed by superiors (their word against the supervisor's), all ramifications of their power disadvantage (Jacobs, 1991).

Imposition of Supervisor's Beliefs

The music therapy supervisor can be the most significant individual in helping to make therapeutic decisions about the client, and indeed has the ultimate responsibility for the client's welfare. Overdirective supervision, however, presents an ethical problem, as " . . . the imposition of the supervisor's beliefs about what is best for the client can take the shape of unbending directives that the supervisee then feels impelled to deliver for fear of failing in supervision or personally insulting the supervisor. Although the supervisor might be acting on beliefs that are manifested because of unclear personal feelings towards the supervisee or the supervisee's client, the supervisee and the client can be compromised" (Kurpius, et al., 1991, p. 51).

In both professional and preprofessional supervision, there is always the potential for a conflict of values according to different theoretical orientations. Allen, Szollos, and Williams (1986) in a study of the best and worst experiences in supervision of psychology students found: " . . . good supervisors modeled respect for both their and their trainees' differences in values experiences and personal privacy. From this nonintrusive and pluralistic base, they provided useful, theory-based conceptual frameworks for understanding psychotherapeutic processes; taught practical skills; and encouraged trainees to experiment using novel strategies" (p. 97).

The music therapy supervisor must be aware of overly directive supervision, perhaps aimed at meeting his or her own needs, be cognizant of the limits of his or her expertise in various theoretical orientations while also remaining open to other perspectives, and maintain clear communication with the supervisee regarding his or her own approach to music therapy to best address the needs of the supervisee.

Transference and Countertransference

In music therapy supervision, because the role of the supervisor is often "parent-like" and the supervision process "therapy-like," and because the supervision process in and of itself is charged with emotional intensity, strong transference reactions may be experienced by supervisees. These can occur in both professional and preprofessional supervision.

Transference can be defined as "feelings that the student experiences in association with a supervisor that are actually displaced—that is, feelings that originated in an earlier significant relationship (often with a primary caretaker) in the student's life. Countertransference refers to displaced feelings that the supervisor experiences in association with a student that have their origin in an earlier relationship in the supervisor's life" (Jacobs, 1991, p. 131).

There are numerous issues that supervisees need to be encouraged to explore within the context of the supervisory relationship. The supervisor's own countertransferences can influence whether or not this takes place. For example, beginning preprofessionals often feel anxious, fearful, insecure, overwhelmed, etc. at the beginning of their practicum or internship experiences. Supervisors may empathetically try to reassure them that these feelings are quite normal and typical within the learning experience, and this can end the discussion of these feelings. Preprofessionals thus get the message that it is not appropriate to acknowledge and explore feelings of discomfort, and that this type of personal examination belongs outside the bounds of the academic setting (Jacobs, 1991; Schmidt, 1976). Obviously, the supervisor's own feelings of discomfort with the preprofessional's discomfort can lead him or her to minimize or ignore what is really happening in the supervisory relationship.

Jacobs (1991) describes a number of these potential supervisee transferences, several of which are included in Table 2 on the following page.

Countertransference reactions to supervisees by supervisors frequently occur when the supervisor uses his or her power within the relationship to meet his or her own emotional needs. This can happen in many ways, including, for example: 1) establishment of unclear boundaries (sexual relationships, therapy, other dual relationships); 2) misuse of power (fostering overdependency, imposition of beliefs, abuse, recrimination); and 3) insufficient and/or incompetent supervision.

Because of the power differential in this relationship, preprofessional supervisees in particular are fearful of protesting any of the supervisor's behaviors (countertransferences). The supervisor has the power to label any transferential reaction as inappropriate, unprofessional, etc., and as a personal deficiency of the supervisee, rather than a result of the dynamics of supervision. Furthermore, the supervisor can utilize his or her knowledge of the preprofessional's personal issues to construct a case for blame (Rosenblatt and Mayer, 1975)

Table 2
Potential Supervisee Transferences

Common Parent Transference Reactions Among Supervisees	
Supervisee as Child	*Transference to Supervisor*
▪ Criticized/unsupported	▪ Difficulty accepting feedback
▪ Emotionally deprived	▪ Expectations of need fulfillment
▪ Family caretaker	▪ Unwillingness to acknowledge own needs
▪ Parent "pleaser"	▪ Approval-seeking
▪ Rebel	▪ Untrusting of supervisor's expertise or authority
Common Client Transference Reactions Among Supervisees	
Supervisee as Client	*Transference to Supervisor*
▪ Lack of power	▪ Responsibility for maintaining boundaries
▪ Overtrusting	▪ Power is used to benefit trainee
▪ Lack of knowledge regarding therapy	▪ Responsibility for defining therapy process
▪ Emotional vulnerability	▪ Power over helplessness
▪ Expectations for personal exploration	▪ Role confusion

Secrecy in supervision may result; discussing transference and countertransference reactions about the supervisory process is difficult and uncomfortable for both the supervisor and supervisee. Supervisees can easily be drawn into protecting the supervisor's discomfort with these discussions, and thereby assume inappropriate roles of taking care of the supervisor, much to the neglect of their own needs as supervisees (Jacobs, 1991).

Jacobs (1991, p. 134) provides the following list of questions (all direct quotations) to help preprofessionals identify "dysfunctional" supervisory experiences and relationships. These questions may also be relevant to professionals in supervision as well:

- Is the student having any feelings about his or her supervisor that the student feels uncomfortable about or that may be interfering with the ability to work comfortably with the supervisor?
- Does the student feel comfortable with the ways his or her supervisor interacts with the student?

- Does the student find himself or herself reacting to his or her supervisor in confusing ways or differently than the student normally reacts to other people?
- Is his or her supervisor generally available to the student? Will the supervisor find time for the student if he or she communicates that something important has come up?
- Does the student ever feel judged or labeled by his or her supervisor? Does the supervisor make the student feel like there is something wrong with him or her?
- If a conflict arises, can the supervisor acknowledge a role in the difficulty, or does the student tend to feel blamed or identified as the cause of the problem?
- Does the student ever feel exploited or abused by his or her supervisor?
- Does the supervisor ever discourage the student from sharing information with his or her fieldwork advisor?

The awareness and appropriate working through of these common reactions of transference and countertransference can increase the effectiveness of supervision as well as contribute to the professional and personal development of the supervisee.

Dual Relationships

Dual role relationships and violations of established boundaries are markers of serious supervisee exploitation (Kitchener, 1988; Stout, 1987). Dual relationships occur when supervisors assume an additional and often conflicting role to that of supervisor with the individual being supervised. Because of the power differential between supervisor and supervisee, there is a diminishment of the supervisee's ability to provide full consent to entering into these additional roles (Jacobs, 1991). Dual relationships are indeed more problematic with preprofessional supervisees, as the power differential may be more negotiable between professional-level supervisees and supervisors.

Dual relationships often have serious consequences: 1) confidentiality can be damaged; 2) the supervisee's autonomy may be impaired; 3) the processes of supervision and/or therapy may be compromised; 4) the needs of the clients involved may not be considered as of primary importance; and/or 5) objectivity can be diminished (Kitchener, 1988).

Examples of dual relationships between the supervisor and supervisee may include: 1) establishment of financial relationships apart from supervision; 2) accepting expensive gifts from supervisees; 3) supervising friends or relatives; 4) creating social relationships with supervisees; 5) creating emotional relationships with supervisees; 6) using supervisees as research subjects; 7) supervising former clients; 8) establishing additional academic relationships with preprofessional supervisees; 9) having sexual relationships with supervisees; 10) providing therapy for supervisees, etc.

Because of the "therapy-like" aspects of supervision, it may be that the provision of therapy for preprofessional supervisees may be the most commonplace boundary violation. Roberts, Murrell, Thomas, and Claxton (1982) found that 35 percent of counselor education faculty considered it permissible to provide counseling to their own or other students. Further, Pope, Tabachnik, and Keith-Spiegel (1987) found a small portion of their sample of psychologists who believed that providing therapy to students was occasionally or frequently acceptable, and in fact 30 percent of respondents had done so.

As the facilitation of personal awareness is one of the essential components of supervision, when does this become therapy? It is suggested that personal exploration during supervision focus on the supervisee's relationship to the client and his or her helpfulness to them.

To be sensitive to the dual relationship issue, the promotion of the supervisee's self-exploration during music therapy supervision sessions should focus primarily on his or her interactions with and helpfulness to the client. Supervision can focus on identifying personal issues that may interfere with music therapy. The supervisee should then be encouraged to work through these issues with another professional. Supervision with preprofessionals is not the context for more in-depth work of this nature if a dual supervision/therapy relationship is to be avoided. In the supervision of professionals, this dual relationship may be either avoided or welcomed depending on the goals or intent of the supervisee.

The issue of dual relationships becomes salient when music therapy experiential methods are used in preprofessional supervision. Experiential methods that require authentic participation and the disclosure of personal information on the part of the supervisee must be handled carefully. Appropriate boundaries and safeguards must be applied and informed consent obtained when these methods are used. Preprofessional supervisees must be given a choice concerning how they choose to participate (authentically or through role-playing another). Supervisees should be informed of the purpose of the methods, as well as the limitations of the types of material that can be addressed (e.g., personal exploration of an in-depth nature). Also, preprofessional supervisees should feel safe that, if personal information is revealed, this will not be included in evaluations or grading (Dileo, 2000).

Obviously, some dual relationships are more dangerous than others. Where is the line drawn between dual relationships, however, that are outright unethical and those that are acceptable when handled prudently? What is the supervisor's responsibility when these are unavoidable? (Kitchener, 1988).

Kitchener (1988) states that dual relationships become problematic when: 1) the expectations between roles become increasingly incompatible; 2) when the obligations of roles become more divergent; and 3) as power and prestige between the roles increase. An example of a problematic dual relationship that meets all three aforementioned criteria is that involving a romantic and/or sexual relationship between supervisor and supervisee. Potential for harm increases the more each of these three areas is violated. Problematic dual relationships are associated with increased likelihood of exploitation, compromised objectivity, and risk of harm.

On the other hand, not all dual relationships are unethical. When the conflict of interests is minimal or small, such as supervisees becoming friends with former supervisors, dual relationships may not be seen as unethical. However, even in these types of situations, the supervisor is responsible for monitoring and being aware of potential role conflicts and buffering their impact if they indeed occur (Kitchener, 1988).

Sexual Relationships

Sexual relationships between supervisors and preprofessional supervisees are a particular area of concern within the context of dual relationships and boundary violations. These relationships are potentially more harmful than other types of violations because of the disparity in power between the individuals involved. Damage to the supervisory relationship may often occur when: 1) the supervisor models this type of power abuse, consequently increasing the possibility that these behaviors will be replicated by the supervisee in relationships with clients; 2) when issues related to sex and sexual attraction are not discussed by the supervisee for fear of illuminating a parallel process; and 3) when objectivity in evaluation is lost, and the supervisee is pressured to acquiesce because of career concerns (Bartell and Rubin, 1990; Conroe, Schank, Brown, DeMarinis, Loeffler, and Sanderson, 1989).

There are currently no data available for the incidence of these relationships in the field of music therapy, however the data available in the field of psychology may be cause for alarm.

According to Pope, Schover, and Levenson (1980) and Pope, Levenson, and Schover (1979), psychologists who teach clinical skills assume the simultaneous roles of teacher, evaluator, and therapist. As educators, professionals are compensated and awarded status in return for maintaining as primary, the needs of the students. The authors contend "a teacher who gains satisfaction for sexual wants and needs through students may have considerable difficulty maintaining the students' interests as primary" (Pope, Levenson, and Schover, 1979, p. 158). Sexual relationships are likely to seriously influence the role of psychologist as evaluator and therapist, compromising objectivity and fairness and threatening the gains of supervision. In these roles, the abuse or manipulation of the power disparity between the sexually involved supervisor and trainee is inevitable.

Pope, Levenson, and Schover (1979) found that 10 percent of 481 professional respondents reported sexual contacts as students with their educators and 13 percent reported entering sexual relationships with their own students. Further, 25 percent of recent female PhD graduates had sexual contact with at least one psychology educator during their training

Results from another study revealed that 17 percent of 464 female members of the division of clinical psychology had had sexual relationships with one or more of their psychology faculty/supervisors during training, and 31 percent were subject to sexual advances from educators (Glaser and Thorpe, 1986).

In another study, 3 percent of psychology supervisors reported having had a sexual relationship with a supervisee, and 8 percent of psychologists reported having a sexual relationship with a current or former supervisor (Ronan-Woodburn, 1994 communicated to Lamb and Catanzaro, 1998). Lamb and Catanzaro (1998) found that 12 percent of professionals surveyed were involved in a sexual boundary violation while a client, supervisee or student. Furthermore, professionals who had been involved in sexual boundary violations while clients, supervisees or students may have a greater chance of becoming offenders themselves while engaged in these same professional roles (Bartell and Rubin, 1990), although this was not found to be the case by Lamb and Catanzaro (1998).

"Sexual intimacy may seriously compromise the disinterest (not lack of interest) crucial to careful, fair, and valid evaluations. The sexual activity may occur in at least two contexts. First, it may be the expression of a profound personal intimacy, as in romantic or passionate love. Second, participation in sexual activity may be traded for academic achievement, as in prostitution or the 'casting couch' tradition in the theater. Both the romantic involvement and the business exchange aspects raise serious doubts about what is being evaluated and on what basis" (Pope, Schover, and Levenson, 1980, p. 159).

Sexual relationships between supervisors and professional-level supervisees are also a matter of concern. The supervisor-supervisee relationship is indeed a professional relationship, and the contract between these parties implies the need for trust that the supervisor will perform according to the best interests of the supervisee. Any behavior that undermines this trust violates the contract. Whereas sexual activity may enhance a personal relationship, it inevitably harms the professional relationship and violates trust (Bartell and Rubin, 1990).

Sexual Harassment

Sexual harassment, another type of boundary violation, may be overt or subtle and may involve teasing, suggestions, etc. No matter how it appears in its numerous forms, it is always demeaning to the supervisees involved.

By maintaining an attitude of respect toward supervisees and an awareness of the implications of the power inherent in the relationship, sexual harassment can be avoided. Supervisors have the pressing responsibility "to monitor their own personal and professional needs so that critical errors are not committed in relationships with supervisees" (Vasquez, 1992, p. 201).

Gender Issues

In a field such as music therapy, which is dominated by female professionals, there appears to be an unrepresentative proportion of males in educational/supervisory roles. Thirty-eight percent of academic program directors are male as compared with 13 percent in the general membership (AMTA, 1999). In situations such as these, a sensitivity to gender role issues is needed to avoid the implication to supervisees that males are more competent, powerful, and superior. "Supervisors must be aware of the socialization issues that contribute to the power differential between men and women in society, because that knowledge has important implications in the issues that surface in therapy" (Vasquez, 1992, p. 200).

Supervisors must be aware of potential differences attributable to gender as well in supervisee development. For example, some female supervisees may have tendencies to overidentify with clients, whereas some males may approach clients in a more cognitive manner. These differences may imply a need for more cognitive interventions with female and more affective interventions for males (Stoltenberg and Delworth, 1987).

The issue of supervisor support may be more critical for women who may respond more effectively to nurturing supervisory styles. In addition, it may be that supervisees can establish closer relationships with supervisors of the same sex (Worthington and Stern, 1985). Stoltenberg and Delworth (1987) suggest that same-sex pairings may be particularly effective for the exploration of ethics and individual differences, whereas cross-gender pairing may provide a different perspective on clients and their issues.

Termination of supervision may also present issues for male and female supervisees. Stoltenberg and Delworth (1987) have observed that female supervisees may have issues around saying "good-bye" in both supervision and clinical work, whereas male supervisees may have similar issues in saying "hello." With same-sex supervisors, these difficulties may become exacerbated: with females, i.e., the "good-bye" may be circumvented and a limbo created. With males, the "good-bye" may occur too abruptly and feelings can be ignored.

Ellsworth (1989) uses the term "voice" as a metaphor for identity, and because of differences between men and women culturally, they tend to communicate in different "voices." Gilligan (1982), in her work on gender differences in moral decision-making, postulates that women speak with the care voice, whereas men speak with the justice voice. The care voice speaks of issues of love, being heard, intimacy, and protection of self and others. The justice voice speaks of fairness, equality, right and wrong, and reciprocity (Gilligan, Ward, and Taylor, 1988). It is the responsibility of the supervisor to listen and attend to "voice" in supervision, as both voices represent ways to achieve a conceptual understanding of the dynamics of supervision (Twohey and Volker, 1993). "It is important for supervisors to be aware of both the voice of justice and the voice of care within themselves and within their supervisees" which can help "supervisors to become more androgynous without ignoring or denying important gender differences" (Twohey and Volker, 1993, p. 195).

Multicultural Issues

"Ethical supervision must include the ways in which individual differences can influence the process" (Corey, Corey, and Callanan, 1998, p. 296). Multicultural awareness includes knowledge of individual differences associated with race, gender, ethnic origin, culture, sexual orientation, socioeconomic status, religion, disability, and age.

Ivey (1986) states that "empathy demands awareness of both the individual and the culture" (p. 320). As this awareness is critical for therapists, it is even more so for supervisors who are ethically responsible for both their supervisees and supervisees' clients (Stoltenberg and Delworth, 1987). According to Corey, Corey, and Callanan (1998) competence as a supervisor cannot be assessed without a consideration of his or her awareness of and ability to address multicultural issues in the supervisory relationship. The supervisor who actively addresses these topics with trainees may provide a model for exploring similar issues with their clients. According to Cook (1994), a variety of direct questions may be raised in supervision which can illuminate the trainee's awareness of cultural differences as well as his or her reactions and responses.

In addition, Bernard and Goodyear (1992, pp. 205–208) provide six areas of emphasis for enhancing multicultural awareness: 1) an open-minded or pluralistic philosophy; 2) cultural awareness and information; 3) consciousness raising; 4) experiential training; 5) contact with minorities; and 6) practica with minorities. (See Chapter 4 for further discussion of this topic.)

Promoting Competence in Supervisees

A primary ethical responsibility of supervision is assuring that supervisees achieve competence in their clinical work and provide adequate treatment for their clients. Implicit in this is the acquisition of specific competencies identified by the professional association, as well as a keen awareness of what the supervisee's limitations are. Ways of accomplishing this include: observations and audio- and videotaping of sessions, discussion of clients, evaluation of written treatment plans, assessment of musical skills, co-leading and assisting with sessions, and so forth.

Besides knowing about the clinical population(s) being served, it is important for supervisees to be aware of gender and cultural issues in their clients as well as their own reactions to these issues and any potential prejudices (Vasquez, 1992). Fostering awareness of the supervisee's own values and discussion of how these influence clinical work is a significant task in this awareness.

Promoting competence in music therapy is the raison d'être of supervision. Competence in its broadest sense also embraces ethical behavior and adequate personal functioning, and a discussion of these two areas follows.

Promoting Ethical Behavior in Supervisees

As supervisors are often "the gatekeepers of the profession, it is essential that they be involved with ethical standards for practice" (Corey, Corey, and Callanan, 1998, p. 293). Bernard and Goodyear (1992) state that supervisors must first model what they hope to teach.

Rest (1984) has identified the four components of moral or ethical behavior as follows: "1) To interpret the situation in terms of how one's actions affect the welfare of others . . . 2) To formulate what a moral course of action would be: to identify the moral ideal in a specific situation . . . 3) To select among competing value outcomes of ideals, the one to act upon; deciding whether or not to try to fulfill one's moral ideal . . . and 4) To execute and implement what one intends to do" (p. 2).

To promote ethical behavior according to Rest's model, music therapy supervisors would do well to focus on the development of empathy, competent decision making (as opposed to rule following), awareness of personal motivation and values, and personal confidence and assertiveness. With regard to the second component, how to evaluate ethical problems, Kitchener (1988) has proposed five ethical principles that may be useful to the supervisee. These are 1) autonomy (freedom to choose and responsibility for one's own decisions); 2) nonmaleficence (not doing any harm to clients); 3) beneficence (doing good for clients); 4) justice (fairness); and 5) fidelity (honesty and fulfillment of responsibilities). Dileo (2000) has proposed an ethical decision making model for music therapists.

Promoting Personal Functioning in Supervisees

A third ethical responsibility in supervision is the assessment of the supervisee's personal limitations and weaknesses, particularly with consideration of how these become manifest in their relationships with clients. This is done "knowing that blindness to those may result in damage to clients and risks to the public, as well as risks to themselves and to the supervisor!" (Vasquez, 1992, p. 199). Ultimately, supervision aims to facilitate self-awareness in supervisees so that they may acquire the ability to identify: 1) their own issues that could be of detriment to the clinical process, and 2) any type of potential harm through incompetence, boundary violations, and/or ethical and unprofessional behavior.

As discussed previously, working with personal issues particularly in preprofessional supervision is challenging because of the potential of establishing a dual relationship of client-therapist. Supervision is "therapy-like" in that the supervisor facilitates personal growth and awareness, and there may be a thin line between this necessary personal exploration and therapy. The supervisor must be aware of when these issues can be dealt with in supervision and when the supervisee needs to be referred for personal work with another therapist. There are no hard and fast rules for negotiating this thin line. However, keeping personal exploration in supervision within the context of the relationship with clients is a starting point. Beyond that, the supervisor must carefully monitor the dynamics and content of the supervision process as well as any possible countertransference tendencies that may lead to the establishment of a dual relationship.

Another challenge for supervisors in this area is the realization that supervisees often demonstrate various types of impairment serious enough to interfere with clinical work, and that this impairment is relatively widespread among professionals as well. Vasquez (1992) cites a survey of professional psychologists wherein 59.6 percent admitted having worked while too impaired to be effective (Pope, Tabachnik, and Keith-Spiegel, 1987), as well as other studies which revealed rates of distress ranging from 2–19 percent (Boice and Myers, 1987; Farber, 1985; Helman, Morrison, and Abramowitz, 1987; Thoreson, Miller, and Krauskopf, 1989).

Signs of impairment in the supervisee include: psychiatric disturbances and depression, substance abuse, excessive grief, recurring medical problems, loneliness and marital discord (Deutsch, 1985; Pope, Tabachnick, and Keith-Spiegel, 1987; Thoreson, Miller, and Krauskopf, 1989; Vasquez, 1992).

As therapists may be reticent to pursue treatment for their problems (Deutsch, 1985), supervision provides an excellent opportunity, resource, and support for helping supervisees identify these issues and seek therapeutic options (Vasquez, 1992).

The developmental tasks leading toward professional competence often are the cause of distress in trainees. This distress is distinguished from the aforementioned types and is often amenable to supervisory interventions (Vasquez, 1988). This issue is discussed in the following section.

Identifying Impairment in Preprofessionals

Lamb, Cochran, and Jackson (1991) and Lamb, Presser, Pfost, Baum, Jackson, and Jarvis (1987) have developed procedures for identifying and responding to psychology intern impairment. Based on the three broad aspects of professional functioning (knowledge and application of professional standards, competency, and personal functioning), impairment is defined as "interference in professional functioning that is reflected in one or more of the following ways: 1) an inability or unwillingness to acquire and integrate professional standards into one's repertoire of professional behavior; 2) an inability to acquire professional skills and reach an accepted level of competency; and 3) an inability to control personal stress, psychological dysfunction or emotional reactions that may affect professional functioning" (Lamb, et al. 1991, pp. 292–293). These authors have also provided useful criteria for distinguishing problematic behaviors from impaired behaviors. Problematic behaviors are those that require attention and remediation but are not seen as unusual or excessive for trainees. Examples include: anxiety regarding clinical performance, discomfort with various types of diversity in clients, and lack of understanding or compliance with agency requirements. Impairment, on the other hand, involves the following: "a) the intern does not acknowledge, understand or address the problematic behavior when it is identified; b) the problematic behavior is not merely a reflection of a skill deficit that can be rectified by academic or didactic training; c) the quality of service delivered by the intern is consistently negatively affected; d) the problematic behavior is not restricted to one area of professional functioning; e) the problematic behavior has potential for ethical or legal ramifications if not addressed; f) a disproportionate amount of attention by training personnel is required; g) the intern's behavior does not change as a function of feedback, remediation efforts, or time; and h) the intern's behavior negatively affects the public image of the agency" (Lamb, et al., 1987, p. 599). In addition, Lamb, et al., (1991) recommend some additional criteria that may be posed to help distinguish problematic from impaired behaviors: 1) the specific behaviors manifested and where, and whether these behaviors are included in evaluation criteria; 2) negative consequences of the behavior for clients and the agency; 3) who witnessed the behaviors in question and their frequency; 4) awareness of the preprofessional and response to feedback; 5) documentation of feedback; and 6) seriousness of behavior on the professional/ethical continuum.

Vasquez (1992) emphasizes the imperative for supervisors to provide adequate feedback in these areas, recommend strategies to remedy the problem, and if necessary, terminate the clinical work of the supervisee. The latter is a very difficult decision for the supervisor to make, one which "requires social assertiveness, integrity, moral commitment, and ego strength," and there may be a "tendency to collude or avoid these important ethical responsibilities that exist to protect the trainee, clients and the profession" (Vasquez, 1992, p. 200). The clients' welfare is of primary concern, in spite of potential conflicts of responsibilities to the parties involved.

Conclusions and Implications

The purpose of this chapter has been to discuss ethical issues in music therapy supervision. The goals of supervision have been defined as: 1) promoting supervisee competence; 2) promoting ethical behavior; and 3) promoting personal functioning. Recommendations for accomplishing these goals as well as issues that may interfere with their achievement have been provided.

There are several conclusions and implications for the field of music therapy that can be drawn from this discussion.

Supervisors need training. Because of the in-depth knowledge of models of supervision, the supervisory process and the skills required to implement this process, graduate and professional-level training should be more accessible for all those who supervise. Knowledge and skill in supervision do not come only from clinical music therapy experience, but from a concerted effort to acquire these.

Training for supervisors may be made available in graduate programs, conferences, workshops, etc. Although there has been discussion of this need in the profession for many years, it is now time for more formal venues to be established. Appropriate and thorough training should be acknowledged by certification.

As it is common practice for graduate students to assume supervisory roles in undergraduate music therapy programs, these students must be closely supervised and trained by music therapy faculty.

Supervisors must also be encouraged to evaluate their own success as supervisors with feedback from supervisees and others. As such, they should be encouraged to model self-confrontation and self-awareness to supervisees.

Competence in supervision also implies sensitivity to gender and multicultural issues of supervisees and clients involved.. This involves knowledge of specific gender-based and multicultural and developmental models of supervision and skill in facilitating multicultural awareness in supervisees and in helping them integrate their ethnic and professional identities (Corey, Corey, and Callanan, 1998).

Supervisors require consultation and support. Supervisors should be encouraged to seek supervision, consultation, support and therapy to maintain the highest standards in what they are doing. Supervisory support services should be accessible following training through the same venues mentioned previously.

The rights and expectations of supervisees should be communicated. Supervisees should be informed of their rights to privacy, respect, dignity, and due process. Similarly, supervisees must be informed of the expectations of supervision and competency, supervisory methods used, experiential training employed, confidentiality safeguards, grading and evaluation procedures, consequences of not meeting expectations, and due process procedures.

In conclusion, "the process of supervision involves intense and intimate relationships with supervisees. As such, we must ensure our competency in the provision of supervision or obtain consultation and training in the areas in which we are lacking. Our effectiveness with supervisees and indirectly with the clients of our supervisees, depends to a great extent on fulfilling our ethical responsibilities as clinical supervisors" (Vasquez, 1992, p. 201).

References

Allen, G., Szollos, S., and Williams, B. (1986). Doctoral students' comparative evaluations of the best and worst psychotherapy supervision. *Professional Psychology: Research and Practice,* 17, 91–99.

Alonso, A. (1985). *The Quiet Profession: Supervisors of Psychotherapy.* New York: Macmillan.

American Music Therapy Association. (1999). *AMTA Member Sourcebook.* Silver Spring, MD: Author.

Bartell, P. A., and Rubin, L. J. (1990). Dangerous liaisons: Sexual intimacies in supervision. *Professional Psychology: Research and Practice,* 21, 442–450.

Bernard, J. M., and Goodyear, R. K. (1992). Fundamentals of Clinical Supervision. Boston, MA: Allyn & Bacon.

Boice, R., and Myers, P. E. (1987). Which setting is happier? Academe or private practice? *Professional Psychology: Research and Practice,* 18, 526–529.

Conroe, R., Schank, J., Brown, M., DeMarinis, V., Loeffler, D., and Sanderson, B. E. (1989). Prohibition of sexual contact between clinical supervisor and psychotherapy students: An overview and suggested guidelines. In B. E. Sanderson (ed.), *It's Never OK: A Handbook for Professionals on Sexual Exploitation by Counselors and Therapists.* St. Paul, MN: Department of Corrections, Task Force on Sexual Exploitation by Counselors and Therapists.

Cook, D.A. (1994). Racial identity in supervision. *Counselor Education and Supervision,* 34(2), 132–141.

Corey, G., Corey, M. S., and Callanan, P. (1998). *Issues and Ethics in the Helping Professions.* Pacific Grove, CA: Brooks/Cole Publishing Company.

Deutsch, C. (1985). A survey of therapists' personal problems and treatment. *Professional Psychology: Research and Practice,* 16, 305–315.

Dileo, C. (2000). *Ethical Thinking in Music Therapy.* Cherry Hill, NJ: Jeffrey Books.

Ellsworth, E. (1989). Why doesn't this feel empowering? Working through the repressive myths of critical pedagogy. *Harvard Educational Review,* 59(3), 297–324.

Farber, B. A. (1985). Clinical psychologists' perceptions of psychotherapeutic work. *Clinical Psychologist,* 38, 10–13.

Gilligan, C. (1982). *In a Different Voice.* Cambridge, MA: Harvard University Press.

Gilligan, C., Ward, J. V., and Taylor, J. (eds.). *Mapping the Moral Domain.* Cambridge, MA: Harvard University Press.

Glaser, R. D., and Thorpe, J. S. (1986). Unethical intimacy: A survey of sexual contact and advances between psychology educators and female graduate students. *American Psychologist*, 41, 43–51.

Helman, I. D., Morrison, T. L., and Abramowitz, S. I. (1987). Therapist flexibility/rigidity and work stress. *Professional Psychology: Research and Practice*, 18, 21–27.

Ivey, A. E. (1986). *Developmental Therapy: Theory Into Practice.* San Francisco: Jossey-Bass.

Jacobs, C. (1991). Violations of the supervisory relationship: An ethical and educational blind spot. *Social Work*, 36(2), 130–135.

Keith-Spiegel, P., and Koocher, G. P. (1985). *Ethics in Psychology: Professional Standards and Cases.* New York: Random House.

Kitchener, K. S. (1988). Dual role relationships: What makes them so problematic? *Journal of Counseling and Development*, 67, 217–221.

Kurpius, D., Gibson, G., Lewis, J., and Corbet, M. (1991). Ethical issues in supervising counseling practitioners. *Counselor Education and Supervision*, 31, 48–57.

Lamb, D. H., and Catanzaro, S. J. (1998). Sexual and nonsexual boundary violations involving psychologists, clients, supervisees and students: Implications for professional practice. *Professional Psychology: Research and Practice*, 29(5), 498–503.

Lamb, D. H., Cochran, D. J., and Jackson, V. R. (1991). Training and organizational issues associated with identifying and responding to intern impairment. *Professional Psychology: Research and Practice*, 22, 291–296.

Lamb, D., Presser, N., Pfost, K., Baum, M., Jackson, R., and Jarvis, P. (1987). Confronting professional impairment during the internship: Identification, due process and remediation. *Professional Psychology: Research and Practice*, 18, 597–603.

Maranto, C. D. (1987). Ethical issues in music therapy education and supervision. In: C. D. Maranto and K. Bruscia (eds.), *Perspectives on Music Therapy Education and Training.* Philadelphia, PA: Temple University, Esther Boyer College of Music.

Newman, A. (1981). Ethical issues in the supervision of psychology. *Professional Psychology: Research and Practice*, 12, 690–695.

Pinderhughes, E. B. (1989). *Understanding Race, Ethnicity & Power.* New York: Free Press.

Pope, K. S., Levenson, H., and Schover, L. R. (1979). Sexual intimacy in psychology training: Results and implications of a national survey. *American Psychologist*, 34(8), 682–689.

Pope, K. S., Schover, L. R., and Levenson, H. (1980). Sexual behavior between clinical supervisors and trainees: Implications for professional standards. *Professional Psychology*, 11(1), 157–162.

Pope, K. S., Tabachnick, B. G., and Keith-Spiegel, P. (1987). Ethics and practice: The beliefs and behaviors of psychologists as therapists. *American Psychologist*, 42, 993–1006.

Rest, J. R. (1984). Research on moral development: Implications for training counseling psychologists. *The Counseling Psychologist*, 12, 19–29.

Roberts, G. T., Murrell, P. H., Thomas, R. E., and Claxton, C. S. (1982). Ethical concerns for counselor educators. *Counselor Education and Supervision*, 22, 8–14.

Rosenblatt, A., and Mayer, J. E. (1975). Objectionable supervisory styles: Students views. *Social Work*, 20, 184–189.

Schmidt, T. M. (1976). The development of self-awareness in first-year social work students. *Smith College Studies in Social Work*, 46, 218–235.

Sherry, R. (1991). Ethical issues in the conduct of supervision. *The Counseling Psychologist*, 19(4), 566–584.

Stoltenberg, C. D., and Delworth, U. (1987*). Supervising Counselors and Therapists: A Developmental Approach.* San Francisco: Jossey-Bass Publishers.

Stout, C. E. (1987). The role of ethical standards in the supervision of psychotherapy. *The Clinical Supervisor*, 5(1), 89–97.

Thoreson, R. W., Miller, M., and Krauskopf, C. J. (1989). The distressed psychologist: Prevalence and treatment considerations. *Professional Psychology: Research and Practice,* 20, 153–158.

Tyler, J. M., and Tyler, C. L. (1997). Ethics in supervision: Managing supervisee rights and supervisor responsibilities. In: *The Hatherleigh Guide to Ethics in Therapy*. New York: Hatherleigh Press.

Twohey, D., and Volker, J. (1993). Listening for the voices of care and justice in counselor supervision. *Counselor Education and Supervision*, 32, 189–197.

Upchurch, D. (1985). Ethical standards and the supervisory process. *Counselor Education and Supervision*, 25, 90–98.

Vasquez, M. J. T. (1988). Counselor-client sexual contact: Implications for ethics training. *Journal of Counseling and Development*, 67, 238–241.

Vasquez, M. J. T. (1992). Psychologist as clinical supervisor: Promoting ethical practice. *Professional Psychology: Research and Practice*, 22(3), 196–202.

Worthington, E. L., Jr., and Stern, A. (1985). Effects of supervisor and supervisee degree level and gender on the supervisory relationship. Journal of Counseling Psychology, 32(2), 252–262.

Chapter 4

Multicultural Approaches
to Music Therapy Supervision

Karen Estrella, MA, MT-BC, ATR-BC. LMHC
Assistant Professor, Lesley University
Cambridge, MA

Introduction

As the music therapy community looks ahead to the year 2002 and the Tenth World Congress of Music Therapy, there can be no doubt of the global presence of music therapy. In 1999, over forty countries were represented at the Ninth World Congress of Music Therapy, which took place for the first time in the United States in Washington, D.C. Music therapy has established itself as a global profession which now takes place in an international context (Maranto, 1993). This international perspective was recognized by music therapists as early as 1974, when the First World Congress of Music Therapy convened in Paris (Moreno, Brotons, Hairston, Hawley, Kiel, Michel, and Rohrbacher, 1990). In 1978, the First International Symposium of Music Therapy Training was held in Germany, and it was then that music therapists began to look at cross-cultural issues in music therapy. Of course, in 1978 there was still little recognition of cultural influences in the fields of counseling, psychology, social work, and education. World music was yet to hit the global stage. Minority populations were given little recognition within mainstream cultures, and the advent of the global community was yet to see the fullness of its potential via the Internet. The image of internationalism which many of us held could be captured by the popular ad campaign at the time, showing people from all over the world holding hands and singing, "I'd like to teach the world to sing in perfect harmony." Little recognition was given to the fact that our "perfect harmony" was based on the English language and diatonic Western harmonic structures.

Not until ten years later, with the publication of Moreno's (1988) ground-breaking article, "Multicultural Music Therapy: The World Music Connection," were American music therapists encouraged to acknowledge the world influences not only on music, but on music therapy as a profession. Moreno noted, "American music therapists tend to be more ethnocentric and to use music in therapy that primarily derives from Western-oriented classical, popular, and folk traditions" (p. 18). At that time there was little recognition that non-Western music might be more appropriate with some clients, and most music therapists had little to no formal training in other forms of music than Western classical music. Moreno encouraged American music therapists to familiarize themselves with musical traditions from around the world, and admonished the music therapy community to value this perspective, by requiring that music therapists in training be exposed to non-Western music directly through their curriculum, via a world music course, or a course in ethnomusicology. American music therapists were beginning to acknowledge the increasing contributions which awareness of world music could have on their practices.

In 1990, Moreno and his colleagues called for the American music therapy community to take a more active role in the recognition of international music therapy practices: "With so many international developments in the field, it is evident that ethnocentric attitudes are untenable" (p. 41). They also recommended that international music therapy research projects be initiated that could learn more about the cross-cultural influences of music on behavior. But was this a call to acknowledge cross-cultural influences, which included those cultures of oppressed people within mainstream cultures? Had music therapy come to recognize its "Western European and Northern American worldview"—the worldview grounding much of what had come to be known as the fields of "mental health counseling" and creative arts therapies (Lewis, 1997, p. 123)? This was unclear. It appeared that most American music therapists had little awareness of differences which might exist internationally with regards to music therapy, not to mention limited awareness of differences which might exist within and between various racial and ethnic groups here within the U.S. It also appeared that American music therapists assumed that most of what constituted international music therapy practice was consistent and resonant with American practices.

The purpose of this chapter is to review the literature on multicultural music therapy, especially as it relates to the practice of music therapy clinical supervision. Multicultural approaches to music therapy is a sparse area of study. Thus, I have attempted to integrate parallel streams of work from related disciplines and to arrive at an overview of the salient issues facing music therapy supervisors who wish to develop their professional cultural competencies, and to provide culturally sensitive supervision.

Music Therapy Training in the U.S.

Prior to the 1990s, little attention was given to the dominance of American training in music therapy. Brotons (1995) speaks of the early American training of European pioneers during the 1960s, when the United States was the "best" and only place to receive training in music therapy. In a survey done by the National Association of Music Therapy (NAMT) Committee for International Relations in 1989, it was revealed that students from thirty-five countries were enrolled in NAMT educational programs (Brotons, Graham-Hurley, Hairston, Hawley, Michel, Moreno, Picard, and Taylor, 1997). By 1990, over seventy approved NAMT training programs existed, and with the programs approved by the American Association of Music Therapy being added to that number, it was clear that American approaches to music therapy education and training had come to dominate the field. Despite these numbers, even through the 1980s, there was little recognition or attention given to international perspectives in music therapy within the United States. At the Fifth World Congress of Music Therapy in Genoa, in 1985, only three American music therapists were in attendance (Moreno, et al., 1990).

In addition, many music therapists, even those who were practicing in Europe and South America, had received their training in the United States. Yet little recognition was given to cross-cultural implications of the dominance of American music therapy training worldwide. No recognition was given to the special perspectives which these students and therapists from other countries were bringing to the field of music therapy. Perhaps because of the many theoretical perspectives within American music therapy training, or because of the limited recognition which counseling and education communities gave to multicultural perspectives, there was, generally speaking, an attitude that music therapy was a "culture-free" discipline, easily adapted to any culture, by just including other musical traditions. While European influences on American music therapy approaches were undeniable (one had only to think of Juliette Alvin and Mary Priestley), these approaches still were embedded in a culturally encapsulated Eurocentric approach (Moreno, et al., 1990).

Much of music therapy training in the U.S. has been grounded in traditional mental health and special education practices, rooted in American and European psychological theories and constructs. The current definition of music therapy posted by the American Music Therapy Association on their Web site (http://www.musictherapy.org) reads, "Music therapy is the prescribed use of music by a qualified person to effect positive changes in the psychological, physical, cognitive, or social functioning of individuals with health or educational problems." This definition embodies the overall mission of music therapists, and contains within it an implied understanding of what "positive change in the psychological, physical, cognitive, or social functioning of individuals" might be. However, what has become clear in the psychology community over the past thirty years is that one cannot define "problems" or "positive change" effectively without an understanding of culture. These influences of culture on definitions of health and pathology, on methods of working in therapy, and on the very way "psychological, physical, cognitive or social functioning" is conceptualized, is only now being fully recognized by the music therapy community.

Psychological, physical, cognitive and social functioning is defined by culture. In addition, "(c)ulture defines what constitutes problems and explains the nature and cause of these problems" (Cheung, 2000, p. 124). Toppozada (1995) cites a study in which low-income Puerto Rican parents rejected the notion of disability for their children who were classified as learning disabled or mildly mentally retarded. "The parents had different boundaries of normalcy" (p. 67). In fact, the very way one experiences emotion, or the boundaries of one's "self" is largely determined by culture (Christopher, 1999; Dosamantes-Beaudry, 1997; Kitayama, Markus, and Kurokawa, 2000). Current psychological research has recently acknowledged that in Western cultures the self is conceptualized as a skin-encapsulated, self-sufficient, autonomous entity with one's own feelings, thoughts, and desires. (While this conception of the "self" has come under criticism by feminist theorists, this autonomous, self-defined person is still the construct of self most valued by the dominant forces in American society—see Miller, 1986; Miller, 1991 for a further elaboration on these themes.) In contrast, the self found in many non-Western societies is "psychologically constituted by one's location in a social network" (Christopher, 1999, p. 147). In individualistic cultures the "independent" self is given meaning as internal attributes are discovered, actualized, or confirmed; while in collectivist cultures the "interdependent" self is given meaning only in reference to the fulfillment of relationships of which the self is a part. (Again, this construct is being challenged by feminists within these cultures, as their freedom to be self-determining becomes more highly valued. See Kitayama, Markus, and Kurokawa, 2000, p. 94.) If culture influences the way we see ourselves, experience emotions, define health and problems, and construct our worldview, than clearly culture must come into play as we assess, diagnose, plan treatment, and engage with our clients.

Multicultural Training in Counseling and Music Therapy Education

Ponterotto, Casas, Suzuki, and Alexander (1995) note that as of 1995, 42–59 percent of counseling programs in psychology required a course in multicultural counseling. In response to these demands, texts and articles on multicultural training, counseling curricula, and multicultural competencies have emerged (see Ponterotto, et al., 1995; Pope-Davis and Coleman, 1997). Within music therapy, two articles have been published which look specifically at multicultural training for music therapists: "Multicultural training for music therapists: An examination of current issues based on a national survey of professional music therapists" (Toppozada, 1995) and "Multicultural perspectives in music therapy: An examination of the literature, educational curricula, and clinical practices in culturally diverse cities in the United States" (Darrow and Molloy, 1998).

Toppozada (1995) found that of the 300 American music therapists that she surveyed, most respondents agreed that the client's cultural background should be taken into consideration when selecting music to be used in a session, and disagreed with the notion that the cultural background of the client was irrelevant. She felt that while this demonstrated a basic support for the "underlying dimensions of multiculturalism," general comments indicated that several of the music therapists surveyed appeared to approach their work in a "color-blind" way, wishing to treat all their clients from a universalist perspective (pp. 79–80). This was again reflected in Darrow and Molloy's (1998) survey of 219 music therapists. They found that while 75 percent of respondents were familiar with multicultural music in general and at least somewhat familiar with multicultural music specific to their clientele, only 50 percent felt that the use of multicultural music and knowledge of cultural differences were important in their own clinical work, and 42 percent marked "neutral" in response to this question, indicating no opinion as to whether they felt this was important or not.

With regards to training, Toppozada (1995) found that most respondents received training in multiculturalism at their professional sites, rather than in academic coursework. Again, this corresponded to the Darrow and Molloy (1998) survey, which found that 78 percent of their respondents received their training in multicultural music on the job, as opposed to 27 percent who received it through coursework. Despite Moreno's 1988 call to music therapists to require a course in world music or ethnomusicology, a decade later NAMT had still not required that music therapy programs offer studies in multiculturalism (specific to music or therapy). Only four out of the twenty-five NAMT programs randomly selected by Darrow and Molloy required a multicultural music therapy course as part of its primary coursework. Most relied instead on elective multicultural coursework (sixteen out of twenty-five), or on secondary courses in which multicultural issues were presented though not as the main focus of the course (nineteen out of twenty-five). In keeping with those results, only 13 percent of the respondents felt that they were adequately trained, either in multicultural music or in working with clients from other cultures. Unfortunately, the professional literature has added little to supplement music therapists' knowledge of multicultural concerns. Darrow and Molloy (1998) found only ten articles pertaining to multicultural issues in music therapy literature from 1970–1994.

The lack of formal music therapy resources for multicultural training, and the perception of most music therapists that they will learn about multicultural issues at their jobs, places the bulk of the current responsibility for multicultural training on the internships and workplaces of music therapists. It is through this on-site training (supervision, workshops, and agency trainings) that most music therapists are learning about multicultural approaches to therapy. So what is meant by multicultural training? What are the multicultural counseling competencies now recognized by most mental health professionals? To fully appreciate the answer to these questions, one must first define "multiculturalism."

Multiculturalism and its Underlying Philosophical Assumptions

The past thirty years have seen a tremendous movement of multiculturalism within counseling in the United States. This sweeping movement to include multiculturalism in the fields of counseling, psychology, and social work has been described as the "fourth force" in counseling (Pedersen, 1991), as influential as psychoanalytic theory, behaviorism, and the humanistic movements. Multicultural counseling has arisen directly in response to the increasing awareness by mental health practitioners of the impact of increasing "cultural diversification" and the "rapid changing demography" within the U.S. (D'Andrea and Daniels, 1997, p. 291). On a practical level, mental health professionals have come to realize that they must provide services which are able to meet the needs of people from a wide range of cultural, ethnic, and racial backgrounds. In addition, practitioners have begun to critically examine their models of therapy, and to see them as belonging to a social and political context. Lastly, many have called for the revision of these same models of therapy, so as to be responsive and effective, with an increasingly diverse population.

Sue (1996) summarized the early impact of multicultural counseling and therapy into five main points:

- The importance of race, culture, and ethnicity in the counseling process has not been adequately considered by traditional counseling and psychotherapy models;
- The history, experiences, lifestyles, and worldviews of culturally different populations have not been understood;
- Euro-American norms have been used as the standard to judge normality-abnormality, and characteristics of "good counseling" are based on these norms;
- Seldom have counseling professionals been adequately trained in the knowledge and skills of systems interventions necessary to acknowledge or deal with the sociopolitical forces affecting the lives of their clients, with professional roles often too narrowly defined;
- If training programs have been intent on producing culturally aware and skilled mental health professionals, education and training of these professionals have to change (p. 279).

On a more controversial level, the multicultural movement has spurred a heated debate among practitioners, scholars, and academicians about the role of political discussion within the fields of counseling and psychology (see Barongan, Bernal, Comas-Diaz, Iijima Hall, Nagayama Hall, LaDue, Parham, Pederseo, Porche-Burke, Rollack, and Androot, 1997; Fowers and Richardson, 1997; Teo and Febbraro, 1997). Can a discussion of multicultural approaches be separated from a discussion of racism, political oppression, or privilege and power? Is acknowledging culture really necessary? Is it possible to "treat all people as equal"? Is there a universalistic approach which is appropriate? Can one ever know all there is to know about the many cultural diversity issues which may arise in one's practice? Isn't it absurd to try to learn about every music tradition and cultural group? Isn't it unethical not to? Doesn't it make sense to just treat each person with respect as a person? These questions have characterized the multiple perspectives which multicultural counseling approaches have taken, each with their own emphasis and set of priorities.

Philosophical Assumptions within Multiculturalism

Trying to summarize the multiple perspectives of multicultural counseling is a little like trying to describe a moving target with still photos. As the multicultural movement within counseling and psychology has developed, there has been an explosion of literature, with a multiplicity of approaches to understanding the importance of culture, race, and ethnicity, each offering a different set of assumptions and priorities. Carter and Qureshi (1995) proposed a useful five-part typology of philosophical approaches taken by multiculturalists during the past three decades: (1) universal, (2) ubiquitous, (3) traditional, (4) race-based, and (5) pan-national. They propose, as do others (see Leach and Carlton, 1997), that training programs, and by extension, supervisors, take responsibility for defining and developing a multicultural training philosophy. Yet, defining this philosophy can be quite difficult, given the many, at times seemingly contradictory, priorities and assumptions laid out by the multiculturalists. Carter and Qureshi's typology describe the range of approaches to multicultural counseling.

The first approach in Carter and Qureshi's (1995) typology, which they label *universal*, assumes "that there is a human bond that supersedes all experience" (p. 245). In the universal approach, while it is acknowledged that our experiences and identity may derive from our race, gender, ethnicity, or other reference group, what is most important is the uniqueness of our "individuality" as a person. This approach is sometimes also referred to as a "transcultural" approach (Fukuyama, 1990), with an emphasis on "universal processes that transcend cultural variation" (p. 7). At its most controversial, some proponents of this approach have suggested that by focusing on cultural differences, one might paradoxically foster stereotyping (Lloyd, 1987) and that by focusing on cultural differences one fails to see the whole person. Critics of the approach, however, propose that to not acknowledge the social and political ramifications of race, gender, ethnicity, etc. is to do an injustice in the treatment of culturally diverse populations.

The main assumption underlying the *ubiquitous* approach is that "any human difference can be considered cultural" (Carter and Qureshi, 1995, p. 246), and that these differences should be celebrated and "accepted." This position allows for the acknowledgment of multiple social group affiliations (i.e., poor, deaf, Catholic, lesbian, Latina, woman), and proposes that "cultural identity" is a matter of choice. Thus the choices one makes with regards to social group affiliation and "cultural identity" are given priority in the therapeutic environment (Carter and Qureshi, 1995, p. 247). By sharing a cultural affiliation, members of a group are seen as sharing a common experience of "different-ness"—so that there is a "culture" of gay people, or women, or people with disabilities. Trainees are encouraged to develop "cultural sensitivity," and prejudices and stereotyping are exposed and eliminated. Critics of this approach note that it fails to acknowledge the historically situated dynamics of power and oppression. Moreover, by seeking to equalize differences, this approach may deny fundamental experiences among some sociocultural groups. For example, although African Americans and women are both "oppressed" cultures within American society, their experiences of oppression have been qualitatively different. The Ubiquitous approach, by focusing on the equivalence of group affiliation, tends to miss something fundamental about how racial identity supersedes gender in U.S. society (Carter and Qureshi, 1995, p. 248).

The main assumption underlying the *traditional* approach is that culture is "determined by birth, upbringing, and environment and is defined by common experience(s) of socialization and environment" as determined by one's national country of origin (Carter and Qureshi, 1995, p. 244). This anthropological definition takes into account a common language, kinship, history, mores, values, beliefs, rituals, etc. as determined by the national culture. All "domains of difference" such as social class, affectional orientation, or gender are understood to find their unique expression through the context of one's national culture (p. 248), but not to be characteristics which, of themselves, create a "culture." Thus, all Americans are seen as experiencing a fundamental "cultural identity" as an American, regardless of race, gender, ethnicity, or other sociocultural differences. However, therein lays the primary criticism of the traditional approach; racism and other influences of intergroup power dynamics are not addressed or acknowledged.

The underlying assumption of the *race-based* approach is that the "experience of belonging to a racial group transcends all other experiences" (Carter and Qureshi, 1995, p. 244) in the U.S., particularly given the American sociopolitical history and the power differences that exist between "visible racial/ethnic groups" (Carter and Qureshi, 1995, p. 251). These groups are understood to be Caucasians, African Americans, Asian Americans, Native Americans, and Hispanics and Latino Americans. Race becomes "the marker or criterion for assigning cultural traits and characteristics" and "is determined by skin color, physical features, and language; and the traits and attributes assigned by classification and group ranking have been and continue to be held as unalterable" (Carter and Qureshi, 1995, p. 251). While ethnicity is acknowledged, race-based theorists propose that it is impossible to become sensitive to another's culture without first "dealing with the overlay of race" (Carter and Qureshi, 1995, p. 253). Racial identity is understood to be a developmental process consisting of both self-awareness, and of awareness of the sociopolitical environment which determines that Caucasian Americans hold the dominant group membership, with the privileges and power afforded that membership. Race-based approaches encourage trainees to become aware of their own racial identity, and to examine the effects of personal, social, cultural, and institutional racism not only on therapeutic relationships, but also in relation to mental health services as a whole. Ethnic and cultural differences are acknowledged as secondary to racial awareness, with an emphasis placed on addressing "the interactive and isolating effect of race on culture" (Carter and Qureshi, 1995, p. 254).

Last, the main assumption underlying the *pan-national* approach is that "racial group membership determines culture regardless of geosocial contingencies" (Carter and Qureshi, 1995, p. 255). Race is viewed in a global context as definitive of culture, and the history of imperialism and colonialism is central to understanding a psychology of oppression. Pan-national approaches include Afrocentrism, which proposes that the European worldview has distorted the worldview of, and denied, people from African heritage from truly understanding or valuing their biogentic makeup, and their "African self-consciousness" (Carter and Qureshi, 1995, p. 255). The proponents of "the psychology of oppression/liberation" represent a second pan-national approach. Their approach proposes that culture should be understood interactively. That is, that the cultures of the oppressor and the cultures of the oppressed should be understood as having developed in relation to one another. Psyche should be understood in relation to social structures, and those structures should be transformed to empower members from all cultural groups. While these perspectives have the advantage of recognizing broad, global understanding of how race relates to oppression throughout the world, and of how groups may be connected by color and common experience, other important factors such as religion or social class may be overlooked.

Priorities and Distinctions within Multicultural Training Literature

Much of the literature within the field of multicultural counseling and training focuses specifically on racial, ethnic, and cultural groups (i.e., Italian Americans, African Americans, Mexican Americans, etc.) and on developing knowledge and awareness of unique qualities and attributes of these cultures (Sue and Sue, 1990). This is true of the limited early literature in multicultural approaches to music therapy as well (see Darrow and Molloy, 1998 for a review). These "culture-specific" models most likely fall under one of three of the aforementioned philosophical approaches: ubiquitous, traditional, or race-based. These approaches differ in the emphasis they place on fundamental ideas, such as whether culture is self-ascribed; on the importance and significance of acknowledging sociopolitical history and power dynamics; on the acknowledgment or prioritization of differences within or between groups; and on whether it is more important to develop cultural knowledge or cultural self-awareness. In addition, critics of culture-specific approaches note that these approaches often overlook important within-group differences. It is important for music therapy supervisors to be familiar with the range of philosophical approaches to multiculturalism in counseling and therapy, and to be aware of their own perspective, and the stand taken by the agencies in which they work.

Throughout the literature on multicultural counseling training and supervision, various definitions and assumptions are reintroduced and prioritized. Stone (1997) distinguishes two approaches, the "inclusive" approach to culture and the "exclusive" approach:

> Inclusives adopt a broad and international approach to defining *multicultural* that often includes the ambiguous terms of *race, ethnicity, nationality, social class, religion, gender, affectional orientation, age, disability,* and more. . . There are others, the exclusives, who prefer to restrict the focus to the "visible racial ethnic minority groups" in the United States, including African Americans, American Indians, Asian Americans, and Hispanics and Latinos. (emphasis in the original, pp. 264–265)

He notes that there are merits and drawbacks to each way of defining "culture," and notes that these distinctions in fact define two different groups. Neither addresses the more subtle distinctions made by the typology offered by Carter and Qureshi (1995).

Another distinction made within the literature is the distinction between "multicultural" approaches and "cross-cultural" approaches. Sometimes these terms are used interchangably, but often they are meant to distinguish between situations in which multiple cultural differences exist, and situations in which two distinctly different cultures are given priority. "Multicultural supervision refers to those supervisory and/or counseling situations that are affected by multiple cultural factors" (D'Andrea and Daniels, 1997, p. 293). They are referring to situations in which for example, a White male supervisor may be supervising an Asian female supervisee who is working with an African-American group of teenage boys, or in which a Latina supervisor is working with a group of supervisees who come from various cultural and ethnic backgrounds. "Cross-cultural counseling supervision is defined as a supervisory relationship in which the supervisor and the supervisee are from different cultural groups (e.g., White supervisor–Black supervisee, Asian American supervisor–White supervisee, Black supervisor–Hispanic supervisee, and so forth" (Leong and Wagner, 1994, p. 118). This cross-cultural approach usually focuses primarily on "visible racial and ethnic groups," that is, on African, Asian, Indigenous, and Latino/Latina Americans (see Helms and Richardson, 1997). While either the multicultural or the cross-cultural approach can take a more ubiquitous orientation, focusing on any cultural difference (i.e., gender, religion, ethnicity, socioeconomic status), the literature tends to offer still more examples of differences between Whites and members of visible racial and ethnic groups.

In addition, one often sees the distinction drawn between culture-specific approaches and universalist approaches within literature on multicultural counseling. These approaches are also sometimes distinguished by the terms *etic* and *emic*. Etic approaches are assumed to be "culturally generalizable or universal" (Fischer, Jome, and Atkinson, 1998, p. 525). Most traditional counseling takes an etic perspective. For example, when one uses a developmental model with clients regardless of cultural background, or a theoretical orientation, such as the person-centered approach with all clients regardless of race or ethnicity. These etic approaches have been criticized as not being sensitive to cultural variations and to the worldview of the client. Supervisors and practitioners are should be able to recognize when counseling theory and constructs reflect Euro-American values. For example, when one "normally" weans one's child can be determined by cultural norms, which differ greatly from those proposed by Freud and the psychoanalytic theorists. Person-centered therapy promotes self-actualization and roots one's growth in self-understanding and unencumbered access to one's inner resources. This perspective, while useful for many clients raised within individualistic cultures, may present a concept of self quite foreign for clients whose worldview includes a more collectivist conception of self, and whose values may include a disregard of one's personal feelings (Sodowsky, Kuo-Jackson, and Loya, 1997). In addition, members of collectivist cultures often realize their cultural ideals by minimizing their distinguishing and therefore alienating features by being self-effacing. This allows them to maintain and maximize a sense of belonging (Christopher, 1999).

Some multiculturalists advocate a "modified etic" approach (Sodowsky, Kuo-Jackson, and Loya, 1997). They propose that one utilize "multicultural constructs, such as racial identity; ethnic identity; worldviews; acculturation; acculturation stress; and immigrant variables" (p. 21). While these constructs represent ideas which attempt to understand the impact of culture on psychological processes, they nonetheless represent a system of understanding the individual within their culture from an outside or imposed set of constructs. It is this aspect, despite its cross-cultural nature, which makes it an etic approach. Etic approaches allow for group comparisons, and give useful information about similarities and differences among different cultural groups, but they do not allow for an understanding of the individual within a particular cultural group (p. 28).

Approaches that describe the individual within the context of their specific culture are described as emic approaches. Emic approaches attempt to discover the constructs and meanings attached to behaviors and beliefs of individuals from within the worldview of their cultural group, rather than applying concepts from outside of the culture. For example, with an African-American eight-year-old male client, you would look at this boy in the context of his family, his community, and his personal development in the context of his surroundings. All stereotypical beliefs about African-American boys would be set aside, and the clinician would attempt to understand this boy's experience through the specific cultural lens (that is, how his gender, race, ethnicity, socioeconomic status, family constellation, acculturation, ethnic identity, etc. interface with the racial, ethnic, socioeconomic, sociopolitical environment) in which he finds and defines himself. From an emic perspective, this understanding must be done from inside this client's cultural world and experience. Once terms are used that are outside of the ways he, and his culture, would define himself, then one is taking an etic perspective.

Being aware of etic and emic perspectives requires that the clinician and supervisor be aware of culture specific and universal factors. Fischer, Jome, and Atkinson (1998) propose that by applying "universal healing conditions" within a culturally specific context, the clinician has an opportunity to integrate the best of both models. They outline four common factors found in most models of psychotherapy and in most healing traditions across cultures, and propose that these factors be seen as "a useful way to bridge the gap between culturally specific and universal approaches" (p. 525). These four common factors are: the therapeutic relationship; a shared worldview; client expectations for change; and a ritual or intervention for alleviating client distress. Fischer, Jome, and Atkinson note that these common factors, while paralleling the work being done by Western psychotherapy integration theorists, differs from the work of these theorists. They note that their approach more closely resembles the work being done by transcultural theorists, who, using an anthropological approach, attempt to find "universal elements found to be operating in all psychological and spiritual healing across cultures" (Fischer, Jome, and Atkinson, 1998, p. 532). I believe this model offers a useful integrationist approach for music therapists. But integration cannot take place unless adequate training and supervision regarding multicultural issues within music therapy happens first.

Multicultural Competencies

Within the past ten years, several professional organizations have taken up the cause of multicultural practices. In 1993, the American Psychological Association published a set of "Guidelines for providers of psychological services to ethnic, linguistic and culturally diverse populations" (APA, 1993). These guidelines include, by example, such practices as recognizing ethnicity and culture as significant parameters in understanding psychological processes; being aware of how one's own cultural background/experiences, attitudes, biases, and values influence psychological processes; identifying resources in the family and larger community; respecting clients' spiritual and/or religious beliefs, values, and practices, and becoming familiar with indigenous practices; and being cognizant of sociopolitical contexts in conducting evaluations and providing interventions. In 1992, Sue and colleagues developed a set of thirty-one multicultural competencies in conjunction with the Association of Multicultural Counseling and Development (Sue, Arredondo, and McDavis). These competencies consisted of a set of beliefs and attitudes, knowledge, and skills in three areas: counselor awareness of own assumptions, values, and biases; understanding the worldview of the culturally different client; and developing appropriate intervention strategies and techniques. These competencies offer similar recommendations to the guidelines offered by the APA, and have provided the groundwork for much of the thinking about curriculum development of courses which address multicultural concerns in counseling. In 1996, the Association for Counselor Education and Supervision formally endorsed these competencies (Daniels, D'Andrea, and Kyung Kim, 1999). This list provides a clear outline of what competencies are needed in the development of a culturally competent mental health practitioner.

The following is a summary of multicultural competencies adapted from competencies listed by Sue, Arredondo, and McDavis (1992, pp. 123–125.)[1]

I. Counselor awareness of own assumptions, values and biases
The culturally skilled counselor holds the following attitudes and beliefs:
- awareness of and sensitivity to their own cultural heritage
- valuing and respecting differences in cultural backgrounds
- awareness of how one's own cultural backgrounds, experiences, attitudes, values, and biases influence psychological processes
- ability to recognize limits of competencies and expertise
- comfort with differences that exist between self and clients in terms of race, ethnicity, culture, and beliefs.

The culturally skilled counselor holds the following knowledge:
- specific knowledge of one's own racial and cultural heritage and how it affects definitions of normality-abnormality and the process of counseling, personally and professionally
- knowledge and understanding of how oppression, racism, discrimination, and stereotyping affects one both personally and in one's work.
- acknowledgment of one's own racist attitudes, beliefs, and feelings. (This may hold particular meaning for White counselors. White counselors should be aware of how they may have directly or indirectly benefited from individual, institutional, and cultural racism.)
- knowledge of one's social impact on others

---

[1] Reprinted with permission from the *Journal of Counseling and Development*, Vol. 70, 1992, pages 123–125.

The culturally skilled counselor holds the following skills:
- have sought out educational, consultative, and training experiences which will improve one's understanding and effectiveness in working with culturally different populations
- ability to recognize limits in one's competencies, and ability to remedy these by seeking consultation, further training or education, referral to more qualified individual or resources, or engaging in combinations of the above.
- the ability to seek to understand one's self as a racial and cultural being
- actively seeking to develop a nonracist identity

II. Counselor awareness of client's worldview
The culturally skilled counselor holds the following attitudes and beliefs:
- awareness of one's negative emotional reactions towards other racial and ethnic groups which may be detrimental to one's clients in counseling
- willingness to contrast one's own beliefs and attitudes with those of culturally different clients in a nonjudgmental fashion
- awareness of one's stereotypes and preconceived notions which may be held towards other racial and ethnic minority groups

The culturally skilled counselor holds the following knowledge:
- specific knowledge about the particular group with who one is working
- awareness of life experiences, cultural heritage, and historical background of one's culturally different clients
- awareness of minority identity development models
- understanding of how race, culture, ethnicity, and other factors affect personality development, vocational choices, manifestation of psychological disorders, help-seeking behavior, and the appropriateness or inappropriateness of counseling approaches and interventions
- understanding and knowledge of sociopolitical influences that impinge of the life of racial and ethnic minorities.
- awareness of issues such as immigration, poverty, racism, stereotyping, and powerlessness, and their impact on the individual, and on the counseling process.

The culturally skilled counselor holds the following skills:
- familiarity with relevant research on mental health and mental disorders of various ethnic and racial groups
- ability to seek out educational experiences which foster knowledge, understanding, and cross-cultural skills
- active involvement with minority individuals outside of the counseling setting, for example via community events, social and political

functions, celebrations, friendships, neighborhood groups, etc. This allows for a perspective that is more than just academic

III. Culturally appropriate intervention strategies
The culturally skilled counselor holds the following attitudes and beliefs:
- respect for clients' religious and/or spiritual beliefs and values, including attributions and taboos
- recognition that these beliefs affect worldview, psychosocial functioning, and expressions of distress
- respect for indigenous helping practices and community networks for help-giving
- respect for bilingualism and lack of judgment towards language skills other than those possessed by practitioner

The culturally skilled counselor holds the following knowledge:
- a clear and explicit understanding of how the culture bound, class bound, and monolingual nature of counseling and therapy may clash with the cultural values of various minority groups
- awareness of institutional barriers that prevent minorities from using mental health services
- knowledge of the potential bias in assessment instruments, and the ability to use procedures and interpret findings in light of the cultural and linguistic characteristics of the clients
- knowledge of minority family structures, hierarchies, values and beliefs
- knowledge of community characteristics and resources within the family and community
- awareness of discriminatory practices at the social and community level which may affect the psychological well-being of the population served

The culturally skilled counselor holds the following skills:
- ability to engage in a variety of verbal and nonverbal helping responses
- ability to send and receive both verbal and nonverbal messages accurately and appropriately, recognizing that helping styles and approaches may be culture bound and being sensitive to limits in that style. When appropriate anticipating and ameliorating potential negative impacts of helping styles
- ability to exercise institutional intervention skills on behalf on one's clients, helping clients recognize when problems may stem from racism or bias in others
- seeking consultation with traditional healers and religious and spiritual leaders and practitioners in the treatment of culturally different clients when appropriate
- taking responsibility for interacting with the client in the language requested by them. When necessary seeking a translator with cultural

knowledge and appropriate professional background or referring to a knowledgeable and competent bilingual counselor

- receiving training and expertise in the use of traditional assessment and testing instruments, understanding of both the technical aspects of the instruments, and cultural limitations
- ability to use testing instruments for the welfare of diverse clients
- awareness of sociopolitical contexts for conduction evaluations and interventions, sensitivity to issues of oppression, sexism, elitism, and racism, and active striving to eliminate biases, prejudices, and discriminatory practices
- taking responsibility for educating one's clients about the process of psychological intervention, such as goals, expectations, legal rights, and one's orientation.

Multicultural Competencies for the Music Therapist

In her article, "Ethical issues in multicultural counseling: Implications for the field of music therapy," Bradt (1997) offers a comprehensive look at the lack of multicultural guidelines in the ethical codes for music therapists. She places the lack of attention to multiculturalism in music therapy in the context of ethical practice. She notes that not only is there not enough attention paid to multicultural issues in the education of music therapists, there is not enough attention paid to ethics in the education of music therapists. She advocates that "(m)usic therapists should have cultural knowledge, insight into their own beliefs, values and stereotypes, and those of their clients. They should be cautious in assessing and diagnosing the clients, in goal-setting and treatment interventions and try to overcome language barriers when working with minority clients" (p. 139). She also notes that there are issues specific to the use of music in therapy. Like Moreno (1988), she advocates that music therapists familiarize themselves with music of many world cultures. She also reiterates the importance of music therapists recognizing and valuing the "meaning of music in different cultures" (p. 139).

Music educators seem to be ahead of music therapists, as demonstrated by a series run in the *Music Educators Journal* beginning in July 1994, entitled "Music in Cultural Contexts," in which they invited ethnomusicologists and music educators to speak specifically about the cultural contexts of non-Western musics and how they might be included in multiculturally sensitive classrooms. These articles provide a rich resource for music therapists. In addition, Sarrazin (1995) has some important cautions to offer music educators (and music therapists) as she writes about the need to recognize the importance and experience of aesthetics cross-culturally. Sarrazin notes that in different cultures music is expressed, perceived, utilized, and conceptualized differently from the way we are used to thinking of it, and she notes that in this way we are likely to be most ethnocentric, failing to even consider that music serves a different aesthetic function from our own. "We have come to accept as a fundamental assumption that the arts are aesthetic or evoke an aesthetic experience"

(p. 34). She notes that we naturally assume that music serves the purpose of "being listened to," and that this assumption makes it difficult for us to recognize and sometimes accept that music may not serve a similar aesthetic function in other cultures. She cites six common factors which comprise the Western concept of aesthetics as outlined by Alan Merriam, "psychic distance; manipulation of form for its own sake; attribution of emotion-producing qualities to music conceived strictly as sound; attribution of beauty to the art process or product; purposeful intent to create something aesthetic; and presence of a philosophy of an aesthetic" (p. 34).

Sarrazin (1995) uses the music of Native American cultures as an example of music which does not adhere to Western aesthetic conventions. She notes that Native American music or ceremonial/tribal music does not conform to the European concept of "art for art's sake." Rather, Native American music is functional. It is "inextricably linked to an action or behavior, as is dance" (p. 34). She notes that in some indigenous cultures the word for music does not even exist as a separate construct (Campbell and Seeger [1995, p. 20] note that the Suya Amazonian people have one word for music and dance—"ngere"). Music for Native Americans is part of everyday life, and is combined with daily and sacred actions and experiences. For example, there are songs for grinding corn and choosing herbs for healing ceremonies. "Traditional music for listening pleasure does not exist" (Sarrazin, 1994, p. 35). Native American instrumental music for its own sake does not exist. The music is inextricably linked to its function and action, each instrument has symbolic meaning, and the music is primarily vocal. Meaning is not attached to the sound of the music separate from its action. (While recordings of Native American instrumental music, new-age renditions of Native flute music, and recordings of Native American songs exist, this music is controversial among traditional members of Native communities. Some within the community embrace the modern uses of traditional music, while others feel it is an objectionable way of using the music.) Lastly, the idea of a composer of the music does not exist: "music is considered to come to an individual through a spirit, either by dreams or by a trance" (p. 35). This different approach to the aesthetic value of music explains much of the controversy and objection which some Native Americans have voiced regarding the use of ceremonial and tribal music in classroom settings (Campbell and McAllester, 1994).

To fully understand the meaning of music in different cultures, we must become sensitive to our own cultural encapsulation. We must recognize the ways in which we take music making and music listening for granted as normal and universal. While music certainly exists as a universal phenomenon, it is by no means a singular universal construct. The meaning and function of church music for a working-class African-American woman, and of pop rock-and-roll for an upper-class white adolescent boy, are different. How culture defines, contextualizes, and prioritizes the experience of music is essential knowledge for music therapists. Ansdell (1995) begins to explore this phenomenon as he talks about the differences between passive listening, and the listening that takes place while playing music together. He calls this "listening-in-playing" or "social listening" (p. 158). Music therapists must write more about these various ways of understanding the experience of music, listening, and aesthetics. Music therapists must know how the fields of counseling, mental health, education, and music are all influenced by the dominant culture. They must be able to identify their own cultural influences, the cultural influences of their clients, and the cultural influences of the field of music therapy itself.

Bernard and Goodyear (1998) note that while it is important to recognize that counseling and psychotherapy reflect the dominant culture, it is also essential to recognize that counseling and psychotherapy, in themselves, constitute a culture. The culture of counseling and psychotherapy has a language of its own; with norms, beliefs, and customs; and its own form of governance. Accordingly, music therapy too, represents a culture. How music is used within the music therapy culture takes on its own meanings. Within music therapy the therapeutic relationship is modulated or mediated via the musical relationship. Ansdell (1995) writes that it is the skill of the music therapist to make music and the qualities of music "accessible to the people" with whom they work (p. 16). Music, creativity, and the creative process are attributed a special status within the music therapy encounter. As music therapists we must be responsible about how our own professional cultural expectations and practices interface with the cultural expectations and practices of our clients.

Multicultural Approaches to Supervision

With the increasing demands of clinicians to provide multiculturally sensitive practice, there has been an increasing literature in multicultural and cross-cultural training and supervision (Leong and Wagner, 1994; Pope-Davis and Coleman, 1997). Compared with the literature on multicultural counseling education, the literature regarding multicultural supervision is quite limited (Bernard and Goodyear, 1998). This likely reflects the limited literature on supervision in general. Bernard and Goodyear (1998) note that studies have found supervision training to be an infrequent occurrence. Traditionally, supervision has been left to more senior therapists, with the underlying belief that if one is a good therapist, one can be a good supervisor (Bernard and Goodyear, p. 5). Unfortunately, this has not always proven to be the case, and more and more mental health professions are requiring that supervisors receive formal training in supervision. In this regard, music therapy appears to be progressive in its policy regarding supervision. As of 1994, the former National Association for Music Therapy required that for a site to become an approved training site for music therapy interns, "the Director must have three years experience beyond the internship in direct music therapy service, and have completed one 5 hour CMTE (continued music therapy education) workshop on Music Therapy Intern Supervision or other documented supervision training" (Clinical Training Policy of the American Music Therapy Association as cited on their Web site).

Clinical supervision is defined as:

> An intervention provided by a more senior member of a profession to a more junior member or members of that same profession. This relationship is evaluative, extends over time, and has the simultaneous purposes of enhancing the professional functioning of the more junior person(s), monitoring the quality of professional services offered to the client(s) she, he, or they see(s), and serving

as a gatekeeper of those who are to enter the particular profession (Bernard and Goodyear, 1998, p. 6).

Supervision takes place prior to graduating with a professional degree during practicum and internship training experiences, often both on-site and within educational supervision courses. In addition, supervision takes place during post-graduate clinical work, initially for many professionals as they prepare for professional licensure and certification, but then afterwards, as well, as part of their ongoing development and the overall treatment coordination of the client.

Supervision is the bridge between theory and practice. Within supervision, clinicians attempt to understand and apply the theory of their profession while meeting the expectations of the demands of their clinical work. Within supervision, the client, the therapist, the supervisor, and the agency or the administration all have a voice. The supervisor and supervisee must attend both to the needs of the client and to the expectations of the larger clinical milieu.

Within supervision of music therapy, I propose that the profession also has a voice. Music therapists, by virtue of their "minority" status within most mental health organizations, are often under a distinct pressure to justify, explain, or translate their work. When music therapists are supervised by other music therapists, the supervisor has a unique role and function. Often the supervisor's role as role model for the supervisee, gatekeeper of the profession, and facilitator of training in profession-specific techniques and methods is intensified. Often the supervisee has no other discipline-specific role models, trainers, or mentors, other than previous educators. This adds an additional burden onto the supervisory relationship, and is intensified by the relationship which the supervisor has with the administration and institution in which the supervisee works. When music therapists are supervised by professionals from other mental health disciplines, supervision is often overlaid with a continual need for the supervisee to translate their music therapy experiences and interventions into a language understood and valued by supervisors. This additional consideration of the impact of the role of the "culture" of music therapy within supervision must be explored in conjunction with multicultural issues, if one is to do justice to the supervision of the music therapist.

Multicultural issues within supervision are as various, complex, and important as multicultural issues in counseling. They parallel the issues raised by the multicultural competencies devised by Sue, Arredondo and McDavis (1992) listed earlier, and include issues which arise from the counselor or supervisor's awareness or lack of awareness of their own cultural assumptions, values, and biases; from the counselor or supervisor's understanding of the worldview of the culturally different client, or of the supervisor's understanding of the worldview of the culturally different supervisee; and from the development of appropriate, culturally sensitive intervention strategies and techniques both in therapy and in supervision. In addition, it is the supervisor who holds partial responsibility, along with educators, for the cultural competence of the clinician. The supervisor is ultimately responsible for the welfare of the client. That responsibility must extend to the cultural knowledge, sensitivity, and skill of the supervisee. In addition, supervisors are in the role of evaluating the competence of supervisees, and as such, retain a position of power in relation to the supervisee. This power is ascribed to supervisors not only because of their responsibilities but due to their credentials and previous training (Cook, 1994). Supervisors must be aware of how their evaluative power influences the discussion of culture within supervision. Given the complexity of these issues, it is clear that, as Bernard (1994) observes, "supervision is not an appropriate place for an awareness of multicultural dynamics to begin—not for the trainee, and especially not for the supervisor" (p. 160).

Yet, given the status of multicultural education for music therapists, we can assume that in fact most supervisees and supervisors have limited exposure to multicultural competency training. Stone (1997) notes that training sites should not carry the burden of multicultural training. Both the supervisor and the supervisee should have had some education in multicultural counseling prior to the student being placed in a situation where they are working with client/therapist dyads and/or supervisee/supervisor dyads where there are cultural differences. This education prepares the way for both the supervisor and supervisee to "possess the capabilities to develop an effective supervisory environment through which the trainer and trainee can learn more about cultural factors in therapeutic practice" (p. 272). Music therapists must begin to incorporate multicultural approaches to music and to therapy within their curriculum. In addition, supervisors must become educated in multicultural issues related to the practice of music therapy.

In a review of the literature on multicultural supervision, Leong and Wagner (1994) note that ignorance on the part of the supervisor accounted for many of the issues raised within the literature. Given that many supervisors are not adequately trained in supervision or multicultural issues this is not surprising. In light of the increasing resources available to music therapy supervisors, we cannot afford to remain ignorant regarding multicultural issues. Steward, Wright, Jackson, and Jo (1998) investigated the importance of supervisors being trained both in their own multicultural awareness, knowledge, and skills, as well as in evaluating the awareness, knowledge, and skills of their supervisees. They utilized the Multicultural Awareness, Knowledge, and Skills Survey (MAKSS) developed by D'Andrea, Daniels, and Heck (1991), and the Cross-Cultural Counseling Inventory-Revised (CCCI-R) developed by LaFromboise, Coleman, and Hernandez (1991). Music therapy supervisors should become familiar with such instruments, and once sufficiently educated themselves should begin to utilize them initially as teaching tools, and then later as evaluative measures. In addition, cultural competency evaluations should include feedback from the client (especially in the cases in which the supervisor and clinician are white, and the client is a person of color) and from colleagues with more extensive multicultural counseling training (Steward, et al., 1998; see also Coleman, 1997 for a description of a portfolio assessment of multicultural competence). Music therapy supervisors should take advantage of advanced coursework in multicultural training offered in most university settings, and in continuing education opportunities offered on this topic.

Racial Issues in Music Therapy Supervision

As music therapy supervisors become more aware of their own assumptions, values, and biases, they will be able to identify and address many of the potential multicultural issues identified in the literature on multicultural supervision. The majority of the literature and empirical research available on multicultural supervision focuses on problems that have arisen when there are cultural differences between supervisor and supervisee. While much of this literature is identified as "cross-cultural," in fact, most of this literature refers specifically to differences in racial affiliation between supervisor and supervisee. Bernard (1994) notes that this reflects the hypersensitivity that Americans still have with racial issues. Cook (1994) proposes that supervisors become familiar with racial identity models, and describes both the people of color racial identity model and the white racial identity model. She notes that "(t)he racial identity attitudes of the supervision partner, circumstances in the clinical agency, or other factors" might trigger a "hierarchy of racial acknowledgment" (p. 135). By this she means that race will be acknowledged in different ways depending on how similar or dissimilar the supervisor and supervisee are in relation to their racial identity development.

Given the preponderance of white music therapists in the U.S. (Toppozada, 1995 indicated that 91 percent of her respondents were white, reflecting the former NAMT membership), the importance of acknowledging white racial identity is particularly significant. Historically, white privilege and cultural encapsulation have contributed to white Americans experiencing themselves as "raceless." White privilege is defined by unearned benefits which whites experience by virtue of belonging to the dominant culture. These benefits include:

> not being questioned or viewed suspiciously every day because of one's race; seeing one's values and history validated and reinforced in the media and popular culture; not having to be the representative of the entire White race in groups or discussions about racial issues; and not having to worry about being targeted by police, employers, or anyone else due to race. Being the recipient of White privilege allows one to neglect or be oblivious to anything outside of the dominant White culture without fear of repercussions. (Fong and Lease, 1997, pp. 391–392)

Cultural encapsulation is characterized by defining reality according to one's own cultural assumptions, minimizing cultural differences, imposing a self-reference criterion for judging the behavior of others, and disregarding one's own cultural biases (Pedersen, 1995). While these processes are likely to be common for many white music therapists of European descent, they certainly cannot be assumed to be true for all white music therapists. Various other sociodemographic variables (including ethnicity, socioeconomic status, gender, and affectional orientation) contribute to the varying degrees to which white counselors are aware of these racial considerations (see Smith, 1991; Richardson and Molinaro, 1996; Rowe, Bennett, and Atkinson, 1994).

In a recent article about racial issues in supervision, Daniels, D'Andrea, and Kyung Kim (1999) identified three issues which arose because of cultural differences between a supervisor and supervisee, when the supervisor was white and the supervisee was an ethnic minority. These included differences in interpersonal style, differences in counseling goals, and differences in the perceptions of the roles of the supervisee and supervisor in the supervision process. Fong and Lease (1997) also talk about differences in style, which they characterize as "communication issues" (p. 395). They note that white supervisors who are unaware of cultural differences may misinterpret basic verbal and nonverbal cues. Behavior such as eye contact, head nodding, and loud rapid speech, or an interpersonal style characterized by direct task-oriented focus, may be seen as normative by the supervisor, leading the supervisor to misinterpret minimal eye contact, quiet deferent verbalizing, or an indirect approach as fear, resistance, incompetence, or low self-esteem. In fact, these behaviors may represent different cultural values such as respect for or deference to authority, or the value of avoiding conflict in the service of sustaining interpersonal contact, or of being self-effacing in the service of belonging (see also Priest, 1994). These differences in interpersonal style and communication style have also been found to exist between men and women regardless of culture. Bernard and Goodyear (1998) point out that "issues of power, sensitivity to feedback, communication style, resolving conflict, and boundary issues are all apt to emerge *for both supervisee and supervisor* when differences exist between genders in this relationship" (p. 46, emphasis in the original).

Stage Models of Multicultural Supervision

When supervisor and supervisee are culturally different, differences in the fundamental approach which counselors take toward establishing goals for treatment, and their understanding of the role of supervisee/supervisor are likely to arise. Worldview and values will inform one's approach to treatment planning, and one's approach to supervision. It is the supervisor's responsibility to be aware of, tolerate, and utilize these differences. Priest (1994) suggests that most effective multicultural supervisors have progressed through a six-stage model of multicultural supervision. In stage 1, supervisors go through a process of denying cultural differences, and being unaware of how these differences influence supervision. In stage 2, cultural differences are recognized, but the supervisor doesn't know what to do with this awareness, and he or she is likely to feel overwhelmed with learning about new cultures. In stage 3, the supervisor attempts to identify the differences and similarities between and among the cultures, and to identify the way these cultures impact the supervisory relationship. In stage 4, the supervisor attempts to understand their own cultural identity, and to be aware of their self-identity and self-worth as defined within a cultural context. In stage 5, the supervisor appreciates the cultural differences and identifies how these cultural attributes can contribute to the supervisee's clinical competence. In stage 6, the supervisor is able to remain professional and respectful of cultural styles. The supervisor is able to use multiple supervisory methodologies and clinical skills to broaden cultural horizons. Bernard (1994) suggests that supervisors accomplish the first four stages of this model in presupervision training. These stages, in fact, correspond with the racial identity development of the supervisor. To the extent that supervisors are aware of their own cultural identity, these stages may be more or less relevant.

Bernard and Goodyear (1998), Priest (1994), and Remington and DaCosta (1989) all discuss some unique challenges which are encountered when the supervisor is a member of a cultural minority and the supervisee is a member of the cultural majority. One issue is the expectation of negative outcomes or the questioning of the supervisor's competence on the part of the supervisee (Priest, 1994). Supervisors are encouraged to bring up cultural issues early on in the supervisory relationship. Issues of power and evaluation often inhibit supervisees from bringing up cultural issues when they involve the supervisory dyad. In addition, supervisors are encouraged to work in consultation with other supervisors. More ethnic minority supervisors need to be trained, mentored, and encouraged to adapt traditional models and develop nontraditional models of therapy and supervision which can meet the needs of a more diverse population. As supervisees are exposed to the experience of being supervised by culturally different supervisors, traditional models and methods will begin to shift (Stone, 1997).

Porter (1994) describes a stage model of multicultural supervision which promotes multicultural competencies in the supervisee. This model assumes cultural competence on the part of the supervisor. In stage 1, the supervisor introduces a culturally sensitive, cross-cultural perspective to the supervisee. "Culture is made salient at every treatment junction, and culturally relative and specific approaches are compared to universalist assumptions about mental health" (p. 46). This stage is task-oriented, structured, and didactic, with the intent of building competence and confidence in the supervisee, and reducing defensiveness. This stage also allows the supervisor and supervisee a chance to build their relationship. In stage 2, a sociocultural framework and an analysis of oppression is introduced. In this stage, the supervisor encourages the supervisee to move from a "more detached, clinical perspective" which may include a pejorative, pathological view of symptoms, to a more contextualized view of the client's behavior in relation to the cultural, historical, and social factors which have shaped that behavior. Issues of acculturation, racism, classism, and other oppressions that affect the client's life are understood as central to an understanding of the client's mental health issues and concerns. Respect for the client's strengths and recognition of the client's cultural resources are critical in this stage. In stage 3, the supervisee's own biases, stereotypes, and racism are explored. As Porter suggests, this stage "is the most personal and difficult stage of the supervision process. . . This stage is the most threatening and requires a great deal of trust between the therapist and supervisor" (p. 50). Certainly this level of work requires that the supervisor have examined their own biases prior to this process, and that a level of trust and open communication be established. Again, one must attend to the issues of power. It must be clear to the supervisee how the issue of evaluation will interface with this process. Stage 4 involves expanding the intervention with the client and the professional development of the supervisee, beyond the individual client "to the realm of collective solutions and social action" (p. 52).

Sinacore-Guinn (1995) describes another stage model of multicultural sensitization, specifically with regards to developing culture- and gender-sensitive diagnostic capabilities, but I think this model can serve as a model for supervisors as well. In stage 1, students (or supervisors) are encouraged to critique the cultural and gender biases inherent in general approaches to diagnosis. In stage 2, students are to examine the cultural systems in their own lives. In stage 3, students identify a personal bicultural struggle. In stage 4, students do an analysis of cultural and gender issues on a series of case studies. In stage 5, students are asked to integrate theoretical orientations and cultural competencies.

These models of multicultural supervision all offer springboards from which to launch multiculturally sensitive treatment. If put into practice, these models can eliminate some of the basic problems identified by Leong and Wagner (1994) in their comprehensive review of the literature on multicultural supervision. These problems include "(a) undiscussed racial-ethnic issues that distort the supervisory relationship or affect patient management, (b) 'overcompensating indulgence' in racial-ethnic issues that were previously denied, (c) overdependence on supervisors and their knowledge and status, and (d) assignment of only minority cases to minority trainees" (p. 120).

Conclusion

Multicultural counseling competencies must become a part of the music therapist's repertoire. These concepts and constructs should become as natural and as familiar as are the concepts of transference and countertransference. Not only must music therapists be aware of a variety of types of world music, and the role and meaning of the music within those cultures, but they must be aware of the nature of culture's influence on the process of identity formation (both their own and their clients'), on the practice of counseling and mental health service delivery, and on the practice of music therapy as a discipline.

Supervisors of music therapy must take an active role in moving the profession forward, by first becoming educated and sensitized to the role and impact of culture on their own lives, on the music therapy encounter, and then on the supervisory experience. Given that American music therapists continue to provide supervision for a large number of international students, it is imperative that music therapy supervisors be aware of multicultural issues within supervision. (A 1997 survey indicated that thirty-eight out of forty-nine international students, representing fourteen different countries, were intending to do their music therapy internship in the U.S. [Brotons, et al., 1997]). Given our current state of multicultural training preinternship, supervisors must assume responsibility for the development and evaluation of cultural competency of their supervisees. Supervisors can also begin to demand that educational programs include multicultural training. Given the overwhelming literature and the force of the multicultural movement in counseling, it is essential that music therapy begin to require multicultural training of students at all levels. Lastly, supervisors must hold the agencies they work for accountable for attention to issues of social justice and multiculturalism.

Music therapists have a unique responsibility to examine and research the question of culture's influence on music. How does culture impact the experience of mutual music making within music therapy sessions? How does culture impact the experience of music, and the definition of aesthetics? How does culture specifically impact the music therapy supervisory relationship? Are there special cultural considerations to which the music therapy supervisor must attend? As music therapists we are acutely aware of the power of music to transcend human boundaries and to provide individuals with a common language. Can music "transcend culture to speak universally to humanity" (Jorgensen, 1998, p. 84)? If so, what is the role of culture in relation to this transcendent function within music? These are the questions which must be answered as music therapy supervisors take up the challenge of multiculturalists within the fields of counseling and mental health. It is the supervisor who can empower the supervisee to empower others. It is the music therapist who explores the cross-cultural potential of the experience of music. It is the client who brings their whole selves to the music therapy encounter. Music therapy supervisors must ensure that their supervisees see this whole-ness, as their whole-ness is seen.

References

American Psychological Association (1993). Guidelines for providers of psychological services to ethnic, linguistic and culturally diverse populations. *American Psychologist,* 48, 45–48.

Ansdell, G. (1995). *Music for Life: Aspects of Creative Music Therapy with Adult Clients.* London and Bristol, PA: Jessica Kingsley Publishers.

Barongan, C., Bernal, G., Comas-Diaz, L., Iijima Hall, C., Nagayama Hall, F., LaDue, R., Parham, T., Pedersen, P., Porche-Burke, L., Rollack, D., and Root, M. (1997). Misunderstandings of multiculturalism: Shouting fire in crowded theaters. *American Psychologist,* 52(6), 654–655.

Bernard, J. (1994). Multicultural supervision: A reaction to Leong and Wagner, Cook, Priest, and Fukuyama. *Counselor Education and Supervision,* 34(2), 159–171.

Bernard, J., and Goodyear, R. (1998). *Fundamentals of Clinical Supervision.* (2nd ed.). Boston: Allyn and Bacon.

Bradt, J. (1997). Ethical issues in multicultural counseling: Implications for the field of music therapy. *The Arts in Psychotherapy,* 24(2), 137–143.

Brotons, M. (1995). International connections: A long tradition. *Music Therapy Perspectives,* 13(1), 7–9.

Brotons, M., Graham-Hurley, K., Hairston, M., Hawley, T., Michel, D., Moreno, J., Picard, D., and Taylor, D. (1997). A survey of international music therapy students in NAMT-approved academic programs. *Music Therapy Perspectives,* 15(1), 45–49.

Campbell, P., and McAllester, D. P. (1994). David P. McAllester on Navajo music. *Music Educators Journal,* 81, 17–23.

Campbell, P., and Seeger, A. (1995). Anthony Seeger on music of Amazonian Indians. *Music Educators Journal,* 81, 17–21.

Carter, R., and Qureshi, A. (1995). A typology of philosophical assumptions in multicultural counseling and training. In J. Pontorotto, J. Casas, L. Suzuki, and C. Alexander (eds.), *Handbook of Multicultural Counseling.* Thousand Oaks, CA: Sage Publications.

Cheung, F. (2000). Deconstructing counseling in a cultural context. *The Counseling Psychologist,* 28(1), 123–132.

Christopher, J. (1999). Situating psychological well-being: Exploring the cultural roots of its theory and research. *Journal of Counseling and Development,* 77(2) 141–152.

Coleman, H. (1997). Portfolio assessment of multicultural counseling competence. In D. Pope-Davis and H. Coleman (eds.), *Multicultural Counseling Competencies: Assessment, Education and Training, and Supervision.* Thousand Oaks, CA: Sage Publications.

Cook, D. (1994). Racial identity in supervision. *Counselor Education and Supervision,* 34(2), 132–142.

D'Andrea, M., Daniels, J., and Heck, R. (1991). Evaluating the impact of multicultural counseling training. *Journal of Counseling and Development,* 70, 143–150.

D'Andrea, M., and Daniels, J. (1997). Multicultural counseling supervision: Central ideas, theoretical considerations, and practical strategies. In D. Pope-Davis and H. Coleman (eds.), *Multicultural Counseling Competencies: Assessment, Education and Training, and Supervision.* Thousand Oaks, CA: Sage Publications.

Daniels, J., D'Andrea, M., and Kyung Kim, B. (1999). Assessing the barriers and changes of cross-cultural supervision: A case study. *Counselor Education and Supervision,* 38(3), 191–205.

Darrow, A., and Molloy, D. (1998). Multicultural perspectives in music therapy: An examination of the literature, educational curricula, and clinical practices in culturally diverse cities in the United States. *Music Therapy Perspectives,* 16(1), 27–32.

Dosamantes-Beaudry, I. (1997). Embodying a cultural identity. *The Arts in Psychotherapy,* 24(2), 129–135.

Fischer, A., Jome, L., and Atkinson, D. (1998). Reconceptualizing multicultural counseling: Universal healing conditions in a culturally specific context. *Counseling Psychologist,* 26(4), 525–589.

Fong, M., and Lease, S. (1997). Cross-cultural supervision: Issues for the White supervisor. In D. Pope-Davis and H. Coleman (eds.), *Multicultural Counseling Competencies: Assessment, Education and Training, and Supervision.* Thousand Oaks, CA: Sage Publications.

Fowers, B., and Richardson, F. (1997). A second invitation to dialogue: Multiculturalism and psychology. *American Psychologist,* 52(6), 659–661.

Fukuyama, M. (1990). Taking a universal approach to multicultural counseling. *Counselor Education and Supervision,* 30(1), 6–17.

Heine, S., and Lehman, D. (1995). Cultural variation in unrealistic optimism: Does the West feel more vulnerable than the East? *Journal of Personality and Social Psychology,* 68, 595–607.

Helms, J., and Richardson, T. (1997). How "multiculturalism" obscures race and culture as differential aspects of counseling competency. In D. Pope-Davis and H. Coleman (eds.), *Multicultural Counseling Competencies: Assessment, Education and Training, and Supervision.* Thousand Oaks, CA: Sage Publications.

Holiman, M., and Lauver, P. (1987). The counselor culture and client-centered practice. *Counselor Education and Supervision, 26,* 184–191.

Jorgensen, E. (1998). Musical multiculturalism revisited. *Journal of Aesthetic Education,* 32(2), 77–88.

Kitayama, S., Markus, H., and Kurokawa, M. (2000). Culture, emotion, and well-being: Good feelings in Japan and the United States. *Cognition and Emotion,* 14(1), 93–124.

LaFromboise, T., Coleman, H., and Hernandez, A. (1991). Development and factor structure of the Cross-Cultural Counseling Inventory-Revised. *Professional Psychology: Research and Practice, 22,* 380.

Leach, M., and Carlton, M. (1997). Towards a multicultural training philosophy. In D. Pope-Davis and H. Coleman (eds.), *Multicultural Counseling Competencies: Assessment, Education and Training, and Supervision.* Thousand Oaks, CA: Sage Publications.

Leong, F., and Wagner, N. (1994). Cross-cultural counseling supervision: What do we know? What do we need to know? *Counselor Education and Supervision,* 34(2), 117–132.

Lewis, P. (1997). Multiculturalism and globalism. *The Arts in Psychotherapy,* 24(2), 123–127.

Lloyd, A. (1987). Multicultural counseling: Does it belong in counselor education? *Counselor Education and Supervision, 26,* 164-167.

Maranto, C. (1993). *Music Therapy: International Perspectives.* Pipersville, PA: Jeffrey Books.

Miller, J. (1986). *Toward a New Psychology of Women* (2nd Ed.). Boston: Beacon Press.

Miller, J. (1991). The development of women's sense of self. In J. Jordon, A. Kaplan, J. Miller, I. Stiver, and J. Surrey (eds.), *Women's Growth in Connection.* New York: Guilford.

Moreno, J. (1988). Multicultural music therapy: The world music connection. *Journal of Music Therapy,* 25(1), 17–27.

Moreno, J. (1995). Ethnomusic therapy: An interdisciplinary approach to music and healing. *The Arts in Psychotherapy,* 22(4), 329–338.

Moreno, J., Brotons, M., Hairston, M., Hawley, T., Kiel, H., Michel, D., and Rohrbacher, M. (1990). International music therapy: A global perspective. *Music Therapy Perspectives, 8,* 41–46.

Pedersen, P. (1991). Multiculturalism as a generic approach to counseling. *Journal of Counseling and Development, 70,* 6–12.

Pedersen, P. (1995). Culture-centered ethical guidelines for counselors. In J. Pontorotto, J. Casas, L. Suzuki, and C. Alexander (eds.), *Handbook of Multicultural Counseling.* Thousand Oaks, CA: Sage Publications.

Ponterotto, J., Casas, J., Suzuki, L., and Alexander, C. (eds.). (1995). *Handbook of Multicultural Counseling.* Thousand Oaks, CA: Sage.

Pope-Davis, D., and Coleman, H. (eds.). (1997). *Multicultural Counseling Competencies: Assessment, Education and Training, and Supervision.* Thousand Oaks, CA: Sage Publications.

Porter, N. (1994). Empowering supervisees to empower others: A culturally responsive supervision model. *Hispanic Journal of Behavioural Sciences,* 16(1), 43–57.

Priest, R. (1994). Minority supervisor and majority supervisee: Another perspective of clinical reality. *Counselor Education and Supervision,* 34(2), 152–158.

Remington, G., and DaCosta, G. (1989). Ethnocultural factors in resident supervision: Black supervisor and white supervisees. *American Journal of Psychotherapy,* 43(3), 398–404.

Richardson, T., and Molinaro, K. (1996). White counselor self-awareness: A prerequisite for developing multicultural competence. *Journal of Counseling and Development,* 74, 238–242.

Rowe, W., Bennett, S., and Atkinson, D. (1994). White racial identity models: A critique and alternative proposal. *The Counseling Psychologist,* 22(1), 129–146.

Sarrazin, N. (1995). Exploring aesthetics: Focus on Native Americans. *Music Educators Journal,* 81, 33–36.

Sinacore-Guinn, A. (1995). The diagnostic window: Culture- and gender-sensitive diagnosis and training. *Counselor Education and Supervision,* 35(1), 18–32.

Smith, E. (1991). Ethnic identity development: Toward the development of a theory within the context of majority / minority status. *Journal of Counseling and Development,* 70, 181–188.

Sodowsky, G., Kuo-Jackson, P., and Loya, G. (1997). Outcome of training in the philosophy of assessment: Multicultural counseling competencies. In D. Pope-Davis and H. Coleman (eds.), *Multicultural Counseling Competencies: Assessment, Education and Training, and Supervision.* Thousand Oaks, CA: Sage Publications.

Steward, R., Wright, D., Jackson, J., and Jo, H. (1998). The relationship between multicultural counseling training and the evaluation of culturally sensitive and culturally insensitive counselors. *Journal of Multicultural Counseling and Development,* 26 *(3),* 205–218.

Stone, G. (1997). Multiculturalism as a context for supervision: Perspectives, limitations, and implications. In D. Pope-Davis and H. Coleman (eds.), *Multicultural Counseling Competencies: Assessment, Education and Training, and Supervision.* Thousand Oaks, CA: Sage Publications.

Sue, D., Arredondo, P., and McDavis, R. (1992). Multicultural counseling competencies and standards: A call to the profession. *Journal of Counseling and Development,* 70, 477–486.

Sue, D. and Sue, D. (1990). *Counseling the Culturally Different: Theory and Practice* (2nd ed.). New York: John Wiley.

Sue, D. (1996). Multicultural counseling: Models, methods, and actions. *Counseling Psychologist,* 24(2), 279–285.

Teo, T., and Febbraro, A. (1997). Norms, factuality, and power in multi-culturalism. *American Psychologist,* 52(6), 656–657.

Toppozada, M. (1995). Multicultural training for music therapists: An examination of current issues based on a national survey of professional music therapists. *Journal of Music Therapy,* 32(2), 65–90.

Acknowledgments

I would like to acknowledge the support and editorial assistance of Dr. Paul Efthim.

Part Two

Preprofessional Supervision

Chapter 5

Group Supervision in First-Time Music Therapy Practicum

Lisa Summer, MCAT, MT-BC
Associate Professor, Director of Music Therapy
Chair, Division of Human Behavior and Human Services
Anna Maria College, Paxton, MA

The practicum is the crucible in which music therapists are forged. No classroom work can compare to the intensity of face-to-face engagement with real individuals; real individuals with real needs, disabilities, and emotions. Like other "first" experiences, the first practicum is emotionally charged and transformative. I have supervised many first-time practica students in my fourteen years as a music therapy educator. My strategy is informed by my own education, experiences as a clinician, and my personal philosophy of music therapy. Each music therapy educator brings these individual influences into his or her stewardship of our future professionals, but there is a commonality that we all share: a desire to promulgate competence in our students and our field. Over the years I have found that my students share a commonality as well: a certainty in confronting basic music therapy issues that I too confronted during my education. Despite differences in cultural background, age, gender, geography, or language, all music therapy students will encounter the same basic challenges as they acquire the clinical skills, theoretical knowledge, musical abilities, and personal growth to prepare them to enter the profession.

In the following chapter I will address the principal obstacles confronting first-time practicum students and my supervisory strategy for guiding students through them. The specific methods of my supervision may differ from yours; for example, I work most effectively in group supervision while you may favor individual supervision, I have worked primarily with undergraduate students, while you may work with graduate students. Nonetheless, I hope that you will find herein a useful summary of the most common first-time practicum issues and various supervision strategies to address them.

The beginning music therapy student should not be treated as a tabula rasa upon which the supervisor impresses her techniques, theory, skills, and style. Music therapy students should not be imitations of their teachers and supervisors, nor should they be trained uniformly as if they emerged from some prototypical music therapy student template. Preferably, the practicum will cultivate within the student the ability to utilize the unique and individual attributes already present within her so that she might best actualize her latent potential to benefit music therapy clients.

An approach to supervision that recognizes and appreciates the differences with which each student enters her training will foster the development of a natural therapeutic style built upon the strengths of each trainee, rather than create a simulacrum, a pale imitation of the supervisor. An effective therapist must be "present" for her client, ready to react spontaneously and unassumingly to difficult clinical situations, not tentatively struggling to recall what her supervisor would do under the circumstances. We as supervisors have a responsibility to countenance independence of thought and action in our charges, not tie them to an artificial dependence on pedantic formulas of our own devices. The initial semester of practicum is the most essential in carrying out an internally driven, rather than externally driven, approach to supervision. Simply put, our goal as first-time practicum supervisors consists of three primary objectives, all of which center on the qualities already present in our beginning students.

The first objective is to reinforce the therapeutic qualities inherent in each student's character. Students have a natural style in relating to people in need (a nurturing style)—the more this is supported, the more naturally therapeutic the student can become. Supervision should begin with the recognition of the student's innate inclinations to help individuals in need so that the student can be as authentic in her service to clients as possible. There is no specific or correct therapeutic style. It is best to begin by identifying the student's natural style and accommodating it to their first client (Forinash and Summer, 1998; Forinash and Summer, 1999).

The second objective is to evoke the student's musical character. Students have already developed a relationship with music. From this relationship they have developed an internal and personal understanding of some of the principles of music therapy from practicing and performing. They have opinions and beliefs about how music is therapeutic. The more these are strengthened, the more the student's learning is internally driven. Their ideas about the functions that music plays in music therapy should be built upon the beliefs they have developed as young musicians. For example, throughout my teenage years, I utilized music primarily as a vehicle for my own self-expression (playing horn by myself, listening and singing to music in my room away from my family and friends). I came to music therapy with a clear personal understanding of how music functions as a vehicle for emotional expression and introspection. Many students, however, come to music therapy with their predominant experience of music being a shared, social experience. For example, a student whose family spends weekends singing songs and playing instruments with each other will come to music therapy with a personal understanding of the socializing and interpersonal, rather than the intrapersonal, therapeutic functions that music performs. The student with a previous use of music as an interpersonal tool will not likely develop music therapy skills along the same line as one whose use of music was predominantly intrapersonal.

Each individual will more readily understand, and implement with their first client, the therapeutic function that they have personally experienced; and each individual will find it more difficult to carry out the functions with which they are not yet familiar. Each individual has only part of the big picture of music therapy clinical practice which, if not made conscious, will hamper the student's overall growth (Summer, 1997).

The third objective is to address preconceived notions about aspects of the music therapy process. Students arrive at the threshold of music therapy encumbered with prejudices about how music can be therapeutic, with peremptory views about what therapy itself means, and often with popular misconceptions about various client populations. Frequently these prior formed opinions can be an obstacle to the student's ability to observe clients with an open mind as well as to perform tasks required for the therapeutic process. The supervisor cannot just ask the student to erase these thoughts, but must help the student to confront the prejudice consciously in order to unseat it.

The development of an effective model for undergraduate first-time practica differs from the graduate model because of the difference in age groups and life experience. A graduate student changing careers has different educational needs than a student who has just graduated from high school. It is common for students who enter a graduate music therapy program with a previous professional identity to experience a narcissistic blow when they are not immediately proficient at basic music therapy skills (Feiner, 1999). For these students, practica that use modeling and imitation of a music therapy clinician is very effective. Because they have a professional identity and independence of thought, they are able to use imitation as the basis for learning without becoming dependent upon a modeling clinician.

Undergraduate students are used to an authoritarian type of teaching model. Students fresh out of high school have an expectation that teachers lecture, students take notes, and at exam time the students repeat back to the teachers the data they have been fed. They are used to a restricted learning structure and externally enforced direction. Since our goal as practicum supervisors is to foster a unique music therapy identity for each student, a first-time practicum that utilizes a music therapy clinician as a model is counterproductive for undergraduate students. Being recently dependent upon the authoritarian high school teacher for motivation, undergraduates are inclined to be overwhelmed by the combination of the new learning environment (the clinical setting) and the authority of the professional music therapist. The undergraduate student may retreat to her previous educational modus operandi and simply mimic the professional music therapist, rather than develop her own identity in relation to the professional.

The initial semester of coursework and practicum is the time to lay down the basic foundation for music therapy clinical practice. The design and implementation of the first semester of practicum is the most crucial developmental step in the music therapy student's training because it is the first hands-on encounter with clients. The educational goal of the first-time practicum is to create a reflective, independent student, not one dependent upon the supervisor. This is the first developmental step toward creating music therapists who are individuals, with a naturally therapeutic style, rather than one inculcated in them by teachers and supervisors.

The knowledge base and skills requirements addressed in the initial semester of practicum establish the program's values and priorities in regard to what is central to the music therapy process. A first-time practicum with no emphasis upon musical skills misinforms students that musical skills are not central to the music therapy process. In order to develop an effective, therapeutic musical relationship over time with a disabled client the clinical goal of the first-time practicum course is to gain basic knowledge and skills in 1) therapeutic presence, 2) musical skills and 3) carrying out the therapeutic process.[1]

The first part of the music therapy process consists of observation and assessment. The emphasis of the initial practicum cannot be on the quality of observation and assessment but rather on the rudiments of observation itself.

Vignette

When a music therapy student visits her first clinical setting, she does not yet know how to make therapeutic contact with a person with significant disabilities. Chelsea,[2] a first time practicum student, had already visited her first clinical site, a nursing home, several times to observe and informally interact with the elderly residents. In the first music therapy session with her individual client, Chelsea initiated contact. Asking loudly she inquired, "Hello, what's your name?" Although the client lifted her head and made eye contact with her, she did not answer Chelsea's question. Chelsea continued, without a pause, more loudly, "What a nice dress. It's such a pretty color and it looks so nice with the color of your hair." The client looked inquisitively at Chelsea, looked down at her dress and rearranged it; but gave no verbal response. Chelsea continued, "I have my guitar right here in this case. Maybe you'd like to hear a song. I'll play one for you and you tell me if you know it. I bet you'll like this song."

Discussion

Chelsea has unknowingly rejected the client's attempt to connect with her because she does not yet understand how to be therapeutically present with a client. Chelsea was sincere in her attempt to make contact with her client, but an examination of her interaction with Linda shows that she approached her with a specific response in mind. She wanted her to respond verbally: "My name is Linda." When she did not get the response she desired, she ignored Linda's actual response to her. Linda's eye contact was her form of response. Chelsea's next interventions actually cut off Linda's response by directing Linda's eye contact to her clothes, to her guitar, everywhere but to Chelsea's eyes. Linda's eye contact is personal contact with Chelsea, but Chelsea did not observe and identify it as such. Instead, she rejected Linda's eye contact and looked for her to verbalize. After Chelsea realized that Linda was not going to be verbally responsive to her, she should have let go of her expectation and made a transition to a mode of nonverbal communication.

---

[1]My first time practicum course is designed so that each student is assigned an individual client, and receives weekly individual and group supervision. However, I have limited myself to discussing group supervision with students who are working with an individual client (as opposed to students who are working with a therapy group).

[2] All names have been changed in order to protect supervisees' and clients' privacy.

Chelsea needs to learn to receive contact from a client in the form that the client is able and willing to give it. This means that Chelsea needs to give up her own expectations and/or preferences about how a client will respond. Rather than go into a session with a narrowed view of what will or should happen, she needs to cultivate an open state of mind. The client's responses, not the therapist's expectations, must dictate how the therapeutic relationship will unfold.

Entering a therapeutic relationship with a client must be accomplished in an open state of awareness and observation. The therapist interacts with the client using evenly suspended attention, (Freud, 1912), a state of mind in which the therapist globally observes the client. In this state, the therapist gives equal and impartial recognition to the verbal and nonverbal aspects of the client. Such a state of consciousness will diminish the chances that the student will circumvent honest communication from a client in favor of what the student perceives as "appropriate."

Chelsea attended a one-hour group supervision session with nine other first-time practicum students, fresh and excited from their first clinical observation session. The class began with Chelsea recounting her interaction with Linda. "I asked her her name, but she didn't respond. I tried to be friendly and talked about her clothes. I don't know why she didn't answer me, but then I played a song for her, hoping that I could help make her feel more comfortable with me." (As I did not take notes during the class nor record the proceedings, this is not a verbatim transcript. After the group supervision sessions recounted here and below I reconstructed as accurately as I could recall the pertinent dialogue. Though much of the discussion is omitted, I believe that the salient material is accurate.) Chelsea was asked to conjecture why Linda did not answer her. She ventured her opinion that Linda might have felt anxious or nervous at seeing a new face at the nursing home.

With further prompting, Chelsea reflected more deeply upon her interaction with Linda. She recalled two important subtleties of the encounter. She remembered that Linda seemed neither anxious nor nervous. She recollected clearly how Linda made direct eye contact with her. Chelsea said that, at the time, she had a sense that Linda had really wanted to respond. Secondly, Chelsea realized that she herself was anxious and nervous, and had become more so when Linda did not readily "respond" to her. (By "respond" Chelsea means there was no verbal response.) This is Chelsea's first step toward recognizing her own state of mind in therapeutic interactions and in observing the subtle responsiveness of disabled clients. This reflection yields two insights which I, as supervisor, could now reinforce to Chelsea and the supervision class: first, the negative impact of one's expectations upon observing clients; and second, the tendency to project one's own feelings upon the client and how one's own feelings affect client observations.

Chelsea was asked to reenact her interaction with Linda through role-playing with another student volunteer; Chelsea played Linda while another student, Jennifer, assumed Chelsea's part as the therapist. They reenacted the encounter as Chelsea had described it. After the role-play, both students were asked to reflect on their experience in character.

Chelsea, as Linda, reported that she felt Jennifer's good intentions, but that she felt rejected by her. She felt that Jennifer (in the role of Chelsea) just wanted to play her song—that that was what she was there to do. Chelsea said, "It was like you had an assignment, something you were supposed to do. . . . Oh, now I get it! When I was with Linda I did think that's what I was supposed to do—to do music therapy I was supposed to play my guitar. I didn't realize that I skipped over the most important part—I missed the human contact with Linda."

Many of the students recognized Chelsea's experience as similar to their own. Chelsea was then asked to reverse roles and to approach Linda anew, with greater openness. Chelsea and the class were given enough freedom to discover on their own, through role-playing, different strategies for approaching a client through music with therapeutic openness. This role-playing constituted a rehearsal for the students' next session with their clients.

In order to address this issue further, the practicum class was given an assignment to prepare them for visits to their clinical sites for the rest of the semester. They were given guidelines for developing a relaxation or centering technique that they would utilize before each clinic visit to put them in an optimal state of consciousness in which they could better observe and respond to their client. This stratagem for improving observation skills and the class discussion and role-playing preceding it are a part of my own pedagogical method. Other teachers and supervisors utilize their own styles and methods; but all first-time practicum supervisors will confront the problem exemplified in Chelsea's situation.

In this practicum supervision session, the students learned, through reflection, role-playing, and centering, the first step in developing "therapeutic presence" with the client: observing the client's verbal and nonverbal expression in a state of evenly suspended attention.

Music therapy students have cultivated, from years of music training, a special state of consciousness for practicing and playing music. This is a highly self-critical, judgmental state of mind in which the goal is to produce a polished musical performance. To meet this goal the musician narrows her observations to a limited area. While playing or practicing, her attention is focused on performing technical musical tasks with a specific outcome in mind. For example, as a horn player I was taught to have a certain dark, velvety tone throughout my entire register; and I was taught that a certain embouchure and hand position would get me that desired tone. Therefore, when I practice horn I am in the self-critical, judgmental state of mind which facilitates my obtaining that technical goal of a velvety tone. I am not in an open, experimental mode; I am product oriented. I use narrowed, selective attention to control my timbre for the desired outcome.

Practicum students may be confused because the narrowed state of mind so beneficial for music practice (and for which they received reinforcement from their music teachers) is precisely the worst state of mind for the proper practice of music therapy. When a therapist is in a state of narrowed expectations, it fosters an inflexible relationship that is based upon the client's compliance with the therapist. The student therapist looks for the client to respond in an "appropriate" way. This kind of expectation may be acceptable later in the therapeutic process in certain instances when a therapist is working upon specific therapeutic objectives, but it is counterproductive to the global perception of the client's behavior and to the unfolding of a basic therapeutic relationship. Because music students are so used to playing music in a performance-oriented state, unless they are taught to shift their state of mind for therapy sessions to one which is open and nonjudgmental, their observation skills and their general responsiveness to clients will be diminished. With diminished observation skills and responsiveness, therapeutic presence cannot be established.

Sometimes students are hampered by the erroneous impression that therapists should eschew involvement or attachment to clients; believing erroneously that the therapist should distance herself from any feelings toward the client. They may deliberately use the music performance state of mind to create an emotional distance from the client. Students are surprised to learn that one's heartfelt caring, concern, and compassion for the client are the life energy of the therapeutic process. The students' positive feelings toward the client must be engaged and utilized actively by the supervisor early in the learning process. Students' conflictual or problematic feelings (those that might interfere with therapy) should also be a part of the supervision process.

My student, Chelsea, has communication skills, social skills, and self-esteem. Her client, Linda, has disabilities in all of those areas. Linda's disabilities and her impairments due to age and institutionalization in the nursing home created an inequity in relating to Chelsea. Initially, Chelsea's approach exacerbated the inequity between them in two ways: first, she approached her verbally; second, she approached her with a guitar. I wanted Chelsea to look holistically at Linda's abilities and limitations and then build a relationship with her based upon what she can do.

Upon discovering that Linda is unresponsive verbally, Chelsea should indeed have approached her with music; but playing the guitar added to the inequity of their relationship. Playing the guitar made it clear that Chelsea is the musician and Linda is not. Chelsea should have begun by making simple musical contact with her. She could have provided an instrument that would have fostered direct eye contact and mutual, musical contact between them. Chelsea needed to provide Linda with an instrument that was simple enough for her to utilize successfully for a nonverbal response. That choice would have provided her with the ability to make contact with Linda in a manner that bypassed her disabilities, not in a manner that ran head on into them.

In the group supervision session, the students continued to role-play the Chelsea/Linda interaction. Chelsea enacted Linda again, imagining her limitations, and other students took turns approaching her with different instruments in different ways. Chelsea, conjecturing how Linda might respond to each option, tried out different responses. Then Chelsea was asked to identify what was helpful in the students' approaches to her to deepen her understanding of how to develop a therapeutic relationship of equality with clients. She and the class discussed fruitfully their ideas about developing a therapeutic musical relationship with Linda and were directed to practice these different musical approaches on their own.

The nature of the music therapy relationship is not an authoritarian one in which the therapist does something musically to the client. First-time practicum students often assume that they are in charge of creating the music, that they are leading the client into the relationship. While a student has this notion, it is not possible to develop a therapeutic relationship that is client-centered, based upon the immediate needs and responses of the individual client.

One of the most detrimental preconceptions harbored by students is the belief that therapeutic nurturance means "fixing" the client. Many students enter my program believing that the goal for a client who is depressed is to "fix" their depression, that the goal for a client who is withdrawn is engagement. Good therapy cannot take place until the student learns to first accept a client's state as he comes into the session. Students must learn to fight the initial tendency upon encountering a disabled client to "fix" him (and thus reduce her own tension). A student usually cannot do this without an understanding of issues of nurturance, in general; and without addressing how they, personally, were nurtured as children. Each music therapy student has his/her own style of nurturing others in need that has evolved in response to the way the student was nurtured as a child. Sometimes the tendency is to pass on nurturance to others in the same way it was given to us; sometimes we nurture in an opposite way (a person might nurture in a very allowing way because her parents were very overprotective.) In the first-year practicum, music therapy students become aware that their heterogeneous clients require diverse forms of nurturance; indeed, that one client will require different forms of nurturance in various phases of the therapeutic process, and that a client will require disparate forms of nurturance on subsequent days within the same phase of treatment. Students need to develop the flexibility to give many types of nurturance; the first step in this process is to address the limited notion of "fixing" as nurturance. After a short period of observation and music therapy assessment sessions, the student learns to integrate the observations into a coherent presentation of the client. The student must understand how a client's identified disability impacts him as a whole person.

For my student Chelsea, this meant coming to her own understanding of Linda's verbal limitations and the relationship of this to her stroke, the natural aging process, and her institutionalization in the nursing home. I encouraged Chelsea to be independent and to develop her own formulations from her own perspective.

The student's next task is to develop a treatment plan for the client. Each student develops an individual treatment plan for the working phase of therapy. The student is guided to design a treatment plan whose primary goal is the development of the therapeutic relationship. Beyond this, the student will also decide upon another goal or goals to address during the semester. These secondary goals are chosen to address specific disabilities or reinforce specific abilities in the client. For a first-time practicum student, it is preferable to limit the work with the client to one or two secondary goals.

The student develops a tripartite session plan. The goal for the opening section is to establish contact with the client; the goal for the working section is the continued development of contact which may also include work upon a secondary goal or goals; the goal for the end of the session is to effect closure. The student designs and develops her own techniques to address each goal. For beginning music therapy students, it is preferable to work with a very simple treatment plan that focuses upon only one goal per technique. In working with Linda, Chelsea developed an improvised greeting song. The only goal for this technique was to develop contact. Despite the fact that Chelsea's secondary goal for Linda was to increase her spontaneous verbal communication, the work on this goal was left for the working section so as not to interfere with the development of the relationship. This type of simple treatment plan is effective in teaching beginning students to work in a goal-oriented manner and to help them understand the natural shape of a therapy session.

Vignette

Paula's first practicum was with Kenny: nine years old, developmentally delayed, and enrolled in a special education classroom in a public school. Paula spent the first three music therapy sessions assessing Kenny's strengths and limitations. By the fourth session she had designed Kenny's treatment plan which began by singing pre-composed and improvised songs designed to improve contact with Kenny.

Prior to working with Kenny, Paula learned from her client's special education teacher Kenny's favorite song. In her fourth session, Paula sang "It's a Small World After All," accompanying herself on guitar. She kept eye contact with Kenny throughout the piece, performing with unwavering tempo, dynamic, timbre, and phrasing. Kenny began to jump up and down in his chair with excitement, continuing sporadically during the entire song; at times in tempo with the song; at other times, not. At one point in the song he clapped loudly in a sporadic rhythm. For parts of the song he had his eyes closed with a smile on his face. At the first chorus of, "It's a small world," Kenny said the word "world" in exact time with the music.

Discussion

Kenny's responses during the song demonstrate that this technique is not working toward the development of their relationship. Kenny's excitement shows that Paula has the potential to make excellent therapeutic contact with him through the song. However, despite the fact that Kenny enjoyed Paula's performance, contact between them was not made. Kenny's body responses—jumping and clapping—were, for the most part, not related to the tempo or rhythms of the song; and closing his eyes was a sign that he was more internally stimulated by this song than stimulated to make contact with Paula. In addition, Kenny's one verbal response was at the beginning of the song, but he attempted no others after that. As the song progressed, Kenny's responses did not grow more responsive to the music. He never accommodated his movements to the rhythm of the music. His responses were more from stimulation and excitement about the music. This indicates that Kenny was not able to use Paula's music as a vehicle for contact; but rather he used the song as a medium for self-stimulation. Had Paula's therapeutic goal in playing this song been to increase Kenny's engagement in the session, then her approach to this song would have been valid. However, there being no issue with Kenny's level of engagement, Paula did not further her treatment plan in this session.

Paula cannot engender within Kenny a sense of trust and therapeutic connection simply by playing Kenny's favorite song, once or repeatedly. "It's a Small World After All" is an excellent context within which to develop their connection, but Kenny needs more than this. Kenny is exhibiting engagement, but not interpersonal engagement. Paula must not only observe Kenny's reactions to the music, she must respond immediately to them. She needs to utilize Kenny's nonverbal responses as a means to make interpersonal contact with him throughout the length of the music. Paula's task is to seek contact with Kenny by spontaneously adapting the song to his responses.

Musicians realize songs by being responsive to the song's lyrics. The musician realizes the meaning of the song, and takes stylistic liberties with the elements of music (viz.: dynamics, timbre, tempo, attack, phrasing) in order to communicate its meaning to listeners. Whereas the musician is responsive to the meaning of the song's lyrics, the therapeutic realization of a song is primarily dependent upon the client's behavior, and the meaning behind the behaviors. "It's a Small World" is a musical structure—a musical container—which should be interpreted by the music therapist not in relation to the song's text but, rather, in relation to the client's in-the-moment responses. Therapists must be accommodating, incorporating the client's responses into the constantly metamorphosing musical container of the therapeutic relationship.

Altering the tempo of the piece through the use of ritardandi, accelerandi, and pauses would permit Paula to mirror musically the rhythm and intensity of Kenny's physical responses. The tempo, phrasing, and attacks should match Kenny's jumping and clapping; the dynamic intensity should be matched to the size of Kenny's gestures and by the look on his face. In order to focus Kenny's attention on Paula, Kenny should become aware, consciously or unconsciously, that his responses are shaping his song. Paula should not be performing "It's a Small World After All," copyright Wonderland Music Co., Inc.; but rather "It's Kenny's World, After All," copyright equally shared by Kenny and Paula.

Music therapy students must learn to make more intimate moment-by-moment contact with clients than they have ever done before in ordinary music-making situations (such as singing in chorus, playing in ensembles, and even playing guitar and singing in social situations).

Paula's rendition of the song was actually unresponsive to the song's lyrics as well as to her client. Her unwavering use of tempo, dynamic, timbre, rhythms, and phrasing is common in beginning music therapy students who are just learning how to play the guitar. Before she can gain enough musical creativity to respond to Kenny, she must first develop musical flexibility on guitar and voice. Most children's songs provide ample opportunities to "play" stylistically because of their simple phrasing and predictable chord changes. Differences in the song's verses can be exaggerated to create different means of contact. Repetition of the chorus can be emphasized, creating a sense of security and trust within which the therapist can musically prompt the client to sing a simple verbal response. Simple, popular songs are flexible musical containers ripe with possibilities for accommodation to make contact with clients. Although pre-composed, they must be significantly altered to become interpersonal experiences with therapeutic significance.

Some students come with an innate ability to realize a piece of music with sensitivity to the lyrics, while some have an innate ability to interpret the client's responses musically. For effective therapy, all students must develop a strategic balance of attention between client and musical responsiveness. Since the therapist acts as the bridge between the client and the music, she should not focus on the client to the exclusion of the music, nor exaggerate the musical interpretation of a piece in a way that excludes the client from influencing the piece.

In group supervision, Paula was asked to describe her session with Kenny to the class. "I was so happy that I had asked his teacher for his favorite song—he loved it. When I started the song, he was distant at first. During the song we had such a good time and I felt so good afterward." She described Kenny as extremely responsive, engaged, and enjoying the music, and characterized the experience as very therapeutic. Paula was very pleased with this experience.

I questioned her further about her own experience during the music. "Where was your attention? What were you thinking about? Did any specific moments during the song stand out to you?" Paula was able to clearly remember and describe in detail Kenny's responses. It is important to initially hear Paula's perception of this experience. As a first-time practicum student, I need to know whether she is aware of the problems I have noticed. Paula and another student, Hillary, were asked to role-play Paula's session with Kenny. Hillary was asked to take on the role of Kenny and to adopt the emotionally distant stance Paula had described him to be in before she began the song. For purposes of learning, Hillary's portrayal was exaggerated. Paula was asked to re-create "It's a Small World" for Hillary in the same way she had for Kenny the day before.

Hillary began the scene by taking a withdrawn stance in relation to Paula. She portrayed Kenny as feeling mistrustful of Paula, unmotivated, and undesirous of any contact. Paula played with strong, mechanical rhythmic strokes, a rigid tempo, and a consistent dynamic through two verses and two repetitions of the chorus. She played with good technical skills on guitar and sang with a clear but unchanging voice quality. She kept eye contact with Hillary throughout the song. As she played, Hillary reenacted Kenny as he became activated in the music. Then, Hillary was asked to report what she had experienced from the client's point of view. Hillary reported that she had, indeed, felt cared for by Paula as she began to play her favorite song. The song had called her out of her withdrawn state and activated her. However, as the song progressed she reported feeling connected to the song, but not to Paula. She reported that as the song progressed she had an impulse to close her eyes in order to enjoy the music even more. She said that the connection with the music seemed to take her inside herself and away from Paula.

I directed Paula back to her original therapeutic intent. "What was your goal in playing his favorite song?" Immediately she responded, "Oh no, I think I really messed up—but it seemed so therapeutic!"

Moments of soul-searching and remorse should be treasured by the supervisor, not immediately assuaged to reduce anxiety in the student and class. Uncomfortable insights are fertile ground for student growth. The first-time student needs to struggle with the recognition that there is much that she does not yet know. True learning is derived from allowing this tension. Students will feel defeated when they have done something wrong, especially when the wrong is perceived to have been committed on a client, but a supervisor is obliged to place students in this awkward position because there is no way to adequately prepare a first-time clinical student for all possible contingencies. Students have to be willing to use their instincts, to take what they perceive as therapeutic action with a client, even when such action may be questioned in the subsequent supervision session. Students will make mistakes, especially first-time practicum students; but these errors need to be handled with sensitivity and an appreciation of their utility in the learning process.

Of course, the supervisor must take precautions to place students in settings which contribute to the learning environment, and to match the student with a particular client where they can achieve a good amount of immediate success. When this is accomplished, the damage will be only to their egos and only fleetingly. Such is the case with Paula and Chelsea. Their errors will help them and their classmates who experience them vicariously through the group supervision session in a twofold manner.

First, examining the error in the clinical practice itself will be turned into new learning and skill development, and second, (and as important,) the students learn to accept the criticism and correction necessary to facilitate their professional growth. My strategy of allowing self-evaluation and peer evaluation to function as the predominant methods of correction, I believe, lessens the deleterious blows to the student's self-esteem that can occur when criticism is directed at them by the supervisor herself. When a student receives too much criticism from a supervisor she can become unwilling to trust her own instincts and to take reasonable risks. A student afraid of stretching herself during the clinical experience, fearful of thinking on her own, perpetually concerned about displeasing her supervisor, is not going to succeed as a music therapist.

By giving Paula the opportunity to direct her own correction through the group supervision process, Paula became an educational leader of the group, not merely a student who had "messed up." I directed a question to Paula: "Remembering that your goal is to make more contact with Kenny, what could you do with 'It's a Small World' in your next session?" I encouraged her not to censor any ideas that came immediately to her mind. When she had generated several ideas, I suggested that she also ask the supervision group to contribute their ideas. Once Paula and the class had generated many ideas, Paula chose one suggestion given by a classmate to try in a role-play. In this second role-play, Paula worked to follow "Kenny's" body responses—jumping and clapping. "Kenny" felt her alterations in tempo and dynamics as a game. The changeable tempo encouraged "Kenny" to pay attention to Paula. She felt a kind of playful contact with Paula, and enjoyment of the song itself.

Through this role-play Paula discovered that choosing a client's favorite song was only the beginning of developing a trustful therapeutic relationship through music and that "performing" music is not quality therapeutic contact. The class learned the concept of flexible responsiveness to the client in the music. A homework assignment was given. Divided into dyads, the students were assigned to 1) play and sing a specific song to their dyad partner with a focus upon the music, in as musical a manner as possible, 2) play and sing the song with their dyad partner, with a focus upon the partner, accommodating the song to the partner, 3) play and sing the song with the dyad partner, practicing a balance between client (partner) and musical responsiveness, and 4) practice free improvisation as a vehicle for developing a relationship with the partner through music.

Students come to their first practicum with the idea that therapy contains recipes. The concept of singing a song with no consideration to accommodating it musically to the client's responses connotes that the therapy is solely in the music—it neglects the heart of the therapeutic process, which is the development of the relationship. Although music therapy sessions (especially with undergraduate students) are, in part, preplanned and task oriented, focusing too exclusively on the preplanned musical task creates the erroneous impression that music-making in the clinic is an external task rather than a container within which the therapeutic relationship develops.

Even when students understand the difference between being task oriented and relationship oriented, there can still be a misunderstanding about the role of enjoyment in therapy. First-time students may become stuck in the idea that music therapy should be fun and pleasurable for the client. They feel a need to be liked by the client, to be a provider of fun. They find it difficult to understand the concept that therapy is not built upon being happy. Musical contact can be light and fun but it is also at times serious and difficult. However, students may continue to hold on to the concept of music therapy as fun to the detriment of their learning.

One reason students confuse the practice of music therapy with the purveyance of pleasure is that they themselves have lost some personal pleasure in their own performing due to the work-load of a college music curriculum. When student music therapists experience a client's unbridled enjoyment of music it helps them to regain their own joy. The student may mistakenly assume that simply the enjoyment of music itself is the quintessential goal of the therapeutic intervention. Although enjoyment may, at times, be a therapeutic goal, it should not be mistaken for the basis of the therapeutic process.

Once the student has developed her first simple treatment plan and has worked with the client for several weeks, she will have developed rudimentary skills and understanding in developing the therapeutic relationship through music. Once that prerequisite is accomplished the beginning music therapy student is ready to take the next developmental step in learning: identifying and working with client resistance.

Vignette

Monica's elderly client, Vince, had been in the nursing home for approximately four years. He was depressed and constantly asked to be taken back to his home. He had little relief from his depression, except for visits from his children. Most days when Monica arrived, Vince was happy to go to music therapy. He engaged easily and developed good contact with Monica through music.

After several weeks of sessions, Vince changed. He was hesitant to begin the music therapy session, and once Monica began the session, he quickly showed resistance. He complained about the nursing home, the room, and Monica; and asked to be taken back to his room. He refused most music saying it "wasn't real music," simple rhythm instruments "weren't real instruments," songs were "boring," music therapy was "boring." He questioned, "Why should I have music therapy?" and "How did you choose me—why not anyone else?" Finally, he declared the session to be over.

Monica listened to Vince and tried to answer his questions honestly. To the best of her ability she tried to help Vince understand what music therapy was and why he had been chosen for music therapy. With sincerity, Monica expressed her concern and caring for Vince. Next, Monica tried to get Vince to sing their usual greeting and engage in their usual music therapy session. Vince rejected this. Next, Monica offered him activity after activity, hoping that she would find something that wasn't "boring" to Vince, or something that he considered "real": singing familiar songs, improvising on simple rhythm instruments, playing autoharp together, playing guitar, movement with scarves, etc. Through her many offerings Monica found one activity that Vince felt was "real": singing his favorite song, "Irish Eyes," on the piano. Monica happily fulfilled this request, feeling that she had found the formula to hold Vince's interest in the session, and hence, holding the session together. But after Vince and Monica sang his song at the piano, he again asked to be taken back to his room. Monica tried again, suggesting other activities, offering to sing "Irish Eyes" again, but Vince refused any song or activity and sat with his head down and arms crossed, making no contact whatsoever with Monica. Monica gave up, ended the session and took Vince back to his room.

Discussion

Naturally, Monica does not yet understand how to deal with a client's resistance and because of this, Vince's resistance escalated quickly and took over the session. Monica's problem is multileveled. Monica had a natural emotional response to Vince's characterization of her and her session as boring. She felt hurt and defeated; by the time she finished the session, she also felt angry since she had tried so hard to accommodate Vince's preferences. Because of her emotional response (and also because she is inexperienced), Monica got stuck in trying to "normalize" Vince and the session instead of accepting and accommodating to the significant difference in Vince's state in the music therapy session. Monica's strategy was to try to concentrate on what Vince was saying (his specific complaints). She was unable to be open to examine and understand Vince's expressed boredom to find out why he was resistant. She was attempting to find an activity—a formula—to combat Vince's resistance.

Resistance must be dealt with by addressing feelings stimulated by the client's rejection and by adapting one's style of nurturance to meet the client's resistance. The solution to resistance is found in the adjustment of the therapeutic relationship in the moment, not in an activity or a task. Through supervision, students can arrive at this conclusion on their own.

In group supervision, Monica brought up her session for discussion. At first she minimized the situation, describing it tentatively, and in an embarrassed manner. With support, she was able to describe in detail, and with feeling, the exact circumstances of the session and how terrible it was for her. Monica reported that after her session, she had left the nursing home in tears. She felt angry from her attempts to deal with Vince's resistance, depressed because of her failure to find a way to re-engage Vince, and inadequate from Vince's harsh insults upon her. She questioned whether she could ever become a music therapist. This is one of the hardest challenges for supervision because first-time students are just getting on their feet and developing confidence. Confronting resistance means acknowledging rejection from the client, which brings up the students' feelings of inadequacy.

At anxious moments like this, it is tempting for the supervisor to reduce the high level of tension by solving the dilemma for the student. I could say, for example, "Monica, Vince was not really bored with your session. He was simply acting out a typical client behavior known as resistance. This is your fourth week of therapy with him and this is what happens at this point in the therapeutic process." However, I believe that answering Monica's dilemma would deprive her and the supervision class of the educational value derived from working together to honestly confront their feelings of inadequacy while acquiring a better understanding of Vince.

Although it may seem reasonable that Monica's classmates would be sympathetic to her situation, it is not uncommon for a usually supportive supervision group to distance themselves from a clinical situation that involves rejection from a client and feelings of inadequacy because these are such emotionally challenging issues. Comments such as, "Oh, that must have been so hard for you; I don't have such a difficult client," and "I don't know what I would do if my client ever did that to me!" are evidence that first-time students tend to deny that they have experienced any resistance from their clients. For beginning students, it is much easier to overlook moments of client resistance, especially when they are fleeting, in favor of focusing upon the exciting gains a client is making in therapy. This common group response threatens the class's integrity as an educational support system and requires an approach to supervision that will aid the student in crisis, as well as help the other students to uncover their own experiences with client resistance. Although dealing with the student's emotional responses to the client's rejection is an important component of addressing resistance, the beginning practicum student first needs to be able to clearly identify resistance, without denial, before tackling her own feelings of inadequacy. Supervisory techniques that are experiential and expressive in nature, rather than verbal techniques, are helpful in allowing students to examine more fully conscious and unconscious aspects of resistance. Role-playing through improvisation is perhaps the most common experiential technique used in music therapy supervision; however, group music and imagery is also an effective technique (Summer, 1996).

The supervision session with Monica utilized music and imagery with a component of art to examine resistant contact in contrast to engaged, quality musical contact with the client. Sitting comfortably on the floor with eyes closed, the students were led through a short relaxation technique and given the following instructions: "Take this time to reflect on your therapy sessions so far with your client . . . let yourself remember a time when you felt very connected to your client in the music . . . you may remember many times, but bring forward a time that you felt the most strongly connected to your client and also to the music you were playing . . . now, open your eyes and let the music that is playing help you to draw this connection on your paper . . . be as expressive as you can be to show the quality of the connection you felt." As the Dvořák String Serenade, Opus 22, first movement played, the students drew with oil and chalk pastels. Subsequently, this process was repeated with the same instructions except that the students were asked to draw the experience in which they felt the most disconnected and distanced from their client during music on a separate piece of paper. For this exercise I substituted Brahms Third Symphony, third movement for the Dvořák. Each piece of music in this exercise was chosen to reflect the general emotional state of the group and to structure and support their imagery expression through art.

Monica's first drawing was pastel and mostly abstract. She drew the therapy room, which Monica explained, was filled half with purple for Vince, half with blue for Monica. Between these two equally sized areas was a yellow area where Monica and Vince "connected" in the music. Each color was clear, but blended together with each other and yellow at the point of connection. In addition, Monica had drawn lines which radiated from and around the room to illustrate the feeling of expansiveness and expressivity she felt present in their music. Monica said that her sessions usually felt like this drawing—smooth, flowing, and natural, like the Dvořák serenade. In her picture of resistant contact, two thirds of the page—drawn in black and red with harsh, disconnected lines, circling around each other—represented Vince, according to Monica. Monica depicted herself in the remaining space with blue, purple, and yellow pastels. The two unequal portions merged at the point of connection. Monica was asked to describe both pictures fully. Regarding the second picture she said, "This is Vince in the session yesterday. He is disoriented. He is paying no attention to me. All these lines are going nowhere, they're all over the place; he's really confused. I can see here that he is really disoriented and he feels very angry. As the Brahms played, I heard the dissonance in the music, and it sounded like how Vince's anger must feel to him. I drew the disjointed lines with the strongly accented rhythms of the music. In the session yesterday, I didn't notice that he was confused. I know that he always says he is angry about being in the nursing home, but I have never felt his anger before."

Monica was asked to describe how she characterized herself in the picture. She said, "I'm trying to reach him, but he is bigger than usual, and my pretty smooth colors are so ineffective next to his sharp lines." I asked, "What is your strategy in trying to reach Vince in this picture?"

She responded, "I can see how different he is in this session than in my other sessions, but I'm trying to approach him in the same way I always do. It's like I'm trying to get him back to his usual self. I can see why he kept rejecting me. I'm not really paying attention to him." Putting her session with Vince into the medium of art gave Monica the ability to examine Vince's state and to examine her interaction with Vince from a new perspective, a perspective that leads her to understand that Vince was not really bored during their session together. To reinforce Monica's change of perception I reminded her of Vince's previous delight with her music therapy sessions. When Monica said, "If Vince wasn't really bored, then it's certainly not helpful to be spending all my time looking for something that wouldn't be boring to him," I believed that she was ready to identify a new strategy for dealing with Vince's resistance. I drew Monica's attention to her second drawing and asked, "Look at this drawing again. Can you see from this visual representation, what kind of contact would be helpful for Vince?"

Monica responded immediately. "I can see visually that he needs colors and shapes as strong as his, not my soft pastels. If I were to draw another picture, I would make myself more complementary to him—I would draw myself in the same colors, with more shape and definition, maybe the same shapes as he is."

I gave Monica a homework assignment to choose a piece of music personally very nurturing and, using the music as support, draw at least one new picture that would represent a new therapeutic approach to Vince: one that uses music to meet, match, and contain Vince's confusion and anger.

That Monica's dynamic work and her new insights impressed the group became obvious during the ensuing discussion. Using their drawings, Monica's classmates also began to identify their own clients' resistances in past sessions, which had not been exposed during previous supervision classes.

As closure, Monica was asked to summarize what she had learned. "I can see that I was trying to change Vince's confusion, to just take it away and make him happy with his favorite song, but that's obviously not possible because the reality is that he is very depressed and angry about being in the nursing home. I have to accept that I can't save him from that."

Students come to music therapy believing that they are self-reflective, and honest with themselves and others. They are not aware of the amount of intellectual and emotional effort it takes to be a therapist. Addressing resistance as described above challenges students to be self-reflective. As their teachers, it behooves us to ensure that self-reflection allows our students to learn and mature, not to make them feel inadequate.

Finally, it must be admitted that some students, even some academically proficient students, will not be able—or they may be unwilling—to develop the therapeutic and musical skills necessary for them to become music therapists. Often, it is during the first practica that this becomes evident. They may be able to successfully mimic the prodding supervisor, but fail to evince that they can adapt to their clients extemporaneously. It is tempting to give a student a passing grade in practicum, especially to students who produce good academic work, but it is of no real value to them or to the field to permit them to camouflage their deficiencies as a therapist. The practicum course may be a single academic credit in an eighteen-semester credit load, so the singularity of a barely passing grade here may appear insignificant. ("C–" is the lowest grade allowed by AMTA for music therapy core classes.) However, this is deceptive. A music therapist studies the academic portion of the training in order to be capable of practicing music therapy. Academicians, such as myself, must be careful not to excuse inadequacy in the practicum as trivial. Practicum supervisors, when they are practicing clinicians and not part of the academic staff, must be careful not to adopt an attitude that is too "therapeutic," allowing any positive growth to constitute success. Each music therapy program director has a standard of competence to be acquired by the student before graduation. Unlike therapy in which a client's growth proceeds at his own pace and without deadlines, music therapy education is time restricted.

In a real sense, the practicum is the crucible in which our future music therapists must learn to thrive. We cannot turn down the heat for individuals whom we respect intellectually nor for those we care about in our role as therapists without sacrificing the transformative energy needed to change the student into a professional.

References

American Music Therapy Association. (1997 Revised). *Standards and Procedures for Academic Program Approval.* Silver Spring, MD: Author.

Feiner, S. (1999, November). *Supervision: A profound creative process.* Paper presented at the 9th World Congress of Music Therapy, Washington, D.C.

Forinash, M., and Summer, L. (1999, March). *Continued explorations into music therapy supervision.* Paper presented at the Conference of the New England Region of the American Music Therapy Association, Meredith, NH.

Forinash, M., and Summer, L. (1998, April). *Supervision in music therapy.* Paper presented at the Conference of the New England Region of the American Music Therapy Association, Hartford, CT.

Freud, S. (1912). Recommendations to physicians practicing psychoanalysis. *Standard Edition of the Complete Psychological Works of Sigmund Freud, Vol. 12.* London: Hogarth Press.

Sherman, R. M., and Sherman, R. B. (1963). *It's a Small World.* New York: Wonderland Music Co.

Summer, L. (1996, March). *Music as mother.* Paper presented at the Conference of the New England Region of the American Music Therapy Association, Springfield, MA.

Summer, L. (1997, December). *The music therapist's relationship with music.* Paper presented at the Lesley College Expressive Therapies Brown Bag Lecture Series, Cambridge, MA.

Chapter 6

A Systems Analysis Approach to
Music Therapy Practica[*]

Suzanne B. Hanser, EdD, MT-BC
Chair, Music Therapy Department,
Berklee College of Music
Boston, MA

I arrived in Stockton, California, to chair a well-known music therapy department with a long history. I was to be the only faculty member, and although I had taught courses in Music in Special Education at Brooklyn College, it was the first time that I would be teaching courses to future music therapists. There was, obviously, much to prepare and much to learn. But, my most urgent task was to coordinate, plan, implement, and supervise more students in clinical practica than I had expected. Of course, the students expected to be out in the field, applying music therapy techniques with real clients and patients as soon as the semester began.

It was this pressured state of affairs that forced me to determine my most significant teaching values and design a realistic and efficient system for supervision. I knew that over time and with practice, students would hone their musical abilities and talents. I assumed that, in the course of their studies, they would learn more and more music therapy techniques and rehearse them in the classroom and in the clinic. I decided that if students could learn a model for designing, implementing, and evaluating music therapy as a treatment, they would have a reliable structure and framework for thinking and making clinical judgments no matter where they worked. If effective, the model could transfer across settings, clinical populations, and treatment modalities.

After much thought, it became clear to me that my most important value in the teaching of prospective therapists was to engender a questioning approach that sought answers to queries, such as:

"How can I contribute to and enhance the well-being of my client through music therapy?" "What do I expect to change or improve by the end of the semester?" "How do I know if and when I achieve this outcome?"

The solution to my problem took the form of an analysis of systems to simplify and codify student expectations and fieldwork practice. Students learned the language used at the beginning of the chapter e.g., goals, objectives, target populations, and target behaviors, to articulate their treatment programs. I was to learn whether it was possible to use this language across populations and a variety of practica.

---

[*] Portions of this chapter are excerpted from Hanser, S. B. (2000). *The New Music Therapist's Handbook.* Boston: Berklee Press. Available from Berkleepress.com

The Systems Analysis Approach

This chapter describes the systems analysis model that I designed in skeletal form in 1975, went on to publish in *Music Therapy Practicum: A Manual for Behavior Change,* and most recently expanded in *The New Music Therapist's Handbook.* The systems I developed for application to student practica were implemented for many years at University of the Pacific and are now adapted and expanded in the practica at Berklee College of Music. Major elements of the system include:

- assigning students to small supervision groups;
- using advanced students to proctor the groups and review weekly assignments at University of the Pacific; currently, using qualified music therapists for supervision at Berklee College of Music;
- allowing supervisors to focus on the quality of interaction between student therapist and client while classroom instruction provides the rationale for treatment activities and planning; and
- utilizing audiotaped or videotaped sessions for supervision.

The details of this system have been described in an article in the *Journal of Music Therapy* (Hanser, 1978). The uses of specific videotape and feedback procedures are the subject of an article by Hanser and Furman (1980). By implementing these schemas, supervision groups provided model treatment teams for students to discuss their observations and learn from peers. Each week, all students had a common assignment which comprised successive steps in the treatment planning process. The present assignments attempt to emulate current clinical practices performed by music therapy professionals who adhere to various philosophies and approaches to treatment.

Borne out of a problematic situation, the system has evolved, offering students the opportunity to participate in the all-important process of treatment planning. The skills learned in this way lead ultimately to the music therapist's contributions to such diverse responsibilities as:

- developing an Individualized Education Plan for a child with special needs;
- preparing a health insurance application for reimbursement of fees for service to hospitalized patients;
- providing appropriate documentation for quality assurance reviews; and
- collaborating on a multidisciplinary team for clinical programming and discharge planning.

It is a pleasure to report that ninety-to-one student-to-faculty ratios are no longer acceptable for practicum supervision in approved music therapy curricula, and individualized supervision by qualified professionals takes priority in curriculum development. In establishing the music therapy program at Berklee College of Music, funds were procured to ensure that students would be properly supervised by practicing music therapists. Practicum classes with limited enrollment help to prepare the student for field work each week. A set of tasks outlines the process of treatment planning.

Rationale for a Data-Based Model

The model implemented in the practicum curriculum is a data-based approach for music therapy. The word "data," however, often conjures up images of computer printouts and massive lists of numerals. I use the term to refer to information obtained through experimentation or direct observation. The series of tasks in this practicum model offer guidelines for constructing the most successful treatment program. The music therapy student not only learns a replicable system, but also benefits as a clinician because the effectiveness of a selected technique may be tested throughout treatment. The clients benefit as they observe evidence of their progress in therapy. The partnership between student music therapist and client is strengthened as both work together to meet selected goals and objectives.

In *The New Music Therapist's Handbook,* I tell an anecdote about how I came to value "data" so strongly. It was when my daughter, Leora, was born. Because I was an only child who never even baby-sat as a teenager, I had no experience with newborns and panicked at the idea of bringing home a person so tiny and dependent upon me. The parenting literature I studied gave few clues for coping with my infant's cries or understanding her needs. Fortunately, I was blessed to have my friend, Sandra, to teach me about collecting data.

"Data?" my family and friends questioned, shocked to hear me use the word in regard to my dear daughter. "Yes," I said. "Data collection has helped me understand her primitive language and allowed me to be a better mother."

Let me explain how:

Sandra bought me a notebook, which she divided into three sections: feeding, diaper changes, and naps. When I nursed Leora, I was to record the time of day and the number of minutes she nursed. When I changed her diaper, I was to record the time and what I found in her diaper. For naps, I noted each time she fell asleep and woke, calculating the length of her sleep.

Very soon, patterns emerged. She would start crying, and I could see that, for example, she had nursed for a shorter duration at her last feeding, and would probably require more milk at this feeding. I could see that diaper changes were required at a certain interval after feeding. I could begin to plan my schedule around her naps, predicting that she would wake at a particular time, replicating her schedule on the day before. When her schedule began to defy my predictions, by changing drastically, I correctly foresaw a medical problem, and her pediatrician diagnosed an early stage infection.

I actually used a stopwatch to time Leora's nursing, prompting the disdain of my family.

"How can you approach your own child in such a cold and calculating manner?" they asked.

I responded that I loved her too much to leave these important details of her care to chance. By learning her routine, I was not only in better control of our interaction, but I became more confident and relaxed as a mother. I devoted more of my energy to our play, getting to know her through singing, talking, touching, moving, and loving her every moment.

I have now been a mother of three children and a music therapist for many years. I have developed my musical talent through study, practice, and performance. I have learned new techniques and become more adept at implementing them while maintaining my primary attention on the people I am serving. I believe that my greatest successes, both personal and professional, have involved my being true to the client-centered and data-based nature of my approach.

The systems analysis model is prescriptive, not by providing a list of music or music therapy techniques for particular problems, but by asking the student music therapist to use creativity, experience, and personal values to determine the most appropriate goals and techniques. Students collect data for the purpose of treatment planning and also, to begin to think as a professional. They learn how collecting data about a client's progress provides evidence of the efficacy of treatment. They see how they may directly and objectively document what is happening in the music therapy session. The model allows students to introduce objective evaluation into the subjective therapeutic relationship.

Student Tasks

There are seven major tasks which students accomplish in addition to completing progress notes on a weekly basis:

- Facility Tour
- Group Activity Observation Form
- Initial Assessment Guidelines
- Setting Goals and Objectives
- Response Definition
- Proposed Treatment Plan Outline
- Music Therapy Treatment Summary

These tasks are discussed below and suggested forms for implementing these are included.

Task 1: Facility Tour

The students' first task is to gather background information about the clinical site. In order to integrate the music therapy plan into existing programs, it is informative to know as much as possible about the facility, its clients, other clinical offerings (e.g., occupational, physical, and recreation therapy), the philosophical orientation of treatment, and the role of music therapy in relation to other departments and services.

At the conclusion of their general orientation, each student observes one client. Students take a lesson in keen observation of human behavior, making an anecdotal record of what they see. They are then able to zero in on behaviors for which music therapy may be an effective change agent.

Students may discuss which of their clients is an appropriate referral to music therapy, based on the following guidelines:

- when there is strength in auditory learning styles;
- when there is responsiveness to sound or music;
- when there is physical inactivity or limited mobility,
- when there is limited cognitive capacity;
- when confrontive therapies are inadvisable;
- when compliance is a problem;
- when there is difficulty communicating or expressing thoughts, feelings, or ideas;
- when there is difficulty getting along with others;
- when there is limited self-awareness;
- when traditional treatments fail or are contraindicated.

Table 1
Assignment for Facility Tour

On your first visit to this facility, take notes related to the following areas:
Type of Facility:
Clientele: Diagnoses, ages, functioning level, etc.
Other Programs: Other therapies, activities, scheduled programming
Therapeutic Orientation
Role of Music Therapy
Anecdotal Record of Observations

Task 2: Group Activity Observation Form

At the next session, each student observes one client who is participating in a group activity. This offers a context for observing a variety of potential target behaviors. The students observe and make comments on the classes of behaviors, scoring each with a + for appropriate response, 0 for no response, or – for inappropriate response. This task prepares the students to conduct a more comprehensive assessment of functioning.

Table 2
Assignment for Group Activity Observation

Date:
Client Initials:
Observer:

Behavior		
Circle + (appropriate), 0 (no response), or – (inappropriate) and anecdotal comments for one client		
+	0	–
Participation		
+	0	–
Responsiveness		
+	0	–
Mood/Emotions		
+	0	–
Social Behavior (Compliance)		
+	0	–
Following Instructions		
+	0	–
Attention to Therapist		
+	0	–
Rapport with Therapist		
+	0	–
Attention to Task		
+	0	–
Client Interaction		
+	0	–
Coordination (Fine & Gross)		
+	0	–
Communication (Language)		

Task 3: Initial Assessment Guidelines

Assessment reveals more about the nature of the problem itself. It determines what the client can or cannot do, knows or does not know. Assessment may involve administering standardized or original tests or observing behavior. It identifies the strengths and weaknesses of the person. A unique feature of music therapy is the assessment of music behavior in addition to non-music behavior.

Students use the outline in Task 3 to describe the client (e.g., age, gender, profession, diagnosis, etc.), and investigate the person's background (e.g., musical preferences, family history, special skills and interests, culture, vocation). They may interview staff of the facility and consult patient records to gather evaluative information in both nonmusical and musical behaviors.

Table 3
Assignment for Initial Assessment

Date:
Student Therapist:

Description of Client (use client initials only):	
Background:	
Musical Preferences:	
Family History:	
Skills and Interests:	
Culture:	
Vocation:	
Nonmusical Functioning Social: Perceptual-Motor: Language: Cognitive: Emotional:	
Musical Functioning Enjoyment: Creativity: Abilities:	

Task 4: Setting Goals and Objectives

Based on the observation and assessment tasks, the music therapy student selects a therapeutic goal. When music therapy is successful, this goal will be met. The therapist defines a specific objective to clarify the goal in an observable way. By defining exactly how that objective will be measured, it is clear when the objective is reached.

To select a goal, the following questions may be kept in mind:

- Will reaching this goal have significant impact on the person's life?
- Is the goal too far removed from present behavior?
- Are there inappropriate behaviors which interfere with achievement of the goals (which might need to be dealt with first)?
- Is the behavior specified in the goal able to be observed and measured over time?
- Was the client referred for a specific reason?
- Do other staff members agree that this is the most appropriate goal?
- Is there a relatively high probability that this goal can be reached by the end of the semester?
- Is there evidence that this behavior truly requires change?
- Is there reason to believe that music therapy is the most appropriate treatment to meet this goal?

When setting objectives, students should describe observable, measurable behavior. They should specify a direction of change and delineate the boundaries, including conditions and criteria for success.

Table 4
Assignment of Setting Goals and Objectives

This task requires you to develop one goal and objective for your client to be accomplished by the end of the semester. You will do this by targeting one area for growth or change, and behaviorally defining one very specific objective.	
The following are examples of possible goals and objectives.	
Goal	Semester Objective
To improve socialization (participation in group)	To sing all the words of one verse to a selected song
To enhance self-esteem	To say two positive statements about self when asked
To focus attention	To increase eye contact with the therapist (eye contact is looking at the therapist) when called upon up to 70% of the time
To decrease fidgeting	To decrease the time spent fidgeting between music therapy activities (fidgeting is the movement of fingers/hands without observable purpose)
Complete the following with your selected goal and semester objective:	
Goal	Semester Objective

Task 5: Response Definition

Defining the target behavior is essential to measure change objectively. To facilitate reliable recording, the behavioral definition must be extremely precise. The complete behavioral description is also known as a response definition. It includes: a descriptor, or concise term for the target behavior; boundaries of the behavior; observational information; and borderline responses.

Table 5
Response Definition Assignment

Write a concise response definition for your target behavior. The definition should be clear enough for all observers to agree that the response has occurred. When you have finished, give it to a classmate to see if it is clear.
How will you observe target behavior?
Does the response occur a certain number of times or length of time?
Does the response occur after a question is asked or during a certain activity? If so, what activity?
When will you observe this behavior? Examples: after a question at the end of the session; during the singing activity; while drumming; in response to call and response.

Task 6: Proposed Treatment Plan Outline

The music therapy plan reveals a navigational strategy for the course of therapy. The students use previous task material to complete the outline:

- Client and Setting (from Task 1). The student determines whether individual or group music therapy is most appropriate for the client.
- Assessment Procedures (from Tasks 2 and 3).
- Goal and Objectives (from Task 4).
- Treatment Procedures.

Students must research the most appropriate music therapy techniques to meet the needs of their clients. Garnering their own skills and talents, they look into the music therapy literature to identify the best strategy.

Table 6
Proposed Treatment Plan Assignment

Student Therapist:
Client and Setting (use client initials only): Briefly state background giving age, gender, facility, reason for referral to music therapy (see Task 1). Under Setting, state frequency and duration of group or individual music therapy.
Assessment Procedures: Summarize observations from Tasks 2 and 3. State Response Definition (Task 5) and describe observations of the target behavior, (e.g., pretest or baseline).
Goal and Objectives: State Goal and Semester Objectives (Task 4).
Treatment Procedures: Describe what you will do musically and nonmusically to achieve the goal. Specify music therapy techniques and music materials.

Task 7: Music Therapy Treatment Summary

As the music therapy plan is carried out, the therapist is well-prepared. However, this does not necessarily preclude additional planning in the form of revisions of objectives, adaptations of techniques, or even redefinition and reassessment of the problem. The student therapist records progress on an ongoing basis, and documents change through graphing behaviors over time or reporting pretest-posttest results. The outline includes: title, author, client and setting, response definition and assessment procedures, goal and objectives, music therapy procedures, results and discussion.

The student uses the relevant information from the music therapy plan in this final report, now written in past tense. Evaluation of the success of the music therapy program involves a comprehensive analysis. The results which are gathered are accompanied by conclusions and recommendations for future action. The student music therapist ends the treatment program and begins another by defining new areas for change. Music therapy, as a process for learning, continues. Termination of this unique relationship between student and client is handled in a professional manner, with appropriate preparation for the client and alternate plans for subsequent treatment.

Table 7
Music Therapy Treatment Summary Assignment Outline

Title of Study (e.g., The Use of Singing with . . . , Percussive Improvisation for . . . , Ensemble Playing to Improve . . . , Managing Disruptive Behavior through Music Listening)
Author
Client and Setting
Response Definition and Assessment Procedures
Goal and Objectives
Music Therapy Procedures
Results (to include graphs, tables and analysis of client progress)
Discussion

Conclusion

I sometimes think that the field of music therapy is one of the best-kept secrets around. Because the profession is younger and less well known than many other established disciplines, the people who make decisions about patient care may not be aware of the potential impact of music therapy. They may not realize that there are music therapists practicing in their communities or that music therapy is a treatment option for individuals with a particular diagnosis. Collecting data about a client's progress provides evidence of the efficacy of treatment. It directly and objectively documents what is happening in the music therapy session. Training therapists in a data-based systems approach to music therapy holds the advantages of accountability to our constituents and to ourselves as professionals.

This model concentrates on the decision-making process regarding the client's needs and the planning, implementation, and evaluation of treatment. It offers a systematic way to structure music therapy experiences and meets treatment goals in an efficient manner. This structure also seems to free the on-site field supervisor to concentrate on the interpersonal process between student therapist and client. It is hoped that the reader will find this material useful in organizing practicum courses for music therapy students, and will experience success in training the future of this profession.

References

Hanser, S. B. (1978). A systems analysis model for teaching practicum skills. *Journal of Music Therapy, 16*(1), 21–35.

Hanser, S. B., and Furman, C. E. (1980). The effect of videotape-based feedback vs. field-based feedback on the development of applied clinical skills. *Journal of Music Therapy, 18*(3) 103–112.

Chapter 7

A Journey through Internship Supervision: Roles, Dynamics, and Phases of the Supervisory Relationship

Susan Feiner, MA, MT-BC, CSW
Associate Director of Music Therapy
New York University
New York, NY

Introduction

Embarking on internship, for both supervisor and intern, is like boarding a small, intimate vessel that cannot sail without the full involvement of two barely acquainted travelers. Waves come from all directions. Every turn brings new territories that can be explored and learned from. Each traveler is dependent upon the other, for if one leans forward, lets out the sail, or changes direction, the other will feel this, and will need to decide how to respond. Each journey is unique and the terrain is full of challenges from within and without.

The potential for both travelers on this journey is rich, full of exploration, accomplishment and self-knowledge. At the end of this journey the intern, now a professional, feels ready to embark upon a career with a foundation of knowledge and experience necessary to meet the challenges that will come. The supervisor feels that he or she has contributed to this exciting journey in the student's life, feels gratified to have passed knowledge to another, and to have participated in such an unfolding. Hopefully both feel honored to have shared this journey together. They feel pleased that they have navigated these waters, in spite of the times there may have been obstacles that were difficult or even scary to traverse.

Many students have spoken of how their internships and relationships with their supervisors have been a time of not only professional growth, but also personal growth and even transformation. Their relationship with their supervisor brought about a major change in how they felt about themselves, even who they were, and their identity. Over and over interns have spoken of how much working with their supervisors has changed their lives. I have been continually awed by what actually transpires in this relationship, much of which goes well beyond the explicit tasks at hand.

This chapter examines some of the vicissitudes of the supervisor-intern relationship in such a way as to illuminate the challenges and potential of this period. I will focus on supervision issues that arise for supervisor and intern, as well as the relationship between them as they journey through the phases of this training experience. The marvelous potential of this relationship, what makes it unique, developmental phases of internship and how roles change, the issues and challenges that arise for both supervisor and intern, along with possible supervisory interventions will be discussed.

Dynamics within the Supervisory Relationship

Assumptions and Expectations

What are some of the dynamics that contribute to the intensity of the supervisor-intern relationship? As a way to begin to understand the dynamics that contribute to the intensity of this relationship, let us start with some of the unrealistic assumptions that both supervisor and supervisee may bring. Looking at dictionary definitions is a remarkably accurate way of describing common preconceptions regarding supervision. If we break supervision into "super" and "vision," the dictionary (Random House, 1978; American Heritage, 1981) define: "super" as: excellent; outstanding; superior; over and above; beyond or to excess; major or greater. "Vision" is the act or power of seeing; unusual foresight; intelligent foresight; unusual competence in discernment or perception; an image or idea of a spiritual nature seen or obtained under the influence of a divine or other agency. Students' expectations are usually not far off from these. They often idealize their supervisor, at least at first, believing that they can see and know all. Supervisors' expectations of themselves, especially new supervisors, are often not far off from these as well. Not only must a supervisor know all clinically and be the perfect model, the supervisor must have a divine understanding of what the supervisee needs. Quite a torch for the supervisor to bear!

Now if we combine "super" and "vision" into one word, and look at the dictionary definition of "supervision" we find that it means to oversee (workers) during execution and performance. When the words are broken into "super" + "vision," this connotes an almost omnipotent being. This being is not only superior and greater, but one who knows all, sees all, and has the powers of divination. When "super" and "vision" are combined, it takes on a very different light, involving judgment and "execution." Beginning interns are insecure about their abilities, even their sense of self and identity, as they enter this new and demanding role. A supervisor often determines whether the intern will pass or fail. No wonder the supervisor may easily be seen as the potential executioner. Supervisors must be extremely sensitive to these expectations and to their power. Supervisors must also watch for unrealistic expectations they put upon themselves to be perfect, to have all the answers.

Given all of these superhuman expectations, in reality the potential of the supervisory relationship is both humble and grand. For the supervisor, it becomes a professional challenge to refine and pass on one's knowledge and to learn with the intern what one does not know. The challenge lies in supervising in ways that could be most helpful given who you are and given who the student is. Each supervisory experience is different because every intern is different. It also depends upon where the supervisor is in his or her life's journey, as the supervisor is always growing and changing over time. A supervisor must be humble enough not to want to fulfill the role of having all the answers, and be willing to learn from the intern how to best supervise, continually revising one's approach. In this give and take comes the creative interplay in this process.

Fears and Uncertainty

For many students internship is the culmination of their studies; others are still completing coursework, but are finally in a position to be fully responsible for a caseload. When starting a new career, one looks at oneself anew. By being intimately observed by another, the supervisor also has the opportunity to look at her or his self anew as well, for each intern brings another part of oneself out for further acquaintance. Interns are often overwhelmed with excitement, fear, as well as unbounded expectations when they first begin. They are usually full of questions. Of themselves they may be asking: Can I really do this work? Will I really like or love this work as much as I imagined? They will be watching their supervisors keenly with trepidation. You will see me inept and vulnerable. I will be so exposed, how will you be? How will you react to my mistakes? I depend upon you to guide and teach me, will you be able to do this? Can I fulfill your expectations of me? Can I trust you? Will I be safe with you? Will you appreciate and respect me? Will you like me? This is a often a time when the student is feeling overwhelmed and disoriented. This is not unusual, and in fact when these feelings are not there I am often on the alert for problems.

Supervisors also begin with similar concerns: Will you respect my work and want to learn from me? How will you react to my mistakes? Will I be able to work well with you? Can I trust you? Can I trust you to represent the music therapy program and to represent *me* in this setting? Will you appreciate and respect me? Will you like me? Through intern and supervisor getting to know each other these questions gradually get answered. This leads to a foundation of mutual trust and respect in most cases, or to potential problems that need to be addressed.

Self-Disclosure and Vulnerability

Issues related to self-disclosure and vulnerability also compound the intensity of the supervisory relationship. The amount of time spent together, the intern's not being able to control the pace and timing of self-disclosure, ongoing observation of the intern by the supervisor, and vulnerability inherent in the process of music, itself, are all significant factors.

At times, internship can feel even more threatening than one's own therapy. In therapy the client usually sets one's own pace, opening up and addressing what one is ready to explore (except during crises). The intern, in contrast, is faced with a constant barrage of challenges and issues from the setting, the supervisor, and clients, whether ready or not. There is no place for the intern to wait, hide, or rest until ready, because s/he must respond to internship demands and clients' needs as they arise. For example, an intern may have difficulty with feelings of anger or loss (is there anyone who doesn't?). In personal therapy, these types of emotions may be triggered by internal stressors, life events, or experiences in therapy. The individual can then address them in weekly therapy and/or on and off between sessions. Within internship, however, a client's anger or fear of death may come up during the session and the intern will need to address this immediately (or in a timely way in the treatment), not necessarily according to the intern's own personal readiness. This poses a challenge for the student and can be quite overwhelming. It is a given that this occurs for all therapists, for we are always responsible for learning about ourselves in the treatment process, but this can be especially difficult for a new intern, intensifying feelings of inadequacy or vulnerability. This also poses a challenge for the supervisor in how to handle these issues without crossing the line and becoming the intern's therapist (this will be addressed later).

Another challenge for the relationship is the format of supervision. In many music therapy settings the intern not only has supervisory meetings, but also is regularly observed doing music therapy. Again there is lack of control for the intern, who is not able to pick and choose what to discuss, or what vignettes of tape to review in a supervision hour. The intern is fully exposed in the moment, and does not have the option to consciously or unconsciously edit what the supervisor is learning. Because the medium of treatment is music, the intern often will also feel vulnerable exposing herself musically. What will the supervisor think of my skills, my sensitivity? How does the music make me feel and can I show this to my supervisor? What will it be like if my supervisor wants to work with me in music? The task for the supervisor is to pace supervision and feedback appropriately to the intern's learning process and remain cognizant of these vulnerability issues.

With this greater exposure and risk comes also greater potential for support and learning. Once the initial fears of exposure and vulnerability are overcome and a trusting environment is established, the student now has an experience of freedom, potentially, to plunge and explore knowing that the supervisor is there in this journey with him or her. A fruitful parallel process can take place—between the student and supervisor and between the student and clients. The intern's self-awareness grows as s/he sees how dynamics or issues with clients will often be mirrored in the relationship with the supervisor.

The following is a quote from an intern's final summary at the end of her internship that eloquently illustrates this:

> *In my interaction with the many therapists at the clinic I have felt respected and revered, accepted and understood. Speaking about them collectively, they each take the time to stop, look, and listen, to me, with me, and for me. It is as if I am a seed that has been planted in this garden we call music therapy, and because of their way of being I am never without sunlight, their warmth, or consideration. This has genuinely affected and subtly guided my process as an intern. I've been able to face issues that I was not comfortable with because of this guidance and support, and actually see them through, see myself grow, and allow myself their years of experience to comfort me. This in turn has been bestowed upon the children I work with each week. It's a bit like passing the torch. I*

dare say there is no other way to learn this technique but through personal experience as the recipient of such gifts.

The Role of the Supervisor

As supervisor, what is our role? Are we educators? Mentors? Therapists? Administrators? Determining our role is not only a challenge, but can be downright confusing. How do we manage all these roles? What happens when they conflict? What does a supervisor do with the intern's personal material or personality issues that become exposed? Where docs a supervisor ethically draw the line in the use of his or her therapy skills working with the intern?

Kadushin (1992), from the field of social work, breaks down the supervisory role into categories that help clarify these questions. He poses that as supervisor we wear three hats, and therefore must juggle the roles of educator, administrator, and supporter.

Educator

As educator, the supervisor is responsible for teaching. Interns must learn a vast body of knowledge by the end of their internship in order to be clinically qualified for graduation. This challenges a supervisor to expand his or her expertise to encompass a new role as educator, one for which music therapists have received little training in spite of their many years of study and practice as therapists.

Mordock (1990) describes this as a new and challenging role for supervisors. As therapists we are trained to react to what a client brings to treatment, but as educators we are challenged to shift from this reactive stance to a proactive stance, focusing on what a student must learn. Supervisors must feel comfortable initiating and more actively giving and modeling information rather than waiting until a student brings it up. The good news is that interns want to be taught and they want feedback. If interns are not given sufficient information and feedback, if they do not get the opportunity to regularly observe their supervisor's work, they often flounder unproductively. They become extremely anxious and focused on "doing good" to meet elusive expectations. Vigilant for reassurance from their supervisor that they are doing well, interns may consequently have fewer resources available to focus on their work with clients. Students want to know what their supervisor does, how they do it, and why they do it. They want a clear understanding of what is expected of them. This educator role is markedly different from a therapist's role.

This poses an interesting challenge for supervisors. How do we offer our work as a model, articulate what our expectations are of our interns, and at the same time help interns develop their own "way" according to their unique qualities, strengths, and skills? The answer is that once interns have a good foundation in the understanding and practice of their supervisor's work, they can use it as a safe home base from which to explore as they progress in their internship. Supervisors can teach their "way" and still support an intern's development of their own unique qualities.

Excellent therapists often need support to be clearer and to "teach" as supervisors. They often fear they would be hampering their intern's creativity and individuality if they teach. What can happen instead are misunderstandings, confusion, and paralyzing anxiety. I usually make this explicit and tell my intern: "I'll show you my way, my methods, and my understandings. Imitate as much as you'd like and when ready you can develop more and more of your own. Don't burden yourself now with 'originality' for the sake of originality before you have a basis to work from. Then take it and fly."

It is enormously helpful and important to teach the intern how to use supervision. Be clear about what an intern's responsibilities entail: paperwork requirements; what she can expect from you during observations and supervision time; how important it is for you to know what she is experiencing (and this means keeping you informed on her personal reactions). Make it your agenda to hear these feelings, fears, and excitements. Details are important too—organizing and prioritizing daily responsibilities, avenues of communication and decision making, whom to contact when a crisis occurs.

Administrator

As administrator, we must juggle the university's requirements (caseload, size of groups, logs, etc.); the site's requirements (numbers of clients, which clients, allocation of supervisor's time); the student's needs (variety of caseload, student's learning style, their special interests); the clients' needs (which clients need services and how these needs fit with your intern).

These varying responsibilities can conflict and cause confusion for both supervisor and intern. Supervisors may be caught in a struggle between the size of groups usually seen at the site and the smaller groups requested by the university. As supervisor you might want a student to be assigned a varied caseload, but the site has more need for a particular type of client receiving services.

A student can become confused and perceive conflict between the supervisor's varying roles: "This is an educator who judges me, an administrator who is my boss. How open can I be during supervision? Will I be penalized for my weaknesses and vulnerabilities? This person can fail me." Successfully negotiating such potential role conflicts and confusion requires clarity and self-awareness on the part of supervisor and a foundation of goodwill and trust between supervisor and intern. One of the important functions of the third role put forth by Kadushin (1992), "supporter" is to build this foundation.

Supporter

Keeping in mind an intern's vulnerabilities, taking the supportive role is to communicate your belief in his or her special abilities and your enthusiasm in being part of the process, and by your actions reassuring the student of his or her worth. This includes resisting the temptation to focus solely on what the student still has to learn, making sure to acknowledge the progress that you see. Interns need reassurance and acknowledgment. They are too quick, too often, to not hear the positive and only hear feedback as criticism. Sometimes I ask students to report back to me the positive feedback they have taken in, and it is remarkable how difficult it is for an intern to "remember" because of their focus on what they did not "do right."

My uncle, an abstract painter, once told a story that I have found helpful in my work with supervisors. He said that the most difficult aspect of teaching is helping a student understand when they've done good work, and what is good about it. I often have to remind supervisors, and myself, to not get carried away in enthusiasm with what there is yet to learn, without balancing with what has been accomplished, otherwise an intern can become easily overwhelmed.

The experience of internship and supervision goes beyond supporting an intern's progress. It *challenges* an intern to stretch and grow; to reevaluate basic assumptions about him/herself and others—clients, peers, teachers or supervisors. It is the push to meet one's potential in the clinical work—the work on oneself, personally and professionally—that drives an intern to grow. The supervisor-intern relationship also provides the "ground" or experience for this development, challenging the intern's personality structure. The internship can thus create a new experience that will change an intern's feelings about him or herself, and relationships with others. This can have a major impact on a student's life, both professionally and personally.

To Teach or Treat?

As supervisors, we learn a great deal about our supervisee's personality in a variety of areas. This brings us to the teach/treat controversy. Questions often asked are, What is our responsibility to address an intern's personality issues as they arise? Should we? When are we overstepping our boundaries as supervisor? What are our boundaries? My answer is that we are not the student's therapists, yet it is our responsibility at certain *times* to deal with personal or personality issues if they are interfering with the student's work as therapist.

Sarnat (1992), a psychoanalytic psychotherapist, has addressed this issue in his writings. He raises the question, "How much should a supervisor allow a supervisee's personality to become a focus in supervision?" I add to this question, "To what extent should the supervisor bring in his or her own therapy skills?" Sarnat suggests that it is important to address the supervisee's personality problems that interfere in the clinical work. One's own therapy skills are used at this time within the supervisor-supervisee relationship. Interns are often quite motivated to explore what is interfering in their work with a client for the sake of their learning and for the sake of the client, in areas that they would be oblivious to or perhaps would be too painful to do otherwise.

It is time to address personal issues when they interfere with students' work in three contexts:

1. When these issues interfere with the intern's understanding or treatment of clients;
2. When issues interfere with the intern's relationship with the supervisor, thereby impeding the learning process;
3. When issues interfere with the intern's relationship with staff on-site.

Once an intern is not able to respond to feedback, or develop in certain areas in spite of it having been pointed out several times, this usually means that "something" is in the way regardless of what a student may consider to be his or her best efforts. Students are often eager to work on this "something." It is at this time that careful interventions are called for so that the issues can be clarified and dealt with, allowing the intern's learning to progress. This is also a time for supervisors to resist the temptation to go beyond the boundaries of the supervisor and venture into the role of the therapist.

The following is an example of when an intern's counter-transference issues interfere with understanding or treatment of clients: A particular member in an intern's therapy group is avoided or overlooked repeatedly, even after both supervisor and intern have discussed the client's dynamics and what his behavior may be communicating. It may be the intern's revulsion to something as simple as drooling or perhaps there is something about that client that evokes emotions that the intern is avoiding. I find that if I make it clear that we all have countertransference reactions in our work—that they are a given to be embraced and explored because of what we can learn from them, rather than we are bad therapists for having them—an intern may then feel comfortable taking the next step in exploring with me what may be going on for him or her.

We are then able to explore the origin of these countertransference reactions. Are they in response to dynamics or transferences that originate from the client? For example, is the client evoking the intern's feelings of anger because of subtle provocations this client always directs toward anyone in an important relationship to him or her? Or is the intern feeling or reacting in such a way because of the intern's own personal past or present experiences that are being triggered?

It is important to give time for an intern's feelings to "blossom" so the intern can reflect back with you over time and really see what you are addressing. For example I may point out a child who has been avoided a number of times before examining why with the intern. Then I can observe with the intern how this has come up a number of times and explore the origin of these feelings. This can be frightening or painful and it is very important to be clear with the student that this happens to everyone. A supervisor giving an example of his or her own countertransference feelings and their interference in the treatment process can often be helpful at these times.

Another way to focus on this is to make the self-reflection a part of the process from the beginning of internship. This sets the stage for future self-inquiry, making it a natural aspect of the treatment process rather than one that is only used when there are problems. For example, at the very beginning of their internship I may ask interns to pick out what clients they are attracted to and which would they rather avoid. We then explore what triggers these feelings. Why are you attracted to the timid child? What is it about you that is attracted to her (i.e., "I like drawing out people, I like this kind of challenge because it makes me feel. . . .")? What is it about the active child that is not appealing (i.e., "I get scared when I feel out of control. . . . ")? What is it about this child that you feel inside of you when you see her—Is this her sadness you are feeling or yours? What about sadness intrigues you? We begin to tease out what reactions we have that are due to what we are picking up about the client, and what is due to our own personal experiences and issues. This sets a precedent so that when problems come up the process of self-examination is already an integral part of the work and a given in our work together. The intern begins to see how countertransference is a useful clinical tool in learning about the client and about oneself.

The following are some examples of other common issues that can interfere in the treatment process: A particular mood of music is absent from an intern's vocabulary, and cannot be accessed when a client needs it; a quality of voice when singing or touch on the piano that is narrow in range. I once had an intern who could not bear to play music that made her feel too sad. To explore this we played music together. First I had her try to improvise a musical portrait of the client and then the child's sadness. When that was too difficult we then just explored sadness musically. Over and over we played until the intern could finally approach the feeling of "sad." Eventually she began to see what she was avoiding and how this particular mood in the music was extremely threatening to her. This new awareness set her free to be more responsive to the client, and she was able to further process the origins of these feelings in her own therapy. Only through musical exploration and then our processing was she able to identify her own unresolved issues, and the impact this was having on the child she was treating.

Another common example of when countertransference feelings may be aroused is when limits need to be set or authority initiated in some way. It can be difficult for beginning interns to be clear and supportive in setting limits due to their own resistance to doing so. "I don't want to be a boss, to be punishing or punitive." One can also see the other extreme, where an intern easily becomes angry, punitive, and authoritarian when limits need to be set. This can be from lack of understanding of how some clients need limits in order to feel safe, but more often it has to do with interns' own past unresolved authority issues or misconceptions about the role of the therapist. In such a case, an intern learns to use his or her own feelings of anger to explore whether these feelings stem from past personal experiences, or if they are evoked by the child and can be used to better understand the child.

The following is an example of when there is interference in the relationship between the supervisor and supervisee: I remember a student, once so eager to work with me, who began to withdraw and even looked pained as I would enter the room for our supervision time. She was still doing everything required of her, and her work with clients was excellent, but I decided I had to confront her about how she seemed with me. I became aware of this because of how *I* felt with her. It was time for me to figure out what was due to my personal countertransference reactions and what originated in her. There was no way I could work with her when I felt so shut out and unwelcome. Gone was the positive spirit of us working together. I saw myself "dancing" in order to "get her back" and when I finally caught on to what was happening I pointed it out. After hearing how I felt she realized that she was dreading her time with me, feeling uncomfortable at how I saw things about her before she saw them. Exploring this together she realized this originated from her past experiences of being intruded upon and abused by an important authority. My way of working with her at that time felt intrusive where earlier, when she was more needy, it felt supportive. I had to evaluate my own countertransference feelings and reevaluate and adjust my supervision style. She was in a different phase of her training now that necessitated my providing more space and independence. She was amazed at having her feelings accepted and responded to without retaliation. She also became clear on what she needed to work on in her own personal therapy.

Sarnat (1992) speaks of how some supervisors are resistant to this type of exploration because of reluctance to see his or her own humanness as a contributor to the impasse with a supervisee. He says that the way to overcome this is through acceptance of one's fallibility. Rather than see personality as flawed when these events occur, he suggests they be seen as ordinary, inevitable, and "subject for analytic curiosity." Again, if we keep our reflective "curiosity" alive throughout, then it will be more comfortably used when there are difficulties for both supervisor and intern.

A third arena in which to explore personality issues is when they arise and interfere with other staff on site. The following are a few examples to look out for: lack of communication and teamwork, or avoidance; competition with other staff; lack of assertiveness when needed for the client's best interests. These areas need to be understood and addressed or the student will be less effective. I remember the relief one intern had that she was able to sit down with a teacher and plan some treatment strategies rather than feel continually thwarted in her work by the teacher's intrusions. This accomplishment gave her the confidence to initiate other contacts with staff and helped her realize that she does have a voice and the respect of fellow team members.

When an intern's personality issues arise, we can then talk about what comes up to the extent that it is appropriate for both of us to become sensitized and united on what needs to be done next. Support systems for following through on the issues are discussed. It is hoped that the student is in therapy where the issues can be worked with in depth. It can become tempting to take on the role of therapist if the intern does not have one, but it is important at this time for the intern to enter outside treatment so that roles and transferences do not become muddy.

Internship Phases

The intern-supervisor relationship, like all relationships, is not static, for it continually changes over time. These changes can be organized into developmental phases. How do these phases evolve and what are the dynamics of each phase? How does the relationship unfold and how can we as supervisors and interns be most effective? Chazan (1990) has divided the supervisory relationship into three phases of development that are quite relevant to the internship. Her use of different theorists to capture the essence of each phase is both illuminating and helpful to supervisors.

Phase 1: The Creation of Space

Chazan (1990) describes the first phase between the supervisor and supervisee as the "creation of space." This "safe space" must be created for the supervisory relationship to develop productively. This creation of space forms a safe home base for the supervisee to return for exploration and experimentation. It is a space where work and play are fused as one, as personal and professional identity become closely bonded. She uses the term "play" as Winnicott (1971) does, a special form of communication between the two individuals that contributes toward growth and health. It is a transitional space similar to the special relationship between mother and baby where through play, they work, grow, and communicate, processing the baby or child's experiences in the outside world and trying out new ways of being. For the intern, supervision is a place to process what has been experienced in the professional world.

Both supervisor and supervisee, according to Chazan, begin this relationship, which is both uncertain and full of promise, with the same questions: Will he/she like me? Can we work together? Can I trust him/her? Can I reveal my doubts? Will I be understood? Will I be appreciated? The first task is for these questions to be answered in such a way that a place safe enough to be creative and exploratory is created for both supervisor and supervisee.

How can we create a safe place in music therapy where interns feel comfortable being just who they are, and safe enough to be open and exposed without fear of condemnation, a place where a supervisor will feel listened to and appreciated, and allowed to be partner in this journey? Much of this has already been discussed in the section on roles, but a few additional points are merited.

A sacrosanct supervision place and time must be set up, with interruptions not allowed if possible. By setting aside this time, interns will immediately feel respected, valued, and listened to. This becomes a sacred joint time of exploration. Listen to and respect the interns' feelings. Help interns listen to their own feelings. Make sure the exploration of these feelings is part of the written assignments, weekly logs, musical explorations, and discussions.

Help the interns feel as safe as possible in this new setting. Educate them about the proper communication structures and decision-making processes. Educate them about some of the challenges they may be confronted with so that they not only know what to expect, but also know that you are sensitized to what it is like for them. An example might be preparing a student for interruptions from a particular unsupportive staff member and how best to handle them. This way your vulnerable student will not take such actions personally, but understand it as part of the package. Tell your intern about and of course introduce him/her to staff that are especially supportive and rewarding to work with. Have a back-up person available to the student who he can have access to if needed when you are not around.

Help your intern understand how much you value communication and need feedback, for understanding each other is a two way street. An intern must feel comfortable bringing up whatever s/he feels is relevant to the internship and supervisory relationship. Communicate this with your words and actions. Structure a space for this type of communication from the beginning: checking in on feelings, being matter-of-fact in assuming that there will be feelings (i.e., about starting, about being in a new role, about clients that are elicited during observations and interactions, about supervision). Really listen. Read your intern's written journals or logs and give them back promptly with feedback that values their perspective while expanding their knowledge. Make sure a section on personal reactions is included, conveying how important it is for you to know how they react to things and what is on their mind. Explore when this is resisted.

I always tell my intern that I will try to do my best, but at times I will get things wrong or unintentionally say something hurtful. I say that the student knows him or herself best, so s/he should tell me when this happens. I want them to know that I want feedback too.

Phase 2: Structure Building

The second phase Chazan (1990) describes as "structure building," using as a model Mahler, Pine, and Bergman's (1975) steps in the separation-individuation process.

Overview

There are two main stages of this phase: twinning and separation-individuation. In the first stage she describes the supervisor-supervisee relationship as "twinning." "I am like her; she is like me." The supervisee "twins" with the supervisor, learning the supervisor's way of working, using the supervisor as a model. The supervisor functions as an alter ego and adjusts herself to the supervisee's individual style, blending and enhancing, rather than negating preexisting patterns. The supervisee will feel this as affirming and supportive, will feel competent in learning, and brave enough to try out new approaches and techniques.

When the supervisee no longer needs this twinning he/she has reached the separation-individuation stage. The supervisee begins to establish more of a separate identity. Interns become less dependent upon imitation of their supervisors. The supervisee continues to venture into clinical forays of exploration, and Chazan describes how they then return to home base for feedback and support in the process of constructing their own therapy model and techniques. The supervisee survives making mistakes, and criticism is accepted better when each little growth step is supported and acknowledged.

During this period there occur differences of opinion and power struggles normal to the challenge of establishing a separate identity. The supervisor's challenge is to tactfully and sensitively support this process, tolerating the differences that arise and avoiding the pitfalls of imposition of authority and domination. At the same time, difficulties that interfere with the intern's clinical work as well as the supervisor-supervisee relationship must be addressed.

Twinning

During the "twinning" period, one of the supervisor's functions is that of role model. The student learns the supervisor's way of working and being with clients, and learns the music as a stepping stone toward developing his/her own way. An intern can then accept and integrate, or reject the supervisor's material and methods as part of the learning process. Interns often place unrealistic pressure on themselves to be spontaneously and prolifically creative. Alleviate the pressure new interns have of immediately developing their own greeting songs, their own repertoire, their own improvisational styles. Let them take yours and then go from there, using your methods and activities as a foundation. (Some students will need to immediately develop their own.)

Develop an understanding of their learning style. Some students feel it is supportive for the supervisor to make suggestions while they are leading a session, while others cannot handle that and may throw up their hands and give up their leadership. How much information or feedback can they absorb before feeling overwhelmed? Do they like to work themselves slowly into the leadership position, or do they work best by plunging in fully? Learn how to go their speed, responding to their questions, observations, and interests as a guide for what to teach next.

It is also important to learn where they are developmentally in their lives. Are they straight out of college and on their own for the first time, still separating from their parents? This brings with it different developmental needs from someone reentering the work force, or changing careers and experiencing the narcissistic blow of being a beginner again. For example, I find that those with a professional identity and sense of competence from their previous professions have an especially difficult time not being proficient and excellent in their own eyes immediately. I need to do a lot of reassuring that their experiences of disorientation and negative feelings about themselves or abilities are common. They may have to leave their expertise at the door and not be able to integrate it into their new professional identity right away. Help them stay in touch with the experiences and skills they possess that apply to this new work.

Learn what cultural challenges an intern may have. Is your intern from another culture? Then it is important to come to a mutual understanding of differing social structures and communication patterns and how these differences may be considered in your work together. For example some cultures have a clear boundary between teacher and student, where divulging personal feelings are taboo and where an individual would not consider developing in one's own way. This must be openly addressed.

Separation-Individuation
After the period of "twinning" and after feeling secure, interns are ready to begin to separate-individuate, to develop their own way as Mahler et al. (1975) would say. The honeymoon is over, the supervisor is no longer so idealized. Part of the individuation process is having issues come up. Expect them to emerge as a result of the intern's past experiences and as a push for separation in the present. As a supervisor you might feel that you are being pushed away. It is normal that challenges arise at this point. Interns no longer need to be so dependent and they are not as comfortable feeling dependent, so there are a host of ways they use to break away. At this time students might finally feel more comfortable with the population and how to manage getting through a session with challenging clients, but may become angry when they are challenged to go deeper in the work. "I am finally comfortable, don't make me see how much more I have to learn. I do not want to feel so insecure again and be so dependent upon you!"

A supervisor's task is to continue to supportively address issues that interfere with a student's work or relationship with you, even as s/he "rebels." Be aware of your own countertransference and reevaluate your supervisory style and determine if it needs to be modified.

I always support independence. For example, during the later part of the internship, when they are ready, I may shift in my role as educator and teach less explicitly, focusing on helping the intern learn how to learn. I am explicit about this. As we evaluate where we have come, and what is ahead, I put forward how my expectations have changed. For example, after a session I observe, I may ask the intern to process the session for me and organize where input is most needed. It is time to help interns identify and further develop their special qualities and strengths even more. Support them developing further their own methods and music therapy materials if this has not already occurred.

Phase 3: Reciprocity and Well-Being

Chazan (1990) borrows from Erikson's (1959) identity formation stage of "intimacy, generativity and integrity" to describe this last phase, called "reciprocity and well-being." In this phase the intern has developed a professional identity and personal identity with an emerging inner experience of "well-being" (fragile as it may be). There is a greater feeling of mutuality and reciprocity between supervisor and supervisee. Chazan states that not all relationships progress to this point, but this is the goal.

During this stage, the termination period in internship, an intern's tasks are to be aware of what was learned, one's special strengths, and what still needs to be learned. The intern is able to communicate clearly about the field and the work that s/he does, and has established him or herself as a professional who has much to offer to clients and fellow staff.

I make a point of relating differently to an intern at this stage. For example, in discussing my work I will seek out impressions and feedback in a more collegial way. I often ask the intern to hypothesize other ways I may have worked with clients during sessions. I want interns to see that there are other good options for working with clients that they may think of. I have to be careful to be open and not dismiss their suggestions due to my own countertransference feelings. I want them to feel a shift in their role with me. I want to stimulate professional interchanges and reinforce the intern's new professional identity. Not only has the intern established a secure professional identity, but also the supervisor feels the rewards of launching a new professional into the field

Additional Considerations

This final section presents some common "issues" or challenges that often come up for supervisor and supervisee in addition to those already discussed. This is by no means a complete list of issues that might arise, rather a examples I've selected from my experience as a supervisor.

- A supervisor, especially a new supervisor or a supervisor starting a new job, can become narcissistically invested in the intern's work. An intern may be seen as a representative of the supervisor's work, so the intern's "performance" will have repercussions on the status of the music therapy department. These feelings can create unrealistic expectations of the student's work. A supervisor may be unable to see the intern's needs due to anxiety about preserving the program's status, even to the point of becoming tense, overbearing and critical. My experience has been that in most cases staff are usually more comfortable with a student than a new supervisor may be. I've also noticed that if I am open to hearing staff's concerns and feedback about a student, they will often align with me to help an intern rather than be accusatory or judgmental.

- Supervisors are often confronted with control issues as they supervise. At times it may be difficult to let a student learn from his or her own efforts and even mistakes. It can be difficult to watch the therapy proceed in a slower manner than what you would have done, or have a client you have worked with not be understood in the way you might. The tendency may be then to jump in too soon, sabotaging the relationship and the intern's leadership.

- It is important to understand the intern's phases of individuation in the supervisor-intern relationship and how they relate to the ways independence is asserted. When a student is learning his or her own way or exploring other ways, this shift may cause a supervisor to experience feelings of rejection or loss of control. Again, watch out that as supervisor you do not feel challenged by this exploration in such a way to feel tempted to squash or "best" it. It is also important to be aware of when the intern shows signs that there is difficulty with the individuation process. Examples may be when a student becomes provocative or belligerent. All of a sudden a supervisor is left out of important decisions. A student might "forget" to check with the supervisor about changes or events, or find other indirect ways to assert and challenge. It is then time to explore your student's feelings and of course any of your feelings or actions that may be contributing to this dynamic. This may be a time to adjust your supervision style or expand autonomy.

- There can be a sense of loss when a supervisor gives up some of one's own caseload and the intimacy of that client contact. This may be especially pertinent to part-time clinicians who no longer have a large caseload when they start supervising. There can be a backlash of feelings when an especially interesting client is assigned or transferred to a supervisee. Don't pass on cases you find so rewarding that you then resent the intern. Watch out for competition.

- Feelings about dependency can be a difficult issue for both supervisor and supervisee. As supervisor, how does it feel to be depended upon, in the way an intern may need you, especially at the beginning of internship? Does it make you uncomfortable in any way? Are any feelings stirred up by being in this role? This leads to the question of how much dependence upon the supervisor is healthy. Norman (1987) discusses this issue in some detail. The amount of dependence is not the question, but rather why it is occurring. She frames this in terms of the "transitional relationship" that I discussed earlier; saying that some supervisees really need to have everything spelled out for them and supported in the beginning in order to feel safe. What is key is how the intern progresses over time. The dependency usually dissipates as the intern becomes more secure. When it does not, it is time to explore with the student what may be interfering. She also gives an interesting case example of a supervisee she had that did not become dependent at all, and was resistant to the supervisor's support and feedback. She had to explore with the supervisee what was getting in the way of the relationship, and only after that was done could the supervisee move on and commit to the supervision process.

- Related to dependence is how it feels to be "separated from," to no longer be needed after all the work invested in an intern. In my own experience I have had to learn not to expect unrealistic amounts of gratitude just at the time when an intern is separating.

- Supervisors should be aware of their own countertransference around the issue of being an authority. The potential exists for the supervisor to take on the dynamics of an authority from the supervisor's own past or reenact an intern's earlier experience with authority. If these authority experiences were problematic, then this may lead to difficulties. Sometimes the supervisor is uncomfortable taking on authority. It can be difficult to assert for fear of the intern's anger, wanting to be liked, or looked up to. It is extremely important for the supervisor to examine one's own feelings about authority.

- A supervisor must sort through what countertransference the intern induces, and what is due to one's own personal issues. In a very short amount of time we learn, by an intern's responses to us, what their previous experiences have been with parental figures and authorities. The intensity of this relationship fosters this dynamic. An obvious example of this is a supervisor who comes to me saying she feels more like a policewoman than a supervisor because she must constantly be on top of her intern to oversee that he gets things done. When the supervisor explored this with him in a supportive way, the intern, who was at first oblivious, was able to identify how this is what he expected from her based upon his past experiences with authority figures. From this experience, the intern saw a pattern of how this dynamic occurred even outside of internship. He could then bring it to his personal therapy, explore it, and then was able to move on and act more responsibly.

- Another interesting dynamic for the supervisor to be aware of is feelings of competition. This can arise especially when an intern is more skilled musically in some area or "has a way" with a particular type of client. What do you find yourself doing in response? Do you go home and feel depressed? Do you feel the urge to show off your great therapy skills and put this intern "in her place"? Or perhaps your intern starts to get feedback from other team members who appreciate her work, perhaps your intern is having success with a client that you did not have. How do you subtly, or not so subtly respond to this? Do you put greater demands on the student so that you are still the authority? Do you withdraw? Do you put your student down? Does your own sense of esteem suddenly dip?

Conclusion

The journey that intern and supervisor together embark upon during internship is both rich and complex, as well as risky and not always predictable. Both partners who join in navigating the various roles and phases share an enormous potential for professional growth, self-knowledge, even transformation. This chapter endeavored to provide a "map" highlighting important features throughout the internship journey. Using this map, the supervisor can develop greater understanding of the demands and dynamics that, at any time, could capsize the fragile vessel that supervisor and intern pilot together. With a broader understanding and perspective regarding the evolution of roles, phases, and issues, a supervisor will become increasingly sensitized to the significance of what takes place and empowered to respond effectively.

References

Chazan, S. E. (1990). On being supervised and supervision. In R. Lane (ed.), *Psychoanalytic Approaches to Supervision.* Philadelphia, PA: Bruner/Mazel.

Erikson, E. (1959). *Identity and the Life Cycle.* New York: International Universities Press.

Kadushin, A. (1992). *Supervision in Social Work.* New York: Columbia University.

Mahler, M., Pine, F., and Bergman, A. (1975). *The Psychological Birth of the Human Infant.* New York: Basic Books.

Mordock, J. B. (1990). The new supervisor: Awareness of problems experienced and some suggestions for problem resolution through supervisory training. *The Clinical Supervisor*, 8(1), 81–92.

Morris, W., (ed.). (1981). *The American Heritage Dictionary of the English Language.* Boston, MA: Houghton Mifflin Company.

Norman, J. S. (1987). Supervision: The affective process. *Social Casework: The Journal of Contemporary Social Work*, 68(6), 374–379.

Sarnat, J. E. (1992). Supervision in relationship: Resolving the teach-treat controversy in psychoanalytic supervision. *Psychoanalytic Psychology*, 9(3), 387–403.

Stein, J., (ed.). (1978). *The Random House Dictionary.* New York: Ballantine Books.

Winnicott, D. W. (1971). *Playing and Reality.* London: Tavistock.

Acknowledgments

I would like to thank Barbara Hesser, who, as my professor, supervisor and then dear friend opened my eyes to the profound potential of the supervisor-supervisee relationship. I also thank my devoted friend and husband, Dr. Marc Goloff, for his tireless support and belief in my work, and superb editing skills that I used to full advantage. Finally, I would like to thank all of the supervisors and interns who have allowed me to accompany them on their most wondrous journeys through internship and beyond.

Chapter 8

Competency-Based Approach
to Intern Supervision

Laurie A. Farnan, MMT, MT-BC
Coordinator, Central Wisconsin Center
for the Developmentally Disabled
Madison, WI

Much has been written about the importance of competency-based education in music therapy. Boone (1989), Greenfield (1978), Maranto (1989), and Petrie (1989), all wrote about the importance of education and clinical training based on student need and demonstration of student mastery. "A competency-based education would be based on student performance, accomplishment, and proficiency, not just completing a course within a specific time frame" (Petrie, 1989, p. 137). The AMTA Code of Ethics (1998) states: "1.1 The Music Therapist will perform only those duties for which he/she has been adequately training, not engaging outside of his/her area of competence." Taylor (1987) defines a competent person as one who has the aptitude, ability, knowledge, judgment, strength, or skill necessary for performing an indicated action" (p. 115). Can a supervisor assist an intern to successful acquisition of the AMTA competencies? If so, how? Is there a relationship between effective supervision and development of intern competence?

The notion that there should be a music therapy supervisor on-site is very popular when discussing the internship stage of clinical training and education. But several questions come to mind regarding the nature and techniques of supervision. Supervising competent interns is easy. Competent interns are on time, can accurately assess clients, implement therapeutic objectives, find their starting pitch, sing and play in the same key at the same time, and figure out where they fit in the larger organization of a facility or agency. But often this level of competence is not present on the first day or even within the first few weeks or months of internship. However, most interns do successfully complete their internships. One could conclude then, that with appropriate support, observation with feedback, guidance, mentorship, and modeling, that through effective supervision, the desired competencies could be successfully acquired. How then, can supervision contribute to the acquisition of the desired intern competencies?

To develop competency-based supervisory techniques it would seem logical to examine the identified competencies learned during internship and coordinate supervisor methods. Several writers have identified competencies that are most often acquired during the internship experience. A survey conducted by the National Association for Music Therapy Subcommittee on Professional Competencies (1997) identified competencies, which appear to be learned in clinical training (internship). Maranto and Bruscia (1988) also reported survey results of competencies learned during the internship phase of education. The topic areas of group techniques, verbal techniques, communicating with clients, client assessment, treatment planning, implementing therapy, treatment and therapy evaluation and termination/discharge planning were common identified competencies between the two surveys (p. 20).

An additional consideration for designing competency-based supervision is intern development. We have identified the competencies to be learned but it would be beneficial to consider when particular competencies are best addressed during the internship. Grant and McCarty (1990) reported that in a six-month internship, "Significant gains were made in personal and professional categories with the greatest gains in months 5 and 6" (p. 102). Glider (1988) described several stages of professional identity formation in psychologists. The first stage is termed "early intern syndrome" and is marked by role ambiguity and search for identity. As students begin to establish a place for themselves within an agency, they may encounter "a period of introspection, doubt and self confrontation" (p. 200). In the Clinical Training Directors Workshop (1994) the NAMT Clinical Training Committee taught new supervisors about the five Stages of Internship. They are as follows:

- Dependency Stage,
- Autonomy Stage,
- Conditional Dependency Stage,
- Fourth Month Blues Stage, and
- Independence Stage.

Intern needs, supervisor techniques, and tools can be identified at each of these developmental stages. Psychologist literature also identifies similar stages of internship.

The purpose of this chapter is to further examine stages of music therapy internship, identify AMTA competencies to be learned at each stage, and suggest supervisory techniques to help an intern successfully achieve the desired competencies. Internships can and do vary in length so delineation by month or hours will be avoided in this chapter. For the purposes of this chapter, internship will be divided into three equal segments—first segment, middle segment, and final segment.

Stages of Internship and Competency Acquisition

Stage I—First Segment of Internship

In the first third of an internship the intern encounters many new sights, sounds, and experiences. Generally their anxiety is high as they attempt to find their place in a new system. The AMTA Clinical Training Committee materials define this first stage as the dependency stage. Care should be taken on the first day of this stage to let the intern know they are welcome. Provide them with a thorough orientation to the environment within which they will be working. This is the time to start to define boundaries and model desired workplace behaviors. Present orientation materials in a number of different ways, both written and oral. Given the general level of anxiety of new interns, it is best not to solely depend on them remembering all oral information they receive at this time. This is a good time to provide the interns with copies of the AMTA Standards of Clinical Practice and the Code of Ethics.

An intern focusing more on himself or herself than on the client characterizes the dependency stage. The intern is spending most of their time observing the therapist work and interact with clients. Concrete observation forms may be helpful supervisory tools at this stage. Therapist questions have to be specific and lead the intern to make more meaningful observations. Farnan (1996, p. 70) provides examples of supervisory forms that might be helpful at this stage including Observation Report, Weekly Supervision Form, and Intern Session Review Form. These forms are provided below.

Table 1
Observation Report

Name of intern:
Names of program staff:
Unit or classroom:
Number of clients:
Client first names:
Date:
1. Describe several client behaviors with and without music.
2. Name activities (songs) used during session.
3. Which interventions were the most successful? Why?
4. What functional skill life areas did the activities address?
5. What did you learn (about the clients, yourself, music therapy, etc.) while observing this session?

Use the Observation Report when interns have difficulty labeling and articulating client responses after a session. It also provides a written reminder of names and locations to help the intern orient themselves to the program and people.

Table 2
Weekly Supervision Form

1. Work week review:
Accomplishments:
Challenges:
2. Personal/professional development:
Recommendations:
3. Objectives for next week:
Recommendations:
4. Client concerns/progress:
Recommendations:

Use the Weekly Supervision Form when interns have trouble brining issues to supervision meetings. This form also helps to specify objectives to be accomplished in a weekly time frame and can help the intern focus on specific elements of competence.

Table 3
Intern Session Review Form

Group:
Dates:
# of clients:
# of staff:
1. What was the most effective thing you did in this session? What made it effective?
2. What was the least effective thing you did? Why was it less than effective?
3. Relate one or more components of the session to one or more of the Sears' Processes of Music Therapy. (Any theoretical model will work here, it doesn't have to be Sears. It could be biomedical, medical, or psychodynamic, etc. It should be relevant to your setting and style of therapy. The purpose of this statement is to help interns gain a grasp of theoretical models as they develop their philosophy of treatment.)
4. Specifically list things you will change in the next session.

Use the Intern Session Review Form to help the intern learn self-evaluation skills. It can also provide a historical record of improvement as the intern progresses and acquires more effective skills.

Competencies also need to be concretely defined. These first few weeks are a good time to work on functional music skills. Individual assessment of an intern's functional guitar, voice, and piano skills is a very good idea within the first two weeks of internship. Formulation of a specific plan for development of skills can follow such a music skill assessment. When designing a functional music skill assessment process, look at the Music Foundations section of the AMTA Competencies. Keyboard skills, guitar skills, voice skills and nonsymphonic instrument skills are listed. Add to your assessment any other functional music skills necessary for your site. For example, if you use Orff instruments or tone bars you may need to assess and then train interns on how to best utilize those instruments within your setting. One possible way to assess voice and guitar skills is to have each intern prepare a piece to play and sing for each other and the supervisor. Assure them this is just so the supervisor can assess abilities and individualize a program for each intern. It is a little less intimidating for the interns if this process is done in a group and not one on one with the supervisor. This approach allows the intern to play and sing in a supportive atmosphere away from clients. The intern needs great assurance that they are on the right track and that there will be a plan to help them improve.

Towards the end of this first stage the intern may be leading specific sections of a therapy session. Sections like opening and closing interventions are usually a good place to start with feedback provided immediately after the session. Specific questions regarding the events in the session are also very good at this stage as a way to develop better focus on the client. Examples of questions and phrases that guide and prompt intern responses are provided in the list that follows. Such verbal prompts can help interns to develop critical observation skills and begin to develop competencies in the Clinical Foundation section, particularly the Principles of Therapy section which includes, basic knowledge of dynamics and processes of a therapist-client relationship. By keeping the focus on competencies the intern can be more forward focused.

Questions and Phrases for Development of Clinical Foundations–First Segment of Internship

- Tell me two client responses you noticed in the sessions.
- What do you think it was about the music that elicited that response?
- I hope you noticed that . . .
- Did you see the way (client) . . . ?
- Tell me why you think we did it that way.
- How do you think your presence affected interactions and interventions in the session?

The final component of this first stage is intern goal setting and defining expectations. Providing interns with their own copy of the AMTA Competencies (1999)[1] helps them to define their own expectations. Within the first week it is very helpful to have the intern write out their expectations of internship. This list is discussed with the supervisor and can be referred to throughout the internship to see how things are going. It can also be helpful to have a written Intern Expectation document from the supervisory point of view, including things like hours of work, work rules, and termination policy. The supervisor and intern are then in agreement on what needs to be accomplished in the period of training and education called internship.

AMTA Competencies–First segment of internship

Music Foundations
Keyboard Skills
- Play basic chord progressions (I-IV-V-I) in several keys.
- Sight-read simple compositions and song accompaniments.
- Harmonize and transpose simple compositions.

Guitar Skills
- Employ simple strumming and finger picking techniques.
- Tune guitar using standard and other tunings.
- Harmonize and transpose simple compositions in several keys.

---

[1] Reprinted with permission from the American Music Therapy Association.

Voice Skills
- Lead groups singing by voice.
- Communicate vocally with adequate volume.
- Sing a basic repertoire of traditional, folk, and popular songs in tune with a pleasing quality.

Nonsymphonic Instrument Skills
- Play percussion instruments alone or in ensemble.
- Demonstrate basic knowledge of care and maintenance of nonsymphonic and ethnic instruments.

Movement Skills
- Move in structural rhythmic and improvisatory manners for expressive purposes.

Clinical Foundations
Exceptionality
- Demonstrate basic knowledge of the potential, limitation, problems of exceptional individuals.
- Demonstrate basic knowledge of the causes and symptoms of major exceptionalities and basic terminology used in diagnosis and classification.
- Demonstrate basic knowledge of typical and atypical human systems and development.

Principles of Therapy
- Demonstrate basic knowledge of the dynamics and process of therapy groups.
- Demonstrate basic knowledge of accepted methods of major therapeutic approaches.

Scenario and Supervision Strategies—First Stage of Internship—Focus on Self

Sixth-week intern Joan[2] had just finished a training class in passive range of motion taught by the occupational therapists. Joan had also received individual instruction with specific clients from another OT staff and had seen passive range of motion paired with music and vibrotactile stimulation in five sessions with the supervising music therapist. When asked to assist and provide range to a client in the next session with another music therapist, Joan looked perplexed, confused, and scared. Her touch was tentative, she appeared unsure of what she was supposed to do, and the range she provided was small and limited, not at all what the client needed. She forgot key elements such as setting the brakes on the wheelchair for resistance, starting with the

---

[2] All names have been changed to protect the supervisees' and the clients' privacy.

least affected limb first, standing on the same side to be ranged, and telling the client what was going to happen.

Intern Joan was experiencing great difficulty generalizing her training from client to client and session to session. When asked about it, she concentrated on herself and the effects she perceived she was having on the client such as: "I think my shirt was too bright and distracting." "I think Bob (client) knew I was new and wouldn't move *for me*." "I was afraid to move his arm because it was so stiff." "I didn't know what to do." "I was afraid I would hurt him." "Does this client have trouble establishing relationships with others?" "How do I know if I am doing the right thing?"

Suggestions for dealing with this overemphasis on self include reminders to the intern that the clients meet many people in their lives and generally make necessary adjustments to the change in care givers and, in fact, may be quite skilled at it. Ask the intern how they felt about the range experience and work from there. Remind the intern to look at the face of the client during range of motion and learn to read responses through facial expressions. Reassure the intern that while being careful is a good therapeutic instinct, being tentative and unsure is not. Reinforce what the intern has leaned already and empower them to apply the knowledge and techniques they are just discovering. While Joan did nothing to harm the client, she probably didn't do him any good either. Encourage interns to take it up to the next level where they will be providing good and effective interventions based on their training.

A reality check at this time is also in order. In this particular case, the "too bright shirt" was a dark, solid color burgundy, therefore, probably not a "too bright" problem. Asking the intern to reiterate how they were trained and by whom helps to remind them they have had training which gave them the tools and techniques they will need. Ask with which clients the intern has worked and ask if there were similarities or differences from client to client and what those difference were. Ask the intern to think about and identify who had similar muscle tone issues in the group. And as for the "He wouldn't move for me," ask why any client should do anything for the therapist. It is not that kind of relationship. The therapeutic relationship is one of empowerment and choice. Then have the intern perform range of motion on the therapist, with the therapist making suggestions throughout the process, praising effective procedures and suggesting how to improve. This is not role-playing but a hands on approach to learning how to literally handle other people.

Stage II—Middle Segment of Internship

The middle segment of internship, the autonomy stage, finds the intern gaining more skill, competence, experience, confidence, and independence from the supervisor. Interns assume increased responsibility for group interventions and eventually begin to run groups without the supervisor. Halfway through this stage the mid-term intern evaluation may occur. With that evaluation, the individual intern expectancies can be revisited to ensure intern and supervisor are on track. Interns should complete self-evaluations and then meet with the supervisor to discuss the overall development of the competencies. It may also be a good idea to review the competency document as part of a midterm evaluation process. When designing internship evaluation forms it would be helpful to use the categories of the AMTA Competencies, which are Musical Foundations, Clinical Foundations, and Music Therapy.

Specific elements of Clinical Foundations such as those contained in the Therapeutic Relationship section can be developed at this middle stage. The intern is establishing relationships with clients and staff that may be independent of the supervisor. The supervisor must be sure to check in often with the intern through observation of sessions and structured supervision meetings where all groups are reviewed and guidance is provided. Establishing a regular weekly meeting time for one-on-one supervision ensures that there will be time to talk about any issues that arise.

The structure of the supervisory meeting is very important. Not all interns are born with the ability to talk about what they are doing so that this skill may need to be cultivated. One way to develop this skill is through written forms analyzing session results and weekly comment forms as those provided by Farnan (1996, p. 70). Another way to help develop verbal skills is to ask the right questions. Therapists learn to ask good questions and so can supervisors. The following questions can be helpful in assisting interns to learn how to articulate what is happening in their sessions.

Questions for Development of Clinical Foundations—Second Segment of Internship

- What are you working on this week?
- What groups are going well for you?
- What is it about those groups that make it go well?
- Are there any groups or individual clients that are challenging you?
- Are you getting everything you need to support your learning?
- Is there anything else you need from our staff?
- Do you have enough work to do?
- Do you have too much work to do?
- Is there anything else that needs our attention for this week?

Elements of the Music Therapy competencies including the Client Assessment, Treatment Planning, Therapy Implementation, Therapy Evaluation, and Documentation sections begin to develop in this stage of internship. Assigning readings about those topics as they relate to the clinical population would be beneficial at this time. Articles or book chapters on assessment and session planning are helpful at this stage. Look through the publications to find articles specific to your own population and treatment planning for that population.

AMTA Competencies—Middle Segment of Internship

Clinical Foundations
The Therapeutic Relationship
- Recognize the impact of one's own feelings, attitudes, and actions on the client and the therapy process.

- Establish and maintain interpersonal relationships with clients that are conducive to therapy.
- Utilize the dynamics and processes of groups to achieve therapeutic goals.

Music Therapy Foundations
Foundations and Principles

- Demonstrate basic knowledge of existing music therapy methods, techniques, material, and equipment with their appropriate applications.
- Demonstrate basic knowledge of principles and methods of music therapy assessment and their appropriate application.
- Demonstrate basic knowledge of the principles and methods for evaluating the effects of music therapy.
- Demonstrate basic knowledge of the purpose, intent, and function of music therapy for various client populations.
- Demonstrate basic knowledge of the psychological and physiological aspects of musical behavior and experience.

Client Assessment

- Communicate assessment findings and recommendations in written and verbal forms.
- Observe and record accurately the client's responses to assessment.
- Identify the client's appropriate and inappropriate behaviors.
- Select, design and implement effective culturally-based methods for assessing the client's assets and problems through music.
- Select, design, and implement effective culturally-based methods for assessing the client's musical preferences and level of musical functioning or development.
- Identify the client's therapeutic needs through an analysis and interpretation of music therapy and related assessment data.

Treatment Planning

- Select or create music therapy experiences that meet the client's objectives.
- Formulate goals and objectives for individual and group music therapy based upon assessment findings.
- Identify the client's primary treatment needs in music therapy.
- Provide estimates of frequency and duration of treatment.
- Select and adapt music consistent with strengths and needs of the client.
- Formulate music therapy strategies for individual and groups based upon the goals and objectives adopted.
- Select and adapt musical instruments and equipment consistent with strengths and needs of the client.
- Organize and arrange the music therapy setting to facilitate the client's therapeutic involvement.
- Plan and sequence music therapy sessions.

Therapy Implementation
- Recognize, interpret and respond appropriately to significant events in the music therapy session as they occur.
- Provide music therapy experiences to change nonmusical behaviors.
- Provide verbal and nonverbal directions and cues necessary for successful client participation.
- Utilize singing skills in music therapy sessions.
- Provide models for appropriate social behavior in group music therapy.
- Utilize therapeutic verbal skills in music therapy sessions.
- Sequence and pace music experiences within a session according to the client needs and situational factors.
- Conduct or facilitate group and individual music therapy.
- Establish closure of music therapy sessions.
- Implement music therapy program according to treatment plan.
- Promote a sense of group cohesiveness and/or feeling of group membership.
- Provide music therapy experiences that assist the client in development of social skills.
- Communicate to the clients expectations of their behavior.
- Assist the client to communicate more effectively.
- Provide music therapy experiences to improve the client's sense of self and sense of self with others.
- Create a physical environment that is conducive to therapy.
- Provide music therapy experiences to elicit social interactions.
- Provide music therapy experiences to promote client decision making.
- Develop and maintain a repertoire of music for age, culture, and stylistic differences.
- Provide music therapy experiences that assist the client in increasing on-task behavior.
  - Provide music therapy experiences to elicit affective responses from the client.
  - Provide feedback on, reflect, rephrase, and translate the client's communications.
  - Provide sensory stimulation through music therapy experiences that allow the client to use visual, auditory, or tactile cues.
  - Utilize nonsymphonic instruments in music therapy sessions.
  - Provide music therapy experiences to encourage creative responses from the client
  - Use music with techniques of relaxation and/or stress reduction.
  - Provide music therapy experiences to improve the client's orientation to person, place, and time. Provide music therapy experiences to enhance the client's cognitive/intellectual development.
  - Recognize and respond appropriately to effects of the client's medications.

Therapy Evaluation
- Recognize and respond appropriately to situations in which there are clear and present dangers to the client and/or others.
- Modify treatment approaches based on the client's response to therapy.
- Recognize significant charges and patterns in the client's response to therapy.
- Revise treatment plan as needed.
- Establish and work within realistic time frames for evaluating the effects of therapy.
- Review treatment plan periodically within guidelines set by agency.
- Design and implement methods for evaluating and measuring client progress and the effectiveness of therapeutic strategies.

Scenario and Supervisory Strategies—Middle Stage of Internship—Focus on Therapy

Ten-week intern Debbie was observed by the supervising therapist in one of her first independent groups. There were two other staff and five clients with profound mental retardation and behavioral issues. Debbie had the good therapeutic instinct that she should try to control the group. But the directions she gave crossed the line of trying to control the group to ordering people what to do because she said so. Examples of her directives to clients were: "I know you don't want to quit playing the drum, but you've got to give it up now, Buddy." "Put the maraca in the box for me now, Cindy." "Jeff, can you play the tambourine?" "Sally, I want you to play the drum now." Debbie also was experiencing difficulty finding her starting pitch and maintaining a tonal center.

While her initial instincts to establish control were very accurate, the phrases she chose served more to make her appear to be dictating participation rather than inviting and supporting it. Suggestions to Debbie started with the phrase, "I am sure you did not intend to create an overly authoritative atmosphere in your group but let's look at the phrases you used and explore how you might have been interpreted." In supervision with Debbie, the written notes taken during the observation quoted her directly which helped to raise her awareness of how she might be being perceived. She was cautioned about the dangers of yes/no questions in asking a client if they can or will play. It is helpful to point out to interns that when a yes/no question is asked, they better be able to honor the yes or no response and if someone doesn't want to play, one can't make them do it anyway. Discussion further explored why she had decided the client who was clearly engaged and enjoying playing the drum was told he had to give it up. Flexibility to adjust the session plan was explored. Samples of empowering statements to substitute for authoritative statements were provided to the intern.

As for development of musical skills, interns are sometimes surprised when they are out on their own that the music doesn't go exactly like it did with the therapist. Suggesting strategies for finding starting pitches can include knowing ahead of time what scale degree to start with, singing a triad to secure the tonal center, carrying a bell with the starting pitch, and of course, more practice ahead of the session time.

Stage III – Final Segment of Internship

The final stage of internship is the independence stage. Interns are running their own groups, attending team meetings, assessing clients, implementing therapeutic objectives, collecting data, and eventually terminating their groups. They also are writing resumes, going to job interviews, and transitioning themselves to an entry-level clinician. They may have questions about the music therapy professional organizations. They may also have questions about how to set up and administer clinical programs. The competencies at this final stage of internship include mostly elements from the Music Therapy Foundations section such as Termination/Discharge Planning, Supervision and Administration, Professional Role/Ethics. The final evaluation of the intern is completed in the last week of internship. This final evaluation should reflect on the gains made by the intern and clearly relate to competencies successfully demonstrated. Supervisory meetings at this stage take on a different tone as the intern, hopefully, is becoming a more independent therapist. The supervisor should also help prepare the intern for finishing by taking time to reflect on how much time remains and focusing on what could be accomplished in the time remaining. Interns benefit from suggestions on how to say good-bye to clients and staff. Suggest specific phrases for them to use such as: "Thank you all for helping me to learn." "Thank you for all you have taught me." "Good luck and keep making good progress."

Questions for Development of Music Therapy Foundations—Final Segment of Internship

- What would your ideal job look like?
- What type of population do you want to work with?
- How do you plan to continue to develop your functional skills?
- Is your resume updated to include internship experiences?
- How are you bringing closure to your groups?
- Are you clear on what paperwork/projects need to be before you finish?
- What changes have you noticed in your clients?

AMTA Competencies - Final segment of internship

Music Therapy Foundations
Documentation
- Write progress notes that accurately reflect client change and meet the requirements of internal and external legal, regulatory, and reimbursement bodies.
- Document clinical data.
- Write professional reports describing the client throughout all phases of the music therapy process in an accurate, concise, and objective manner.

- Communicate orally with the client, parents, significant others, and team members regarding the client's progress and various aspects of the client's music therapy program.
- Document and revise the treatment plan and document changes to the treatment plan.
- Develop and use data-gathering techniques during all phases of the clinical process including assessment, treatment, and evaluation.
- Demonstrate knowledge of professional standards of clinical practice regarding documentation.

Termination/Discharge Planning
- Inform and prepare the client for approaching termination from music therapy.
- Establish closure of music therapy services by time or termination/discharge.
- Determine termination of the client from music therapy.
- Integrate music therapy termination plan with plans for the client's discharge from the facility.
- Assess potential benefits/detriments of termination of music therapy.
- Develop music therapy termination plan.
- Demonstrate knowledge of professional standards of clinical practice regarding termination.

Professional Role/Ethics
- Adhere to professional code of ethics.
- Interpret and apply ethical standards of the music therapy profession.
- Adhere to professional standards of clinical practice.
- Demonstrate dependability: follows through with all tasks regarding education and professional training.
- Accept criticism/feedback with willingness and follow through in a productive manner.
- Resolve conflicts in a positive and constructive manner.
- Meet deadlines without prompting.
- Express thoughts and personal feelings in a consistently constructive manner.
- Demonstrate critical self-awareness of strengths and weaknesses.
- Interpret and apply laws and regulations regarding the human rights of the clients.
- Demonstrate basic knowledge of professional music therapy organizations and how these organizations influence clinical practice.

Interdisciplinary Collaboration
- Demonstrate a basic understanding of the roles and develop working relationships with other disciplines in the client's treatment program.
- Define the role of music therapy in the client's total treatment program.

- Collaborate with team members in designing and implementing interdisciplinary treatment programs.

Supervision and Administration
- Participate in and benefit from supervision.
- Manage and maintain music therapy equipment and supplies.
- Perform administrative duties usually required of clinicians.
- Write proposals to create and/or establish new music therapy program.

Music Foundations
Keyboard Skills
- Accompany self and ensembles proficiently.
- Play a basic repertoire of traditional, folk, and popular songs with or without printed music.

Guitar Skills
- Accompany self and ensembles proficiently.
- Play a basic repertoire of traditional, folk, and popular songs with or without printed music.

NonSymphonic Instruments
- Play autoharp or omnichord with same competence specified for guitar.
- Demonstrate basic understanding of technologically advanced instruments.
- Demonstrate basic skills on several standard percussion instruments sufficient to facilitate rhythm-based experiences for groups and individuals.

Scenario and Supervision Strategies—Final Stage of Internship—Independence and Closure

Facing the end of internship can be both liberating and scary. It can be helpful to start to talk about the final evaluation, final projects, and final client reports about six weeks before the end of the internship. Readings on how to terminate groups are beneficial at this time. Finishing intern David was experiencing separation anxiety as the end of internship loomed large on his horizon. He had no future plans, didn't know where he was going to move, had not applied for any jobs, and was having great difficulty completing his final paperwork assignments such as compositions and client summaries.

In supervision it is good to start focusing on the intern's future with questions directed toward helping the intern develop a plan (see questions on page 128 for examples). Firm due dates also provide an effective strategy for interns who don't want to leave. Make the dates manageable and provide frequent reminders that you will be looking for the reports on the date they are due. In some cases, a due date and a due hour of submission of reports is necessary. Mention frequently how important the final reports are that the intern writes. Also mention how the reports will be used by the therapists and interns in the future to provide continuity of treatment and care. Remarking on contact with past interns can help to reassure a finishing intern that the relationship with the supervisor will not necessarily be severed by successfully completing the internship. Provide suggestions on how to say good-bye to groups. Suggest to the intern that they thank both clients and staff for helping them to learn to be a better therapist. Though David struggled through all his final reports and stayed late on his last day, he came back several times to visit certain residents, and finally successfully found a job in the same city as his internship.

Elements of Competency-Based Supervision

Writers have commented on the importance of student-centered, competency-based education and training in music therapy. NAMT sponsored two symposiums, which were held on education and clinical training in 1988 and 1989. Each meeting produced recommendations and the following list is a compellation of ideas from both meetings.

- The competencies of entry-level therapists should be identified.
- Students applying for internship should be required to pass functional music examination in voice, keyboard, guitar, improvisation, group ensembles, and adapted methods.
- Students' learning style should be considered in designing education and training programs in music therapy.
- Competencies for music therapy education and training should be identified for the bachelor and master's level.
- Students should be informed of expectations and responsibilities prior to the internship and at the onset training.
- Clinical training should be process oriented.
- Competencies should be used as the basis for developing and approving educational curriculum and internships (Maranto, 1989, pp. 82–84; 1989, pp. 108–109).

From these recommendations we get a clear picture of the need for competency-based training. It is imperative that the internship supervisor be familiar with the AMTA competencies and design a training program based on a systematic plan to assist interns to acquire those competencies. "The primary task of educators and clinical training supervisors consists of identifying competencies required in music therapy and refining techniques for shaping the competencies"(Greenfield, 1978, p. 15). How does an internship supervisor design such a program?

The internship supervisor must first look at the competencies and identify how the structure of their setting will contribute to the acquisition of the desired competencies which characteristically are acquired during internship. Next, the supervisor must divide up the segments of internship to allow the intern to deal with manageable skill acquisition. Expectations of the intern and of the supervisor need to be crystal clear. The supervisor needs to be able to adjust supervisory methods depending on intern learning style and abilities. In other words, the supervisor needs to individualize the training for each intern. Basing the internship on the AMTA list of competencies can contribute to clear expectations. This would include developing the midterm and final evaluation forms based upon the categories of the AMTA competencies.

A variety of tools are available for internship supervisors. Written forms, guided questions, and of course, direct observation followed by feedback provide the supervisor with a few choices. Maranto and Bruscia (1988) provide an analysis of supervisory techniques: "As in the educator's survey, clinicians were asked to describe their three most successful methods of supervision. The majority of respondents (62%) indicated that observation and feedback was the most successful method. Other successful methods mentioned were supervisory conferences or discussion (33%), modeling (20%), and written or form evaluation (14%)" (p. 33). As in the case with intern Debbie, direct observation followed by both written and oral feedback provided her with concrete ways to improve. She did change the way she related to clients and changed phrases she used when leading groups. Gellerman (1968) stated that ". . . real motivational changes occur only when the individual learns that his environment had changed or that his earlier ideas of what it was like were not completely accurate" (p. 34). Observation, with written and oral feedback, can help the intern to more accurately assess the effects they may be having on clients. It is interesting to note that modeling, the "watch me do it this way and then you do likewise" approach was reported to be effective only 20 percent of the time. Interns do need more than ever a stellar role model of a clinician in order to more fully develop their potential. They need to be able to see their internship as a time when they know what they need to learn and they know how and when they will learn it.

Memory, Unkefer, and Smeltekop (1987) stated "Supervision is an integral part of practicum and internship clinical training and is most beneficial when it is individualized to meet the particular needs of each student, supervisor, client group and clinical setting. Effective supervision is therefore a partnership between student and supervisor, both of whom are responsible for sharing information and concerns" (p. 161). One way to individualize clinical training is to base that training on the desired, identified competencies.

The supervisor can ask these questions:

- What does the intern need to learn?
- How do I teach what they need to learn?
- When should I teach it?

The answers to these questions will vary slightly from intern to intern and setting to setting. But in general, the answer is that the intern needs to learn the identified competencies. The supervisor teaches those competencies through a variety of techniques including observation and feedback, assigned readings, modeling, written forms, and well-structured supervisory meetings.

Summary

Competency-based education in music therapy implies competency-based training. Basing supervision techniques on the progression of competency skill acquisition can be a very effective way to structure the clinical training of internship. There is, of course, overlap of competencies from segment to segment. And, certainly, there is greater breadth and depth of each competency as the intern progresses through all the stages. But it is helpful to both intern and internship supervisor to examine which competencies could be the focus at each segment of internship. Such an approach can bring an overwhelming task down to manageable, achievable parts and skills and help transform a student to an intern and an intern to competent entry-level music therapy clinician.

References

American Music Therapy Association (AMTA) (1998). *Code of Ethics*. Silver Spring, MD: Author.

American Music Therapy Association (AMTA). (1996). *Professional Competencies*. Silver Spring, MD: Author.

Boone, P. C. (1989). Future trends and new models for Clinical Training. *Music Therapy Perspectives* 7, 96–99.

Farnan, L. A. (1996). Issues in clinical training: The mystery of supervision. *Music Therapy Perspectives,* 14(2), 70–71.

Gellerman, S. A. (1968). *Management by Motivation*. American Management Association, Inc. New York: Vali-Ballou Press, Inc.

Gilder, J. S. (1987). Trainee distress and burn out: Threats for music therapists? In C.D. Maranto and K. Bruscia (eds.), *Perspectives on Music Therapy Education and Training*. Philadelphia, PA: Temple University, Esther Boyer College of Music.

Greenfield, D. (1978). Evaluation of music therapy practicum competencies: Comparisons of self- and instructor-ratings of videotapes. *Journal of Music Therapy*, 15, 15–20.

Grant, R. E., and McCarty, B. (1990). Emotional stages of internship. *Journal of Music Therapy,* 27(3), 102–118.

Maranto, C. D. (1989). The California symposium: Summary and recommendations. *Music Therapy Perspectives*, 6, 82–84.

Maranto, C. D. (1989). California symposium on music therapy education and training: Summary and recommendations. *Music Therapy Perspectives,* 7, 108–109.

Maranto, C. D., and Bruscia, K. (eds.) (1987). *Perspectives on Music Therapy Education and Training*. Philadelphia, PA: Temple University, Esther Boyer College of Music.

Maranto, C. D., and Bruscia, K. (1988). *Methods of Teaching and Training the Music Therapist*. Philadelphia, PA: Temple University, Esther Boyer College of Music.

Memory, B. C., Unkefer, R., and Smeltekop, R. (1987). Supervision in music therapy: Theoretical models. In C. D. Maranto and K. Bruscia (eds.), *Perspectives on Music Therapy Education and Training*. Philadelphia, PA: Temple University, Esther Boyer College of Music.

National Association for Music Therapy (NAMT). (1994). *Stages of Internship. Clinical Training Committee.* Clinical Training Director workshop handout. Silver Spring, MD: Author.

National Association for Music Therapy (NAMT). (1997). *Competencies Which Appear to be Learned in Clinical Training (Internship)*. NAMT Subcommittee on Professional Competencies. Silver Spring, MD: Author.

Petrie, G. E. (1989). The identification of a contemporary hierarchy of intended learning outcomes for music therapy students entering internship. *Journal of Music Therapy*, 26, 125–139.

Taylor, D. B. (1987). A survey of professional music therapists concerning entry level competencies. *Journal of Music Therapy*, 24, 114–145.

Chapter 9

Student-Centered Internship Supervision

Caryl-Beth Thomas, MA, ACMT, LMHC
Adjunct Faculty, Lesley University
Clinical Training Director, Community Music Center
Boston, MA

Introduction

The following chapter will be devoted to exploring and understanding the developmental process of music therapy students in internship. Process is defined as a "systematic series of actions directed towards some end" (Flexner, 1987, p. 1542). The focus of this chapter is on how the intern's development is indeed a process, and that a supervisor must be open to the distinct and unique needs of each student and support his or her development accordingly. Each supervisor and supervisee bring to the relationship of supervision their own expectations of how the process may unfold. In some ways this process has many similarities to the process of therapy itself, yet it is an educational process. One must be very careful to not confuse the supervisory process with the therapeutic process. Supervision is an interactional process between an experienced person (supervisor) who supervises a subordinate (intern). Hart (1982) defines supervision as an "ongoing education in which one person in the role of supervisor helps another person in the role of supervisee acquire appropriate professional behavior through an examination of the supervisee's professional activities" (p. 12). The relationship of supervisor and supervisee is a dynamic process in which both parties "negotiate a personal way of using a structure of power and involvement that accommodates the trainee's progression of learning. This structure becomes the basis for the process by which the trainee will acquire knowledge and skills—the empowerment of the trainee" (Holloway, 1995, pp. 41–42). In this chapter various aspects of the internship process will be discussed along with the roles and responsibilities of the supervisor. This process mainly focuses on the support and facilitation of the intern's personal and professional development and the promotion of music therapy competencies.

Walk Right In, Sit Right Down
Gus Cannon and Hugh Woods

The beginning of an internship needs to be a period of orientation and adjustment to this new phase of their music therapy training. The student comes in asking, "Where am I and what am I doing here?" It is most helpful at this time for the supervisor to thoroughly discuss and familiarize interns with their new environment, as it is so often very foreign territory. Every site, be it a school, clinic, hospital, day program, or community center, has its own specific set of ground rules and expectations for all who dwell there. There are many rules, regulations, and roles to understand; those of the staff, the clients or patients, and the student. The role of music therapy in the site must also be clarified, as it may vary from the student's previous preinternship clinical experiences. Each site has its own unique way of incorporating music therapy, and the intern needs to know "How do I fit in?"

Interns generally feel very unsure of their role at this time. Are they a participant, an observer, a client? These questions often occur for any new intern, but may be particularly difficult for a music therapy intern, since the role of the music therapist itself is often quite unique. Music therapy interns are often unlike other students-in-training at their facility.

The supervisor needs to make an effort to reduce the initial anxiety and apprehension of an intern by orienting students as much as possible about the site and their upcoming internship. A certain amount of comforting and reassurance is needed, while at the same time making overall expectations very clear from the beginning. Providing some kind of overview and general time frame of the internship is important so that interns can actually see that there are clearly defined parameters to this experience, and that it is not just a frightening, unfamiliar place they are expected to now walk into and feel at home. These expectations can be somewhat overwhelming and may initially create more anxiety on the part of interns, but it overall serves to help them establish a foothold and begin to define their role. It provides them with some clarity in the vagueness of these new and unknown experiences.

Elaine[1] spent the first day observing me run four groups of clients with varying needs and functional levels. She participated in the groups and was engaging with clients, but generally was very quiet throughout the day and made few comments. When we met afterward, she was tearful and said she had no idea that it would be so hard. She did not think that she could ever remember all the different people's names or the music, let alone know what to do with clients who had such differing needs. After first acknowledging how different this was than any experience she had prior to her internship, we then reviewed what I actually did and discussed the common elements to the treatment approaches. We also talked about how I had learned to manage a large number of cases and populations over time, and that she was not expected to take on such diversity until she was ready.

Providing structure, guidance, and support are all ways of helping to reduce anxiety for interns. Providing a consistent supervision time and place to meet, giving full attention to the intern's needs and helping them to understand how supervision can and will be used is essential throughout this process, but of particular importance early on. Establishing a clear structure for the supervision session is a helpful start. Specific time frames and the use of an agenda for the session are both important, and it is the supervisor's role to initially provide this structure. The agenda should cover specifics regarding the week's plans and expectations, any business that needs to be

---

[1] All names have been changed to protect both the supervisees' and the clients' privacy.

tended to, as well as outlining future meetings and plans. Early supervision sessions should be primarily informational and acquaint the intern with the training site, population(s), and approaches to treatment and methods utilized. The intern's perspectives and feedback are always encouraged and increasingly incorporated into supervision and he most likely begins to formulate many questions of his own as this process continues to develop. As the intern's confidence grows, the supervisor should reduce the amount of structure provided in supervision and encourage the intern to be more autonomous. With each passing week, the intern will be encouraged to add to the agenda, and eventually will be primarily responsible for the basic structure of the supervision session.

Sue came to me in supervision with a completely stunned look on her face. She had just observed two group sessions that had been very intense. Sue knew that she would be taking over one of these groups later in the year. She discussed feeling overwhelmed and unprepared to run such "difficult" groups. After listening to her thoughts and concerns I gave her a clear time frame as to when she would be responsible for the group, and that there would be ample opportunity for her to observe, co-lead, and discuss these types of clients and issues with me. We talked about what skills we would need to address prior to her taking leadership of the group such as dealing with conflict in music and limit setting. We agreed to include these issues as part of the supervision agenda.

Do You See What I See?
Noel Regney and Gloria Shane

Interns need to initially develop some type of identity relative to their new environment. They know they are not professionals and yet are expected to behave as if they are. They have learned a lot about music therapy in their training thus far, yet they are only just beginning and often feel they don't know anything. They have many ideas but are unclear about how to execute them. They believe they can be a competent therapist in one moment, and certain that they have chosen the wrong career the next. There is some comfort in having a specific purpose and role initially to allay some of the anxiety of that which lies ahead for the following six to nine months. This process of understanding where they are now going to be spending most of their time, what is it they are going to be doing, and who they are expected to interact with is not only the orientation process but an ideal arena to practice fine-tuning observation skills.

I offer new interns a full month to "be a sponge" and to be totally immersed in the process of observation. They are only to be involved in the process of taking it all in, with no other responsibilities. They are asked to observe as much as they can in this initial time period, generally the first month to six weeks. This may not be limited to where they will eventually be spending all of their time as interns, but with other music therapists and related professionals, both within the agency and in the local geographical area. They are given a list of contacts, expected to make the arrangements with these professionals, and create a schedule of visits, observation, and processing with the therapists they are seeing. They are also expected to document these experiences. I encourage them to write as much as they can in a process note about what they actually saw happening, and to then write separately about their personal responses to the experience as well. In this way they begin the practice of separating the objective from the subjective, a vital skill they will utilize throughout their career.

In supervision sessions, I begin by asking them to tell me specifically what they observed and how the session progressed. This information is presented by the intern and then discussed, helping him to practice the skills of oral presentation of case material, as well as talking about his personal experiences.

This phase of the internship helps to expose interns to a variety of role models and situations in which a music therapist may function and the various methods utilized by music therapists. Even though they may have done a fair amount of observing earlier in their training, I feel that they will be observing differently now that they are an intern and preparing to do the work themselves.

This may seem somewhat daunting to interns as they are likely to observe a wide range of client populations, clinical settings, and music therapy methods and techniques. At the same time it may serve to demystify the music therapy process, demonstrate that each therapist has found his or her personalized way to conduct their work, and that as interns, they too will begin to develop their own path and approach. It can also be the early stages of developing and fostering a sense of professional identity, as they witness how others have established their own.

Strong observation skills are so essential to being an effective music therapist: being able to listen, hear, see, identify, and separate the facts and the feelings. By initially providing interns with an opportunity to intensively focus on this part of the work without having to think about any other aspects, they become more confident in this skill area. Through this part of the process, they are developing a clearer understanding of different approaches or philosophies of music therapy. They may encounter concepts or methods that are unfamiliar or that they have questions about. They may also begin to identify their own philosophy of treatment in the course of their observations, as well as philosophies of treatment where they may feel less comfortable or in fact resistant. This provides the supervisor with some insight into how an intern understands the practical applications of music therapy in the workplace, not just in the academic sense, which has been their primary experience prior to their internship. It also provides information about an intern's current ability to report clinical information, maintain objectivity about what was seen, and identify a client's areas of strength as well as potential areas of concern.

There tend to be two main areas interns talk about at this point, or that I will ask about if they are having difficulty responding to the question "What did you see?" The first area of focus is what literally happened in the session; having interns describe the client's presentation and what types of interventions and methods the music therapist utilized. They might talk about how and where the session was set up, the music and the instruments used, the client's manner of participation, the music therapist's interventions and role, and sometimes their own reactions to all of this. The second area of focus is more about the therapist's actual interaction with the client(s) and vice versa. Here the details of the session are not as important, but the focus is more about being witness to the participants, their relationships to each other and to the therapist during the session. These early stages of supervision can be utilized to discover what it is that each intern tends to see as most valuable in sessions—the music therapy techniques or the therapeutic relationships and process they have observed. By discussing these observations with them, the supervisor gains an understanding of the nature of that particular intern's perspective of the music therapy process and the areas that he gravitates toward most comfortably. This shared knowledge helps both the supervisor and the intern to early on identify potential areas of strength and familiarity, and those they may be less comfortable with and will most likely need further exploration and development.

Sarah was a very talented and enthusiastic new intern. She had very strong and negative reactions to her first observation, and immediately questioned whether she had made the right decision in her own choice of study. She felt she could have done as well or perhaps better musically than the therapist. She was also highly critical of the "therapist's choice" of clients and the setting, which she found unpleasant and nonconducive to what she thought of as music therapy. This student often had unrealistic expectations and very high standards, not only of others but also of herself. Over the course of her internship this proved to be an ongoing challenge for both her and the supervisor. Another student, Ellen, observing at this same site on the same day spoke about how difficult the situation was, and how she admired the therapist's efforts to provide music therapy for them despite the challenges and limitations of the setting and the clients. Her positive attitude served her well when working with others; however, she later had issues with limit setting and was often not as assertive as she needed to be when requiring assistance or cooperation from staff.

Jean observed a music therapist in both individual and group music therapy sessions. She spoke about the therapist's inspirational manner with the clients; that it was a beautiful experience to observe and how moved she was by the respectful and caring approach toward the clients. She spoke of how important the unconditional regard that she had observed was as an all-important life philosophy for her personally, and how she knew it to be a great strength, yet sometimes quite challenging, when working in the field of human services. She did not comment at all on the music aspect of the session until asked. Todd observed the same therapist in the same setting at a different time and spoke only of the music used, asking many questions about what the therapist's training had been, why certain chords were used, and about the intent of musical choices. He was solely focused on technique and method, which came to be somewhat of an obstacle for him later in his training, in the area of therapeutic relationship and presence.

Stand By Me
Ben E. King, Michael Stoller, and Jerry Leiber

As interns begin to settle into a regular schedule where they are assigned to specific groups or individuals, they are expected to begin the process of moving from the role of observer to that of co-leader. They begin to more keenly observe and more fully understand the client's needs. They generally have some ideas of their own, with opinions about what is being done and how to implement treatment, but from the viewpoint of a much more involved observer.

Before interns actually take any leadership role in the sessions themselves, this role of active observer further develops. This is the time where supervision becomes a more in-depth discussion and exploration of what an intern did or did not see, what they understood about what they took part in, and how they are able to process this with the therapist as a co-leader. They continue to discuss their experiences both objectively and subjectively, not only about what they saw and experienced but how their role in it is developing and taking form. This is again a time where interns may start to feel more confident about taking on an active role, but also increasingly anxious regarding the expectations that come with the responsibility of moving to a more advanced level.

Up until this point the supervisory sessions have been more of a "list" of what, how, and who was seen, and their experience of the work. The expectation is now to begin to talk more about the therapeutic experience from the inside out rather than the outside in. There is still somewhat of a reporting by the intern of what was done, how it occurred, who did what, etc. The supervisor is beginning to ask more about not only how they experienced the sessions, but also how they are beginning to interpret them, and if they might have done things differently. The supervisor's questions moves from "What did you see?" to "What do you think about that session, what meaning does it have?" This helps to support that they have their own perspective of the session that is valid, and that it might differ from that of their supervisor. It also supports the concept that music therapy is a process involving various participants with no exact formulas, just as the process of training interns must be individualized.

This phase of internship is the next stage of an intern's discovery and the beginnings of establishing his or her own professional identity. Interns are beginning to think more as therapists. In this phase they are also challenged to question why something occurs in session, or why a certain technique is utilized, or why it may have been successful or not. It is also the time where they become more aware of how they feel about what they are witness to and participating in. They may begin to think more in terms of what they might have done if they were leading the session. This starts to lay the groundwork for having their own preferences and instincts about how to best implement treatment, even though it may not be the same as their supervisor's. This inevitably creates some feelings of anxiety for an intern, as they are being asked to give their own input even though they have limited experience, and to a situation of which they are not in charge. They are being encouraged to think more for themselves in preparation for the act of taking on more of a leadership role. It is important to discuss this phase of an intern's involvement in the sessions—their thoughts, feelings, and ideas in supervision prior to their actual functioning as a co-leader.

There may be times when interns will work with an individual or group on their own and never go through the process of co-leadership. If at all possible, interns should have some opportunity to explore this process with a co-leader prior to working on their own, so that they have some type of modeling and support as they begin to identify their own style, philosophical approach, and preference of methodology.

Don was a student with a strong music background who was particularly interested in songwriting. He was working with a music therapist in an adult psychiatric setting, and was familiar with the rock and roll and rhythm and blues music that the clients enjoyed. After observing for a few weeks, he began to play guitar along with his supervisor during the sessions. Supervision focused on taking these traditional tunes and playing them with varying dynamics, tempi, and word substitutions, so that he could learn to use this music improvisationally and spontaneously. As he became more familiar with some of the therapeutic applications of these styles of music, he also began to question and explore ways in which he might begin to incorporate his own songwriting skills in addition to the traditional songs being used in the sessions.

Pat had been working with a music therapist on site for several weeks and was reporting in supervision that she found the music to be very limited in dynamics. She said that the same songs were always sung but weren't "going anywhere" and didn't seem to serve much of a therapeutic purpose for the clients anymore. She acknowledged that the clients loved the songs being used, but she was sure that the same music could be different or more therapeutic, although was unsure how that might be done as she did not yet possess such skills. She talked to me in supervision about adding movement (being something she was familiar with and loved to do herself) and we experimented with how that could add to the experience of music in our own sessions. She was then encouraged to offer that suggestion to the site supervisor as a complement to the familiar songs being used. This proved to be very successful not only for the clients, but the music therapist became motivated to collaborate more on the idea of creative movement and music.

Put Me In Coach, I'm Ready To Play
John Fogerty

The next phase in the process of co-leadership is that of an intern actually taking on some part of the leadership role. On some level it is an evolutionary process for all interns as they enter this more mature phase, in which they naturally begin to demonstrate a stronger presence in the session, and begin to participate more actively. This may be by singing or playing an instrument with a stronger and more functional presence (i.e., harmonic instrument or drum), or adding verbal contributions, responses, and directives. It is at this phase of an intern's development that it becomes quite clear that there is no way to clearly identify when this level of participation will occur or even how it will occur. Given that each student is completely unique and brings his or her own history, experience, personality, and skills to this work, it is impossible to give a specific time frame for leadership skills to appear. Although clear expectations and competencies must be met throughout the process, some competencies come more easily than others for each intern, and generally develop at highly individualized rates.

It is essential for the supervisor to review and keep in mind the intern's individual process and development at this point. One must consider the rate of independence demonstrated thus far in their actions, behaviors, and expressions of their thoughts and feelings about their work, and how to best support their developmental process. It is always contingent on the intern's initiative and willingness to take the risk of moving to the next level. There are interns who have been "ready" since early on, being more self-directed and outgoing, but trusting in the supervisor's guidance. There are students who have resisted the process and structure provided by the supervisor, and are certain that they should be further along than they feel that they are in their learning and internship experience. And there are students who will never make a move toward more involved levels of participation without strong prompts from the supervisor, and then often need additional support and encouragement to do so. Particularly at this point, the intern's personal needs and who the supervisor knows him or her to be are critical factors to be considered and dealt with, and accordingly so the supervisor's approach must be quite different with each student. A supervisor's choice of when and in what manner to require more of an intern can be quite crucial at this point in their process.

This is when students are often faced with some of their greatest fears about being able to do this work. Many of their insecurities and self-doubts may surface and need to be processed and understood by both the supervisor and the intern. These feelings may be relevant to the specific situation in which they find themselves, or they may be old patterns that arise in times of challenge and uncertainty. These are important considerations for the supervisor when asking an intern to be more involved in the sessions, and it is often the supervisor's responsibility to help them confront personal issues as they relate to their professional performance. Student interns are strongly encouraged to do the necessary work of discovering, understanding, and working through their personal issues outside of their internship in their own therapy. Whereas it is not in any way the supervisor's job to provide therapy for the intern, they certainly may need to assist them in clarifying how their life experiences may strongly impact their work.

This phase of the intern's development is also one in which the supervisor is faced with a few of his or her own challenges. Supervisors must be able to both move aside and create the space for the student to assume more of the leadership role. Some clinicians find it difficult to do this, and not to step in and take control of the session during these early stages of co-leadership. Supervisors need to be quite conscious about their choices of when to continue to model, when and how to support the student's process, and when an intern must be allowed to find his or her own way. Many supervisors find themselves "rescuing" a struggling intern and must examine what motivates them to do so. There are many considerations here: the greater good of the client or group, the best interests of the intern's growth and development, the therapist's ability to let the session take a different course than she would have pursued, or the need to do it her way, just to name a few.

Denise has been asked for several weeks if she would be willing to try the hello song in the next session. She says she feels she is learning so much from observing the therapist's techniques and wishes to continue this a while longer. She has been singing along for quite a while and the supervisor knows that she has adequate guitar skills. After acknowledging and reinforcing that she clearly has the needed skills, she is confronted with the fact that she needs to take this next step. Using the supervision session to practice the song in a role-play, she is then told she will be leading the hello song in the next session. She is able to do this very well, and is surprised that she was much less anxious doing so than she had anticipated.

Bob had been given an assignment to have an activity of his own choice prepared for a group in which he had been actively involved. He had led the hello and good-bye, as demonstrated by his supervisor, for several weeks. When the time came to bring his own ideas, he stated that he had not had time and was not yet ready. His inability to come prepared was explored later in supervision and related to his fear of trying something he had not yet seen modeled by the supervisor. Bob felt certain that he did not yet have enough skills to initiate anything in sessions on his own. It was agreed that he could work with new ideas in supervision sessions in order to troubleshoot areas in which he felt insecure. He built a larger repertoire of skills and ideas that he could then utilize as he transitioned into a position of more responsibility.

Despite consistent feedback from her supervisor, Dana brings in activities that are too challenging and complex for the clients. She does not understand why the clients seem increasingly distant and that she feels inadequate. She is frustrated that they are never able to have a successful experience in the sessions. The supervisor eventually assigns a specific activity for Dana to try with the clients and they later discuss how it felt more realistic for both the clients and the intern. After reviewing the basic treatment goals and objectives, the intern is asked to plan in simpler terms and utilize stepwise progression in her activities. The intern begins to understand that she does not have to always present highly challenging activities in order to feel that she or the clients are really working toward accomplishing something, which she also has spent much of her life doing in her personal endeavors.

There Will Never Be Another You
Harry Warren and Mack Gordon

Another major factor at this point in an intern's process and development is the potential for feeling intimidated by their supervisor's ability as a music therapist. These feelings can sometimes hinder their ability to move forward with the development of their own identity. Students often feel that they cannot ever measure up to their supervisor or be as good as their supervisor in thought, word, deed, or music. This coupled with the not so unrealistic feeling that they are being evaluated, and also judged, by the supervisor often results in becoming paralyzed and unable to develop their own identity. This is one of the strongest arguments in support of fostering the process of the intern's development and identity early on.

If interns have been given the opportunity to work through these phases that allow them to gradually gain skills and some level of confidence in applying them, they will be better able to utilize them in a leadership role. An intern will not be able to recognize or acknowledge his own skills or accomplishments if he has primarily focused on what the supervisor has done, and has not felt validated and comfortable processing his own thoughts and potential contributions to the work along the way. Likewise the supervisor needs to recognize and acknowledge the intern's developing skills as separate from their own "style," so that they are then better able to support and give feedback to continue the development of the intern's professional identity and growth as a music therapist.

Other contrasting dynamics that can develop between supervisors and interns are that of mentorship or competition. One is a desire to be cared for and to strive for sameness, and the other is to resist the relationship and always try to "outdo" or be superior. Both types of relationships could be motivating or destructive to the intern's sense of individuation. An intern may strive to work hard to become as skilled and proficient as, or even better than, the supervisor and it may serve as great motivation. However, the intern's own personal needs and desires must be taken in to account when trying to emulate or be "as good as" their supervisor, or they will not be authentic in their skills, but rather risk adapting them for the wrong purposes. This is particularly true for the music therapist. Since our main tool is music, and its creation and delivery is so very personal in nature, it is impossible to be reproduced, copied, or judged as "better than." Each therapist's musical and therapeutic presence is completely unique and incomparable. Supervisors can only serve as guides and partners in the intern's discovery of themselves as a music therapist, much as all therapists ultimately function in a similar role for their clients.

Bob improved in being prepared for sessions as his internship progressed but he had continued difficulty implementing his plans. In discussing this, he stated that he did not know what made it so difficult but that he often found himself feeling "frozen" and unable to continue what he had begun. He was able to identify that he was "trying to do it like you do" (re: his supervisor) but knowing he could not, he then felt unable to do anything. He realized that he was not allowing himself to try approaching the work in his own way for fear that it would not be "good enough." Bob was validated by his supervisor as having more than adequate skills and was encouraged to focus more on beginning to develop his own style. He also explored his expectations of having to be like someone else in order to be successful instead of believing and trusting in his own abilities.

Paula also struggled with feeling inadequate about her skills, and said she would feel much more confident it she could run her sessions on her own with the supervisor out of the room. She felt she would be less anxious and better able to be herself if she were not being observed and critiqued in the session. She felt that the supervisor was always comparing her skills to her own and that consequently she felt scrutinized and doomed to fail. She felt sure she had the skills, but was too overpowered by the supervisor's presence to utilize them. The supervisor felt strongly that this might allow the intern to "just do anything" and there would be no way to give her feedback or to know if she was learning anything. Both supervisor and intern needed to re-evaluate their working relationship at this point, as the dynamics between them were interfering with the training process. They agreed that the supervisor would not observe the session, but that the intern would discuss her plan with the supervisor before the session. Together they would then review an audiotape of the session in their supervision.

Out Here On My Own
Leslie Gore and Michael Gore

As interns begin to function more independently and are more established in their role as student therapists, supervision begins to take on a somewhat different purpose. Supervisory feedback has less impact as interns develop a more solid frame of reference of their own in the implementation of music therapy. It is at this stage that the intern is developing the capacity to "envision survival without the full support of the supervisor" (Friedman and Kaslow, 1986, p. 42). This shift generally begins more than halfway through the internship and is often a time when interns may become either rebellious or more passive in the supervisory relationship as they begin to make treatment decisions and choices on their own. It can be a challenging time, somewhat likened to adolescence, that the supervisor and intern have to work through together as they become more separate in their working relationship.

It is also at this stage that interns start to recognize their own core issues and stumbling blocks and how these may be effecting their clinical work. Whereas much of the focus prior to this has been on developing and refining specific competencies and techniques of music therapy, interns are now moving toward beginning to integrate these two experiences of their lives and work. This often is the time where supervisors must be willing to challenge interns regarding these issues in order to help them move on in their work.

This move toward greater independence and development of a separate professional identity can sometimes be slow and stressful, but provides the opportunity to explore and discuss their work as music therapists on a more in-depth and reflective level. The focus on music skills, therapeutic techniques, and interventions always continues, but there is now another level of awareness developing in their work. Interns begin to move toward solidifying their own professional identity, which is very exciting, though still filled with questions and uncertainties. There are often feelings of empowerment, of being much surer of themselves, but frequently there are also feelings of being pressured and that they must learn everything there is to know before they finish their internship. This is particularly true as the intern realizes that they are getting closer to the end of their training. It is an important time of integration as well as great anticipation.

At this point, interns have a better understanding of the connections between theory and practice in relation to their clients. There is also a decreasing need for direction from their supervisor. Supervision sessions are much less about going over the list of what happened and why. Ideally, interns have become more aware of their own strengths and areas of need, and are able to address how this is applicable to their work as music therapists. They may talk about certain clients that they have difficulty working with and are able to explore what this may be about for themselves. They may realize that they feel stuck in certain musical ruts and desire to break away but are finding it difficult.

They may take on a client who is very challenging in order to work on certain musical or other therapeutic skills they know they are in need of strengthening. They may come to understand that there are certain areas or clients that may always be difficult for them, and that they may not be well-suited for at this time. They may begin to recognize how integral their identity as a person is to their identity as a therapist.

Jenny had been working with a group of geriatric clients for several months and began to feel that she was not providing enough meaningful experiences in the music therapy sessions for them, and that the group was "sluggish." She stated that the clients still appeared to be engaged in the group and making progress, but she felt they must be bored and getting tired of hearing the "same old thing." She was sure that she needed to bring new activities or techniques to this group if they were going to progress any further. The supervisor felt that this intern was doing a good job musically and that it was not the group lacking in energy, but the student. The focus of supervision was then to explore Jenny's own feelings of disinterest and boredom with the music, and that it was difficult for her to be objective about the clients' experiences when she felt this way. Although very resistant to this initially, she began to acknowledge that sometimes her motivation and choices were being driven by her own needs and not that of the clients. The necessary styles and repetition of the music for this population was far from her personal tastes, and she recognized the need to keep her focus more on the responses of the clients and less on the style of the music.

George was beginning to talk a lot in supervision about feeling "stuck" while working in both individual and group sessions at his internship. He also felt that the work was becoming somewhat stagnant and he felt he was not being very effective. His style was very directive in the sessions and he was making choices based on treatment plans that he felt would be helpful for these clients. He was recently finding that the clients were becoming resistant and there was less participation overall. When asked about making choices based on the clients' immediate needs or requests in the session, George said he felt very anxious about breaking away from his plan. He was fearful that "it will all fall apart" if he abandoned his session plan, and followed their lead. In discussing these sessions, it became clear that he was not allowing a more engaging and reciprocal level of involvement with clients to occur in the music-making, because of his need to keep "everything under control" and "not to make any mistakes." He was able to relate this to other areas of his life in which he became anxious if he felt a situation might be getting out of control. We began to explore greater risk taking in supervision by improvising music together, where there were no mistakes. It was important for George to have more experience with not always knowing where the music or the client may be going, but to still feel able to maintain a sense of leadership in the group.

And Now the End is Near . . .
Paul Anka

As interns enter their last phase of training, they generally have a stronger sense of their strengths and weaknesses, and are able to focus on areas in need of development with more perspective and less resistance. There is more mutual sharing between interns and supervisors of their impressions, experiences and information, about their work, and the supervisory relationship becomes more collaborative than in previous phases. The intern is increasingly personalizing his own style of treatment and continues personal and professional integration in his work as he moves toward the closure of this important experience. The intern's experience of the termination process with clients, the site, and their supervisor often is very profound and a distinctly unique experience, as most students have not encountered such long-term relationships in their past training. Reexamination of their work helps to highlight the areas in which they have made remarkable progress as well as where they may still have much work to do. After having moved toward a more collegial relationship with their supervisor, interns may often need extra support and feedback during this period of termination. It is often the most valuable experience they have in which they come to clearly understand the impact of their work as music therapists with the clients. It is also often the time that they really begin to integrate the impact that this work and these relationships have had on them as well, both as a music therapist and as a person in relation to others. They come to understand that all relationships, be they with clients, supervisors, teachers, co-workers, or the music itself, develop through a process and a period of time. So must adequate time and space be given and honored as they end these processes and say good-bye.

In the final weeks of internships, there is the opportunity to evaluate a great deal about one's experience of the last six to nine months, both for interns and supervisors. It is a time to reflect on the process of all parties involved in the course of this interactive music therapy experience and training. Final evaluations of client progress are made, as well as that of the student intern, the site, and the supervisory experience. Most supervisors find this to be an important time to conduct some type of self-evaluation, as they review their own role with interns, in order to have closure for themselves in this particular process and to prepare for the next training period and intern.

The process of supervision is one where important learning and knowledge can and does occur on many levels. After moving through the stages of this journey together, which may include instructing, advising, modeling, consulting, supporting, and sharing, interns and supervisors can take a greater understanding of themselves and their work with them from their collective experience. It clearly provides opportunities for continued growth and development both personally and professionally, particularly when the work is based on the respectful and cooperative efforts of these two individual's actions, emotions, perspectives, wisdom and music.

References

Anka, P. (1969). "My Way." C. Revaud and C. Francois (original French lyrics and music). New York: Spanka Music Corporation.

Cannon, G., and Woods, H. (1930). "Walk Right In, Sit Right Down." New York: Peer International Corp.

Flexner, S. B. (ed.). (1987). *Random House Dictionary of the English Language* (2nd ed.). New York: Random House.

Fogerty, J. (1985). "Centerfield." New York: Warner Brothers Publishing.

Friedman, D., and Kaslow, N.J. (1986). The development of professional identity in psychotherapists: six stages in the supervision process. In N. J. Kaslow (ed.).

Supervision and Training: Models, Dilemmas, and Challenges. New York: Haworth Press, Inc.

Gordon, M., and Warren, H. (1942) "There Will Never Be Another You." New York: Morley Music Co.

Gore, L., and Gore, M. (1980) "Out Here on My Own." New York: EMI Music, Inc.

Hart, G. (1982). *The Process of Clinical Supervision.* Baltimore, MD: University Park Press.

Holloway, E. L. (1995). *Clinical Supervision: A Systems Approach.* Thousand Oaks, CA: Sage Publications, Inc.

King, B. E., Stoller, M., and Leiber, J. (1961). "Stand By Me." New York: Progressive Music Publishing, Inc.

Regney, N., and Shane, G. (1964) "Do You Hear What I Hear?" New York: Regent Music Corp.

Acknowledgments

I would like to acknowledge the music therapy students with whom I have worked over the past fifteen years. Each one has helped me to better understand the value of an individual's life experience to his or her work and how it shapes him or her as a professional. These collective experiences have been my greatest teachers and made clearer to me the necessity of honoring each supervision process as unique. I would like to express my thanks to all of the students for their contributions to this work.

Chapter 10

The Creative Arts in Group Supervision

Trudy Shulman-Fagen, MA, MT-BC, LMHC
Adjunct Faculty, Lesley University
Cambridge, MA

Introduction

Group supervision in an off-site academic setting is rich with the grace of transitional growth from student to therapist and laden with the complexities of evolving professional identities coupled with rigorous academic demands. The cycle of training with its episodic peak performance requirements (evaluations, exams, etc.) as well as vacation hiatus provide a well-defined rhythm to training and at times provides shape for the supervision group. Stages of the therapeutic process are often influenced by academically predetermined models of internship or practicum (e.g.; "It's your third month of internship, you must be leading four independent groups and seeing a few individuals," or "It's May and time to terminate!"). In academic settings, a balancing act is performed by supervisors and students alike in cultivating their therapeutic leadership skills with their abilities to satisfy academic schedules. While often well thought out by sites and training institutions, the "ripeness" of the student can be asynchronous with the complexities of a clinical setting or health-care system.

There is a lot to be covered in supervision, including: clinical skills, transference issues, the development of professional identity, arts applications and repertoire, comprehension of pathologies and medical systems, interdisciplinary articulation, leadership development, along with grounding in the "business" end of therapy (marketing, job searches, grant writing, providing in-services, etc.). Simply put, students are expected in a few semesters of training to begin to gain clinical skills and professional judgment that really take a lifetime to develop.

This chapter will describe the developmental stages of a weekly three-hour music therapy supervision group. The students are completing internships at various local sites. This supervision group takes place at the academic institution and occurs in addition to the on-site weekly individual supervision provided by the music therapist at the internship site. Supervision groups meet for two sequential semesters during which the students complete their internship along with other academic coursework.

Overview of the Supervision Group

It is helpful to create structures for the boundaries of the supervisory relationship and the supervisory meeting. This can include addressing technical issues such as providing an overview of the supervision course syllabus, academic and written expectations, class participation requirements, required readings, attendance, and assignments (including personal journals and professional documentation). In addition, creative rituals for beginning and ending the supervisory meetings can also be useful in shaping the supervision experience.

Supervisory sessions include several components. A designated "check in" time at the beginning of the session allows students a place to explore the current state of their internship. The check in is often followed by a lecture oriented component in which theoretical issues are explored including styles of therapy, treatment planning, review of psychopharmacology, or new theories on illnesses and recovery. The final component of the supervision group is focused on music and arts experientials designed to address clinical issues of clients or issues in academic supervision.

The roles of student intern and supervisor must be clearly defined at the outset of clinical training. The student's role is to refine clinical skills, gather information regarding illness, develop musical repertoire, understand health-care systems, develop a professional identity, and learn how to use supervision. Students must be willing to take professional and sometimes personal risks when it is clinically indicated, develop leadership skills, and learn how to "actively listen" while setting their own issues aside. Awareness of transference issues to coworkers, supervisors, clients, the illnesses encountered, and the systems in which they work must be heightened. Altruistic motivations should be investigated, empathic awareness must evolve, and the ability to use the creative arts in treatment must be developed. Students make mistakes and must embrace learning from them. Students must learn to take care of themselves, know their own capabilities and respect their own pace and style of growth. They must find and know their own voices and then use them, even in what may sometimes be an unfriendly arts therapy environment.

As supervisors it is our primary responsibility to provide a fertile and safe environment for students to develop the above skills and ways of being as a therapist. Our job as supervisors is to create and maintain the container for learning and clinical creativity, and to provide the maps for the professional journey. There are ethical responsibilities of training well-equipped therapists (Malchiodi and Riley, 1996). We must focus on skill building as well as on consciousness raising of our students and we must draw boundaries between supervision and therapy. We balance and mediate the concerns of the academic program advisor with the site supervisor without triangulating the process, while at the same time provide support, empathy, respect, and mentoring to the students. We must respond to the expectations of the sites and academic institutions while honoring the individual and group dynamic process of the supervision group. We lead, and follow. We intervene, facilitate, listen, wait, catch the falling, and reel in those in danger of flying too close to the sun. We take the stance of "not knowing" in order to help students find out. We model that it is okay to be "good enough" and we provide creative arts processes to inspire and motivate. We must know what is in "the box" and think outside of it. We facilitate and model when to tread lightly and when to press forward. Like any powerful experience, gates and borders must be in place to provide sanctuary for learning. Helping the supervision group to become responsible for their own creative learning process provides safety.

Through music-making and arts, we are provided with the gift of creative language. Delving into the creative process provides a forum for expanding our awareness of our professional identities. It is incumbent upon supervisors to use the arts in the process of working through issues and challenges in order to continue to model the efficacy of the arts.

A myriad of factors dictate the process of the supervision group, including factors such as the various personalities and readiness of the group members, style and skill of the academic supervisor, style of the on-site supervisor and how this fits the student, as well as the daily roller coaster of clinical experiences. Latent skills and insecurities bloom under the stress of internship; our best and worst moments are faced privately and in relationship with others. It is a very vulnerable time and one with great opportunity for learning.

Stages of Development in Group Supervision

Creative arts internship supervision groups in academic settings are contiguous on three levels: individual professional growth; the evolution of the group dynamics of the supervision group; and general clinical skill development. What follows are four stages of group development and suggested arts experiences designed to address each stage in the group process as well as the various levels mentioned above.

Stage One - Building the Container

For supervision to proceed fruitfully, the development of "the group" as an entity and safety of the individual members within the group has to be established first. On the academic front, the nuts and bolts of internship responsibilities should be reviewed to create clear expectations and professional boundaries; this covers not only academic standards but also the distinction between supervision and therapy.

Building the container refers to the process of looking within to develop the internal therapeutic space and outwardly to create the therapeutic space at the internship sites. Creative arts experiences can provide the opportunity for self-inventory and help identify issues that influence the building of the container at this beginning stage. Developmental issues in these first few weeks include: Who am I as therapist? What will the relationship with my supervisor be like? What are my expectations from my site supervisor? Can I meet them? Are my music skills strong enough? Will I know what to do? Can my supervisor accept my feelings? I realize there is so much to learn. Am I prepared? Where am I in this supervision group? What can I expect from this group?

Suggested Arts Experiences
Making the Connection: Analytic, object relations, and relational models of music improvisation are helpful in examining the process of establishing connections

(Horney, 1993; Jordan, Miller, Striver, Surrey and Kaplan, 1991; Winnecott, 1992). Connections can be made internally (becoming aware of how one is feeling, how these feelings may be rooted in one's past experiences, etc.) or externally (becoming aware of how one is relating to the instruments, how one is relating to other group members, etc.).

To explore this ask students to improvise in a group using percussion instruments, guitar, and piano with the task of finding a connection. After the improvisation ask students about the kinds of connections they made, both internally and externally, (to themselves, to the instruments, to each other). Ask them to look at what made it easy or difficult to make these connections. Discuss strategies they might employ when they or their clients have difficulties in making connections. Ask students to look at patterns in their own lives. How do they usually make connections and when do they feel most connected? At their sites, what might help them feel connected to their supervisors and clients? How do the instruments function in the process?

Help the group explore these questions by asking them to use "I . . ." in their responses and discourage them from interpreting each other's responses. If a group member was unable to make connections, see if the group can find a creative arts strategy to assist this member in making a connection. It can be helpful to validate that feeling disconnected occasionally happens and is normal, yet also worthy of exploration.

It is important to bring a clinical perspective to the discussion. Ask questions such as "What happens if a client has difficulty making a connection?" Explore the concept that there are times, such as in codependent relationships and in addiction, when it might be healthier for clients to be disconnected from a situation. It is important to validate that exploring a lack of connection is not necessarily fragmenting the group process, in fact it can even bind a group together. Other questions to explore include: What does it mean to become a member of the group? What does being part of a group mean if you struggle with mental illness? What if a client does not want to be part of the group?

Building the Container: This refers to the process of helping students define the therapeutic space or culture they wish to create within themselves as a clinician and as the therapeutic environment they wish to provide for their clients. An arts experience for building the container could include Jungian synchronicity-style drum circles (Diallo, 1990; Jung, 1981). Have the group start with a simple rhythmic pattern on a drum, and explore its dimensions in terms of dynamics, tempi, etc. (for example, try Middle Eastern, African or Latin rhythms). Discuss the impact of the rhythmic pattern on the container. Did it help build? Was it secure? Was it overpowering?

Another example would be to have group members start playing a drum in synchrony with their heartbeat. After individual rhythms have been established ask students to develop this individual sound into group synchrony. Discuss the experience and ask questions such as: What might this type of experience be like for your clients? What might the negative aspects of group synchrony be? Discussing the focus on the "we" as therapists and the "they" as clients and in what way both are parts of the container can also yield interesting insights.

Flexing the Container: Once the container is established students can begin to examine the flexibility of the container. This refers to the process of change and accommodation in one's internal and external therapeutic space. Movement experiences can be especially helpful in this exploration. While in a circle, ask students to try expanding and contracting as a group using stretch bands or other props that provide kinesthetic awareness. Have one member initiate a movement and then pass it around the group so that each member experiences the movement in turn. Have students discuss what it is like to feel the expansion and contraction of the group as container. Explore questions such as: What is it like to experience movement initiated by someone else? Do clients take on each other's movements? Can taking on someone else's movement be pathological? When is it useful to walk in someone else's shoes?

Authentic movement (Starks Whitehouse, 1999) exercises based on a theme can be used to explore the concept of container on an individual level. Working in dyads, have one student move, exploring the shape and texture of his internal therapeutic space, while another student bears witness. Have the students first share their experiences as mover and witness in the dyad and then with the group as a whole.

Students can also build representations of their concept of containers from clay or other art materials paying special attention to their idea of the therapeutic space. Explore issues such as: What kind of space can I create in myself for therapy? What kinds of things might fill my container (therapeutic issues, countertransference)? How much can I hold right now? Can I create more space? Is there easy access to my container? Can it be closed? What are my thresholds for closing and opening? How strong is this container? Are there places that need strengthening and are there places that might seem rigid? Can this container be too flexible?

While this exercise often takes a lot of time to both do and process it can be used successfully over the course of supervision. It is important to examine our therapeutic containers and notice how their shapes and capacities change over time.

Music psychodrama is another technique that is useful in exploring the container. Working in dyads, have one student enact or personify the concept of container using movement and music. The partner takes the role of a "double" who provides a simultaneous description or gives a voice to this exploration. Have students discuss both in dyads and in the larger group what they learned from both the movement and music experience as well as having that experience set in words by the partner.

Stage Two - Filling the Container

It is essential in creating safety of the supervision group to explore the ability to maintain connections. Themes of safety and connection parallel each other. Students need to learn to create a holding environment for the clients they treat.

As therapists we heighten our abilities and strategies for creating connection and engagement and take a close inventory of the personal issues we bring into the therapeutic holding environment. It is important to sort out whether what we bring to the therapeutic relationship is useful to the process or obscures the clinical intent. We need to know what is in our container, and choose whether or how to hold onto it.

Personal styles of creating a holding environment need to be explored on a personal/professional level, in relationship to other students, and in relationship to clients and various systems in which we work.

Suggested Arts Techniques and Structures

In examining the relational issues in therapy, it is helpful to use the work of Karen Horney (1993) who provides us with perspectives on relational strategies. She suggests people engage "toward," "against," and "away from" others in relationships. Directional styles used by a healthy individual are dependent on the context (e.g. in a threatening situation one might move "away"). In deeper and more intimate relationships there is fluidity in directional style and the use of more than one strategy simultaneously. For example, in the healthy parenting of an adolescent we might move toward lovingly by encouraging independence and move away with respect and trust, or against and toward by placing limitations on behavior as with a curfew where we are expressing a responsible form of love. Pathology is often expressed with a lack of fluidity in directional style (as with the catatonic whose directional style is perpetually "away"). A lack of attunement to the directional flow and needs of a relationship are often seen in dysfunctional families (enmeshment, codependence, domestic abuse, etc.).

It is helpful for students to begin to examine music and movement improvisation with this Hornerian lens. Improvisations can provide elucidating data on the styles and functions of students' relational directions. Using percussion and melodic instruments have students find connections and then create a holding environment to maintain them. Afterward explore the kinds of connections students made, including where it felt easy and when they experienced difficulties in connecting to themselves or others. Explore how they created a holding environment and relate how the patterns of connection and holding appear in their clinical work.

Countertransference issues can also be explored through the relational styles. Appropriate professional boundaries sometimes encourage a moving away strategy and site mandates can also dictate relational strategies. Negotiations in relational style between students and the site, or students and supervisors can be accentuated through improvisation and discussion.

In examining the music that comes out of these experiences it is critical not to interpret specific musical data. There is no single drum stroke that indicates a relational style. Rather the musical elements are available to aid in inquiry. For example, one might ask: John, in this group improvisation I noticed you played in rhythmic synchrony with Jane for a little while, do you remember this? What was this experience like for you? Is this familiar to you? Was it fruitful for you? Is this a relational style you use with clients? Others in the group may be may be also asked these questions: Jane, did you notice that John played in synchrony with you? Did anyone else in the group notice?

Hornerian style movement improvisation can be structured similarly to music improvisations by having students notice movement patterns in themselves and in others in the group. These improvisations can be employed singularly and in tandem with music making.

Perspectives on relationships can also be drawn from familial patterns. In making and holding connections, we can play the roles of parent, child, and adult. As with the Hornerian model, healthy individuals respond with fluid strategies in changing circumstances. The more intimate a relationship, the more complex the strategies become. A dysfunctional or ineffective relationship can often times be seen easily through this model, as when a married couple exclusively parent without relating to each other as adult to adult, or in families struggling with addiction where children can become exclusively parentified.

Music and movement improvisations can provide a way to access relational strategies that emanate directly from musical and movement processes. It is interesting to work with these strategies in an exaggerated or inverse manner. For example, if students find themselves often parenting a client or one another in the group, we can do improvisations that are childlike in order to let them experience this different interactional style. This situation becomes most apparent when a young intern finds himself working with clients who have many more years of life experience then he has. The transference and countertransference issues can become quite powerful and the intern can become stuck. These issues can be explored though the arts processes and result in personal insight into the particular dynamic along with strategies for change.

To explore the concept of relationships have students move about the room physically greeting each other without any sound. They are asked to meet, exchange movement, gesture, and energy, close the short encounter, and then move on to do the same with another group member until all group members have been met. In discussing the experience one can ask questions such as: Where in your body do you find yourself open to greet someone? In what ways do we consciously or unconsciously stay closed? Are there emotional blocks that impact your ability to relate to others in clinical situations that we would like to address in supervision? How do these issues effect your therapeutic container and space for holding? In what ways does it feel too vulnerable or professionally inappropriate to hold? What are the gender issues that arise?

In further examining relationships students can focus on the experience of being inside or outside. This can refer to being inside or outside of the therapeutic relationship, the supervisory relationship, etc. In dyads have students use visually permeable scarves to explore though movement the polarities of inside and outside. Recorded music can be used to both support and contain the movement Very different sound arenas can be created for this experience depending on the music used. For example Carlos Nakai's Native American music will create a different space and container for this process than a Bach Brandenberg Concerto. Ask questions such as: What is it like to be outside of the process? Where do you feel more comfortable, outside or inside? What might being inside or outside mean to your clients?

Using the work of Thomas Szasz (1984) as a model for understanding the human condition, it is possible to use polar opposites on a continuum of experience for exploration. The concept of boundaries, with one end of the continuum representing firm and rigid boundaries and one end representing no boundaries, is one that is usually fruitful to explore with students. In this experience ask students to work in a small group, of up to eight, exploring musical boundaries. Have them explore both ends of the continuum as well as where on the continuum they feel most comfortable. After the improvisation, explore the students' experience of internal and external boundaries. Ask them to notice if the boundaries ever shifted. Have them explore their sense of personal boundaries. How might these issues of boundaries affect someone struggling with mental illness or within a dysfunctional family system?

Stage Three - Individuating, Finding a Therapeutic Voice

As the supervision group develops, students begin to define their roles as novice therapists. Similarly, the relationship between site supervisor and intern evolves. In the healthy relationship, the mentoring supervisor begins to encourage individuation in the intern by gradually sharing and then passing group leadership to the student. This is not always a smooth process and many of the issues that arise in this process of individuating can be addressed through creative processes. The arts structures provide the forum for students to work on developing their therapeutic identities and provide the supervisor with additional avenues for supporting this process. This opportunity for deepening the understanding of students' styles of expression and communication as well as continuing to identify places that might need strengthening is valuable for students and supervisors alike.

Suggested Arts Techniques and Structures

Experientials that focus on the use of breath can help students explore what they take in from their surroundings and what they put out into the world. This balance of being effected and learning how one effects others is a part of helping students find their voice, or their style as a therapist. Some of these experientials can also help to de-stress anxious students and create a sense of healthy individuation. Yoga practices can teach therapists innumerable methods of breath work. The following are only a very few culled from an enormous body of knowledge (Lee, 1997).

Have students breathe in though the nose and slowly exhale from the mouth counting backwards from ten to one with each exhale. As they are exhaling have them listen to the sound of the breath. As they breathe have them notice the places of tension and relaxation in their bodies. Examine how those areas of tension impact their therapeutic voice and how the sense of relaxation impacts their clinical presence.

Finding one's voice is critical in claiming an identity as a therapist. While on one level the voice is a fundamental therapeutic tool—it is intimate, vulnerable, and direct—on another level, the voice can be a charged issue. As musicians, our expectations of our vocal prowess can be high, and our self-doubt significant or counter to this—we might find ourselves "over polished" or professionalized vocally. Claiming ease with our voices requires an embracing of the self as therapeutic container without unnecessary baggage.

Open-ended vocal play can be a lighthearted way help break the ice in terms of using one's voice. It can be helpful, in supervision and in many therapy situations when students or clients are stuck.

Have the group sit in a large circle where they can easily see one another. Have students vocalize as a group on singular vowel sounds. Do each vowel sound separately. Invites students to see how many vocal expressions they can explore with each other using the vowels. Encourage students to express different feelings in the vowel sounds: have them nurture each other, argue with each other, and tease each other. Add gestures and movement to the dialogue. In the discussion ask questions such as: Where does the sound start in your body? How can you modify its resonance? Can you be spontaneous with inflection, pitch, articulation, and intonation? How might your voice be perceived by your clients?

Amplifying the voice can be the next step in developing one's therapeutic voice. A natural extension of the vocal play delineated above is to move to a structure of simple chanting. Indigenous chants from Native American, African, Hasidic, Quaker or other cultures can be used. Supervision groups may also choose to write their own chant. The essential elements are that the chant is simple, repetitive, easy to sing with a limited range, and symmetrical in rhythm. As students feel their own comfort within the structure of the chant they can be invited to begin to improvise vocally around the basic chant and encouraged to stretch themselves, finding their own edges of comfort and creativity. In discussion one can help students examine their places of comfort and areas where they need to grow both musically and in terms of the symbolic exploration of their voice as a therapist.

Learning to take appropriate risks is a natural part of the individuation process. Improvisation can be helpful in this exploration. Have students improvise using their voices and the instruments on the theme of risk taking. After the improvisation discuss the actual risks they took in the improvisation along with the awareness of risks they might need to take to further their individuation process. Ask how they might negotiate these risks. What were the conditions that supported or negated the risk taking? Were the risks taken familiar to them or did they stretch beyond their usual patterns? How might risk taking relate to their work as emerging therapists? In taking risks, have students look at the internal and external expectations they have of themselves. Are there differences in what is "needed" as a therapist or what you "should" do as a therapist? Look at the risk taking of individual group members as well as the risk taking as a group. What relevance does risk taking have to clinical work with clients?

A movement experience that can be helpful in this exploration of individuating is to use a large elastic stretch band as a prop. Ask that the group stand inside the band and let each student in turn explore his or her style of moving in and out of the elastic support of the group. In the discussion ask students to reflect on their style of separating from the group. Ask questions such as: Was it hard to separate? Did you do it quickly or slowly? Ask students how they experienced each other separating from the group.

Another experience to further this exploration can be adapted from a body of work created by the modern dancer Bill T. Jones (1997). After having witnessed the painful struggle of his partner who had AIDS, Jones traveled across the country creating moving workshops for and with people negotiating the survival of their own life threatening illnesses. From these workshops Jones then choreographed dance repertoire.

We can adapt Jones' idea of choreographing the journey of his workshop participants. By narrowing the focus of the movement experience to the developmental process of individuating as a therapist, we can help students gain perspective on the obstacles and challenges that they negotiate in this process. Have students create a movement piece that represents their development as a therapist. Have them include the struggles they face and have faced and ways that they have overcome these issues. They can do this in dyads or in the large group. In the discussion have them articulate how they have developed, how they have met the challenges and what the next step in their development might be.

The moving experience can be designed as follows: A theme, such as "internship" can be chosen. Students form a chain staying in some physical contact. Often, one person begins in the front, the next is behind the first with a hand on the first person's back, etc. The student in the front of the chain initiates movement related to the theme of internship. The students in the chain "shadow" and bear witness to the movement. When the student in the front position feels ready, he or she moves to the back of the chain and the next person continues the exploration through movement. In the discussion ask questions such as: How has the experience of internship been different for different members? How has your growth as an intern impacted your clients?

Stage Four - Autonomy and Termination

At some point in the internship process students begin assuming responsibility for planning and running their own therapy groups as well as becoming responsible for individual clients. As they take on more of a separate identity and have more responsibility they may be feeling a mixture of emotions. Some students are excited to finally be "on their own" while others may struggle with the weight of treating patients struggling with illness. In either case the student's role at the site is no longer totally filtered through by the supervisor.

The arts can serve as a fruitful way to both support the sense of autonomy and examine the questions that arise as the student begins the move into the role of professional. Supervision at this stage requires sophisticated listening and respect for the student's professional path. It is often a time of stepping back and waiting for the student to approach with questions.

As the internship of music therapy students draws to a close, supervisors are also faced with a mixed bag of termination issues. There are those students who are racing to graduate and find employment, others grieving over the loss of a student life role who may have trepidation regarding the transition to "real life," and still others who may prolong and avoid the termination process. It is helpful to assist each student defining their own path on this journey, give permission for rejoicing, grief and confusion all to surface. It is important as well for supervisors to be vigilant of our own issues at this time. We too often grieve the loss and miss guiding students who have grown so much.

Suggested Arts Techniques and Structures

Meditation and Music: The following exercise includes several arts modalities: a guided kinesthetic meditation with music followed by a visual art process. This exercise can use prerecorded that encourages reflection or improvised simple drumming. Have students begin by focusing on the inward and outward movement of their breath. When grounded in their breathing, ask that they imagine that a line is drawn down the middle of their bodies from the top of their head to their toes. Have them slowly examine the feelings, tensions, and areas of relaxation on left side of their bodies. Ask them to then focus on their ability to "receive" in the world. Ask questions such as: How easy or difficult it is to receive from others? Are there types of receiving or conditions that make it more fruitful for you to receive? Attend to your ability to receive in different places in your body. It is likely that some places will be more open and others more protected. Focus on your left hand as a receptor.

When this exploration is complete, begin to examine the right side of the body in the same way only focusing on their ability to "give." In the manner suggested previously, heighten awareness of giving abilities and traits and focus on your right hand as a giver.

One can follow this experience with artwork. Suggestions include having students draw the left and right hands with their different capacities to receive and give. Sculpt the hands out of clay or other materials. In the discussion have students share insights gleaned from this experience focusing on the questions posed during the experience.

Using a variety of arts materials students can also be encouraged to create a mask that represents their autonomous professional identity. Once completed have students create a dialogue between the students in their new identities. In the discussion ask students to examine their mask and what it represents to them. What are the qualities they hope this mask emits to other professionals? To clients?

One can also have students explore various archetypal characters or images that represent their identity or issues that they are facing as they finish their clinical work. These images can be traditional archetypes (the trickster, etc.), or ones that are designed by the group (musical master, etc.) Ask students to individually select an archetype that resonates the most with where there are at this point in their internship. After the selection has been made ask the students to reveal their archetypes and then partner with someone else in the room, who has selected either the same character or relative character (an opposite or complement). Students can then use a creative process, such as songwriting, to explore how these archetypes are played out in their clinical work. In the discussion have the students explore the images they used. Ask questions such as: What does this image mean to you now? What part of it do you want to take with you into your new professional identity?

Conclusion

The internship is a time of growth and development as students move from student music therapist to professional music therapist. This journey is not always direct and predictable but rather full of surprises and unexpected detours. This however is the beauty of the experience, that all students have a unique journey of development and that we as supervisors have the honor of witnessing and guiding this process. We must always hold that for each stage of development our students move through, the creative arts can function as a way to encounter, examine, hold, work through and resolve the issues that arise.

References

Diallo, Y. (1990). *The Healing Drum: African Wisdom Teachings.* New York: Inner Traditions Intl. Ltd.

Jordan, J., Miller, J., Striver, I., Surrey, J. L., and Kaplan, A. G. (1991). *Women's Growth in Connection: Writings from the Stone Center.* Boston: Guilford Press.

Horney, K. (1993). *Our Inner Conflicts: A Constructive Theory of Neurosis.* New York: W. W. Norton & Co.

Jones, B. T (1997) *Still Here.* Film. David Grubin Producer, Films for Humanities, Inc.

Jung, C. J. (1981). *Archetypes and the Collective Unconscious.* New Jersey: Princeton University Press.

Lee, M. (1997). *Phoenix Rising Yoga Therapy: A Bridge from Body to Soul.* New York: Health Communications Inc.

Malchiodi, C., and Riley, S. (1996). *Supervision and Related Issues: A Handbook for Professionals.* Chicago, IL: Magnolia Street Press.

Starks Whitehouse, M. (1999). *Authentic Movement,* Philadelphia, PA: Jessica Kingsley Publishers.

Szasz, T. (1984). *The Myth of Mental Illness: Foundations of a Theory of Personal Conduct.* New York: Harper Collins Inc.

Winnicott, D. W. (1992). *The Family and Individual Development.* New York: Routledge Inc.

Chapter 11

The Fostering of Not-Knowing Barefoot Supervisors

Brynjulf Stige
Associate Professor in Music Therapy
Sogn og Fjordane College,
Sandane, Norway

I Heard It On the Radio

In this chapter I will present experiences with and perspectives on role-playing of supervision in the training of music therapy students. The context is the music therapy education in Sandane, Sogn og Fjordane College. This education was established in 1988, ten years after the first music therapy education in Norway was established in Oslo. But where is Sandane? You may pick up your atlas and look at the map of Scandinavia, and still not find the place, since it is a small town in a rural area. So I will help you. In western Norway, north of Bergen—where the fjords are deep and the mountains steep—you will find a long fjord called Nordfjord. At one of its sidearms, underneath some high mountains and wide glaciers, you will find the town of Sandane. About 2000 people live here. Around the center you will find several small and steep farms and a few small-scale industrial enterprises. The town of Sandane, tiny as it is, has been one of the centers of culture and education in the region, and since 1983 music therapy has been a part of the scenario. This started with a three-year project to stimulate the social and cultural integration of handicapped people. Out of this grew an approach to community music therapy that was ecological (Bruscia, 1998) and cultural (Stige, 1993/1999), and the foundation for a new Norwegian music therapy education was made (Stige, 1992).

It is a two-year full-time program, which qualifies one for a graduate diploma.[1] The background of our students is varied. All of them have minimum three years of education at the university level before they attend our program. Some of them are musicians, others are teachers or health workers. This—and the fact that students learn competencies differently—makes it important for the students to define personal goals for their own development. These goals are a theme of communication between the educators and the students, both in the classes, in the fieldwork, and in

---

[1] The Norwegian system of education is somewhat different from the American. The Norwegian two-year music therapy education leads to a degree somewhere in between a bachelor and master's degree in the American system. After that the students may take a two-year full-time (four-year half time) "research major" in music therapy, which will be somewhere between a master's degree and a Ph.D. After that it is possible to study for a doctoral degree.

supervision. We want to educate music therapists that are able to integrate theoretical knowledge, musical skills, and personal integrity and sensitivity, including a political awareness; they should understand how societies and communities could make it more easy or difficult for people to promote health and quality of life.

These goals ask for the development of *reflexivity* (Stige, in press) in the students. Part of my reason for working with role-playing of supervision is that I think it enhances my students' possibility to reflect upon the supervision they receive themselves, both how they contribute themselves and on how their contributions are colored by context. My idea is that supervision is a very context-sensitive form of interaction (Kvale, 1998). Generally therefore the students need to develop their awareness about how context influences their communication about music therapy. An illustrative example, although related to an untypical situation, is the following:

In one of the first weeks of 2000 our faculty and students experienced a couple of hectic days. Our college had established a new prize to stimulate the program with the best learning milieu, and the music therapy education became the first-prize winners. We received a decent amount of money, which we decided to use for a study visit to Lithuania later that spring. Two days later we received a fax from the Norwegian ministry of education, telling us that we had permission and money to start a new "research major" in music therapy together with the State Academy of Music in Oslo.[2] Since our school is located in a small, rural county, news like that is of public interest. A local radio reporter came to interview our students. One of the students he chose to interview was Irene, who told about her fieldwork, which she at the time was doing together with another second-year student. They were working together in a local school, with pupils in the first grade. Irene told that the teacher that had referred her class for music therapy wanted the students to work with the *class milieu*, to help the pupils develop their abilities to collaborate in a group, with fewer conflicts and more reciprocal communication. She also told the radio reporter how important it was to acknowledge the cultural background of each pupil.

Irene and her fellow student received supervision from me on this work, and a few days later we had one of our sessions of supervision. In the stories that the students told me from their clinical work *one* pupil and her individual problems were in the foreground most of the time. I felt that these problems needed to be dealt with, but I also felt that some themes were missing in our conversation; the interaction *within* the class and also *between* the class and the two students. In response to my questions the students even started to become vague about if the focus of the clinical work was on the individual or on the collective level. I asked: "A few days ago I heard it on the radio that the teacher that referred this class for music therapy wanted you to work on the class milieu, isn't that correct?" "Yes," Irene responded, "but . . ."

All three of us started laughing. It was amusing to see how different the stories told in these two contexts actually were. The lesson learned from this incident was *not* that Irene had been pretending when talking to the radio reporter. She had been sharing the reason for referral to music therapy, and she had been sharing her personal and professional values. The interesting thing was that these themes for a while had been marginalized in the discussions in the supervision context. What could that tell

---

[2] See footnote 1.

us? The students could see that this probably revealed some limitations in their thinking concerning class milieu and group processes. They had had problems with seeing the forest for all the trees; that is, the problems they had with one child had led them to restrict their thinking to the didactic area while the referral had asked for an ecological approach.

More positively it could be said that the differences in the stories told in these two contexts also revealed that supervision for these students was a place were they could "be human," could feel safe enough to share and explore difficulties and problems. This emotional aspect then is an important part of the lesson learned: context influences the stories we tell about our clinical work. The stories we tell are dialogic in the sense that they are responses to the situation and to our previous experiences. They are also dialogic in the sense that they anticipate possible responses and new questions in the audience (as perceived). In short: a narrative perspective might be helpful for our understanding of what is going on in supervision.

The Role of the Supervisor

The example above was taken from supervision of music therapy practice in a school setting. Since music therapists work in a number of settings and areas, we could learn from the treatment of supervision in several related disciplines, such as education (Acheson and Gall, 1997) and psychotherapy (Watkins, 1997), although I certainly would suggest that we also need to develop our own approaches to supervision. But why should we bother with supervision anyway? Watkins (1997, p. 3) suggests:

> Psychotherapy supervision is important because, among other possibilities, it provides supervisees with feedback about their performance; offers them guidance about what to do in times of confusion and need; allows them the opportunity to get alternate views and perspectives about patient dynamics, interventions and course of treatment; stimulates or enhances curiosity about patients and the treatment experience; contributes to the process of forming a therapist "identity"; and serves as a "secure base" for supervisees, letting them know that they are not alone in their learning about and performing of psychotherapy . . . Furthermore, psychotherapy supervision serves a critical quality-control function, ensuring that (a) patients are provided with acceptable care, (b) therapists do no harm, (c) therapists possess sufficient skills to function as "therapists," and (d) those who lack such skills are not allowed to continue without some form of remediation.

To my judgment this quote summarizes many of the arguments that have been used for the legitimization of the increasing focus upon supervision, not only in psychotherapy but in several professions within health and education. I will suggest that it is possible to condense Watkins' statements by considering three aspects of the supervisor role: the *teacher*, the *therapist*, and the *gatekeeper*.

To oversimplify: When the supervision helps the supervisee with his[3] development of skills and knowledge, the supervisor's role is close to that of a teacher. When the personal development is in focus, the supervisor's role approaches that of a therapist or a counselor.[4] Ideally a supervisor will switch flexibly between these two roles, depending upon the learning needs of the supervisee. The supervisor has a third responsibility though, which is essential in a training course; he has an evaluative function. In some way or another the supervisor is a gatekeeper and he has a responsibility concerning the quality of the service delivered to clients. Supervision as an integrated facet in a music therapy training endeavor then usually focuses upon all these objectives.

To balance these three roles flexibly—and not to neglect any of them—is a challenge for the supervisor. It is also a responsibility, which reminds us of a fact that is often taken for granted but which deserves to be reflected upon: the supervisor is almost per definition a person in power. A supervisor has authority by the effect of his competency but also by the effect of his role responsibilities. This is illuminated in one of the most quoted definitions of supervision, as:

> . . . an intervention that is provided by a senior member of a profession to a junior member or members of the same profession. This relationship is evaluative, extends over time, and has the simultaneous purposes of enhancing the professional functioning of the junior member(s), monitoring the quality of professional services offered to the clients she, he, or they see(s), and serving as a gatekeeper for those who are to enter the particular profession. (Bernard and Goodyear, in Watkins, 1997, p. 4).

Authority is of course not necessarily authoritarian, but criticism has been offered on what has been perceived as traditional and hierarchical models of supervision. Feminist perspectives on supervision have extended such criticism and advocated alternative supervisor roles, as suggested by the concept of a partnership model of supervision. Feminist therapists hold that more equality in power and authority is a basic notion both in the relationship between client and therapist and between supervisee and supervisor (Munson, 1997).

If there is total equality there is no supervision, but certainly feminist theorists have brought in some important criticism, and I would suggest that the balancing of the three roles previously mentioned needs to be balanced with a fourth role, that of the supervisor as a *listening coauthor*.[5] This fourth metaphor that I choose for

---

[3] For the sake of simplicity I have chosed to use "he" and "his" throughout this chapter instead of more polically correct constructions like s/he and his/her.

[4] The roles of teacher and therapist/counselor could of course in themselves be extremely differentiated. A teacher's role could for instance be focused upon instruction or upon learning through interaction.

[5] For sake of brevity, I will continue by calling this fourth role as the role of the *listener*. That the role of a listener so closely is related to the role of a co-author is probably not obvious in itself. It is a common suggestion within narrative therapy, though. A similar juxtaposition— concerning written texts—is made by Jon Fosse (1989), who suggests that to read open-ended

description of the function of the supervisor is in an uneasy relationship with the three others, which all three are metaphors for a professional role. To be a listener is hardly a profession, so I have here chosen a metaphor that could not be juxtaposed with the three others. And this is my point. To be a listener could not be an alternative to being a teacher, therapist, and gatekeeper; it needs to be an addendum at the same time as it needs to be integrated in the three others.

Supervision is not just a personal relationship, it is also an institution in a society. The supervisor has a certain responsibility toward the society—his task is to help the supervisee learn and to develop his professional personality, and his task is to conduct some kind of quality control, for the benefit of the clients but also of the profession. To neglect the roles of being a teacher, a therapist, and a gatekeeper is therefore not possible. If you combine this reality with a vision of the role of the supervisor as one that supports the supervisee in his search for reflexivity and autonomy, you have a seemingly paradoxical situation: you are in power and your task is empowerment of the other. This is not a completely unknown paradox for most of us, though; we do for instance meet it in our private lives as parents and in our professional lives as therapists.

A Narrative Perspective on Supervision

The challenge for the supervisor then becomes to develop attitudes and strategies that make empowerment of the supervisee possible. To take the role of a listener might be such a strategy. The importance of the role of the listener is of course not a new idea. We find it underlined in Carl R. Rogers' (1951) client-centered psychotherapy, in music therapy for instance in Gary Ansdell's (1995) discussion of Creative Music Therapy with adults. The perspective on the listener that I will take here is a specific one, though, inspired by narrative theory and the literature of narrative therapy. How is the role of the listener influenced by taking a *narrative* perspective?

In the last decade there has been an increasing interest for the text analogy in therapy theory. Users of this analogy usually focus upon narrative and storytelling, the basic idea being that people's problems are constructed as performances of oppressive, dominant stories of knowledge. Therapy then means to help the client to (co)author and perform alternative and liberating stories (McLeod, 1997; White and Epston, 1990). The text analogy has not been very influential in music therapy, but lately we have seen some contributions, such as Bonde, (1999), Frohne-Hagemann (1998), Ruud (1997, 1998), and Stige (1999).

My interest for narrative perspectives is based upon a general interest for questions of meaning and language in music therapy (Stige, 1998). Neither music therapy nor supervision exist beyond culture and language. In supervision the supervisee is telling stories about his clinical work. That is a foundation of this interaction. Even if the supervisor also might listen to audio examples, watch a videotape of the work, or observe the clinical work in vivo, the supervisee's

---

texts is very close to being an author. This suggestion is related to Bakhtin's (1929/1984) dialogic concept of text.

representation of his own work remains essential. It is suggested then in narrative theory that such representation is more than a "mirror" or a "picture," but it is framed as a storied world. This is hardly something to avoid, nor possible to neglect, and needs to be explored.

In psychotherapy at least three perspectives on storytelling and narrative have been taken: psychodynamic, cognitive constructivist, and social constructionist (McLeod, 1997). I am not undertaking an evaluation of these three perspectives here. It would have been relevant to do so if I was focusing upon a therapy-based approach to supervision; that is, if I was suggesting that the clinical practice and the supervision should be guided by the same theory. I am not making this suggestion. In this context I am more interested in how narrative perspectives can enhance our understanding of the supervision situation and process, regardless of the theoretical perspective taken by the clinician. "Regardless of the theoretical perspective taken" does not mean "with little interest for the theoretical perspective taken." Almost the contrary is true: clinical theory is part of what shapes the language we use when describing music therapy, and to take a narrative perspective means—among other things—to take interest in language.

A premise for me when writing this chapter is the relevance for music therapy of the "linguistic turn" in philosophy. One of the contributors to this turn in thinking has been Ludwig Wittgenstein (1921/1961, 1953/1967). His later work illuminated problems in his earlier and quite influential theory of language as a picture of the facts of the world. The meaning of language—according to the later Wittgenstein—is not mainly established through the use of logical rules but through social use. Where there is social use there is history and power, a perspective on language and knowledge that clearly has been developed by Foucault (1961/1991). Language is not a transparent medium, showing us how the world is; it is a medium with which we also construct our world. To take this suggestion seriously means that to reflect upon music therapy means to reflect upon discourse, a perspective that has elegantly been taken by Gary Ansdell (1999) in his recent doctoral thesis.

The stories told by the supervisee therefore could be explored from several angles. In some way or another they reveal something about the clinical world as experienced by the supervisee, and indirectly as experienced by the client. While most supervisors would reflect upon the veracity and completeness of the information given, to take a narrative perspective also implies to take a direct interest in the story itself. What does it reveal about the social and moral world of the supervisee? Supervision then includes an aspect of discourse analysis in action. What words and constructs are used? How are these related to other stories known and/or told by the supervisee? What is the plot of the story? Who are the agents and what are their roles? Etc.

If the supervisor takes the role of the expert knowing the answers of such questions, I would not expect the supervision process to be very helpful for the supervisee. This would just add a new aspect to the supervisor's authority role. The task will rather be that of creating a safe space for stories to unfold, and I will suggest—as indicated in the title of the chapter—that the supervisor needs to take the role of a *not-knowing listener*. Exploration of the story then becomes an act of reciprocity, and the active part of the supervisor's contribution becomes closer to that of a co-author than to that of a critic or reviewer.[6]

By focusing upon reciprocal exploration of the stories told, the interaction develops an element of "side by side" communication. While there is usually a basic element of "nose to nose" communication in supervision, it has been suggested that side by side communication—where both participants look at, analyze, and interpret some information given—is helpful for the development toward more equality in power and authority (Acheson and Gall, 1997). Such side by side communication with a focus upon the stories told gives the supervisee opportunities to do much more than digesting advice. He is given tools to reflect upon how his understanding of his clinical work is situated in culture and language. Reflexivity then does not mean to transcend this situatedness, rather to acknowledge it and by that possibly achieving some flexibility and fluidity.

To tell is to create something in the other, for myself, and for the relationship between us. Questions therefore arise: What and how do I want to create? What stories can I tell to this person, and in what way?[7] A narrative perspective on supervision therefore also includes examination of the relationship between the supervisee and the supervisor. Storytelling is an interpersonal and emotional situation. Is the supervisor opening or closing a space for stories? How is he listening and responding to the stories? As soon as the supervisor responds verbally, he is constructing his own narratives, which of course then demands self-reflexivity in the supervisor. We will return to this after I have shared how I use narrative perspective on supervision in my work with students as future "barefoot supervisors."

Who Would Want to be Barefoot?

The accessibility of—and thus knowledge about and interest for—supervision is obviously related to the stage of development of a profession. In the early literature on music therapy little is written about supervision. In the 1970's and 80's you will find some interest, and lately this interest has been increasing in several countries, for instance in England (Brown, 1997), Germany (Weymann, 1996; Frohne-Hagemann, 1999), and U.S. (Dvorkin, 1999), to give some examples of the existing literature.[8]

So far supervision has not been a major topic in the discussion of the discipline and profession of music therapy in Norway. To this day most music therapists in my country have been "pioneers"; they are usually working as the only music therapist in their community, school, institution, or hospital. They are rarely or never receiving supervision from a more experienced music therapist, simply because there is no one

---

[6] See footnote 5.

[7] Cf. the example in the beginning of this chapter, where a student discovered how different she told a story in two different contexts.

[8] In the Nordic countries not much has been published yet, but some master theses have touched upon this topic. I also want to mention that Ingrid Hammarlund in Stockholm (S) and Inge Nygaard Pedersen in Aalborg (DK) have been working with supervision for quite some time and are engaged in a process of developing an education for music therapy supervisors.

around. At best—and still not very often—they are receiving supervision from a colleague in another profession, for instance from a psychologist or psychiatrist. But this is changing. Some music therapists are starting to give, and ask for, supervision, and I am sure that a discussion on how to develop a strategy for the development of more professional music therapy supervision is coming.

Already quite a few of our students end up as "barefoot supervisors." After having worked for a few years they are asked to supervise students or less experienced music therapists, although they have no official training in supervision themselves. They are also sometimes asked to be consultants for workers belonging to other health and education professions, still without having any specific training for doing this. Some will define all this as a problem and as an illustration of the lack of development of the music therapy profession. There is some truth in that, and I certainly will welcome initiatives for the establishment of training courses for music therapy supervisors. My focus though has been to show interest for these barefoot supervisors—I think they are important—and to prepare my students for that role.

I use the term barefoot supervisor in allusion to the Chinese tradition of barefoot doctors, and to the more recent use of that term in both developing and developed countries. As the term Barefoot Doctor originated in China it stands for people in the community trained to take care of health problems. These practitioners would walk— barefoot, I presume—from village to village and treat diseases with the tools they had available. During the Cultural Revolution the term was revitalized, and paramedical workers with some—but still minimal—formal training were stimulated to provide part-time medical service, primarily in rural areas. They promoted basic hygiene, preventive health care, and family planning. They also treated some common illnesses. In sum: they acted as primary health-care providers at the grass-roots level (De Geyndt, Zhao, and Liu, 1992).

The last few decades the term barefoot doctor has been used in several developing countries. Some government agencies have trained and used barefoot doctors as a part of their strategy for the development of better health services in a situation where there is a lack of both financial resources and educated personnel. This has for instance been the situation in several African countries (Werner, Thuman, and Maxwell, 1993). I first became aware of the tradition of barefoot doctors myself when living in eastern Africa in the early 1970s. Although young at the time, I then also realized something which has been a part of my understanding of this concept till this day, and which is why I want to allude to it in this context. These barefoot doctors have some specific qualifications that are different from those of a university-trained doctor. They do not just know less than a doctor proper; they know different things. By their close relationship to the local culture they are able to negotiate meaning and understanding in ways not so easily accessed by doctors trained in the western modern tradition.

Lately the term barefoot doctor also has gained popularity in some rich and developed countries. The need for such doctors is then only to a little degree related to the lack of available university-trained personnel, and is probably more related to a search for alternative roles and relationships between the helper and the person in need. One barefoot doctor trainer in the U.S. gives this "mission statement":

And though the methods may be similar to our healers/doctors using diagnostics, therapeutics and prognostics, the Barefoot Doctor usually only advises on a course of action, recommending a path that seems most suitable for the person. The responsibility of the Barefoot Doctor is to let people be responsible for themselves, to let people choose their own course of action. A Barefoot Doctor may review the options, help weigh the risks and benefits, and offer suggestions when asked for advice, but ultimately, like a good coach who stands on the sidelines and lets the players play their own game, they expect that the person must be responsible for their own path, hopefully a path conducive for healing (Berg, www.barefootdoctors.org).

Although I bear in mind that some of the so-called barefoot doctors in western countries today are rather close to the speculative New Age movements criticized by Summer and Summer (1996) and others, I do think an elaboration of alternative roles between helper and client is justified. When I in this chapter use the expression barefoot supervisor I therefore want to allude to two related but distinct meanings. First: while waiting for more professional trained music therapy supervisors to be around I will suggest that we need to train and support barefoot supervisors. Second: in the role of the barefoot supervisors there exist possibilities for innovative developments of role relationships between supervisor and supervisee. The integration of the role of *listener*—understood in a narrative perspective—is the approach I have chosen.

Playing Supervision

The last few years I have tried to develop an approach to how I could work with my students so that they could prepare themselves for a future role as barefoot supervisors. The context I have chosen for this work is the improvisation course of our music therapy education, a course that is scheduled throughout the two years of the program. The first year I give an introduction to improvisational music therapy and also an introduction to the Nordoff-Robbins tradition of clinical improvisation. The second year we focus upon different forms of role-playing, giving the students opportunities to explore other approaches to improvisation, approaches they choose and/or develop themselves, as they find them relevant for the problems and clients to be worked with.

We work quite systematically with this role-playing, and I think it is a major element in the students' learning process this second year of their education.[9] There

---

[9] I am grateful to Professor Tony Wigram at Aalborg University (DK) who during the years has shared some of his experiences with role-playing in the training of students. Many of the ideas I work with concerning role-playing of music therapy have been inspired by his work, while the role-playing of supervision—the topic of this chapter—is an approach that I have developed myself.

are four roles to be taken: the therapist role, the client role, the supervision role, and the video filmmaker role. One or two students will be therapists, one or two or more will be clients, depending on the format chosen, (group therapy or individual therapy with or without co-therapist). A description of the client role is given in written text, as a "vignette" describing a client and his problems and resources, including context and social network. This text is given to students at least seven days before the role-playing, which makes it possible for the "therapist," "client," and "supervisor" to *prepare* themselves for the role-playing.[10] In part this will be to study relevant literature on client populations and on approaches to music therapy, but just as important is the time needed to prepare oneself emotionally for participation in the role-playing. If practically possible the students choose the role they shall play, based upon their understanding of their own learning needs, for instance as experienced in their practical fieldwork. This might of course be a topic of discussion in itself, since there might be a need for reflection upon how and why they choose a particular role. Some students also choose to submit written proposals for roles to be played.

Usually we have been working in this sequence: 1) introduction; the therapist presents what he will do, what his ideas and theoretical perspectives are, etc.; 2) role-playing of improvisational music therapy; 3) "thinking minutes" for the therapist, preparing himself for the role of being a supervisee; 4) role-playing of supervision; 5) discussion (in plenum) and reflection upon the role-playing of supervision; and 6) discussion of the role-playing of music therapy. When "going back" to reflect upon the role-playing of music therapy we quite often choose to study the videotape that has been made of this role-playing, so that we have several perspectives on the same event: a) the observations made by all the participants[11] of the in vivo event, b) the stories told and reflected upon in the supervision, and c) the observations and reflections based upon the video-documentation of the event.

Let us now take a look at the role-playing of supervision. After the role-playing of a music therapy session, the student who played the role of the therapist role-plays a supervisee asking for supervision from a supervisor, which then is role-played by another student. Quite often the student playing the role of supervisor in the beginning finds this bewildering and difficult. Am I qualified to give any advice? What shall I tell him? How could I guide him? Usually, of course, the more bewildered the supervisor is the more bewildered the supervisee. These difficulties could be perceived as "natural" since no student is trained to be a supervisor. Often, though, I find that they reveal a limited concept of what the supervisor role is or could be. As discussed in the beginning of the chapter, this role includes aspects of the role of a teacher, a therapist, and a gatekeeper. Sometimes the students focus upon supervision as teaching. They need to free themselves from ideas that suggest that they can help by being more knowledgeable than the supervisee. Other times they might fear the therapist or gatekeeper role, feeling that it asks more of them than what is possible.

---

[10] I will proceed by using the terms "therapist" and "client" in singular, although—as said—the format sometimes is group therapy or individual therapy with two therapists.

[11] Therapist, client, supervisor, audience (fellow students and teacher).

These perceptions of the supervisor role needs to be dealt with,[12] but a good practical place to start when working with the role-playing of supervision is to refocus, and help the students to start *listening* to the stories presented. The supervisor can be helpful for the supervisee as a listener and co-author. This then suggests a role more active in listening than in questioning and suggesting. While listening the supervisor might ask himself questions such as: How is the story told? What is the style of the narrative? What is the focus of the story? Who is acting and what is the plot? How is music integrated in the story? If the supervisor then thinks that his role is to figure out the answers to such questions, there will be problems. Then the supervisee easily will think that the supervisor has a "secret agenda," and he is not really listening but rather analyzing the story told. The task is instead to create a safe place for stories to unfold. By creating such a space—for instance by allowing the well known and trite to be—one also opens up a space for the new, and a hermeneutic circle of understanding is already in its development.

This is not to say that the questions mentioned previously are irrelevant. When a safe space is established, when the supervisee feels that this is a place where he also can present stories that make him look bad, then a mutual examination of such questions might be helpful. A basic premise for a narrative approach is that helpful supervision is not to give the supervisee the correct idea or answer, but to help him develop his own flexibility, his ability to look at his own work from several perspectives. In this a "not-knowing barefoot supervisor" actually can be quite helpful. Without the authority of an experienced therapist and supervisor his words will not so easily be interpreted by the supervisee as sacred words of wisdom. And the supervisor can use all his human sensitivity and all his knowledge of and love for stories when listening and sharing questions with the supervisee.

The supervisor might perceive the story as too fragmented, so that it no longer is a story. He might perceive the story as too logical, too linear, too obvious, and might find a point in this linear logic to question. He might find some discrepancies in a story that at first seemed coherent. He might wonder about something concerning one of the agents in the story. He might also have questions to the way the story is told more than to the content and structure of the story. Such simple questions are not always easy to share. The right timing, the right phrasing, the right formulation, attunement to the affections of the supervisee—all these are important factors contributing positively or negatively to the creation of the safe space mentioned earlier. So while this approach to supervision takes the limited competency of a barefoot supervisor into account, it is no easy approach. The supervisor needs to use and develop his sensitivity to the other person, to language, to stories, and to music and culture, and—not the least—to develop self-reflexivity.

Role-Playing and Reflexivity

Music therapy has a lot to do with the spontaneous and emotional experience of the moment, of the here and now. At the same time music therapy is about meaning as

---

[12] See the discussion of reflexivity later in the chapter.

social use; that is, history and power. So, rather obviously, creativity, sensitivity, and flexibility are necessary but not sufficient conditions for good music therapy supervision. *Reflexivity* also needs to be part of the process. The concept of reflexivity refers to the process where the thinking is reflected back or turned toward itself, so to say. (Self)-reflexivity then could be understood both as the supervisor's and supervisee's exploration of their own roles in the supervision process, and as their exploration of their own role in the community and society they are living in. Since I earlier in this chapter have argued that supervision is both a personal relationship and an institution in the society I will argue that both meanings have relevance here.

Reflexivity is to some degree possible to understand with the help of psychological concepts.[13] Even Ruud (1998), one of very few music therapy theorists to use and discuss the concept of reflexivity, advocates the importance of a broader perspective though. He argues that there is a correspondence between our values and interests and how we perceive the world. Reflexivity then to Ruud (1998, p. 17) includes awareness of our presuppositions and values. With reference to Anthony Giddens he also connects this to a concept of identity: ". . . what characterizes identity in our (post)modern culture is, in large part, reflexivity. Identity no longer comes to us ready-made, because identity is a process, something never fulfilled" (1998, p. 37). What Ruud suggests, could be described as "culturally informed hermeneutics"; reflexivity means reflecting upon your own position in the culture you belong to and its influence on the work that you are conducting.[14]

In clinical music therapy as well as in supervision I think there often will be a need to reflect upon the interaction between a psychological and a cultural level; both a psychological process of self-inquiry and a culturally informed hermeneutics are essential assets of such processes. What has this to do with role-playing then? Maybe a lot. Ruud (1998) refers to the anthropologist Don Handelman and his reflections upon the reflexive nature of play in general. "Play tells us not how things *should* be but rather how things *might* be" (1998, p. 119). "Through play, we create a dialogue with outside reality: we comment on this reality, change it symbolically, play roles, and so on without running into the consequences of the real situation" (1998, p. 179).

We know when we play. There is a certain metacommunication present telling us that this is "just play." This is not reducing the value of the act of playing; rather it contributes to its value as a medium of self-reflexivity. Role-playing of supervision seems at first to include several limiting factors—the supervisor is inexperienced, the time is limited, there is an audience disturbing the private space usually associated with supervision, etc. I then will suggest that the other side of this is that the situation of *play* gives room for other types of reflections than in "ordinary supervision."

The students can compare their different experiences of the supervisor's role, think about how context influences their stories, reflect upon how they approach the situation themselves, etc. As mentioned earlier, reflections upon the supervisor role

---

[13] Psychological concepts—as tools for reflection upon one's role and contribution to an interpersonal process—have been developed within several traditions, for instance the concepts of countertransference within the psychodynamic tradition and of authentic communication within the humanistic tradition.

[14] Which in the context of the music therapy profession could be clinical work, research, teaching, or supervision.

usually enter these discussions early. Students often find that they have had limited or unbalanced concepts of this role; for instance by expecting the supervisor to be an instructor-type teacher, by showing resistance to the therapy-element of supervision, or by fearing the gatekeeper aspect of it. A narrative approach does not in itself solve such problems; in fact, taken into its extreme, it can be experienced as abdication from the roles of responsibility connected to supervision as an institution. But a sensitive approach to narrative supervision might open up a space for explorations of roles and for flexible reflections. A good place to start is usually to remind the supervisee of his responsibility in the supervision process. In the role-playing of supervision the supervisee knows that the supervisor has observed the role-playing of the therapy process, so it is tempting to start the supervision by saying something like: "Now, what do you think?" An important part of the learning experience then is to acknowledge that the role responsibility of the supervisee is to present stories about the clinical work, and to be willing to explore them together with the supervisor.

Pretty soon a question essential to music therapy pops up: "How do we talk about music?" Some insist that it is impossible to talk about music, but the fact is that we keep doing it all the time, and many will suggest that this speech about music co-constructs the music experience (Feld, 1994). If music is a part of the story told—and most music therapists agree that it should be—we need to ask ourselves *how* it can be included. Do we talk about sound as such, musical syntax, musical meaning, or the ontological world of the client (Forinash and Gonzalez, 1989)? Do we talk about music as identity (Ruud, 1997, 1998)? Do we use metaphors and personal language when describing music, or more technical terms belonging to the discipline—as for instance the descriptive terms in IAP (Bruscia, 1994)? Do we talk about music as an object, or about musicking as a verb (Small, 1998)?

Part of the value I have found in working with role-playing is related to the possibility of reflecting upon supervision in a public space. Supervision is usually a personal experience. That is some of its possibilities, while also some of its problems. When supervision becomes a major element of the students' learning experience, there is always a danger that there will be a decline in critical discourse, since discussions are taken from a public space and transferred to a more private space. This problem is especially poignant in education programs with close relationships between teachers and students (Kvale, 1998), which I suppose is the situation in most music therapy training programs. For several of the learning challenges in music therapy I consider supervision an adequate approach to learning. A solution to this problem is then not necessarily to reduce the amount of supervision. To create possibilities for critical reflections is one alternative. Role-playing of supervision, as discussed in this chapter, has the potential to be developed into such a more public space for critical discussion. The students enter the role-playing with several experiences of being supervised, both in their three placements during the first-year practicum and in their second-year independent fieldwork. When role-playing supervision they then have the possibility to compare and reflect upon these other experiences of supervision, and ask questions such as: Which issues are relevant to work with in supervision, which belong to other forays? How is the paradox of power versus empowerment dealt with?

It Takes a lot of Knowledge to Take a Not-Knowing Perspective

A barefoot supervisor—although with little specific competency in supervision—is hardly not-knowing in a traditional sense. He already knows a lot, both about music, stories, clients, and therapy. When I have chosen the term "not-knowing," it is with reference to Anderson and Goolishian's (1992) specific use of that term. They express a criticism to therapy models that define humans as information processing "machines." Instead they focus upon man as a meaning-generating being. The term "not-knowing therapist" is then sometimes used within the tradition of narrative therapy, to express the idea of a client-centered therapy that also is willing to question the authority of the therapist. A not-knowing therapist respects the client's narrative truth, and enters a dialogue based upon this rather than upon his own predefined knowledge.

This does not mean to forget all of one's preunderstanding. Supervision in a narrative perspective is closely related to hermeneutics, where preunderstanding is considered a condition for any understanding, provided it is reflected upon. A not-knowing approach therefore has more to do with openness than anything else. It should not be an excuse for abdication of responsibility. A not-knowing approach is not to neglect the value of the supervisor as a *qualified* listener, but to stress that his main task is to be a *qualifying* partner by trying to create a space where both partners can take the humility of a beginner's mind.

When I ask my students to take a not-knowing approach, that of course then is not contradictory to a student's search for knowledge. My experience as a teacher and supervisor has taught me that it takes a lot of knowledge to be able to take a not-knowing approach. Lack of knowledge—of oneself and of the topics covered in a conversation—usually contributes to closing stories instead of opening them. In working with the role-playing I have tried to communicate this, by stressing the importance of the students' emotional and theoretical preparations for the role-playing. What we are searching for is freedom and openness for new and diverse stories, which is related to the freedom and openness we search for in a musical improvisation. And as the Indian musician Shankar wrote in his autobiography: ". . . this freedom can come about only after many years of basic study and discipline and organized training . . ." (Shankar, in Weisethaunet, 1999, p. 146).

Conclusion

My conclusions so far are: 1) I think it is important to help music therapy students prepare themselves for a role as barefoot supervisors. 2) I think a not-knowing narrative perspective on supervision might be helpful, by enhancing the students' reflexivity and ability to be good (enough) listeners to a wide range of stories. 3) The not-knowing approach suggests an ethics "of being with the other" (Bauman, 1993). Ethics in supervision is more than knowing what you are doing and what you should not do—it is related to tolerance for diversity. The stories told might reveal that the supervisee (and his/her client) has values that are very different from those of the supervisor, who needs to be able to respect and acknowledge that.

My experience is that the process of reflecting about their own future roles as barefoot supervisor also has enhanced my students' ability to reflect upon and use the supervision they receive themselves during the music therapy education.[15] If the future of music therapy should bring us plenty of qualified music therapy supervisors I will be happy, but I still believe there are lessons to be learned from the "not-knowing barefoot supervisor." The barefoot aspect both points toward developments of future peer supervision within music therapy, and toward a more general discussion of the knowledge base and of the role relationships in supervision. The not-knowing narrative approach remains relevant also for the qualified supervisor, by reminding us of the meaning-generating aspects of any conversation, supervision included.

References

Acheson, K. A., and Gall, M. D. (1997). *Techniques in the Clinical Supervision of Teachers: Preservice and Inservice Applications.* (4th ed.). White Plains, NY: Longman Publishers.

Anderson, H., and Goolishian, H. (1992). The client is the expert: A not-knowing approach to therapy. In S. McNamee and K. J. Gergen (eds.), *Therapy as Social Construction.* London: Sage Publications.

Ansdell, G. (1995). *Music for Life. Aspects of Creative Music Therapy with Adult Clients.* London: Jessica Kingsley Publishers.

Ansdell, G. (1999). *Music Therapy as Discourse and Discipline. A Study of "Music Therapist's Dilemma."* London: Unpublished Doctoral Thesis, Department of Music, City University.

Bakhtin, M. (1929/1984). *Problems of Dostoevsky's Poetics.* Minneapolis: University of Minnesota Press.

Bauman, Z. (1993). *Postmodern Ethics.* Cambridge, MA: Blackwell.

Berg, J. "On The Art of Barefoot Doctoring." [online] Madisonville, LO: *Barefoot Doctors' Academy.* Available from: http://www.barefootdoctors.org [Accessed 15 February 2000]

Bonde, L. O. (1999, November). "Metaphor and Metaphoric Imagery in Music Therapy Theory: a Discussion of a Basic Theoretical Problem—with Clinical Material from GIM Sessions." Paper presented at the 9th World Congress in Music Therapy, Washington, D.C.

---

[15] My approach to working with role-playing of supervision is new and under development. Writing this text has given me several new ideas that I want to work with in the years to come. For instance: Could the fact that the role-playing is videotaped be used more systematically? Such documentation opens up for what Kagan and Kagan (1997) call mutual recall, where both agents in a dialogue reflect upon and share the experience they had in the in vivo event (therapy or supervision), while watching the videotape of it.

Brown, S. (1997). Supervision in context: a balancing act. *British Journal of Music Therapy,* Vol.11.

Bruscia, K. (1994). *IAP. Kartlegging gjennom musikkterapeutisk improvisasjon.* [IAP. Improvisation Assessment Profiles]. Translation and introduction by Brynjulf Stige and Bente Østergaard. Sandane, Norway: Sogn og Fjordane College.

Bruscia, K. (1998). *Defining Music Therapy.* (2nd ed). Gilsum, NH: Barcelona Publishers.

De Geyndt, W., Zhao, X., and Liu, S. (1992). *From barefoot doctor to village doctor in rural China.* World Bank (technical paper; no. 187), Washington, D.C.

Dvorkin, J. (1999). Psychoanalytically oriented music therapy supervision. In T. Wigram and J. De Backer, *Clinical Applications of Music Therapy in Developmental Disability, Paediatrics and Neurology.* London: Jessica Kingsley Publishers.

Feld, S. (1994). Communication, music, and speech about music. In C. Keil and S. Feld, *Music Grooves.* Chicago: The University of Chicago Press.

Forinash, M., and Gonzalez, D. (1989). A phenomenological perspective of music therapy. *Music Therapy* 8(1), 35-46.

Fosse, J. (1989). Frå telling via showing til writing. Essays. [From telling via showing to writing. Essays.] Oslo, Norway: Samlaget.

Foucault, M. (1961/1991). Galskapens historie i opplysningens tidsalder. [Madness and Civilization—History of Insanity in the Age of Reason]. Oslo, Norway: Gyldendal.

Frohne-Hagemann, I. (1998). The musical life panorama. *Nordic Journal of Music Therapy,* 7(2).

Frohne-Hagemann, I. (1999). Integrative supervision for music therapists. In T. Wigram and J. De Backer (eds.), *Clinical Applications of Music Therapy in Developmental Disability, Paediatrics and Neurology.* London: Jessica Kingsley Publishers.

Kagan, H. and Kagan, N. (1997). Interpersonal process recall: Influencing human interaction. In C. E. Watkins, Jr. (ed.), *Handbook of Psychotherapy Supervision.* New York: John Wiley and Sons, Inc.

Kvale, S. (1998). At blive vejledt i en spejllabyrint i tåge. [To be supervised in a mirror labyrinth in the mist]. *Uniped,* Vol. 20, No. 3.

McLeod, J. (1997). *Narrative and Psychotherapy.* London: Sage Publications.

Munson, C. E. (1997). Gender and psychotherapy supervision. In C. E. Watkins Jr. (ed.), *Handbook of Psychotherapy Supervision.* New York: John Wiley and Sons, Inc.

Rogers, C. R. (1951). *Client-Centered Therapy.* London: Constable & Company Ltd.

Ruud, E. (1997). Music and identity. *Nordic Journal of Music Therapy,* 6(1).

Ruud, E. (1998). *Music Therapy: Improvisation, Communication, and Culture.* Gilsum, NH: Barcelona Publishers.

Small, C. (1998). *Musicking: The Meanings of Performing and Listening.* Hanover, NH: Wesleyan University Press.

Stige, B. (1992). Small is beautiful: The music therapy training program in Sandane. *Music Therapy International Report,* Vol. 8.

Stige, B. (1993/1999). "Music Therapy as Cultural Engagement. Or: How to Change the World, if Only a Bit." Paper presented at the 7th World Congress of Music Therapy, Vitoria-Gasteiz, Spain. In D. Aldridge (ed.), (1999): *Music Therapy Info. Vol II.* (CD-ROM).

Stige, B. (1998). Perspectives on meaning in music therapy. *British Journal of Music Therapy,* 12(1).

Stige, B. (1999). "Hypertexts in Music Therapy." Paper at the 9th World Congress of Music Therapy, Washington D.C.

Stige, Brynjulf (in press). *Music Therapy: Toward a Cultural Matrix.* Gilsum, NH: Barcelona Publishers.

Summer, L., and Summer, J. (1996). *Music: The New Age Elixir.* Amherst, NY: Prometheus Books.

Watkins, C. E. Jr. (ed.). (1997). *Handbook of Psychotherapy Supervision.* New York: John Wiley and Sons, Inc.

Werner, D., Thuman, C., and Maxwell, J. (1993). *Where There Is No Doctor: A Village Health Care Handbook for Africa.* London: Macmillan.

Weisethaunet, H. (1999). Critical remarks on the nature of improvisation. *Nordic Journal of Music Therapy,* 8(2).

Weymann, E. (1996). Supervision in der Musiktherapie. *Musiktherapeutische Umschau,* 17.

White, M., and Epston, D. (1990). *Narrative Means to Therapeutic Ends.* New York: W. W. Norton & Company.

Wittgenstein, L. (1921/1961). *Tractatus Logico-Philosophicus.* London: Routledge.

Wittgenstein, L. (1953/1967). *Philosophical Investigations.* Oxford: Blackwell.

Acknowledgments

I want to express gratitude to my students. I also want to thank Dan Gormley for the discussions we had on role-playing of supervision and for the comments he offered to an earlier version of this chapter.

Part Three

Professional Supervision

Chapter 12

Peer Supervision in the Development of the New Music and Expressive Therapist

Elizabeth Baratta, MA
Crossroads/May Behavioral Health,Cambridge, MA
Michael Bertolami, MA, MT-BC
Perkins School for the Blind, Watertown, MA
Andrew Hubbard, MA, CMT
Riverside Community Care, Upton, MA
Mary-Carla MacDonald, MA, MT-BC
Assistant Professor, Anna Maria College, Paxton, MA
Deborah Spragg, MA
Wild Acre Inns, Boston, MA

Introduction

Peer supervision in the transition from student to professional is a topic that has been given limited treatment in the supervision literature, especially when music and the expressive arts are brought into the equation. Although some of our colleagues have continued to meet in a supervisory capacity after their graduation from degree programs, there is little reference to this in the literature. The idea of exploring our own group experience, with the intent of sharing this information, was received by our supervision group with great enthusiasm. We felt as a group that what we have in the form of peer supervision had been very valuable to us during a difficult period of transition. We were all ready and willing to attempt to discern what it is that has allowed us to thrive as a group up to this point.

The main focus of this chapter is to address the transitional period from student to professional. For us as a group, the developmental process began while we were graduate students in an off-site internship supervision group that was held at our academic institution. An academic supervisor at the college led this group. At the time, there were six students in the group, all at different sites in the local area. Currently, the five of us that remain of that original group (one moved out of the area) are each relatively settled into work in music or expressive therapy. In reflecting on our development from a group led by an academic supervisor to an independent one co-led by peers, we found several stages to our process. A model describing our growth from a "learning space" through a "transitioning space" and into a "containing space" is presented at the end of this chapter.

As students in the mental health profession we are introduced to supervision in both group and individual formats. If we are fortunate, our supervisors become containers, mentors, and guides for us as we begin to explore the world of the therapist. Together in a group, or as individuals, we develop relationships with our supervisors that will hopefully encourage our healthy development into full-fledged therapists. At times we run to the supervisor for support, guidance, understanding, and nurturing; at other times we strain against her as the adolescent pulls away from her parents, testing her wings but needing solid roots.

As a group of second-year interns, we were very fortunate to have a dedicated academic supervisor. Demonstrating faith in the arts process, in the group process, and in the strengths of the individual group members, our supervisor moved with us through the stages of the internship process. As students, this learning space had certain qualities that formed a part of our value system as new therapists: it was playful, safe enough, explorative, nurturing, and challenging. Our compatibility as a group is important to recognize here: over our nine months together as interns, strong bonds of respect and trust were nurtured in the space provided for us. When it came time to stretch our wings and fly from the nest, we decided to find a way to maintain our supervision group. The arts had become, over the course of our training, a means of self-care and nurturing which we wanted to take with us beyond the academic environment. By making art together we found the strength of the creative process becoming more available to us, and we wanted to use this principle in a peer supervision group. The stress of termination from our teacher was eased somewhat by the knowledge that we would remain together as we moved out into the work force.

It has now been nine months since our graduation. We are new professionals who have helped each other through a difficult transition period; we now look back with appreciation at our journey together to this point. It is difficult to find resources on the topic of peer supervision for new professionals, and we offer what we can in this chapter to help those searching for such information. We hope the peer supervision group in the making will find something of value within these pages.

In this chapter we present our experience of how a peer supervision group can be used to help during the transition from student to professional. We discuss our understanding of what peer supervision is and why we feel peer supervision is so valuable to the new professional. The technical aspects of running a peer supervision group are also explored, with the intent of giving the readers some practical suggestions to facilitate the development of their own format. Such concepts as finding an appropriate meeting space, setting up a schedule, structuring time, and understanding boundaries within the meetings are presented. How we share leadership roles and have assumed personal and group responsibility for the continuation of a healthy supervision process is outlined. The integral role of music and the arts in the supervision process for both continued professional and personal insight as well as self-care is demonstrated in the examples provided. Finally, we discuss our three-stage model of peer supervision group development as defined through our experience.

What Is Peer Supervision?

We use the word "supervision" as it has come to be understood in the mental health field to date. Supervision is usually understood to be ". . . the process by which therapists receive support and guidance in order to ensure that they are addressing the needs of the clients" (Edwards, 1993, pp. 216–217). This is perhaps a good basic definition but one which does not convey the holistic functioning of our group. The use of the word supervision generally implies a person in the position of supervisor. In our use of the word, we "supervise," or support and guide *each other,* we have no single overseer, but maintain shared responsibility for the well-being of our group. This shared responsibility comes about because we are a peer group. According to Webster, a peer is "one that is of equal standing with another: one belonging to the same social group"—or in our case the same professional group (Webster, 1987, p. 867). As a peer supervision group our role has been to listen, examine, discuss and share mutual problems of therapy to help each other cope with professional difficulties (Feingold, 1968, p. 517). Over the past year and a half we have come together from the world of the student into the world of the professional music or expressive therapist.

Coming through this transition evokes Webster's second definition of "peer"; "to look narrowly or curiously; to look searchingly at something difficult to discern; to come slightly into view; emerge partly" (Webster, 1987, p. 867). This image is most descriptive of our journey together to this point. Peering around metaphorical bends in the road, turning the search inward to the group and to ourselves as individuals, we have worked together. Whether we have been supporting, challenging, holding, or creating music or art with each other, all of the work has taken us forward into the realm of professional. With each corner we turn, the importance of what we are doing, as a group, has become more evident.

Why Have Peer Supervision?

Toward the end of the final semester in our music and expressive therapies graduate program, group members began to feel anxious, to varying degrees. The anxiety sprang from the realization that within a short time we would each be finished with our training and "out there" on our own. With this came the expectation that we would each obtain a position in our field. Finishing school meant disconnecting from a strong creative arts community, leaving the support and understanding we received around this work. We also experienced the loss of a physical space, which had connected us emotionally to each other and the work. More specifically, it meant losing an academic supervisor and a group that had sustained us emotionally and creatively for nine months. This realization occurred concurrently with the beginning of the termination phase with clients and staff at our internship sites. The upcoming losses felt overwhelming. Our group supervision experience had been, for many of us, the core support while juggling classes and internship. It was a place to explore clinical issues, music and arts therapies questions and processes, internship culture and politics, and finally the task of initiating our search for work in the field.

When our group began to explore termination issues at our sites, from our school and from our academic supervisor, the idea of continuing to meet as a group quickly caught on. The six-member supervision group was a piece of this creative arts community that we could choose to hold on to. During the last weeks of the school semester we each agreed to commit to our group, although one member was intending to leave the area within a couple of months. Our commitment helped to decrease the anxiety each of us felt about all of the endings that we were experiencing. Still, we would be without the strong teacher who had gently guided us each week. To clarify for ourselves how our supervision group might continue beyond school, without such a leader, we each agreed to try to articulate just what we wanted from this group. We met for dinner having each considered our own answers to the question "Why have a peer supervision group?"

Initially our supervision group's main purpose was to continue the work we had started together as students: exploration of our strengths and weaknesses, countertransference, growth and general struggles as therapists using music and the arts in that exploratory process. To stay connected in this way meant to stay connected to a creative community, albeit a much smaller one. Over time, the reasons to meet grew, due partially to our transition from student to professional and partially from the deepening relationships between us as group members. One of the many important ideas we had internalized as students was to make time for self-nurturing activities. Neglecting self-care, we understood, might lead to feelings of isolation, feeling overwhelmed, or being dissatisfied with one's work. At peer supervision, we gather to receive support and understanding, along with letting go and allowing ourselves to freely engage in the arts—to play music, to make art, and to move. It gives us a structured way to keep alive the creativity that was ignited in our music and expressive therapies training program. Our biweekly meetings have proven to be a grounding experience. Peer supervision has become a rich resource—a place to regroup and put things into perspective.

Speaking a shared language has become a very important aspect of our group. It is often the experience of music therapists and expressive arts therapists that other mental health professionals we encounter can misunderstand the work we do. This can occur for a variety of reasons. First, because of the relatively short history of the formalized profession, being a music or expressive therapist is simply not as common as being a mental health worker or a social worker. There are fewer of us employed in the helping field. Second, a general familiarity with projective assessments has lead many people to connect music and expressive therapies to interpretation. Third, the difficulty that many arts therapists have in conveying what it is we do in clinical language can lead to confusion to some degree. This confusion may reinforce mistaken assumptions on the part of some mental health professionals. For example, there is the stereotype that expressive work leaves clients vulnerable and without adequate containment. The fact that a range of expressive interventions can be used toward a range of clinical goals—including containment itself—is not always understood. For all of these reasons, we are often faced with a feeling that we have to prove ourselves. Additionally, we may find ourselves the single music or expressive therapist at a site, and may feel the burden of representing an entire field. Peer supervision provides a "homeland" for our own terminology; on returning to the group our guard can drop, we can speak of intermodal transfers or the creative process and know that we are respected for our experience and understood.

The transition from student to professional is a struggle and a process that our peer supervision group is continually exploring, both verbally and through arts processes as will be described below. There is the letting go of the student role, with both its benefits and its drawbacks. As students at our internship sites we did not bear the full weight of responsibility regarding every aspect of our work (from paperwork to clinical matters). This was experienced partially as protection from the reality of working full-time with difficult populations. We tended to receive extra support and understanding from staff in our roles as student interns. Along with the internship support on-site, there was also the support one received at school. With these benefits, however, there are a few very real disadvantages to being a student. Most obviously, you don't get compensated for the work you are doing. It might also be your experience that you are not fully treated as part of the staff or that your ideas, feelings, and clinical input are not respected. These scenarios can make for a very difficult work environment, especially for those using music or other expressive modalities.

In moving from student to professional how and when do these situations resolve themselves? Our group's experience has varied with each individual. The work load, responsibilities, and pressures certainly increase as a hired professional, which leads to feeling like a "real" music or expressive therapist. Yet when we return to the group, oftentimes there is a sense that we are still students very new and inexperienced. Whether we are struggling with understaffing, site politics, or clinical matters, our group has become a place where it is okay to feel insecure in the new role, whereas in the workplace we may not wish to reveal this part of ourselves so freely.

One important function of our peer supervision group is that it has helped us articulate our individual values regarding this work. As a student, one's supervisor guides one around values and/or ethical issues. In fact, the supervisor ultimately held the responsibility in terms of ethical dilemmas. Moving into a professional role, one begins to form one's own value system around therapeutic work. The peer supervision group has become a forum to discuss our values as music and expressive therapists. It reconnects us to these values when we feel discouraged by the challenges of our clients, our sites, and the mental health field as a whole.

Logistics

Among our first tasks in continuing our peer supervision group was to establish the criteria for an appropriate meeting space. Since we had agreed that the arts should continue to be an integral part of our meetings, the space needed to be large enough to accommodate creative movement activities and activities that would involve visual arts. Moreover, it would also need to be suited for music-making experiences. Perhaps of greatest significance was that we locate a safe space that would allow us to explore supervision issues and creative processes without the risk of being interrupted, breaking confidentiality, or interrupting others within the vicinity of our meeting place. Finally, the logistics of the location was another important factor to consider. Our meetings would need to take place at a location that was within reasonable traveling distance for all group members.

Once the requirements for a meeting place were determined, we began to explore potential locations. During initial discussions, the idea of meeting at someone's home was quickly ruled out. This was primarily due to a lack of space that could accommodate our needs. Also, it seemed necessary to find a more neutral space that would be less subject to the possible distractions that could be presented by meeting at someone's home. Eventually, we found a workable space at a local academic institution, where we began to meet.

Initially, meetings were scheduled on a weekly basis for two and a half hours. However, as our meetings progressed over time, our primary wish to have full meetings, with all five of us present, ultimately resulted in a biweekly schedule. Meetings are always on the same day of the week, and at the same evening time, but we are somewhat flexible week to week. We may shift by a week, for example, to accommodate individual schedules so that we can achieve full participation. Perhaps most important to our ability to maintain consistency, given the flexibility in our meeting schedule, is our commitment to meeting with each other. We all have a strong desire to be a part of this group and share a common respect and admiration for the sacred space we create together. We realize the value and importance of maintaining our supervision group, and have come to look forward to the cleansing and revitalizing that each of us experience as a result of our meetings. Without this shared commitment and strong belief we have entrusted to this process, the group would likely deteriorate and eventually dissolve as a whole.

Structure of Meetings

Since our meeting time was limited, the focus of our first few meetings was to decide how to best structure our time. Reflecting upon our supervision experience as graduate students, we were able to identify several areas that seemed critical to creating safety and boundaries while nurturing openness in our group. A discussion of these areas will be elaborated further in the following sections.

"Check-In" Time

Our individual transitions from graduate student to professional and the challenges that ensued seemed destined to become a key area of focus during initial meetings. Many group members were struggling with financial insecurities and searching for a job. Even those able to secure jobs immediately after finishing school struggled with the notion of now being a professional. As professionals, concerns were shared over the ability to handle certain clinical situations while feeling somewhat isolated without the support of a graduate program. The intensity of our life changes, it seemed to us, demanded that we structure time within every meeting to allow each group member to "check in" with the group and to report the present status of their professional lives. This check-in period has served as a valuable means for allowing group members to process where they are in their professional lives, and also receive support from other group members.

Due to time constraints, it was necessary to provide some containment around the process of check-in. Although we were opposed to assigning group members a specified duration of time, it seemed reasonable for each member to make efforts to be aware of time during our check-ins. To help concretize the awareness of the time passing during our check-ins, we created a "talking stick" during our first arts activity as a peer group. The talking stick serves as a way to help focus during check-in time. Each individual would maintain possession of the talking stick during their check-in time, and would pass it to another group member when finished. Holding this ritual object, which we had all participated in creating, seemed to enhance our awareness of and respect for time. As a result, it served to help us contain our individual issues within the given structure.

Since authenticity was a critical factor in the original development of the group, personal issues and feelings were an important part of the process. While no subject matter was off limits during check-in time, our prior experience with using this type of format in graduate school had provided a shared understanding of its ground rules. Even in difficult circumstances members remain aware of the groups boundaries; we are careful to maintain the group as a supervision group rather than a therapy group.

While having some containment around check-ins is necessary, it has always seemed important to have flexibility within this structure. In some instances, it seems important to allow group members additional time to process difficult issues and emotions. Periodically, the subject matter of an individual's check-in lends itself to further exploration and discussion during the remainder of the session's time. This is especially true in cases where several group members can relate to an issue raised during an individual's check-in time. These tend to be issues in the professional realm, and further processing has been invaluable in addressing (and sometimes resolving) difficulties for an individual, as well as providing insight for the group as a whole. We each bring different strengths to the many challenges of our work, and this process has deepened our appreciation of each other, in all of those differences.

Leadership

During our graduate training experience, supervision meetings were often focused around subject matter and activities brought forth by a group leader. As a student group, our academic supervisor always took on this responsibility. In our experience, the group leader helped provide containment around the group's experience as a whole, and provided direction that helped us to gain insight into specific areas of clinical practice and our experiences at internship sites. Moreover, the academic supervisor helped facilitate the group's development and maintained a sense of safety within the group, allowing us to bond and develop as individuals.

Since the role of a leader was so valuable to the group in terms of organizing the focus and direction of each session, it seemed sensible to continue having some form of a group leader. Rather than assigning this responsibility to any one individual, it was divided among all members of the group. Within this model, a different group member assumes the leadership role for each meeting by setting forth the agenda or focus of the meeting. The designated group leader may structure this time however they choose. In our experience, this has involved such things as arts-based explorations of clinical issues, sharing clinical applications of music therapy or expressive therapy, case presentations, and simply exploring the arts as a way of nurturing our creative beings. It is important to note that within our supervision group, a group leader is never pressured into determining the agenda for a meeting. Although the role of the leader was maintained to help focus the direction of our meetings, it is not meant to be a burden to the prospective leader of a session. Therefore, the designated leader of a meeting only provides the session's agenda if they are able to identify an area of focus within the time that their schedule will allow. In the event that the leader does not have an agenda, the group determines the focus of a session as a collective unit. The leadership role has rotated through the group in an unstructured way on a volunteer basis. The person that volunteers to lead the next group takes the "talking stick" home with them until the group next meets. In this way, as in check-in, there is a certain sense of "holding the space" for the group. As it happens, even though the process is voluntary, leadership seems quite evenly spread among the five of us.

More recently, the group has been exploring other means for determining the agenda or focus of meetings. At the present time, the group generally decides upon the agenda for a meeting prior to the next scheduled time, rather than assigning this responsibility to a single member. Once an area of focus has been identified, the group negotiates how the agenda will be brought forth in the next meeting. Ultimately, either someone will volunteer to take responsibility for the upcoming agenda, or it is shared between several members or the group as a whole. In our experience, we have found both of these approaches to be effective in organizing the focus of meeting time.

Meeting Agenda

Once the group has completed its check-in process, the remaining session time can be structured in diverse ways. Among some of the areas that are frequented most often are clinical applications of music therapy and expressive arts therapy, and formal and informal case presentations. The group may process issues that are raised within each of these areas either verbally or creatively. Music and the expressive arts have remained an important part of the group's process and are generally used to either help gain further insight into specific issues or subjects, or simply for the sake of nurturing our creative selves. The following sections will further explain how these areas are explored within the context of group meetings.

In our meetings, clinical applications of music therapy and expressive therapy are generally explored in an informal manner. Typically, group members will describe aspects of their work that may highlight a way in which they are using music or the creative arts to address specific clinical issues/conflicts that may arise within a session. Oftentimes this may involve sharing specific interventions and creative activities used to help facilitate a therapeutic process. For example, a group member working with children that have special needs may describe how they are using music to help enhance their social skills and communication. While clinical applications are usually shared through verbal processing, group members will sometimes use the creative arts to help enhance or clarify the way in which an intervention or approach was used (i.e., sharing a specific song, or actual materials used on-site). Since not all members of our group work with the same population, this usually presents a valuable opportunity for group members to expand their knowledge and understanding of how music therapy and expressive therapy are used within different settings.

As a group, we treat clients with major mental illness, with developmental delays, with severe physical disabilities, medically compromised children, and clients struggling with terminal illness and with addiction. Our sites range from residential schools and treatment centers to day treatment facilities. It is remarkable to note that, given this variety, we feel both met in our own work, and able to offer each other support and insight. Our common use of music and expressive arts therapies is an overarching and powerful bond. Even when some of our work lies outside of these modalities, our perspective on treatment is shaped by our dedication to them.

Periodically, case presentations are used to provide the group with further insight into the clinical work being done by an individual group member. In addition, it also provides the clinician presenting the case with the opportunity to receive the group's commentary, which in some cases is invaluable to the future direction of treatment. Again, case presentations may allow group members the opportunity to gain valuable insight into client populations and treatment approaches that may be different from their experience. Within this structure, individuals have presented cases in both a formal and informal manner. A formal case presentation usually entails presenting a detailed description of the client's history, the presenting problem or issue, the current treatment approach, and the challenges that exist within the therapy itself. An informal case presentation may consist of a scaled-down version of the formal presentation, or might be focused on one specific session or interaction that occurred within the treatment process. In either case, time is generally allowed for the group to discuss the materials presented and provide suggestions for specific interventions when appropriate. Although our case presentations have been based in verbal processing thus far, we have discussed methods of bringing the arts into this process as well. Some of these possibilities may include the use of role-playing to "act out" specific interventions or therapeutic moments. Audio or video recordings from sessions would help exemplify how the arts were actually used within the specific case being presented. Finally, creating art or music in response to a specific case is another way of incorporating the arts into this process. It is our belief that by utilizing the arts, we may be able to gain valuable insight into our work that might otherwise not be realized through verbal processing alone. As a result, this will continue to be an area of exploration in future group meetings.

While the use of music and other expressive arts has not yet become an active part of case presentations, they are incorporated into many other aspects of our meetings. In our experience, we have found that the arts can be extremely valuable in providing further exploration of issues related to clinical practice. An example of how this has worked within our group is a music-based process that was used to explore issues around our entrance into new professional environments. At the time, many of us were engaged in starting new jobs and dealing with issues related to being the "new" professional within an already existing system. By using this experiential, we were able to gain new insight into previously unconscious patterns associated with the transition from being an outsider to an insider within the workplace.

Ten- and twelve-inch frame drums with mallets were given to all but one member. The member without a drum was the "outsider," or new therapist entering the workplace. The members with the drums were the established "insiders." Each participant took on the role of both outsider and insider. No words were used, and the main expressive tools were the drums, bodily movement, and vocalization.

In some cases the insiders' drums were used physically to create boundaries around that group. At other times the volume of the instruments was raised and lowered like a metaphoric barrier. Some insiders used the instrument to provide outreach toward the outsider. In some instances this resulted in two or more participants improvising on a single drum. In another instance an insider gave a drum to an outsider temporarily, then snatched it back.

Participants enacting the outsider role used physical gestures or vocalizations as representations of their personal styles of seeking contact with the group. One member chose to carry a chair around to place it in the middle of the insider group. This represented one way of entering the established professional system. Another outsider was noted to pace around the group, apparently studying it before approaching with smiles and handshakes.

In discussing this process afterward it was generally felt to have allowed members to express some anxieties as well as strengths regarding the entry into the workplace. For some of us the experiential process brought to consciousness skills and abilities used in other settings, which could be adapted to this transition.

Another example of how we have used the arts to gain insight into clinical issues, and their impact on us as clinicians, is an art-based exploration that we used on the theme of "hope and hopelessness" in dealing with clients with major mental illness. This experiential arose out of a case presentation involving a particularly frustrating client. We first did a group mandala painting on a circular board. In this painting, one image was particularly evocative—of water which either filled or flowed out of a container, depending on the orientation of the painting (which, being circular, had no "correct" orientation). This image led us through an intermodal transfer to a group poem created on a blackboard. This poem affirmed our hope amid the feelings of hopelessness, and the ebb and flow of these feelings.

The jug of hopelessness
empty   expansive   karma
motion, fluid, swirling
and I think
Is there any hope at all?

The space to grow
Washing, raining, washing
Looking deeply into
Faces emerge from the storm
I feel cleansed

10/10/99

Perhaps as important as our use of arts to address specific clinical issues is our use of the arts freely for self-expression. As with any area of skill that is developed over time, our ability to remain creative is dependent on our commitment to the exercise of our creative minds. Since our field and our effectiveness as clinicians relies so heavily on our ability to be creative, it is our ethical responsibility to maintain the creative abilities we have established within ourselves. By engaging in creative play, we are also able to maintain our belief in the power that lies within the use of the creative arts. In a sense, our own experience within the process of creative play is healing and helps foster our ability remain creative. In doing so, we are then allowing ourselves the ability to continue using the creative arts to effectively aid others in achieving their own therapeutic growth (Rogers, 1993, p. 13). Although it is also beneficial to explore the creative arts on our own free time, there is a certain dynamic quality that is lost outside of the group setting. Within the group, the unique dynamics presented by each individual helps shape the creative process as a whole, providing us with a different perspective and understanding of the creative process. Based on this belief, we try to allow ourselves at least some time to explore the creative arts freely within our meetings.

An important practice that has helped ensure the success of our meetings has been our ability to analyze and discuss the current status and functioning of the group. Periodically, the group creates time to discuss possible structures or topics that might be valuable for future exploration. Oftentimes, these discussions will allow group members the opportunity to identify areas of focus that they believe are receiving too much or too little attention. It may give group members an opportunity to present new ideas for structuring the time of future sessions. For example, in a recent meeting one group member observed that we had not been allowing any time for free creative play during our last several meetings. As a result, we agreed to restructure the group's time so that future sessions would once more allow for this important element of our meetings. By committing to the maintenance of the group and communicating with each other about our individual needs, we are able to ensure that our working space remains valuable and resourceful to all members of the group.

Our Model of Peer Supervision

As we noted in the introduction, our learning space as students was playful, safe enough, explorative, nurturing, and challenging. It provided us with a grounding in the use of creative processes—both our own and our clients. Making art together had provided us each with personal insights regarding our involvement in our profession, and we wished to continue learning from these explorations. Our peer group was formed in the hopes that we could nourish each other in our common commitment to music therapy and expressive therapy.

In the development of our own group, beyond the school setting, we have identified three "spaces." While not entirely sequential in a discrete way, these stages together may represent something of a fluid model of peer supervision for those students emerging from a training program in music or expressive therapies into the mental health profession.

Return to the Learning Space

The group has integrated the qualities of the learning space by moving through the graduate school experience and emerging as new professional music and expressive therapists. When we meet for peer supervision we have discovered that we can consciously return to the nourishing arts-based learning space. We regain feelings of support, safety, nourishment, and refreshment by revisiting the space of our earlier creative work together. We often experience a mood of having "come home" since the internalized learning space is triggered by our coming together in an arts-based environment.

As new professionals we had our peer group available to help us stay grounded during the transition into clinical work. As a peer group we have a place to return to from our individual work environments where we can share our insecurities and successes. While some of our members work with other music or expressive therapists, others of us do not. As new professionals we often find ourselves asking many questions about the uses of music and the arts within our particular work settings. In our peer group we can regain access to the original inquiring, playful learning space in order to find some of our own answers.

Transitioning Space

The transitioning space was defined by the act of completing our graduate program, and seeking entry into the professional world as music or expressive therapists. The essential pattern of change within this space was from the role of students, reliant upon our teachers and supervisors, to the role of professional therapists, responsible for our own work. We emerged as individual clinicians from our group training able to make functional work alliances beyond the original learning environment. Some group members found themselves feeling quite vulnerable "out there" interacting as a new clinician with groups of other, more experienced professionals. At various times we all found ourselves saying "I don't know what I'm doing."

The transitioning space was marked by a quality of individual activity outside the peer group, and then return to the relative safety of the group environment. In this space members made emotional bonds around searching for work, saying yes and no to various employment prospects, and quitting new, but perhaps inappropriate, jobs. We built connections through our common struggles as graduates seeking a place in the professional world. As a group, we gave each other permission to be present together within the difficult transitional space. It was this attitude of the peer group that constituted a return to our internalized learning space. The ability to revisit the mood of the learning space during this period of turbulence and difficult change enabled us to adapt flexibly to our new roles. We had to learn how to depend upon our own resources, each of us individually at our own clinical work sites. However, the group ability to reconstitute the original learning space strengthened the foundations of those early experiences in each of the group members. It is in part this foundation within each individual member that allows us to engage with the world of professional work with clear clinical values and realistic expectations of what music and expressive arts therapies can provide to our clients.

Containing Space

In our development as a peer supervision group we are currently located in a containing space. This space is defined by the mix of our individualizing professional identities and personalities. Because we have internalized the learning space of common values and power equivalency, we can provide each other with supervision, feedback, and problem solving. We can meet with feelings of safety, equality, and balance as well as an honest respect for all of the different strengths we bring to the work. There is a common commitment—a choice to remain involved in the group. We are able to delineate boundaries, make choices about group goals, and create our own structures based on the conscious perception of group needs. As professionals we have become self-contained, where as students we required external containment. We are members of a developing field that is gradually gaining recognition among other professional clinicians. When we are together, we form a creative arts community of people who have similar experiences in the work world. The peer group provides us a place to bring concerns best answered by other music or expressive therapists. "Inside" the peer group we can get away from the work site and find support for a professional identity as an expressive therapist, which may not be validated "outside."

Conclusion

In the "return to the learning space," we ground in the ways we were held during our internship year, in our teacher-led supervision group. We create a consistent container: we find a place and time to meet, we find an agreeable way to structure our time together, we share leadership, we use check-ins. In the "transition space," we begin to move out into the world of our professional lives, returning to touch base with our peers, but bringing the ever-increasing challenges of our work, now independent of the structures that an academic institution provides. Our check-ins may now provide jumping-off points for further discussion. We provide each other firm support for many painful moments en route to a satisfying job. We use the arts to explore our own ways of being in a professional environment. We present each other with our case material, with stories of burned-out coworkers, with our confusion and our joy in working with clients. Finally, in our current "containing space," we find that we are beginning to have a more cohesive sense of our own work experience, partly as a function of having had the opportunity for peer supervision. We are reaping the benefits of our work together. We find validation in our group, and a place to continue to build confidence and repertoire, and to find support and reliable feedback. We find re-connection to the arts in the midst of our busy lives, we find re-affirmation of the depth of expressive work. We find humor, compassion, and strength in each other. Out of our stories and our art, out of the sharing of both our challenges and our successes, we have built a container that grows both fuller and firmer with each meeting.

It was evident as we discussed the writing of this article that our excitement in reviewing our history was both personally affirming and had value for the community of emerging music and expressive arts therapists. Our exploration provided important feedback and increased clarity concerning why we have each stayed so committed to "showing up" for group. Music and expressive therapists should be strongly encouraged to make the effort to create peer supervision groups as they emerge from school. Especially during that critical transition, the benefits of such a group for members of our field are potentially enormous.

References

Edwards, D. (1993). Learning about feelings: The role of supervision in art therapy training. *The Arts in Psychotherapy*, 20, 213–222.

Feingold, A. (1994). *Peer Supervision and HIV: One Groups Process*. Washington, DC: APA Press, Inc.

Mish, F. C. (ed.). (1987). *Webster's Ninth New Collegiate Dictionary*. Springfield, MA: Merriam-Webster Inc.

Rogers, N. (1993). *The Creative Connection*. New York: Behavior Books, Inc.

Acknowledgments

Among their many wonderful supervisors, the authors would especially like to thank Trudy Shulman-Fagen, in whose group (during the second year at Lesley University Graduate School of Arts and Social Sciences) and under whose wing they began their journey together as peers in supervision. Trudy's commitment to the supervisory process was joyful, intelligent, and wholehearted.

Chapter 13

The Journey of Two:
Supervision for the New Music Therapist
Working in an Educational Setting

Dorit Amir, DA, ACMT
Professor, Head of Music Therapy
Bar Ilan University, Israel

Introduction

In Israel, the two main employers of music therapists are the government offices of education and health. Most music therapists whom I supervise work within the school system (regular and special education); some work within the health system (state, city and private medical and psychiatric hospitals, centers and institutions). Usually, music therapists take private supervision and pay for it themselves. Recently the situation has been changing, and there are more workplaces that pay for supervision and/or give supervision by one of its staff members.

In the past year, it has become clear that music therapists have to be registered by the ministry of health in order to be able to get jobs. As of now (2000), the registration goes according to the professional scale of the Israeli Association of the Creative and Expressive Therapies (I.C.E.T.). Therefore, I would like to devote a paragraph explaining the requirements of the association. The I.C.E.T. has a developmental scale of four professional stages: stagiaire (a new music therapist who just started working as a professional music therapist), regular member, registered member, and registered supervisor. Supervision hours are mandatory in order to advance from one stage to another. A stagiaire has to work 2,000 hours and to get 200 hours of supervision (at least 100 hours from a music therapist) in order to become a regular member.[1] A regular member has to work an additional 1,000 hours and get 100 hours of supervision (at least 50 hours from a music therapist), if they want to move on to be a registered member. A registered member who wants to supervise music therapists has to take fifty hours of supervision on supervision (at least twenty-five hours from a music therapist) during two years in order to become a registered supervisor. Supervision hours at all stages need to be taken from a psychologist who is a registered supervisor *and* a music therapist who is a registered supervisor.

My supervision practice consists of three kinds of supervision: Individual and group supervision (for students, new and advanced music therapists) and supervision on supervision for advanced music therapists who want to become supervisors. In this chapter I focus on individual supervision for the new music therapist who works

---

[1] According to the national association, a stagiaire is not allowed to work privately.

within the educational setting. By new music therapists I mean supervisees who have been working in the field for less than four years. Special attention is given to the very new music therapist who just graduated from a music therapy program.

Supervision Approaches

Alonso (1985, in Kron, 1994) divides supervision of psychotherapy into three categories: cognitive-didactic approaches; approaches that are based on the experience of personal-emotional growth; and approaches that emphasize the interpersonal process that is based on empathic connection. Grinberg (1990) divides supervision into approaches that are based on the client and approaches that are based on the supervisee. I find myself moving from one approach to another according to my supervisee's needs, stage of professional development and maturity as a person and according to my own inner intuitions and feelings. I can be didactic and deal with the issues that are brought up cognitively, I can focus on the supervisee's feelings and explore them with him, I can share with him my own feelings, images, and sensations around his client, and I also bring up the relationship between he and I in case he is ready to see it and deal with it. There are times when I share with my supervisee my own personal experience from being a therapist, and at other times I share with him some things from my private, personal life. I try to use my whole self and pay attention and listen to my physiological, cognitive, emotional, intuitive, and spiritual areas.

For the beginning therapist, my supervision approach includes the following:

1. Giving primary, basic tools for the exploration and understanding of verbal and musical therapeutic techniques and activities; offering interpretations of clients' certain behaviors and musical material, suggesting technical means and procedures such as what to look for while observing the client, how to approach parents and what questions to ask them, how to prepare a child kid who comes to music therapy, and so on.
2. Dealing with the supervisee's feelings concerning the client, the therapeutic process, her own being, and intervening during treatment.
3. Dealing with the supervisee's feelings around her own private life that come up in the supervision process.[2]

The Beginning of the Journey

In general, I see my role as a supervisor consists of the following tasks: to give support and empathy; to contain the supervisee and make it a secure place for him; to give information, offer interpretations, suggestions, and ideas; to encourage the supervisee to create, shape, strengthen, and trust his "inner guide" (Casement, 1985)

---

[2] For a further discussion on points 2 and 3 see my article on musical and verbal interventions (Amir, 1999).

by encouraging him to give his own understanding, interpretations, suggestions, and ideas and by helping him see what he cannot see, so that he can find his blind spots and eventually become more aware of the phenomenon's many levels and layers.

At the beginning stage, I find that most of the supervision time needs to be devoted to technical, organizational, and staff problems. I need to listen empathetically, give a lot of support to the therapist, and share my knowledge and experience with him. My role at this crucial stage consists of several functions:

- To provide "first aid" and give specific advice concerning how to cope with these kinds of problems (what to do, how to get started, what to buy, where to buy, how to get donations, how to raise money, etc.).
- To allow and encourage ventilation and expression of feelings and release of emotions both verbally and musically (I wonder how you feel about it? Can you play it? What instruments can express your anger and frustration? What would you have liked to do right there and then that you couldn't?).
- To listen with empathy and to support the therapist in these difficulties ("Yes, this is a rough situation, no wonder you feel so frustrated and tired.").
- To encourage the therapist to describe the situation verbally and musically.
- To provide a safe environment so that the therapist can feel secure to release his feelings of frustration, anger, resentment, helplessness.
- To encourage the therapist to explore his ways of reacting to the situation (i.e., keeping it all to himself and becoming very tense, losing his patience and temper and becoming aggressive toward the principal, the teacher, and/or the kids, becoming completely paralyzed, etc.).
- To help the therapist explore the possible reasons for the teacher's (or someone else from the staff) behavior and to help him gain empathy for the teacher (teacher feels jealous and has a power struggle with the therapist, teacher needs to be in control of her class—after all, it is her class, it is the teacher's way of helping the "young" therapist by providing valuable information, etc.).
- To guide him in how to talk to the teacher/helper in order to gain the teacher's support and cooperation.
- To help him set boundaries and be clear concerning what role he wants the teacher to play in the group.

Common Issues at the Beginning of the Journey

Here I will talk about common issues that are brought to supervision from both "outside the therapy room" and from "inside the therapy room." In order to illustrate some of these issues, I will be using case vignettes later in the chapter.

The new music therapists, who just graduated from a training program, usually spend a few weeks or even months in searching for a job. (There are very few lucky ones who get hired in the same place where they did their internship.) Usually, they find several part-time jobs and start working in several places. It is the first time that they are working in the field without being under the warm umbrella of the training program. The new music therapists usually feel scared and confused, lonely and isolated, flooded with feelings, suffering from a lack of confidence, yet at the same time feeling excited and highly motivated as they start their beginning stage of professional development.

During the first few weeks of their work, the common issues that are brought to supervision are from "outside the therapy room." These issues have to do mainly with practical management of arranging the work space, getting oneself known among the staff members, understanding one's role of being a music therapist within the educational setting, and dealing with referrals and how to chose clients.

Practical Management of Arranging the Work Space

At their initial phase of working as professionals, music therapists most likely find out that in many of the placements there are poor conditions or no conditions, thus making it impossible to start clinical work right away. The new therapists have to put a lot of their time and energy in bureaucratic and management aspects of getting space and setting it up. Quite often the music therapist has to share a space with other professionals. That means that there are many things in the room that don't belong to music therapy and have to be taken into consideration while arranging the space and trying to make it as aesthetic and inviting as possible.

Many music therapists start working in a room that is available but not appropriate, while some have to move from one room to another according to what is available at the time. Many of them bring their own instruments because there aren't any in the place and there is no money to buy instruments. Very few places have pianos.

Getting Oneself Known Among the Staff Members

Usually it takes time until the staff members get to know the music therapist and understands that he is part of the professional team and not "just doing music with the kids." Most teachers do not know anything about music therapy and treat it as another class. Frequently I hear stories about teachers (or even the principal of the school) who come into the therapy room without asking permission or without even knocking on the door; teachers who decide to take the student for private tutoring exactly at the time of his music therapy session; teachers who don't inform the music therapist of field trips that will not have the child back in time for the session, etc. At the very beginning the therapist may find out that professional meetings happen without him being informed, and the same happens with parents' conferences.

Direct contact with parents is very often not allowed, and the therapist has to go through the main teacher or the social worker if he needs to contact the parents. The caseload is usually heavy. Sessions' length has to be adjusted according to the school's time schedule, sometimes with no flexibility at all. In some schools individual work is not allowed, and group work is usually expected to be with all of the class members which can mean up to twenty students at a time.

Understanding One's Role of Being a Music Therapist within the Educational Setting

In many schools, music therapists are being asked to conduct shows and performances with the pupils (clients) (see vignette 3). Music therapists have the same responsibilities as the teachers, such as keeping an eye on the children during recess outside, going with the children on trips, etc. Many music therapists feel confused about their role: Are shows and performances part of music therapy? Are these within my responsibility? Do I, the music therapist, have the same duties that other teachers have? How does my role as "recess monitor" go along with my role as a music therapist? What if such duties interfere with the intimate process of therapy and confuse not only me but also the children who are also my clients? Other issues have to do with where therapy should take place—in the classroom or in a different room? Is therapy confined to the music therapy room or can therapy take place in the school's playground in case the child does not want to come to the therapy room?

Referrals and How to Choose Clients

Another issue has to do with determining who to work with and how. In some schools, it is the school's psychologist or counselor's task to make these decisions and to refer children to the music therapist. Here the questions are not with whom to work but how to work with the children: As a group? In dyads? Individually? The problem gets more complicated when there are no referrals and the music therapist has to make these decisions himself. Usually, there are more children who need therapy than the therapist can take, and there is a need to choose.

Facing all or some of the common issues discussed above, the new therapist feels frustrated and discouraged. He feels completely lonely and isolated. At this crucial time, my main tasks as a supervisor are to contain the supervisee and make supervision a secure place for him. I try to do this by acknowledging his difficulties and by giving him support and empathy. I find it very important to encourage him by reminding him that these problems are common and that his feelings are very natural as a beginning professional who faces all or some of the above dilemmas. I also offer practical suggestions and ideas concerning the above issues, yet, at the same time, I encourage him to see if he can solve some of the problems and find creative solutions to specific situations. For example, I offer him some help in determining criteria concerning whom to work with; discuss with him ways of making this decision (i.e., observing the children in the classroom and in other places, talking to the teachers, etc.) and ask him what feels more comfortable for him and why.

Once there is a room to work in, instruments to play with, and children to work with, the new music therapist can start working. At this time, many of the issues that are brought to supervision are from "inside the therapy room." The following are some of the common issues.

Setting Boundaries

Many supervisees have problems with setting boundaries with their clients. Supervisees feel that setting up boundaries is an educational issue that makes them take the role of a teacher and look like the bad, strict teacher or a policeman and not like a therapist. They find themselves saying "no" to the child many times and thus creating a negative atmosphere. I try to convey to my supervisees my belief that setting boundaries is a necessary and integral part of therapy. Supervision on music therapy with children needs to address the fact that clinical work with children, unlike adults, includes educational aspects, setting up boundaries, and treating behavioral and discipline problems (Bixler, 1949; Reisman, 1980). These basics are part of the mirroring and interpretation in the process, but they are an integral part of understanding reality from the very fact that they set up a frame without which no therapy is possible (Arazi, 1994).

Boundary issues exist not only with clients, but with staff members as well. The new music therapist who works in an educational setting faces the dilemma of how to deal with staff members (teachers or aides) who stay during the session (sometimes because they have to) and feel free to intervene and interject comments regarding the student's performance, personal situations, as well as telling the therapist what to do, and how to deal with a specific student, etc. The supervisee is often confused about the role of the teacher or the class aide during the group music therapy session. Setting boundaries for the staff members can be much harder than with children. The supervisee experiences feelings of frustration and helplessness.

The main question, as I see it, is *how* to set up clear boundaries. I try to help the supervisee sort out and understand the nature of this difficulty, its external and internal sources, and to encourage him to look for verbal and musical ways to deal with boundaries, for both clients and staff members, in an efficient way that will enable the clients as well as staff members to cooperate in a useful way.

Feelings of Boredom

The supervisee reports that he feels bored and helpless. This happens a lot with supervisees who work with autistic children, children who are perseverative and exhibit a stereotyped behavior (the child does the same thing over and over again), or supervisees who work with very disturbed, depressed adolescents (see vignette 2). The supervisee tries to intervene, but whatever he tries to do does not work, and he does not know what to do. I find that musical improvisation on this title helps a lot in understanding what is going on. Is this countertransference? Is this projective identification (the therapist feels what the group or the client really feels)? Is this a cover for anger? Sadness? Feelings of helplessness? Another variation is that the therapist feels fine, but the child (or the group) tells him that he is bored (see vignette 1). The therapist is very surprised when this happens. He cannot understand how this can be. Some therapists feel angry and blame themselves for not being sensitive enough to their client, while others get angry at the client and blame him for being manipulative and competing with the therapist. I try to examine each situation from all angles so that we can understand the reason for this dichotomy.

"There Is no Music in the Room—Is This Music Therapy?"

This is a question I hear many times in supervision. As I already mentioned, in many educational settings, the music therapy room is shared by other professionals such as occupational therapists, physiotherapists, and art therapists and therefore there are lots of other types of equipment in the room. The supervisee complains that the child who comes into the room does not show any interest in the musical instruments but wants to do other, more stimulating things such as playing ball, or playing with other toys and games that are in the room. The question the supervisee brings to supervision is two-fold: How do I bring the child to the music? If the child does not want to play music, what is my role?

This is a complicated issue. The supervisee, especially the new therapist, feels frustrated and confused, stuck and helpless. For him, no music in a music therapy session means unclear professional identity and many times an indication of a failure. He has to compete with so many stimulating things in the room, and usually he is defeated. The child does not choose music, but other games. I find myself being empathic to the supervisee's feelings and giving him empathic reactions such as: yes, it is very difficult and frustrating to work in such a room.

At this point I try to lead the supervisee to see if there is a possibility to rearrange the room in a more suitable way: to put away or hide some of the games, to put a curtain that will divide the room and create a corner for music therapy, etc. Sometimes I will ask the supervisee to picture the room as he/she wants it to be in his imagination, and that by itself can create a shift in perception and feelings. It is a creative way to find solutions to rather complicated situations. On another level we may focus on the child and try to understand why the child is more interested in other things. We also focus on the supervisee. There are two common things that I see here: first, a narrow perception of what is defined as music—if there is no playing there is no music. Here we discuss ways of looking at things that are happening in the room in a musical way (i.e., rhythm, dynamics, speed, etc.) and try to find the music in the nonmusical activity. The second is a narrow perception of the role and function of the music therapist. Many of my supervisees feel that they should not be "too active," meaning they should not play if the child is not playing, but "be with the child." Here I share with them my belief that it is the supervisee's responsibility to bring the music into the room and one way of being with the child is to accompany his actions by playing music that will resonate with him. We discuss ways of bringing the music into the session—what kind of music to play, what instrument to use, etc.

The Format of the Supervision Session

The Supervision Room

I usually give supervision in my music room at home, where I also work with my clients and play music. It is a small and cozy room, with lots of instruments. There are two comfortable chairs in one corner of the room, facing each other, with a small table in between them. There is a tape recorder on the table that serves for listening and recording. The sitting corner creates a feeling of intimacy yet allows for some distance.

First Session

Here is where we both get the first impressions of each other. I want to get to know the supervisee and I start by asking him to give me the relevant professional information: Which program did you graduate from? Where did you do your internship and fieldwork? Where are you working now? What is your main instrument? Did you get supervision before? What kind? Then I proceed and ask him to tell me about himself. Whatever he wants to tell me about his personal life is okay with me. Sometimes I ask specific questions but I try to be sensitive to his boundaries and careful not to be intrusive. I ask him if he wants to ask me some questions about myself. The contract for supervision is then discussed and includes the following:

- Issues of payment, time duration, and frequency of the sessions. There are therapists who come once a week for a one-hour session, there are therapists who come once every two weeks for a one-hour session, there are therapists who come once a month for a two to three hour session, and there are therapists who come only when they feel they need a supervision session.
- Establishing the general focus of the supervision process: there are supervisees who want to devote the entire supervision process to one group. That means following the specific chosen group on a weekly basis and looking very closely at this specific group and examining it from its various aspects throughout its various developmental stages. There are other supervisees who want to bring something new for every session according to their here-and-now needs. Some want to focus mainly on the musical aspects of their work and others want to focus mainly on their countertransference issues with their clients.

Typical Session Format

Before the session I try to prepare myself both emotionally and content wise before my supervisee comes in. I read what I wrote in the last session and try to tune myself into the supervisee who is going to come now by sitting quietly for a few minutes before she comes.

A typical supervision session can be divided up to three stages: In Stage One I listen to the supervisee and try to sense and find out to which area the material belongs in. Here are a few examples:

- Inside the therapy room—understanding the client's music; understanding the therapist's music; understanding the musical relationship and the interpersonal dynamics between client and therapist; understanding the client's words in terms of content and shape, the obvious and the hidden, the external and the internal; understanding the therapist's verbal interventions in terms of timing, reasons for making the interventions, countertransference.

- Outside the therapy room—understanding the interpersonal dynamics in the workplace and the practical management in the workplace (Brown, 1997).
- Inside the supervision room—understanding the interpersonal dynamics in the supervision room (Brown, 1997): dealing with the relationship between me as the supervisor and the supervisee in the supervision.

In Stage Two once the area has been identified, I work with the supervisee on that area, musically or verbally or in combination of both. I use three main ways of working with the material:

- Listening to the recorded musical material that was brought by the supervisee and analyzing it according to the following parameters:
  - Client's choice of instruments and use of musical elements—client's rhythmic patterns, basic beat, melodic shape and feeling, time order, harmonic patterns, dynamics, speed, structure, repetitions, texture, use of pedal, physical use of the instrument, gestures, style of playing, intensity
  - Client's intrapersonal parameters—degree of organization, energy level, degree of motivation, degree of being active, sense of imagination, creativity, emotions, feelings, sensations
  - Therapist's musical interventions and reactions—the use of musical elements and instruments
  - Therapist's intrapersonal parameters—understanding where they come from: unconscious reactions (countertransference, own issues, projective identification); conscious reactions (musical modeling, the use of various techniques such as supporting, grounding, motivating, stimulating, etc.)
- Playing live music. Supervisee demonstrates his client's music by reconstructing the client's playing at the session through role-playing (I ask the supervisee to be the client, and to play and/or talk as the client); I ask the supervisee to play his feelings concerning the client (how do you feel about your client or other significant figures in the client's life); I ask the supervisee to play a musical portrait of the client (how you see your client, how you describe him/her musically); I can ask the supervisee to reconstruct his musical reactions; I might suggest exercising various musical responses; I might suggest that we play together and experience various musical techniques and activities.
- Talking about the case/the situation. The supervisee describes the situation (verbally or musically) and we talk about it and discuss interpretations and reflections; I ask questions, I talk about my inner feelings (what the description made me feel), I direct the supervisee to see his blind spots, I offer suggestions, guidance, and support. The supervisee asks and sometimes answers questions and deepens his understanding of the case/situation by verbally exploring the issues and getting insights. At times I refer the supervisee to the appropriate literature on a specific issue being discussed in the session.

In Stage Three I bring closure to the material being discussed and move to the next material. At this stage I ask the supervisee how does he feels and check if we can bring it to a closure or if there are still some aspects that feel unfinished and need to be dealt with now. At times I suggest to leave it as is, let time bring a new perspective on the matter, and continue to deal with it at another time in the supervision process.

After the supervision session, I sit a few minutes and reflect on my own reactions, explanations and interpretations, feelings and images that occurred during the session. I try to see if there are some unresolved issues that I need to focus on such as where I felt blocked and didn't find the right approach, why I had such intense feeling about the supervisee or about the client (Does he reminds me of someone?). Some of it I write down and at times I bring it to my own supervisor or discuss it with some of my colleagues.

Vignettes

Vignette 1

Linda,[3] a music therapist who has been working professionally for almost four years, comes to supervision and starts talking about Steve, her client. He is a six-year-old boy, who was referred to music therapy by the psychologist of the school, due to severe hostility and behavior problems such as physical violence toward his peers. He comes from a broken home. The father is drunk most of the time and the mother is a sick woman and does not function very well as a mother. He has two older brothers and one younger sister. Linda sees him individually in the music therapy room within his school. It is the third session and she says that she feels stuck with him. She tells me that he comes to the room, sits down, and declares that he is bored and that he doesn't have anything to do here. She offers him activities such as playing various instruments or writing a song, but he says no and does not want to participate in anything. It has been like this from the start. She keeps offering him things to do and he turns down everything she offers. I ask her how this makes her feel and she says that she feels frustrated and inadequate. She does not know how to reach him. I ask her to describe this boy and she describes him as a very sweet boy and that she really likes him and wants to work with him. She feels that if she gets over this barrier, they will be able to work together and she will be able to help him.

The way she talks about him makes me feel somewhat uncomfortable and I find myself wondering how she really feels about Steve right now. I suggest that she explore her feelings musically and she agrees. She goes to the piano and I ask her to close her eyes and to imagine Steve as he is in the music therapy room and then start to play. At the beginning her playing is very gentle at the middle part of the keyboard—both hands together. The right hand plays a melody and the left hand plays harmony in E minor, mezzo piano.

---

[3] All names have been changed to protect the supervisees' and the clients' privacy.

Then, she starts playing loud arpeggios with both hands up and down the keyboard and this becomes like a storm. The storm quiets down and the improvisation comes to an end. She immediately says: "Well, I guess I am angry at him. He doesn't let me work with him! He doesn't let me reach him! How can I work with him if he doesn't do anything in the room and turns down everything I offer him to do? I am trying so hard to connect with him but he doesn't seem to want my help." At this point Linda became quiet. She realized all of a sudden that she was working too hard in order to make a contact with him. This last sentence she said was the key to it all. She was able to see in a very clear manner that she was choking him with ideas.

I said that it seems to me that her way of trying to make contact with him was by being very busy on the realm of "doing"—offering him activities and making suggestions of what they can do together in the room—but she wasn't really tuning in to him and was not listening to his being. The piano improvisation brought to the surface her anger toward Steve, and by realizing it and talking about it in a more open and direct manner, she was able to get an insight concerning her way of trying to reach him, and why wasn't it working.

Then we tried to understand his being. Why was he so resistant to her? I suggested that maybe this was his way of testing her to see if he can trust her. Maybe he wanted to check out if she accepts him even if he behaves this way and makes her hurt, frustrated, and angry. Maybe the only way he learned that he could trust an adult is by giving him tests to see if he is strong enough to pass. Maybe the only way he knew how to make contact and get attention was by resisting and doing the opposite from what the adult wants.

We talked about ways to be empathic to him in order to be able to reach him. She suggested letting him be the way he is and reflecting his being on a small instrument; telling him that it must be so hard for him to trust other people and that she has the patience to wait till he is ready to do something; playing for him without asking him to participate, etc.

Linda wanted to explore more why was she intervening the way she did. I suggested exploring it via music, and asked her to play her "working too hard." She chose the bongos and the cymbal and played them in a very structured rhythm of eighth notes in a loud and clear manner. The rhythmic pattern was repeated over and over without a pause. I noticed that I felt very tense and was not breathing. I felt like I had no air and wanted to get out of the room so I can breath.

When she finished we were silent for a while. I asked her if she saw a connection between this experience and her own life. We then talked about how by keeping herself so busy she is running away from feelings. She does not stop and listen to herself. I suggested that she might want to further explore it in her own therapy. This experience helped Linda feel the intensity of her intervention and made her realized that this countertransferential intervention needed to be explored in depth in her therapy. By being aware of it she could now be more open to Steve's being and try out more subtle ways of making contact.

The music in this session was used twice. In the first time, the music brought out the hidden feelings. By experiencing them musically Linda could acknowledge them verbally, and it brought further realizations. In the second time, the music functioned as a sound amplifier: it gave sound to the theme and by that intensified and exaggerated the experience. Only after experiencing the feeling could we examine its relation to the supervisee's life.

Vignette 2

Dona is a music therapist who just finished her studies in music therapy and started to work in a school for disturbed adolescents. She gets psychological supervision from a clinical psychologist who works there and she comes for music therapy supervision once every two weeks. After telling me a little about herself she says that she wants to focus on the music within her therapy sessions.

She brings a tape with a recording of a first session with Eden, a fifteen-year-old male teenager who is very depressed. He hardly talks, and she describes him as apathetic and in his own world, without much contact to reality. When Dona asked him if he would like to explore the instruments in the room and make some sounds, he agreed to try. He chose several instruments: hand cymbals, several hand bells, castanets, Tibetan bells, a small drum, and a big cymbal on a stand. What we hear on the tape is the music he was making.

First I ask Dona to describe the musical structure and elements: she says that his music is very slow, the structure is one small sound after sound, very low dynamics. The use of each instrument is the same: one small sound, even on the big cymbal. Then, I ask Dona to tell me her impressions of the music. She says that when she hears it she feels heaviness, apathy, no life. She says that the music was created without enjoyment or spark of creativity.

I then asked her how she feels when she hears the music and she says that she feels helpless and bored. Eden is obviously very depressed, not into music, and she feels that it is going to be a waste of time. She says that this is how he has played every session from the beginning. I asked her if he seems to be bored and she said that she is not sure, and if yes, why does he keep coming to her for music therapy. (Therapy is not mandatory and this teenager, together with his psychologist, chose to come to music therapy.)

I asked her what she does when he plays and she said that she sits and listens to him. I asked her if she tried to play with him and she said no. She felt that she needed to respect his space and to accept him the way he is. I then asked her if she is willing to re-create the situation using live instruments and taking the role of the client. She agreed and she chose the same instruments as Eden and played them in the same way he played them. I asked her how she felt while doing it, and she said that she felt very depressed and empty.

By becoming the client and imitating his playing she was able to experience these feelings in a more intense way and that shifted the attention from herself to Eden's being. Then, I asked her to do this again and this time I took some of the same or similar instruments and played an echo to each sound she created. Even though it had the same quality of sound, it changed the improvisation. It wasn't so empty; it was a tiny bit more alive. Also, Dona realized that by me doing this with her it meant to her that I was with her, there was some kind of a connection between us. Dona said that the fact that I was with her and did not change any of the musical elements made her feel supported by me.

Here I used modeling (by me being the therapist and Dona the client) and showed her a musical activity that she can use with Eden. Then we reversed roles and I became the client. We did the same thing and Dona explored different ways of responding to the sounds and being with her client. We also talked about the fact that he comes regularly to music therapy, accepts her suggestion to play music, makes choices concerning what instruments he wants, and uses all the instruments he chooses as signs of his healthy and alive parts. We tried to understand the meaning of his choices and we saw that he chose mainly small instruments (except for the big cymbal) and mostly metal ones (except for the castanets and the drum).

I suggested that maybe the fact that there was one big instrument and two wooden instruments are signs for good prognosis: right now he chooses mainly small instruments but there is an opening for a big one to be used differently.

I find that role-playing and modeling are very useful tools in my supervision. By being the client and acting like the client, Dona was able to shift the attention from herself and put her client in the center. These experiences made it possible for her to be more empathic to him and get a clearer picture not only of the way she perceived him, but also of what can she do in order to be with him musically.

Vignette 3

David is a twenty-four-year-old therapist who has been working almost two years in a special school for autistic children. The school's philosophy is based on behavior modification and each child has a chart with weekly points that he gets for "good behavior" and reduction of points for "bad behavior." David feels very frustrated because he hates this approach and does not know what to do. He has struggled with it since the beginning of his work. Also, the principal of the school expects him to conduct the end of the year performance, and to be in charge of the musical part of the holidays' celebrations. David does not get extra hours for these additional responsibilities and he needs to do rehearsals during therapy hours. Also, the principal wants David to create a choir and an orchestra in the school and to devote two hours weekly for rehearsals.

David has been coming to me for supervision every other week since he started to work in this school, and these were the issues that he brought to supervision. David feels frustrated and angry. He feels that the principal is very demanding and controlling and does not understand him and his work. David feels that he does not succeed in standing up for what he believes in. On the other hand, he enjoys working with the children and feels that his work is productive. Overall, he feels trapped and told me that since he cannot do his work properly, he is thinking of quitting his job.

During the first six months of supervision, I listened to David and acknowledged his difficulties with a lot of empathy. I said that it is hard to work in a place that forces you to be part of a philosophy that is quite opposite to your belief system. At this initial stage I let David ventilate his feelings and verbally release his frustrations and anger. At one time, when I suggested he try to release his anger musically, he refused and said that he is afraid that the sound will be so big and frightening that he won't be able to tolerate it. Together we tried to look for ways to deal with the situation, to see how can David be part of the system and go along with the school philosophy yet allow himself the freedom to work according to his own philosophy inside the therapy room.

We discussed what this solution requires from him and he said that he needs to be more flexible and try to see things not in just black and white, but in colors too. When I asked him if there is a price he has to pay for that kind of flexibility, he said that he needs to give up total control and this is hard for him. Also, he has to give up "being right" and being the only one who knows what is good.

I helped David to separate the various issues. We had discussions about performances, celebrations, choirs, and orchestras. Again, we found out that this had a lot to do with David's rigidity with what he feels is right and wrong, with how he sees his job description and what he believes is not part of his job. We talked about the therapeutic potential of performances in front of others, as well as its potential damage. We could slowly see together that with some of the kids it would be a wonderful thing to do, while with others it would be counterproductive. Slowly there started to be a shift in David's way of approaching things. He went from the general to the individual, starting to look at the uniqueness of each and every situation instead of going by his principles in a rigid way.

Only after this shift occurred, we could move to another, more personal area. All along the supervision process I suspected that the principal of the school represents a harsh father figure to David, and that David's reactions to him are transferential. I suggested doing a musical role-play, but David was still afraid of it, so we did verbal role-playing. I asked David to close his eyes, to see the principal and talk to him. When he did that, it became obvious to me and to him that he was talking to his father, who was a very harsh and dominant figure in David's life. In this role-play David told the principal that whenever he was talking to him he felt like a child— small, helpless, and hurt—and that he could not be himself. This realization opened the way for us to look at the transference, and to separate the two figures. David took this issue to his own therapy and in our supervision we were able to look at things with more clarity.

Later on, we added music to our sessions. David was willing to release his anger via making music. His piano improvisations started with anger, then became heavy and mellow. We could hear and see how much sadness there is beyond the anger. It was easier for David to get angry than sad in his life. However, exposing the sadness through the music gave way to acknowledge it and again, he could take it to his therapy and process it there.

David continued working in the school. He no longer thought of quitting his job. He started bringing other issues to supervision, issues from the therapy room. We continued to work on all levels now, the personal and the professional: understanding the child's music, actions, and behaviors; understanding David's reactions; analyzing the dynamics between him and the child in the therapy room and comparing it to the dynamics between him and me in the supervision room, or between him and another significant person in his life. We did that through words and music.

The Use of Music in Supervision

I always try to use music in my supervision session. I believe that this is crucial for supervision in music therapy. Music can serve many functions. In summary, the use of musical instruments gives the supervisee a chance to explore new ideas and to enrich himself with musical possibilities (Stephens, 1984); to experience the power of music in leading to insights and solutions and to understand the unique influence of the music on the therapeutic process (Stephens, 1984). It helps the supervisee develop musical intuition, encourages him to use the child within—the enthusiastic child, the child who is willing to try—and nurtures the free and open child within him. It also encourages the experiential learning, helps the supervisee to shape and strengthen his professional identity as a music therapist, stimulates the supervisee to develop his musical and professional skills (Frohne-Hagmann, 1998); creates a way to break through the block that the supervisee feels in the therapy process and to see other explanations, solutions, or ways; helps the supervisee to discover his own blind spots; can answer questions such as: How do I perceive the client? How do I feel about the client?; clears countertransferential issues and any projections the supervisee is making concerning the client (Frohne-Hagemann, 1998).

The use of recorded clinical material gives the possibility to listen again to the session and explore certain things; allows for a thorough analysis of the musical material of therapist and client; and allows for reflection and sheds light on certain things that the supervisee forgot.

Even though I always try to use music in my supervision sessions, it does not always happen. We could see in the example of David that for quite a long time he was not ready to use the music in supervision. I had to respect that and not to force it on him. It did open up a very crucial issue: If you are so scared of the music, how can you offer it to your clients? I also had to deal with my own reactions to David's resistance to use musical means, something that is hard for me not to use it when I see the potential of it in supervision.

Summary

There are supervisees who I love and adore. There are supervisees whose intellect I appreciate and others whose hard-working attitude, seriousness, and devotion to their clients I admire. There are supervisees who touch me very deeply and move me a lot, while others impress me with their growing understanding and the way they deal with difficulties and complications. There are supervisees with whom I find it very easy to bring more of my personal and intimate self, while with others I am more official and didactic. There are supervisees who press my buttons and usually succeed in making me angry, tense, frustrated, and helpless, and others with whom I feel at ease and at home. There are supervisees who look up to me, admire and even idealize me, while others see me as an equal and can argue and disagree with me. There are supervisees with whom I feel challenged and stimulated and others with whom I tend to get bored.

There are times when I stay very focused, completely in the here and now, and there are other times when I find myself drifting away. There are times when I find myself looking at my watch and wanting the hour to be over, and other times when the hour goes so fast that I find it hard to believe that the session is over. Sometimes I know exactly what to do and where to go with the material that comes up, and other times when I feel blocked and don't know how to approach the material. There are times when I feel that I work very hard (sometimes too hard) and other times when I feel that I didn't work at all.

As in therapy, I need to tune myself before the session. I remind myself that each supervisee is unique and I try to look for the things I like and appreciate in each and every one in order to create a positive and welcoming atmosphere. I need to tune myself during the session, to listen and try to understand what is going on in the session, and I need to stay a few minutes after the session, listen to myself, reflect and process my thoughts, feelings, and reactions. Supervision is a journey of two. It is like an improvised song: It creates itself in the here and now, out of material from the past. It starts from a specific title, word, or sentence, and travels to the unknown, that is based on the known.

References

Alonso, A. (1985). *The Quiet Profession: Supervision of Psychotherapy*. New York: MacMillian.

Amir, D. (1999). Musical and verbal interventions in music therapy: A qualitative study. *Journal of Music Therapy, 36*(2), 144–175.

Arazi, S. (1994). Supervision of psychotherapy of the child and his parents. In T. Kron and H. Yerushalmi (eds.), *Supervision of Psychotherapy*. Jerusalem: The Hebrew University, The Magnes Press.

Bixler, R. H. (1949). Limits are therapy. *Journal of Consulting Psychology,* 13 1–11.

Brown, S. (1997). Supervision in context: A balancing act. *British Journal of Music Therapy, 11*(1), 4–12.

Casement, P. (1985). *On Learning from the Patient*. London and New York: Tavistock Publications.

Frohne-Hagemann, I. (1998). *Integrative approaches to supervision for music therapists*. A paper presented at the 4th European congress for music therapy, Leuven, Belgium.

Grinberg, L. (1990). *The Goals of Psychoanalysis: Identification, Identity and Supervision*. London: Karnac Books.

Stephens, G. (1984). Group supervision in music therapy. *Music Therapy 4*(1), 29–38.

Reisman, J. M. (1980). Child psychotherapy. In A. K. Hess (ed.) *Psychotherapy Supervision*. New York: John Wiley & Sons.

Acknowledgments

I would like to acknowledge Professor Barbara Hesser for our stimulating dialogues on the subject over the years. I also want to acknowledge all my supervisees from whom I have learned so much about supervision.

Chapter 14

Experiential Music Therapy Group as a Method of Professional Supervision

Gillian Stephens Langdon, MA
Director of Creative Arts Therapies
Bronx Psychiatric Center, Bronx, NY

Introduction

It was with an urgency of purpose that I began my first music therapy group supervision in the late 1980s. As music therapists, I saw all of us seeking out social workers, psychologists, and other professionals outside of the music therapy field who had a great amount to offer us. Yet if music therapy was a special modality able to tap into unique aspects of our understanding, why shouldn't it also be used to help us untangle our own supervision puzzles?

Although it is no longer a new concept, I come to this topic with the same sense of mission today. The current world of the music therapist is rich and engaging as new knowledge of music and the brain is uncovered daily. The field of practice for the music therapist is also changing daily. Music therapists need support in designing innovative programs and navigating the systems of changeable institutions. One of the most important needs for support is in nurturing the way of thinking that allows us to move back and forth between words and music and, particularly, being able to nurture what can be called the "musical mind."

In this chapter we will look at how music therapy group supervision can nurture this musical mind and then see how the group can address needs and issues in the early stages of professional development (post internship) and later as mature professionals.

The Music

We are surrounded by ideas and words. As clinicians we are constantly being called upon to verbalize descriptions of musical events and regularly produce written records of our work. And yet, I'm sure most music therapists have struggled as I have in trying to explain to the treatment team a pivotal moment in a session only to find ourselves at a loss for words.

For a long while, I thought it was my inability to articulate what had occurred—or worse, that the event was not so important after all—that made me uncomfortable as I listened to the neatly verbalized group dynamics set forth by the psychologists, psychiatrists, and social workers where I worked. Yet when I co-led a group with one of these psychologists who was particularly articulate, I could see an interesting process in action. She had been playing music in the group and perceived the development of the group as she played. When it came time to report on the session in our supervision group she was unable to bring forth the words. She stopped in the middle saying, "This is really hard! Doing the switch to words." She had a vast clinical knowledge yet when she remembered the music therapy session it was with her musical mind. She had to work to cross over into her rich verbal realm.

Most of us need practice in this quick back and forth between immersion in music in our groups to the verbal and analytic mode. We need a forum where we can practice this and nurture both modes equally. It is interesting that without a conscious effort even in the music therapy supervision group we can find ourselves getting stuck in the verbal mode. The group members begin to report their groups, analyze them, and find verbal solutions. Yet just as we would lose the specific, the analytic, and the didactic by avoiding words, by avoiding music in supervision we lose the dynamic, the intuitive, and the integral healing of music. What we are looking for is a synthesis of both modes.

The Experiential Music Therapy Group

It is useful to begin the music therapy supervision group with a musical improvisation. This can serve several purposes. The first is to open up the musical mind and to allow this to be available to the group. This is important whether one has just been playing music, traveling on a bus, or writing a lengthy verbal assessment. It also serves as a release of the tension and burdens of the week, as well as a way of bringing the group to an aware present. This may crystallize for individual group members what the core concerns are for this session.

I have found that at times this beginning music becomes a joyful free expression. This freedom and this joy may be remembered in the next music therapy encounter. If one is sensitized with this experience one is more likely, in the immediacy of the music therapy group to grab the moment—the foot that is already tapping—the segment of a melody already being sung by a group member, rather than starting with that "perfect" treatment intervention that had been planned.

After the first "gathering music" there is time to verbalize issues or concerns the individual group members have. These can be addressed in many ways: through verbally shared group discussions, didactic information, verbal or musical role-playing, musical improvisation, etc. Throughout the group, the supervisor listens for the possible musical intervention. Whatever is most useful is what should be used. Because we get so easily "stuck" in the verbal mode it is important to keep the musical possibilities in mind. But, of course, we should never use the music just for the sake of using it.

If there is time at the end of the music therapy supervision group after the main issues are worked on, one can also close with a musical improvisation. This can be a time of renewal, a way of expressing particular needs, or a way of experiencing the group support. This music reaffirms music as the root and inspiration for the work of the participants as therapists and as group members.

As the supervisor listens and guides the group, he/she can be aware of what mode is being used. The following is helpful in studying the use of music and verbal interventions (revised from Stephens, 1984; Stephens, 1987). Although in the music therapy supervision group there should be a fluid intermingling of verbal and musical modes, for the purposes of studying them and bringing them to awareness, I will separate them here into discreet modes.

Modes of Intervention

Verbal–Verbal

The issue or problem is stated verbally and the mode of solution is verbal. This is most effective for specific analysis and for clarity of content. For example, the therapist may wish to reflect on group cohesion within a particular music therapy group and what might be done to develop cohesion. He/she can reflect on the specifics of a series of sessions: what individual clients played, eye contact observed, to whom conversations were addressed, etc. The supervision group members may become involved in this discussion perhaps by assisting the therapist in identifying points of resistance between certain clients or patterns that are beginning to emerge. Once the specifics are clearly articulated, possible musical strategies to enhance the connection between group members may be discussed. Later, if these are tried out in the group, we can think of the mode as expanding to verbal–verbal–music.

Music–Verbal

In this situation the therapist may use his or her own playing to uncover material which can become the focus of verbal discussion. For example, one therapist might present a session where he or she is unsure of the full meaning of a particular improvisation and how to develop this material in future sessions. The therapist might be encouraged to play this improvisation, playing the remembered music of the client, shaping his or her body posture and movement to the remembered image of the client. The muscles, the arms, and the fingers re-create the client's melodies, rhythms, dynamics, and phrasing. After playing, the therapist can verbalize the experience: what unexpected emotions were discovered, what specific needs were experienced. These feelings can be analyzed for their relevance to the client's history. The group can provide verbal feedback to the therapist regarding observations and hypotheses.

Music–Music

In this mode, the therapist works from the music and lets the music bring him or her to a solution. In the above example, instead of a verbal discussion of what it felt like to play as the client played, the therapist would be encouraged to keep playing as the client played and let the music be the guide to what needs to come next. Is it a loud crescendo? A lyrical melodic phrase? An invitation to others to join in?

Another example would be a therapist presenting a case of a client who continues to play in a very rigid style. He or she wants to encourage more freedom of expression. The music therapist might be encouraged to re-create this rigid style of playing and develop it into a freer style. By playing in this rigid style and observing the transitions necessary in order to move into a freer style, the therapist may discover a need for a more gradual move into this freedom of expression, rather than hurrying to force an abrupt transition.

Verbal–Music

In this mode, music is used to deepen the therapist's understanding of a particular issue or to help the therapist come more in contact with him/herself regarding specific issues. A therapist, for example, may be quite adept at observing the interpersonal dynamics of a group and discussing group process, yet may exhibit a certain distance from the material—an inability to be truly present as a leader in the moment. Thus the therapist's work reveals a lack of spontaneity and a rigidity of style. The music therapist can be encouraged to explore musically his or her feelings about being a leader and to notice where he or she feels cut off. Movement and breathing might be used to strengthen the therapist's musical expression.

Working with the Issues of the Professional Music Therapist: Early Stages

The music therapist's job is particularly challenging because of the constant need to educate and pioneer. Many clinics and facilities still have rudimentary knowledge of music therapy and even if one works in the most organized and prestigious of programs, one still needs to educate the public of the specific benefits of music therapy. Many music therapists just starting out need to design and develop their own programs at a site. There are often many compromises that have to be considered to match one's ideal of a job with the actual expectations of the administration.

In the early stages of a music therapist's career there are four primary needs that can be met by the experiential music therapy group. They are 1) the need for creativity in dealing with the challenges of a new career; 2) support for the emerging identity as a music therapist; 3) the need for continuing development of the ability to move between the musical and verbal modes as the verbal challenge grows with professional reporting and documentation; 4) a place to share music freely with a community of understanding peers.

In the first example, the music therapist may be faced with the need for programming in a site which has just moved into a skills development model that uses "classrooms," "courses," and a "core curriculum" and skills development topics such as anger management, problem solving, etc. The music therapist is required to lead a series of verbal groups and sees her role as music therapist shrinking. She comes to the supervision group with feelings of discouragement. She is asked to improvise this feeling. Perhaps the sound is subdued and she uses a small amount of space to move in. With the group support the therapist finds room for her sound within the larger sound of the group. She becomes gradually more assertive and alive, able to fill the space available with her own sound. From this experience in the music, comes a new way to bring music therapy to her work. Perhaps she will talk with her supervisor or perhaps she will create a series of skills development music therapy groups such as anger management through music therapy or problem solving though improvisation.

At the end of an internship and the beginning of a new job the music therapist is usually at the stage of shaping his/her identity. With the challenges of a new music therapy job this identity is often under siege in terms of the job description. It can also be a time of identification with peers who are professionals in verbal therapies. As one learns from these professionals, it is easy to begin an attempt to "translate" verbal concepts into musical activities. This can have great value but it can also be limiting. As one expands one's knowledge of psychological issues and group dynamics, one needs to continue to deepen one's awareness of the basic power of music itself to heal. With a continued self-exploration through regular musical experiences and through accompanying others in their explorations using music, the music therapist can continue to develop his or her deep sense of this music therapy work. The therapist delves into a deeper understanding of group dynamics and transference issues as they are expressed and felt through music. The group members voice their dilemmas, all sharing the common goal of using music therapy to the full and continued growth as music therapists.

As issues are presented verbally, the group can discuss possible solutions. Yet the leader looks for openings for introducing the music wherever this makes sense. This work helps to develop the fluidity of moving from verbal to musical thinking that may have been at the beginning stages during an internship.

Above all, at the early stages of a music therapist's career is the need for peer support. The experiential music therapy group can be a haven to return to—a community of peers who understand one's ideals and aspirations and who love to play music together.

Issues of the Professional Music Therapist: Advanced Stages

Many of the issues of the music therapist at the early stages continue on throughout one's career. Music therapists are constantly pioneering programs, educating other professionals and the public about music therapy, and carving out a place for music therapy. As paradigms change under each new administration the relevance of music therapy often needs to be fought for all over again.

Other roles also become important: the music therapist as intern supervisor, the music therapist as administrator, the music therapist as writer, the music therapist as active participant in the music therapy organization.

The music therapy supervision group provides a forum for verbal sharing of different music therapy systems; ongoing restructuring within facilities; city, state, and federal laws and changes in the laws; clinical opportunities and development of private practice. It is a place to try out new possibilities with other professionals with similar ideals. It is the place to keep up with the latest techniques and ideas in the music therapy field.

It is also the place to keep nurturing the musical mind. In this stage sometimes the music is used to solve dilemmas that are about systems in addition to personal therapy issues. The music therapist can improvise the feeling of being overwhelmed with multiple responsibilities and difficult choices in programming, staffing, and hiring. The intense strategizing and working and reworking systems in the mind and on paper can be played out through music into a creative solution that could not emerge in the verbal mode. Staff conflicts can be broken up into their affective components through music to deepen the understanding of the music therapist's transference and countertransference issues as a supervisor.

A music therapist/administrator may present the overwhelming pressures at work of complying with shifting administrative paradigms and changing survey requirements accompanied by low staff morale. He/she can be encouraged to improvise his or her feelings being in the midst of this. The music may evolve from a quiet sound into a loud cathartic release. As the music progresses the therapist might be encouraged to find a sound that reflects an inner strength or sense of purpose while the group plays a supportive improvisation. In a further development, the group may create sounds reflecting the pressures surrounding the therapist. The therapist can travel through this maelstrom, experimenting with attempting to maintain a centered feeling. Discussion can follow to uncover in words what has occurred: Was it possible to maintain a centered feeling? What got in the way of maintaining it? What concrete changes might need to be made to allow room for this to occur? The group can share their feelings of "being" the pressure instead of having to "survive" it themselves.

As the music therapist continues on day by day, the isolation and the seeming repetitiveness of the work may lead to burn out. With a group of peers one can improvise and receive the healing that is necessary to continue on. Perhaps one captures a new perspective, listening to another music therapist's solution. Perhaps a free musical improvisation revitalizes the sense of the healing power of music and renews one's sense of creativity. We are all growing and changing as human beings, traversing the different stages in our lives. The music therapy we do should be changing alongside this growth. The experiential music therapy group helps to keep a sense of balance of our needs, whether musical, intellectual, or spiritual.

Conclusion

As the music therapist deepens his/her musical connections and expands his/her understanding of the dynamics of a session—through the continual search for solutions using music as a primary mode—the therapist expands the ability to move back and forth between music and words. The role of an experiential music therapy group is to provide shared experiences, a forum for experimenting with new ideas, a musical support and, most of all, a music therapy support. The group can provide a sounding board for feelings that arise from unexpected turns in the road; a nurturing place for music therapy ideals to flourish and tools to develop. As the music therapist hears of shared struggles he or she can feel less isolated. As he or she compares strategies in handling a difficult situation he or she can feel strengthened. Having exposure to the healing of music at each meeting supports the difficult mission of educating others of its effects. Because music is used extensively the musical mode is encouraged and the sense of identity as a music therapist is supported.

The gathering of other music therapists provides not only a forum for support of music therapists' issues but a tangible community which is able to affirm the mission that we all share in creating opportunities for people to benefit from the healing power of music.

References

Stephens, G. (1987). The experiential music therapy group as a method of training and supervision. In C. D. Maranto and K. Bruscia (eds.). *Perspectives on Music Therapy Education and Training*. Philadelphia, PA: Temple University, Esther Boyer College of Music.

Stephens, G. (1984). Group supervision in music therapy. *Music Therapy*, 4, pp. 29–38.

Acknowledgments

Special thanks to Gary Hara, MA, MT-BC and Sumi Paik-Maier, MA, CMT for taking the time to remember.

Chapter 15

Peer Supervision in Music Therapy

Diane Austin, MA, ACMT
Adjunct Faculty, New York University
New York, NY
Janice M. Dvorkin, PsyD, ACMT
Assistant Professor and Coordinator of Music Therapy,
University of the Incarnate Word
San Antonio, TX

In 1988, the authors, along with several other music therapists, began meeting informally at music therapy conferences to talk about our work, our developing ideas, and theories. We found a common ground in our struggle to integrate the ideas and concepts of music therapy with psychotherapy. In 1991, several of us felt the need for a more frequent and ongoing way to continue these discussions, which led to the formation of a peer supervision group in music therapy. While we had different therapeutic orientations, we had many commonalties. We all believed in a psychodynamic model of therapy (e.g., Jungian, Kleinian, and Object Relations theories), all had graduate degrees in music therapy, and all had pursued advanced psychotherapy training through institute or doctoral programs. We all worked primarily with a combination of improvised music and words and all worked primarily with adults.

We agreed to meet in a peer supervision group once a month, for a two-hour period. After four months, another person was invited to join. The new person practiced privately and at an institutional setting. She also had a background in psychodynamic music therapy. For the next three years, this peer supervision group consisted of four female members.

There were several factors that created the impetus to form this group. At the time there were very few music therapists who were educated and experienced enough to provide in-depth, analytically-oriented music psychotherapy supervision services in our local geographical area. While in school, all of the group members had received music therapy supervision. But, this supervision focused on the basics of working as a music therapist, assessment, goal planning, specific techniques for specific populations, increasing musical skill used in therapy, and support. We felt the peer supervision group would be a place where we looked to each other to provide help integrating the knowledge obtained from advanced training, personal therapy, and our experience as music therapists. Most of the members sought, or continued to be in verbal supervision, in order to increase the depth of knowledge in psychodynamic clinical theory and technique. However, supervisors of verbal therapy could not, or would not address the use of music within the process of therapy. While in school, all group members had received music therapy supervision.

Another impetus for creating our peer supervision group was to combat feelings of isolation that we all shared. Feelings of isolation are not an unusual experience in a private therapy practice. However, music therapists can also feel isolated when they work in a school or institution, whether or not there are other creative arts therapists at the work site. Our peer supervision group helped to reduce feelings of loneliness and isolation by offering validation, support, and empathy (Singo, 1998). When one member brought clinical issues to the group, our problem solving increased her sense of empowerment and enabled her to continue the work that had not been understood or appreciated on the job. Through permission from the group to try out new ideas, or ways of working, we each gained confidence to trust our creativity and clinical understanding, which helped to increase spontaneous responses with our patients.

This group met another need as it provided the opportunity for group music making. The group was a place to play self-expressive music with colleagues. These opportunities for emotional release and musical self-expression were particularly important to those, who had little opportunity to play music with peers. At times, the peer supervision group, also allowed for a creative music making experience that was cathartic for all involved. This type of experience often occurred in response to role playing a therapy group being presented (Evans and Cohen, 1985; Hardcastle, 1991; Ladany and Lehrman-Waterman, 1999; Richard and Rodway, 1992).

Beginning

The inception of our group came about during an informal dinner, where we decided that we would meet monthly as a peer supervision group. We originally attempted to alternate the meeting place between our homes, although after several months it was eventually decided that we would meet at one member's centrally located home/office. Aside from being an easy commute for everyone, her office was also fully equipped with a piano, a variety of instruments from which to choose, and access to a tape deck.

Supervision often brought up personal issues for members. Therefore, we needed to be aware of how and when personal and clinical issues were becoming merged. We needed to focus on personal issues only as they affected our clinical work. Because we already knew each other well and had an ongoing relationship with each other, self-disclosure was a minimal issue, but, at times, the boundaries between supervision and therapy became somewhat loose (Prieto, 1997; Richard and Rodway, 1992).

One of the major functions of these early meetings was the constant encouragement we all gave to each other to put our feelings and ideas into music. For example, when Brittany[1] began to talk about her "identification with a female clinic

---

[1] The names that appear in this chapter are composites that have been devised to represent different group members at different times. They are not representative of the individual members of this group.

patient, who was struggling to become more independent," Elizabeth said, "Can you play her?" Brittany continued to share that she believed that she "was stuck in working on helping her with her struggle to become more independent." Elizabeth said again, "Can you play her?" Brittany said, "Yes," but kept talking. Donna offered an interpretation of Brittany's countertransference issue and the discussion continued. Elizabeth again asked Brittany to play the patient. At this point, Brittany stated, "I don't think I can." Donna asked what her resistance was. Brittany replied, "I don't think I can play the right music to really describe her." Elizabeth then responded, "Then play your feelings about her." Brittany began to play a narrowly ranged, repetitive group of minor chords on the piano. As the sounds became faster and louder, Brittany suddenly stopped playing. When Donna asked, "Why did you stop?" Brittany replied, "I don't know." Elizabeth asked her if she could continue. Brittany again started playing the music, but, this time, she began talking as she played. With further encouragement from Elizabeth and Donna, Brittany began to musically and verbally express the frustration and fear that she and her client had in common. Elizabeth said, "Can you stop talking and just play?" Brittany complied and started crying softly after a few minutes. Elizabeth moved to join her at the piano and offered musical support for expression of her feelings. She played holding chords in the bass. Donna then came to the other side of the piano and musically mirrored Brittany in the upper register. As Brittany continued playing, her music changed. It became more fluid, with a greater melodic and harmonic variety. The session ended with the members improvising together in response to Brittany's realization that it was all right for her vulnerability to be seen and heard by the supervision group. The musical support enabled Brittany to better empathize with the client's feelings of fear and vulnerability in relation to her struggle for more independence.

Each group began with an informal catching up (who was presenting their work, who was writing articles or chapters, etc.), checking in, and exchanging personal information. A ritual developed in which this social conversation was accompanied by dessert and tea. Sometimes the group would let off steam by joking and kidding around. When the group was "warmed up" (which took no longer than a half-hour), someone would say, "It's time to start." The next ninety minutes would be spent briefly following up on the last case, in relation to the client or the therapist, to see if there were any developments due to the previous supervision session. Then, a member would say, "I have a case to present tonight." The presenting member would begin by verbally describing the client or situation. At times, this information would also be conveyed through musical imitation, audio and/or videotapes. At a minimum, the group offered feedback to the presenter in the form of reactions to the music and/or behaviors, as well as suggestions on how the therapist might proceed beyond this point in the therapy process. However, most of the time, someone would say, "Can you play the client?" or "Can you play your feelings about the client?" This intervention might lead to further musical role-playing (e.g., another group member coming to the piano and playing the role of the therapist). At other times, it might lead to more in-depth musical exploration of personal feelings triggered by, or related to, the client. One example of this is when Elizabeth presented a client, Sandra, with whom she was experiencing difficulty. Donna asked her, "Can you play the client?" Elizabeth chose the drum and began playing softly. Her rhythm was erratic, with a lot of stops and starts and an overall tentative feeling to the music. When Elizabeth stopped, she had little to say. So Donna suggested, "Why don't I play Sandra now. I'll play what you just played and you'll play yourself." Donna took the drum and began imitating what Elizabeth had just played. Elizabeth went to the metallaphone and began playing loud and dissonant sounds. As the music continued, she picked up speed. This seemed to make the music more intense. At one point, Elizabeth was hitting the instrument so hard, that a few bars flew off. Gradually, the music subsided, then stopped. Sue asked, "What did you just experience?" Elizabeth said, "I feel like Sandra really won't connect with me. She stops and starts, as if to connect and then withdraws. As if she's withholding from me." Donna shared what it felt like for her to role-play Sandra. She said, "I felt like Elizabeth was impatient and might be angry with me. It made me feel like withdrawing even more into myself." Sue asked Elizabeth, "Have you ever felt this way before with anyone—unable to connect, and feeling frustrated?" Elizabeth then made an association to her mother and her anger at her mother's withholding behavior. The group shared their impressions of the music and gave interpretations and/or suggestions on how to work with the client. At the next supervision session, Elizabeth told the group that her work with Sandra had been going much better. She said, "My experience in group last time helped me to differentiate Sandra's issues from my issues with my mother. I'm not taking Sandra's behavior so personally anymore. I realized at the last session that Sandra isn't withholding from me, but is withdrawing because she feels unsafe. That's what she does when she feels afraid." Brittany said, "It sounds like you've broken the cycle of her withdrawing because she doesn't feel secure, which frustrates you, and causes Sandra to withdraw even more and it continues over and over again." Elizabeth replied, "Yeah, I think that's true. I think that Sandra's responding to the change in my attitude toward her withdrawing behavior. And she's coming out of her shell. She seems more comfortable expressing feelings verbally, and in the music."

Evolution

During the third year, the major focus of our group continued to be the integration of improvised music with verbal processing. By the end of the third year, Sue suggested inviting a colleague, whose work as a music therapist was music centered. Sue said that his approach would help the group focus more on music and less on verbal interpretation and intervention. So, when the group resumed after the summer vacation, David became a regular member. After a few months, not only did the ratio of four women to one male feel out of balance, but we also began to realize that having a diversity of music therapy styles enhanced the group's value by offering a variety of possibilities and perspectives. So, another male member of the local music therapy community, Phil, was invited to join. At this time, we considered six to be an ideal size, and did not want to expand it further.

We minimally changed the group's structure due to the expansion of the group. The night of our meeting changed to accommodate everyone's schedule. In addition, we decided to schedule case presentations in advance. Initially, presentations were made on need and/or desire. With a larger group, the system did not seem to work as well. It seemed as if the same therapists presented all the time, while on the other hand, a few members needed a great amount of encouragement to contribute case material. This new system was created to offer every member a chance to present. This system involved the assigning of future supervision sessions to each member for his/her case presentation. This seemed to provide more structure and organization.

As in any additions to a group process, the group returned to the forming stage. For our group, this included concerns about trust, safety, and confidentiality. Direct expression of these concerns was more obvious and frequent. Case presentations tended to stay within the safer parameter of facts and observations about the client, and descriptions about what occurred during the sessions. However, there was a reluctance to disclose personal feelings and information. This was resistance to disclose countertransferential thoughts and feelings. The new group initially attempted to resolve this problem through a negotiation of personal boundaries. For example, the group had to find out each member's comfort level, in terms of answering questions about his personal history, as they related to countertransference material. (Ladany, Lehrman-Waterman, Molinaro, and Wolgast, 1999; Shaten, Brody, and Ghent, 1962). The group members encouraged each other to participate at a level that felt safe to them. With the recognition that we belonged to a well-connected community, we needed to respect boundaries, while emphasizing the importance of the therapist's countertransferential thoughts and feelings. Those members who felt more comfortable working on this level were able to model risk taking by revealing personal material, when it impacted on the case presentation. As each member, in turn, shared personal feelings and associations, he usually received support and validation. This allowed all group members to see how the new group would respond to taking this risk. In time, the group became a safer container, as the fear of judgment decreased.

Music was valuable during this transition period, because it seemed to be a less threatening way to express oneself, as well as facilitating group cohesion. An example is when Phil returned, after missing two sessions, looking very depressed. The group expressed their concern for him, which prompted him to talk to them, for the first time, about the personal problems he was facing. Phil said, "I tend to isolate myself when I'm having a hard time and it's difficult to reach out for support." The group encouraged him to not only talk about the problem, but to also express his feelings in music. Phil picked up the guitar and began playing quietly. As he played, he seemed to withdraw into himself, so the group asked if they could join him. Phil nodded his agreement and the group members gradually joined him. This improvisation changed in mood, as Phil and members of the group interacted through the music. By the end of the improvisation, the mood changed from minor and slightly somber to a more playful minor blues. This event seemed to bring the group closer, while increasing the group members' willingness to be vulnerable (Evans and Cohen, 1985).

It is important to keep in mind how thin the line between supervision and therapy can be at times. As experienced therapists, used to working on our own countertransference reactions, it seemed natural and necessary to approach clinical presentations in an analytic style. This meant that we not only looked at case material, but also believed that the therapist's feelings, personal associations, and reactions were just as, if not more, important in understanding the clinical work than the data about the client. In our group, once the trust level was established, it was not unusual to see a group member work on a supervision issue in the music and have his own repressed or unconscious material come to the surface. This can occur in verbal supervision, but is even more apt to happen when working in music, since music has the ability "to mediate content from the personal and collective unconscious to the conscious mind" (Austin, 1996). Music transcends verbal defenses. We have found that when a member sang or played, the musical expression was often a catalyst between the therapist's unconscious defenses and clinical insights. The former brings to consciousness the therapist's countertransference and the latter provides overt information about the client. We therefore believe that a member's feelings are something to be embraced, not avoided.

During one meeting, David was having trouble finding words to describe a client, Pierre, whom he had just started seeing. Phil asked, "Can you play a musical portrait of him?" David came to the piano and began playing a repetitive, atonal pattern. Sue said, "It sounds like whirling, perpetual motion." David did not respond to her comment, but seemed absorbed in his own sound. He soon became so involved in the sound and movement of the music he was playing that he appeared lost in his own world and unaware of the group. After a while, Brittany got up and approached the piano. She waited until there was an opportune time to provide a simple rhythmic chordal structure to ground David's music and enable him to emerge from the perseverative pattern in which he seemed lost. David started to play slower and look over at Brittany, who was poised at the upper register of the piano. They began playing together for a few moments and, then David brought the music to a close. David, and the group, talked about their experiences from the last half hour. David spoke about his feeling of withdrawal into the music and lack of awareness of the people around him. Elizabeth said, "Would you say that what you just played was an accurate picture of your client?" David said, "I hadn't thought about it that way, but it makes sense. Pierre does have a spacey quality to him. Sometimes I feel that he leaves during the session, when he's playing music. And I'm not sure what to do, or say, or play." Donna said, "That's really interesting. That's how I felt while you were playing." As the group members gave their impressions of what he was playing, David shared, "That was the kind of music I used to play while I was growing up. It helped me escape from the sounds of my mother and father fighting." Phil made a connection between the way David and Pierre had used the music. When David heard that, he realized that his client was probably dissociating while playing music during the session. He speculated about a possible traumatic history that Pierre had not as yet talked about. He realized that Brittany's intervention was one that he might use the next time he thought Pierre was dissociating. Was David correct about Pierre's traumatic history? The greater the degree of education and experience, the more the clinician is able to listen and observe what is occurring in the field between the client and therapist, and differentiate what belongs to whom.

Another example of how our group worked by understanding the therapist's countertransferential feelings was when musical improvisation was used to work through the anxiety related to a new job. Donna came to the supervision group wanting to talk about her upcoming job with an adolescent program. As she was talking, she realized she had a lot of anxiety and dreaded starting the following week.

Brittany asked her, "What do you think you're afraid of?" and Phil asked her, "What would be the worst-case scenario?" But she continued to repeat that she could not explain the intensity of her fears. Elizabeth suggested, "Why don't you play 'Adolescents'?" Donna was reluctant, but agreed. She chose the piano. She began playing loud, dissonant chord clusters, with no consistent rhythm. The overall feeling was chaotic. After several minutes, Elizabeth approached the piano and began playing a repetitive, steady bass line. At first, Donna did not seem affected by Elizabeth's playing. But, eventually, her playing slowed, her body posture relaxed, and she began to breathe deeply. Donna's music became synchronous with Elizabeth's music. She began to form chords from the dissonant clusters and, harmonically, they ended together. During the verbal processing, Donna said to Elizabeth, "When you first started playing, I was annoyed. What were you doing? I felt like you didn't want me to have my anger. After awhile, the bass line felt kind of nice. I started to like it. By the end, I was really enjoying the music." David asked Donna, "Did you ever have any feelings similar to what you just played?" Donna made a brief reference to her own adolescence. She said, "It was really hard. My mother dominated and tried to control me all the time." She was silent for a few minutes and then said, "When I expressed my anger just now, it reminded me of the times I got angry at my mother. The painful part was that she couldn't deal with my anger and I felt she abandoned me whenever I tried to express it." These insights helped Donna recognize her anticipated identification with the adolescents, as well as the possibility of becoming like her mother when in the therapist's role. As the group continued, David asked Donna if she could imagine how the job might go if she responded to her clients as herself, and not as her mother. The group then shared their ideas and experiences of working with adolescents. As the group was ending, Donna told the group, "I don't feel quite as anxious about starting the new job. I think I can begin to separate the issues of my adolescent clients from my own adolescent experiences. This really makes me feel more confident."

Parallel Process

A peer supervision group is a teaching tool in which the supervision process does not recognize one clinician as the leader, or "supervisor." It is the group as a whole that functions as teacher for each member. Each member of the group is the supervisee and supervisor within a mutual process of support and education. A strength of our group was that each member had various types of advanced training, so that we were equipped to recognize and work with the complex psychodynamics that emerged during case presentations. Some of these dynamics included parallel process and various forms of resistance.

Parallel process, the recognition that the relationship between the client and the therapist is often reenacted between the supervisee and the supervisor, was also evidenced in our peer supervision group. Sue was presenting an audiotaped selection from a session with a client who had been sexually abused. The client was playing the cello and Sue was playing the piano. The client had been resistant and missed several appointments. Sue was trying to understand the dynamics of the transference and countertransference. The group agreed that the music sounded merged. It was hard to differentiate Sue's music from her client's music. Phil, at the piano, provided some musical examples of how Sue could maintain the boundaries between therapist and client, while containing the client's music. A victim of abuse herself, Sue admitted to feelings of identification with her client, Annie. Sue said that she wanted to explore her feelings about Annie through music. She went to the piano and began plucking the strings, one at a time in a random manner. As she continued to play, she added more strings and was plucking them very loudly. She ended with dissonant groupings of tritones. Several people remarked that the music sounded aggressive and harsh. Sue said, "Maybe that's how I feel I came across when I confronted Annie about the missed sessions." A few members began to ask Sue questions in a challenging manner. As the tone of the group seemed to become more critical and confrontational, she appeared to become more passive and compliant. At one point, Brittany asked her if she was all right. Sue responded, "Yes, I'm fine." At the next meeting, Sue confronted the group. She said she felt judged and attacked at the last meeting. She continued, "At first I was upset, but when I thought more about it, I realized that a parallel process had occurred." Sue wondered if she had induced sadistic impulses in the group members, as her client seemed to induce sadistic impulses in her. Just as the group responded by becoming critical and hurtful, Sue realized she had made interpretations to Annie that could have been heard as critical and hurtful. Just as Sue couldn't protect herself even when asked if she was all right, Annie couldn't stand up for herself either. This is a common occurrence when working with abused clients. The client unconsciously attempts to reenact their trauma with the therapist as perpetrator (Herman, 1992; Kalsched, 1996; Pearlman and Saakvitne 1995). Sue said, "I discussed this possibility with Annie and she said that she had felt angry at my persistent interpretation of her missed sessions as resistance. Annie said that she was too depressed to come in, and told me that I didn't understand." Sue's empathic failure became "grist for the mill" and a turning point in the therapy.

Conclusion

Despite changes in membership, this peer supervision group continues to meet. The group is now composed of five music therapists, including four of the original members. The authors believe that the reason this group was, and remains, so effective, is the members' knowledge of group process and how to work in the music, as well as our willingness and ability to address countertransference issues. The members were usually aware of the process occurring both within the session as well as the process that evolved from session to session. Due to the fact that our members had undergone (or were continuing) their own personal therapy, they were able to allow themselves to develop enough trust in the group to be vulnerable and share their problems, insecurities, and questions about their work. They were open to looking at how their own countertransference and behavior may be contributing to these issues. In agreement with the literature on verbal group supervision, we believe that members in psychodynamic peer supervision groups need to have enough postgraduate experience to provide at least adequate supervision to the other group members, and to utilize feedback from the group. Our depth of experience allowed us to provide feedback that helped our group move beyond a peer study, or support, group (Benshoff, 1993; Borders, 1991; Clarkson, 1998; Feingold, 1994; Gomersall, 1997; Hardcastle, 1991; Powell, 1996).

To our knowledge, there has been little, or nothing, written on music therapy peer supervision groups. For this reason, the citations for this chapter contain information exclusively on verbal peer supervision groups, which are usually within the areas of counseling and social work. Various concepts that are related to structuring peer supervision groups are listed in: Benshoff, 1993; Borders, 1991; Crutchfield and Borders, 1997; Crutchfield, Pruitt, McGarity, Pennington, and Richardson, 1997; Feingold, 1994; Remley, Benshoff, and Mowbray, 1987; and Roth, 1986.

The unique contribution of a peer supervision group is the exposure it provides to a variety of theoretical orientations and styles of working (Clarkson, 1998). This is separate from a supervision group in which the leader has the role of teaching a specific way of working. Our music therapy peer supervision group also provided a wealth of musical expression that we, as individual therapists, might not have considered, at little or no expense. This included learning about the symbolism of different instruments, the effect of playing instruments in different ways, and working with unfamiliar musical styles or idioms.

There are many advantages to a music therapy peer supervision group. Its unique qualities provide continuing education for advanced clinicians. But, most important, it constantly reinforces how essential the music is to the therapeutic process, the supervision process, and to the therapist, for his own clinical and personal development.

References

Austin, D. (1996). The role of improvised music in adult psychodynamic music therapy. *Music Therapy,* 14,(1), 29–43.

Austin, D., and Dvorkin, J. (1993). Resistance in music therapy. *Arts in Psychotherapy,* 20, 423–429.

Benshoff, J. (1993). Peer supervision in counselor training. *Clinical Supervisor,* 11, 89–102.

Borders, D. (1991). A systematic approach to peer group supervision. *Journal of Counseling & Development,* 69, 248–252.

Clarkson, P. (1998). Supervised supervision: including the archetypal of supervision. In P. Clarkson, (ed.), *Supervision: Psychoanalytic and Jungian Perspectives.* London: Whurr Publishers, Ltd.

Crutchfield, L., and Borders, D. (1997). Impact of two clinical peer supervision models on practicing school counselors. *Journal of Counseling & Development,* 75, 219–230.

Crutchfield, L., Price, C., McGarrity, D., Pennington, D., and Richardson, J. (1997). Challenge and support: Group supervision for school counselors. *Professional School Counseling,* 1, 43–46.

Evans, M., and Cohen, P. (1985). Borrowing a vision: A creative use of countertransference feelings in peer supervision to release barriers in the intuitive analytic process. *Current Issues in Psychoanalytic Practice, 2,* 111–121.

Feingold, A. (1994). Peer supervision and HIV: One group's process. In S. Cadwell (ed.), *Therapists on the Front Line: Psychotherapy with Gay Men in the Age of AIDS.* Washington, D.C.: American Psychiatric Press Inc.

Gomersall, J. (1997). Peer group supervision. In G. Shipton (ed.), *Supervision of Psychotherapy and Counseling: Making a Place to Think.* Buckingham, U.K.: The Open University.

Hardcastle, D. (1991). Toward a model of supervision: A peer supervision pilot project. *Clinical Supervision, 9,* 63–76.

Herman, J. L. (1992). *Trauma and Recovery.* New York: Basic Books.

Kalsched, D. (1996). *The Inner World of Trauma.* New York: Routledge.

Ladany, N., Lehrman-Waterman, D., Molinaro, M., and Wolgast, B. (1999). Psychotherapy supervisor ethical practices: Adherence to guidelines, the supervisory working alliance, and supervisee satisfaction. *Counseling Psychologist, 27,* 443–475.

Ladany, N., and Lehrman-Waterman, D. (1999). The content and frequency of supervisor self-disclosures and their relationship to supervisor style and the supervisory working alliance. *Counselor Education & Supervision, 38,* 143–160.

Murdon, L., and Clarkson, P. (1998). The ethical dimensions of supervision. In P. Clarkson, (ed.), *Supervision: Psychoanalytic and Jungian Perspectives.* London: Whurr Publications, Ltd.

Pearlman, L., and Saakvitne, K. (1995). *Trauma and the Therapist.* New York: W.W. Norton & Co.

Powell, D. (1996). A peer consultation model for clinical supervision. *Clinical Supervision, 14,* 163–169.

Prieto, L. (1997). Separating group supervision from group therapy: Avoiding epistemological confusion. *Professional Psychology, Research & Practice, 28,* 405.

Remley, T., Benshoff, J., and Mowbray. C. (1987). A proposed model for peer supervision. *Counselor Education & Supervision, 27,* 53–60.

Richard, R., and Rodway, R. (1992). The peer consultation group: A problem-solving perspective. *Clinical Supervisor, 10,* 83-100.

Roth, S. (1980). Peer supervision in the community mental health center: An analysis and critique. *Clinical Supervisor, 4,* 159-168.

Scheiby, B., and Montello, L. (1994, June). Introduction to psychodynamic peer supervision in music therapy—'dancing with the wolves' in the client-therapist relationship. *Proceedings of the American Association for Music Therapy Conference, USA* 214–223.

Shatan, C., Brody, B., and Ghent, E. (1963) Countertransference: Its reflection in the process of peer group supervision. *International Journal of Group Psychotherapy, 12,* 335-346.

Singo, W. (1998). *The Effects of Peer Group Supervision and Individual Supervision on the Anxiety, Self-Efficacy, and Basic Skill Competency of Counselor Trainees in Practicum.* (Doctoral dissertation, Wayne State University, 1998.) Dissertation Abstracts International, Section A, Humanities & Social Sciences, 59, 0738.

Acknowledgments

We would like to sincerely thank the members of our supervision group for their help, their suggestions and their good will as we wrote this chapter. Our group is a very special entity.

Chapter 16

Integrative Techniques
in Professional Music Therapy
Group Supervision

Isabelle Frohne-Hagemann, PhD
European Academy for Psychosocial Health
Fritz Perls Institute,
Hückeswagen, Germany

The Integrative Approach

Professional music therapy supervision is a very young discipline. In Germany, there are few publications on this subject and there is a lot of research that has to be done in order to develop this field to a serious discipline. As a music therapist and supervisor with an "integrative" background, I see the task of those involved in professional music therapy supervision as needing to develop multiperspective views (Petzold, 1998, p. 101). These multiperspective views on supervision situations take into consideration different theories (aesthetic, psychoanalytical, social psychological, social ecological, systemic, and social constructive) in order to respect the great variety of different "social worlds" (Strauss, 1978) in which we live.

A "phenomenological perspective" (Petzold, 1998, p. 88) would focus on the perception of the phenomena (situations/systems) in their environment (Gibson, 1979) which means to sense, to listen, to watch, and to feel in accordance with the way of perceiving we have learned from the social world in which we were brought up. Phenomenological perception thus is not naive, but always interpreted perception. The affective involvement and the subjective experience are important information channels for the other perspectives.

A "hermeneutic perspective" (Petzold, 1998, p. 88) is described as the theory and method of interpreting meaningful human action. It takes into consideration that our understanding of meaningful behavior develops in a circular relationship which consists of a movement back and forth between the particular phenomenon and the general context. The meaning and significance of specific actions, situations, or systems are always seen in relation to the whole (Koschnik, 1992, p. 453). In this perspective phenomena are regarded as expressions of lived experiences which we can interpret to their structures with the help of empathy, resonance, and interpersonal contact (which we consider as corporeal abilities based on sensory-motor activities). These give meaning to cognitive perceptions. Understanding is only possible because the people concerned share a common humanity.

An "evaluating perspective" (Petzold, 1998, p. 88) would consider the ethical and political dimensions of our assessments and would reflect the way we interpret various situations in terms of understanding why. This is a multilayered reflection and because of the need to create some distance from ourselves this reflection can only take place with the help of other supervisors or supervisees in a group.

An "action-oriented perspective" (Petzold, 1998, p. 88) would then take into consideration all the interventions and techniques that could be helpful in changing reality (situations) and models of reality (systems).

At the present time there is certainly no longer any excuse to accept in supervision only one perspective on all of the different personal problems in and with therapeutic relationships, social interests, different discourses, and cultural and political developments. A purely psychoanalytic perspective will not be able to reduce and explain the whole complexity of possible systems of interpretation; neither will a systemic theory or any other theory by itself. Therefore we should try to look at supervision situations with many different viewpoints and different perspectives. This inclusion of different viewpoints becomes a "multiperspective approach" (Petzold, 1998, p. 120).

Supervision is a large domain and here I will restrict myself to the area of case supervision although other areas, for example team supervision, are also very important. A "case" is a clinical situation or process and it has to be supervised as a figure in front of the following variables.

What is the *field* in which the music therapist works? Is it in the field of psychosomatics, psychiatry, social health service, childcare, etc.? A supervisor should have some field competencies in these areas. The problems in each field can differ greatly, and thus the supervision of a music therapist's work has to take into consideration the laws, traditions, clinical theories, etc. of the field in which he or she works.

The same is true for the *institutions and organizations*. It makes a big difference whether the music therapist works in a hospital, a prison, a center for drug addicts, or a recreation center. It is important to have some knowledge about the structures and traditions in these institutions or organizations.

The *supervisor's competence* must also be considered. What training and experience does the supervisor have as a clinician? Which psychotherapeutic and social scientific theories does s/he use? What is her/his music therapy background?

What is the *function of the supervision*? What is the supervisee seeking from the supervisor? Is the supervisor there to counsel, teach, coach, support, prevent burnout, and analyze musical improvisations and their relational dynamics, or something else? It is very important to be aware of the function of supervision in order not to get involved in conflicts that arise from unclear supervisory contracts.

What are the *supervisory relationship and the supervisory process*? What kind of relationship exists between the patient and the music therapist, between the music therapist and his supervisor, between the supervisor and the institution that pays the supervisor? What does the supervisor focus on: object relations factors, the transference viations, parallel processes (reenacting the patient-therapist in relation to the supervisee-supervisor relationship and the supervisor-institution relationship) or others?

What is the *personality of the supervisor*, the *personality of the supervisee* and the *personality of the patient*? How do the salutogenetic aspects of their personalities (vitality, resources, skills, motivations, hopes, longings, etc.) fit with the pathogenetic aspects of their personalities (deficits, conflicts, disturbances, trauma)?

What is the *social world of the patient*? In what kind of social reality does the patient live? Is his/her world compatible with the supervisor's world? What kind of music therapy with what goal does the patient need for his/her social world?

What *clinical theories* come into play? What kind of classification theories does the supervisor use: structure theories, developmental theories, relational theories, etc. and what does the use of only one theory mean for the supervisory situation?

Anthropological and sociological theories[1] must also be considered. Which social psychological and social scientific theories does the supervisor take into consideration if the patient suffers from unemployment, isolation, stress, and burnout, from ethnocultural problems? (See Holoway, 1995; Petzold, 1998.)

Group Supervision

Professional music therapy supervision can be done in either individual or group supervision format. I will focus here on group supervision, because it gives me the chance to demonstrate the advantage of the joint competence of group members. The members of supervision groups bring in different positions, viewpoints, frames of understanding, and patterns of intervention. These various positions can be discussed in regard to their compatibility and integration. Integration here means to find bridges and connections between different views on the actual problem without randomly mixing them together. The variety of clients and the variety of theoretical perspectives make supervision rich; the process of finding bridges for integration promotes collegiality, and tolerance for different ways of doing and analyzing clinical work. Group supervision, to a great extent, connects different music therapy "schools"—different theoretical backgrounds and philosophical approaches to how one works as a music therapist. These different perspectives serve to create a supervision group that is regarded as a competent group—one that has the resources to help each member grow and learn from supervision issues.

The supervisor in such a group may sometimes be a moderator, a teacher, or a counselor, who helps the different music therapists ally their potentials and competencies. The supervisor is not a therapist and s/he works on personal problems of his supervisee only to the extent as is helpful for the supervisee's work as a

---

[1] A mother with two children who left her violent husband and lost her job has to cope with different problems than a person who suffers from depression because of trauma in early childhood. The supervisor must help the supervisee look at problems from a social scientific view. It would not help this client at all if the music therapist would only try to uncover repressed material or focus on defense mechanisms and resistances in the therapeutic relationship that are understood as a result of disturbed relationships in early childhood. The supervisor would have to develop the supervisee's awareness for interventions that focus on the stabilization of the client and her resources—for example, developing ideas on how to share (musical) experiences with her supporting social network and with her children in order to feed herself emotionally, share her emotions with others and stay in emotional interaction with her field.

therapist. Of course the supervisory techniques will also have a salutogenetic therapeutic influence, as we understand therapy as also being a promotion of resources, potentials, and competencies.

Techniques used in professional music therapy supervision are meant to have influence on the supervisee and his world, the supervisee's patient and his world, and their therapeutic relationship. The supervisor is *always* participating, directly or indirectly, because the relationship between the patient and his environment will be reproduced between the music therapist and the patient. It will be transferred further into the relationship between the music therapist and her supervisor and/or the group and eventually even further into the relationship between the supervisor and his intervision group (a group of colleagues that discuss their cases without an external supervisor—a peer supervision group). In Integrative Supervision this is referred to as a "model of several levels" (Petzold, 1998, p. 203).

During the last thirty years music therapy in Germany has developed different approaches to the client. They are mostly relationally oriented with a depth oriented psychologic, psychoanalytic, developmental, humanistic, systemic, or integrative focus in music therapy. The dominant models today are Analytical Music Therapy, Anthroposophical Music Therapy, Integrative Music Therapy, Morphological Music Therapy, Nordoff-Robbins Music Therapy, Orff Music Therapy, Regulative Music Therapy, and Social Music Therapy. These models often seem to use the same therapy techniques, but their theoretical backgrounds and goals are very different. In supervision these background theories have to be identified in order to prevent misunderstandings.

The Process of Supervision

I now will present a supervision situation, the process that unfolded and the use of supervision techniques. In supervision the supervisor will focus on music therapy as a method of psychotherapy *and* on music therapy as a therapeutic medium with specific aesthetic qualities. Professional music therapy supervision integrates general supervision and specific music therapy supervision. Techniques can be verbal or nonverbal and include free verbal association, imagery, sculpting persons in scenes and contexts, role-plays or identification with an instrument as a symbol for a certain person, a function, or an emotional quality. Here certain psychotherapeutic techniques are "translated" into music therapy supervision. However, there are music therapy techniques such as free improvisations, musical expression of atmospheres, affects and relations, listening to music, and others that are specific to music therapy. These again, of course, can be verbally worked upon from different psychotherapeutic perspectives and theoretical explanations. A free improvisation can be looked upon with the theory of contact (gestalt), the theory of object relations (psychoanalysis), the theory of development psychology (learning and communication theories), the theory of systems, and so on.

A supervisor who is a trained music therapist will use specific music therapy techniques which make the hermeneutic understanding of the nonverbal much richer, because the supervisee can experience the meaning of relationship. A supervisor that has no music therapy qualification still can use techniques like music therapy role-play or identification and so on in order to have the supervisee *experience* an understanding of his/her actions.

However, the musical process itself and free improvisations need a special supervision hermeneutic in order to understand what is going on (Frohne-Hagemann, 1999a, p.107; 1999c). How can we diagnose the musical process between the therapy partners? What is the "theme," what is the "message," what is the "scene," what is the "relation," what is going on psychodynamically, group dynamically, interpersonally, and emotionally? Questions like these can only be answered if we are open for discussions that try to uncover our thinking and talking traditions and our ways of understanding music. Musical improvisations in therapy have their own specific language. It has to be considered whether the patient's musical improvisation began with or without any directions and if so, what kind of instruction had been guiding the improvisation.

My experience shows me that many supervisees need help especially in this hermeneutic area, because often they do not find the right words about the improvisation that allow them to communicate with the patients. This is because, as Dvorkin states, ". . . a lack of understanding about what is occurring between the therapist and the patient neglects at least two-thirds of what is happening" (Dvorkin, 1999, p. 280). She thinks that it is necessary to have "basic knowledge of psychotherapeutic techniques and framework" (p. 279) in order to understand the musical relationship within the therapy. The understanding of the musical relationship in respect to the psychoanalytical object relations theories is, however, only one dimension to be considered. There might be time and space enough for a multiperspective approach and who knows whether an improvisation could give answers to questions that have not yet been asked, yet those which could lead to new theories.

Regarding general and specific music therapy supervision, I have described earlier (Frohne-Hagemann, 1999c) a hermeneutic model that is useful to integrate different perspectives on the problem discussed in supervision. This model is based on Integrative Theory (Petzold, 1993) and shows a never-ending spiral of the supervision process as follows.

Figure 1
The Supervision Process

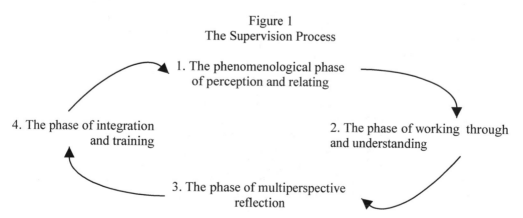

1. The phenomenological phase of perception and relating

2. The phase of working through and understanding

3. The phase of multiperspective reflection

4. The phase of integration and training

Each of the four phases of this spiral focuses on the presented problem in a specific way. With the help of music therapy and verbal techniques the problem can be worked upon with multiperspective glasses.

Vignette

I will describe the supervision process with a young music therapist (I will call her Mary) who introduced an improvisation (videotaped) to our supervision group and I will use the hermeneutic model as a heuristic.

The Phenomenological Phase
of Perceiving and Relating

Mary (age 34) reports on a music therapy situation. She has worked for the past two years in a hospital that deals only with psychosomatic illness and today she presents a group of five patients she has in music therapy. Mary says she would like to reflect on her relationship to one of the patients, Mrs. P, because she does not understand her personal reactions toward this woman. Mary describes the group members: Mrs. A, age 34, suffering from colitis ulcerosa; Ms. T, age 22, suffering from headaches; Mr. R, age 30, suffering from asthma; Mr. S, age 32, suffering from generalized pain; and Mrs. P, age 58, a nurse, suffering from back pains, but unwilling to talk about it. Mrs. P *always* plays the large and deep drum. Mary reports with anger in her voice that Mrs. P is dominating all the others and forcing them into her rhythmic pattern. Mary had already tried to confront her musically by provoking some other rhythmic structures, but Mrs. P held onto her rhythm. However, all the other patients seemed to be happy with the improvisation and even supported Mrs. P's playing against Mary. Mary felt incompetent.

The members of the supervision group are invited to musically express their countertransferences to the unspoken level of Mary's report and by expressing their corporeal resonance to get a feel for the dynamics and relations of the group. Countertransferences can become conscious by a psychoanalytical-oriented technique called "Balint-group improvisation" (Loos, Strobel, and Timmermann, 1988, p. 277). Countertransferences may risk interpretations that only refer to psychoanalytical theories. Musically expressed corporeal resonances consider much more somatic and sensory-motor information, and may help to prevent the risk of one-sided theory, because images, associations, thoughts on a supervisee's report, and his/her appeal are in their phenomenology much more concentrated on our senses. The questions are: What exactly are we aware of and what exactly do we see, hear, smell, get in touch with, etc? The next step is to answer the questions: What do these perceptions feel like, what structures are they composed of, and where are these structures of our experience from?

The phenomenological corporeal approach is characteristic of Integrative Music Therapy and supervision. Our corporeal abilities help us to sense and to track what we experience physically through seeing, hearing, touching, and smelling, and to sense and track what we experience through imagination and thought. This gives reality to cognitive perceptions (see also the research of Damasio, 1994).

Our corporeality is not a state, but a process. Sensing and resonating do not give information about feelings as psychic states, but they help to understand phenomena as dynamic processes. The dynamic process of a widening (instead of the experience of width) or the dynamic process of a contracting (instead of a contraction) is an experience that lets us understand better the dynamics of music. There is a correspondence or an "analogy" between music and movement (Frohne, 1981; Klausmeier, 1978; Smeijsters, 1991; Zuckerkandl, 1963). There is a dynamic correspondence between our corporeality and music. Corporeal impulses like widening and contracting or accelerating (accelerando) and slowing down (ritardando) are basic qualities of music and of emotions. Emotional states like joy and sadness are basically flowing. (If an emotion is frozen as in a depression, it can be considered to be pathological. Depressed patients are not able to be in resonance with others. And who can flow with a person who is stuck in a constant smile?)

The basic experience of any emotional state, thought, or memory is a dynamic movement. Daniel Stern described wonderfully in *Diary of a Baby* (1990) our corporeal resonance to somebody, somebody's report or somebody's improvisation which enables us to flow with the inner movements of a situation or system. The fundamental dynamic vibrations or movements may be sensed as atmospheres, visualized as scenes and experienced as different role configurations (such as "concordant," "complementary" or "reciprocal" countertransferences as Jacobi, 1987 described them). In a way we create different "social worlds" out of the dynamics that make up situations and systems. Thus techniques like these help to reenact therapy situations and systems on several levels and by parallel processes in the supervision group. These connect us with our own experiences, and in this case with Mary's world and her patients.

In this phase it could, of course, have been helpful to have Mary express her feelings musically. This would have been a useful technique in order to get Mary herself in emotional contact with her verbal report. But Mary first wants us to watch a videotape showing her improvising with the patients. It seems to be important for her to show us something and for her to look at the problem from a more distant position. It is possible that she at this moment is afraid of her emotional reactions that cause her to be the center of attention. She feels safer to first *look* at the problem with us. However, the group tells her about the resonance her verbal report left:

Mary's report and the way in which she had reported had been experienced, corporeally, in the group as helplessness and irritation, especially when she described Mrs. P. Mrs. P was experienced as if she were growing and Mary was experienced as if she were shrinking. The members of the supervision group experienced a concordant countertransference to Mary (because of her helplessness) which related to her own reciprocal countertransference to Mrs. P (where Mary unconsciously changed roles with Mrs. P, as she became the patient and Mrs. P appeared as a dominant nurse). How could this happen and why?

After having watched the videotape the group members report their impressions and observations: In the video Mrs. A starts to play the xylophone, searching for a way to find her place. Ms. T. looks out the window and joins Mrs. A with the rainmaker. Mrs. P looks at both and comes in with the deep large drum initiating a rhythm which gives the music of Mrs. A and Ms T a frame and stabilization. However, they seem to ignore Mrs. P. Mr. R now plays a melody on top of this that sounds a bit like a children's song, but his facial expression is quite serene. Mr. S joins Mrs. P on a djembe, his rhythm shortened to the minimum. The music sounds quite fixed and the players have little eye contact. Now Mary comes in with the "Big Bom" (a very big—120 x 60 x 60 cm—wooden slit drum) and plays a swinging walking bass in a rhythm that irritates the others. This stimulates Mrs. P to play harder. The impression of conflict between them arises. Mrs. P avoids looking at Mary. It seems that the patients play hard and firm in order to stay in the rhythmic frame, however, the music sounds as if the whole does not want to move and open up. There is indeed an impression of a prison, and of hard work. We can understand why Mary wanted to stimulate the group to become more open for movement.

As every observation is already informed by our experiences and internalized models of perception, any interpretation should be declared as a hypothesis that has to be verified in the following phases.

The video gives additional information from the pure music. When watching the video (and watching video is not as intensive as pure listening) we *see* the behavior of the patients as individuals trying to find their way, and we *see* how they communicate or have influence on each other. In our case we saw six individuals that played together in a group, but we did not experience the group as one being. As pure *listening* gives different information we decide to hear the music again with our eyes closed. Listening is directed to the whole gestalt, which is something other than the sum of the single observations. Listening in the corporeal way helps us experience the dynamic, impulses, and movements of the whole and the parts within the whole, the need to move or not to move and the necessity for adequate expression.

We use the technique of listening with closed eyes and resonating to the dynamic of and within the group. What we now experience seems to be a much more salutogenetic part of the improvisation: we hear that the individual patient is part of the scene and busy with creating a certain scene he/she is part of. We hear a search for contact and this is found in a rather firm rhythm. There is no contact among the instruments like interactions or interaffectivity, but there is contact because of a shared common rhythm. An outsider tries to disturb this identity and by that stimulates the group to stick even more to the firm rhythm. Thus the therapist who was the outsider caused the group to feel a good rapport with each other. We understand why they enjoyed Mrs. P's rhythmical play.

She gives a basic heart rhythm that provides the feeling of stability and continuity. The music does not *sound* as irritating as our *eyes* had experienced the scene. Thus there is a discrepancy between what we see and what we hear.

In this phase of the hermeneutic model we found out aspects about the individual patients, their behaviors, attitudes toward each other, gestures, mimic, choice of instruments, and their functions for the moment. Then we listened to the music and discovered it as an indicator for resources, potentials, and needs. In this situation Mrs. P had, with her rhythm, an important role which was accepted by the other patients. We understood why Mary was irritated. Her perception of the scene part of the session and her perception of the relational part of the session did not fit together.

What did this have to do with Mary? At this moment it seemed that only Mary had a problem. Was she a scapegoat in the actual session (systemic perspective) or did she have a transference of her own biography (psychoanalytic perspective) or did she have a problem with the hierarchy in the hospital that caused her to see the situation as she did (social perspective)?

The Phase of Working
Through and Understanding

The next phase is that of working through and understanding, where we have a closer look at the problems the music therapist has to cope with. This phase has therapeutic aspects, but personal problems are worked on in supervision only to the extent it is necessary for Mary's work.

I ask Mary to tell us more about her problem. She says: "The problem I have with Mrs. P is that she takes the role of the therapist in the group—my role. But she avoids real contact with me. The group is relaxed, but I am very irritated and feel more and more incompetent because she makes me angry and that is not therapeutic." She also reports about her situation in that hospital and the feeling of conflict among the different therapists.

When now invited to express her feelings musically she chooses the drum and beats it really hard in anger. Mary feels that she really would like to beat Mrs. P. She suddenly feels like a severe mother who wants to punish the daughter that is not obeying. It feels strange to her, because some minutes before she felt like a helpless child that was being dominated by Mrs. P. In fact, Mary feels that she is quickly moving from one extreme to the other. The drum apparently gives power which both Mrs. P and Mary seem to need.

Now the question in this phase is: What is the underlying emotional context and the underlying scene that provokes the problem? Asked what it feels like to have chosen the same instrument Mrs. P had played, Mary becomes curious to identify with Mrs. P. The supervision technique of identification (and role-play) is often used by gestalt therapists. It is not based on the phenomenon of resonance or countertransference, but on our ability to be empathic. Mary plays the deep drum identifying with Mrs. P while some supervision group members play the other patients and their instruments. I play the therapist's part on the "big bom."

In this improvisation Mary experiences Mrs. P in the following way: "I have to lead the group and care for everyone. I am the oldest of six brothers and sisters (the patient group and the therapist are also six people!) and it was always my job to be responsible. The music therapist Mary, is very young and is not interested in harmony. I am not happy with the way she holds the group together. She searches for problems, but I do not have any except some pains in the back. I have always taken responsibility for everybody's problems and I am proud that I succeeded. The fact that I have pain myself has nothing to do with this and therefore I have to stop the therapist from further investigating our emotions and interpersonal affects and suggest that musical experiments lead nowhere."

Mary now understands Mrs. P better. In fact, this is, in a way, Mary's own story. She tells us she also had to take care of her family, and she became a therapist because she felt responsible for people that needed help. She did not take care of her own problems. She had to function. Why? Mary had an alcoholic mother who was not reliable. Her mother accepted help only when she was drunk. When she was sober she rejected help and did not want to hear anything about her problems. In a sober state she was very rigid and unjust, and in a drunken state she was disgustingly overflowing and confluent. Mary knew that she did not want to become that weak so she became a therapist in order to protect herself from becoming like her mother. She understands that Mrs. P, as well, possibly cannot afford to become weak.

The supervision group members share their feelings and experiences as "patients" during the improvisation and give feedback. As patients they experienced Mrs. P as the oldest among them who gave them support. In fact is she more than twenty years older than all the others. They felt the pressure of being forced by the therapist to relate to something they did not understand yet—a pressure psychosomatic patients always express toward their therapists. It felt comforting to feel Mary's (Mrs. P's) steady rhythm on the deep drum. They felt the need to stick together under the rhythmic blanket and not be threatened by a therapist who tried to disturb the nice harmony. The therapist also appeared threatening simply because of the fact that she belonged to the group of therapists in the hospital.

Looking at the situation from a position where we are not involved, we can reflect on what happened: An old scene was reenacted where Mary as the oldest child (like Mrs. P) protected the family against her mother and where she wanted to "help" her mother (projected on Mrs. P). This did not work because in this particular scene Mary met her projected mother (Mrs. P) in a "sober" state where she was rigid and clear in avoiding emotional disturbances. So the structure became clear and Mary started to understand her own transference and countertransference to Mrs. P. Mrs. P had entered the scene in Mary's world as a 58-year-old person that seemed to fit precisely into the role of Mary's mother. She was not only forced into this role because of her age, but also because Mary wanted to have therapeutic influence on her which she—like Mary's mother—could not (yet) accept. Any change would mean a change in her attitude toward life and this might be painful. Both Mary and Mrs. P needed to "help" in order to protect themselves and that was their common world. But did Mary also understand Mrs. P? Both had a social profession (music therapist/nurse), but a nurse does not often have time to be empathetic with each patient. A nurse has to function much more practically than a therapist does. Their strategies are quite different. Mrs. P wanted to harmonize everything in a way like mothers care for little babies, whereas Mary wanted to find out about the "person" by searching for contact. Mrs. P went into the direction of harmonization and stabilization whereas Mary went for differentiation and confrontation.

The question is what did Mrs. P really need at this stage of the therapy?

Before the supervision group discusses the consequences the supervision work had so far on further therapeutic interventions and techniques, it is useful to look on the situation again from a mutliperspective reflection.

Phase of Multiperspective Reflection

The topic in this phase of the supervision process is the hermeneutical understanding of the overt experiences from different perspectives (Petzold, 1996, 2ff).

Mary's professional problem has more than this one dimension we had discovered. We have to consider the following

One must examine the *political dimension*. What is the actual situation of the public health service, what are the traditions and cultures of the institution Mary works in? Mary works in a hospital for psychosomatic patients. How long do the patients stay on average? Who pays for the therapy? What are psychotherapeutic and medical treatment concepts in this hospital? What status does Mary have? Is she allowed to do diagnosis in order to choose the right patients for music therapy or not? Is she allowed to work on conflicts or relations or is she supposed to "relax" the patients and make them forget their problems? Mary is extremely poorly paid for the work she has to do, and her status in the hierarchy is low, yet the work she has to do requires a great deal of responsibility. She is constantly under stress, because she has to prove that music therapy is a serious and valuable form of psychotherapy. How much is her work accepted and appreciated in the hospital?

Considering this dimension Mary's problem also reflects her own actual frustration of not being adequately accepted by the institution. So her transference to Mrs. P stems from not only her childhood, but is also rooted in her current situation. She should become aware of this fact and consider her frustration and possible burnout effects also in this regard.

The *theoretical dimension* must also be considered. What are Mary's philosophies? What are her concepts of cognition, knowledge and diagnosis, personality, psychological development, health and illness, therapy in general, music, and especially of music therapy? What are her theories of music therapy methods and processes?

In Mary's case we looked at her problem from a psychoanalytical perspective. She has a professional background that is relational oriented. Mary did not know much about modern psychosomatic theories.[2] She wanted to confront the patients perhaps too early with relationship, disregarding the fact that a psychosomatic patient first must have the chance to feel valued before he/she is able to accept his/her dysfunction and pain and be able to relate to his/her experiences. In respect to the analysis of the video we interpreted the phenomena in respect to the roles, scenes, behaviors, and communication. In respect to the aurally and corporeally resonated understanding of the musical improvisation we

---

[2] If a patient suffers from psychosomatic disorders, it is important to know whether the music therapy interventions should be concentrated on the entodermal (vegetative), mesodermal (emotional) or ectodermal (actional, relational) functions of the body (Frohne-Hagemann, 1999b; Wyss, 1987). A headache can be a healthy reaction toward too much stress from inside or outside, and thus a helpful warning. In this example the best music therapy intervention could simply be to offer relaxation techniques and other techniques that help get one in contact with the signals of one's body. However, a headache can also be an expression, perhaps the end of a process of functions that started with the loss of a beloved person that could not be mourned, of impulses that were not possible to live with. Here the right music therapy intervention could be the offer to improvise together with the music therapist in order to express the affects or to listen to music that could express the repressed wishes of the patient.

took in a salutogenetic perspective based on the gestalt theory position that psychological impulses and motivations are always striving for the "good gestalt" or that the psyche is always busy with forming new gestalt formations (Frohne-Hagemann, 1990; Tüpker, 1998). Mary apparently underestimated the important "holding function" of the patients' music at that time and she wanted to interpret (too early) the music defense mechanisms against the therapist.

Another consideration is that of the *practical dimension*. What professional background does Mary come from? What kind of training did she have as a music therapist? Mary's psychoanalytical background made her interpret with too much emphasis the patient's musical activities as defense mechanisms. She wanted to uncover repressed material, work on conflicts, confront patients with their defense mechanisms. It seemed incompetent to her if she allowed patients to have fun.

The *ethical position* concerns Mary's basic ethical attitudes toward any person. What is a "patient" to her? How much is she part of the therapy system: may patient and therapist learn from each other and teach each other or is the therapist the one who knows everything? Why could Mary not bear that Mrs. P "knew everything better"? What does it mean to lead a patient, to support a patient, to be a "therapist"? In my opinion, for example I *am* not a therapist, but *become* a therapist in one of those meaningful moments when it comes to an exchange and understanding between my patient and myself. To be a therapist is neither a state nor a role, but a meaningful moment in a process that has to be achieved.

It was very important to discuss Mary's "responsibility" as a severe mother or therapist, her fear that the family will fall apart if the members do what they want or if someone regresses and just wants to experience joy. Many therapies have been developed over the years on a therapist's basic experience of fear. Therapy for many therapists must be a painful process. Fun and joy are interpreted as pure defense mechanisms!

As a result of these experienced reflections we finally enter phase four.

Phase of Integration and Training

Mary's desire to be a competent music therapist must be seen as a figure in front of several backgrounds. One must consider the hospital and her position in the hierarchy, her analytical approach in music therapy and the humanistic orientation of her colleagues, her biography with responsibility, having to care for others, her frustration about the dependence on the institution and on her mother, her unconscious interpersonal arrangement with Mrs. P's social world, and its potential of mutual therapy as could be heard in the original music.

The music showed the way. Music indicated that a changing and meeting would only be possible in a holding and caring attitude toward each other. Not paying attention to who played which instrument had already be experienced in our supervision group. The group made suggestions to Mary and they gathered together ideas for future interventions and music therapy techniques for the next settings. How could Mary follow the patient and still have the position of leadership?

Mary thought about regaining the therapist's role by accepting Mrs. P's "help" and her effort to take responsibility. This possibly would give Mrs. P a feeling of being accepted and appreciated. Mrs. P would have a witness for all the efforts she made to be accepted. To be witnessed has great therapeutic value that can be shared musically and turned into an experience of being valued. Mary could initiate this in an improvisation where Mrs. P would play again the deep drum in her supporting way, but this time—and this is the important factor—being esteemed by the "daughter" Mary. A change of roles might set free new experiences (for both): Mary could give rhythmical support on the drum and Mrs. P could play what it feels like as a person who does *not always* need to take responsibility. Maybe Mrs. P by then would develop enough trust in the relationship to express her pain and sorrow.

We are at the end of our supervision. We know that the spiral will move on and what we found out today will be reviewed under another perspective in our next supervision—and this will also include the reflection of my interventions as the supervisor—a perspective that possibly did not show up today but that will only show up *because* of today's work.

References

Damasio, A. R. (1994). *Descartes' Irrtum. Fühlen, Denken und das menschliche Gehirn.* Dtv, München.

Dvorkin, J. A. (1999). Psychoanalytically oriented music therapy supervision. In T. Wigram and J. De Backer, (eds.), *Clinical Applications of Music Therapy in Developmental Disability, Paediatrics and Neurology.* Philadelphia and London: Jessica Kingsley Publishers.

Frohne, I. (1981). *Das Rhythmische Prinzip—Grundlagen, Formen und Realisationsbeispiele in Therapie und Pädagogik.* Eres Verlag, Lilienthal.

Frohne-Hagemann, I. (ed.). (1990). *Musik und Gestalt. Klinische Musiktherapie als Integrative Psychotherapie.* Paderborn, Junfermann. New edition Vandenhoeck and Ruprecht: Stuttgart, 1999.

Frohne-Hagemann, I. (1999). Integrative supervision for music therapists. In T. Wigram and J. De Backer, (eds.), *Clinical Applications of Music Therapy in Developmental Disability, Paediatrics and Neurology.* Philadelphia and London: Jessica Kingsley Publishers.

Frohne-Hagemann, I. (1999a). Zur Hermeneutik musiktherapeutischer Prozesse. Metatheoretische Überlegungen zur Integrativen Musiktherapie. *Musiktherapeutische Umschau*, Heft 2.

Frohne-Hagemann, I. (1999b). Musiktherapie in der Behandlung psychosomatischer Patienten. In: *Einblicke—Beiträge zur Musiktherapie,* Heft 9.

Frohne-Hagemann, I. (1999c). Überlegungen zum Einsatz musiktherapeutischer Techniken in der Supervision. In *Integrative Therapie 2–3, 25. Jg.,* Junfermann Verlag, Paderborn.

Gibson, E. J. (1979). *The Ecological Approach to Visual Perception.* Boston: Houghton Mifflin.

Holloway, E. I. (1995). *Clinical Supervision: A Systems Approach.* Thousand Oaks, CA: Sage Publications.

Jacobi, M. (1987). *Psychotherapeuten sind auch nur Menschen.* Walter, Olten.

Klausmeier, F. (1978). *Die Lust, sich musikalisch auszudrücken.* Rowohlt, Reinbek.

Koschnik, W. J. (1992). *Standard Dictionary of the Social Sciences,* Vol. 2. K. C. Saur München.

Loos, K., Strobel, W., and Timmermann, T. (1988). *Die musiktherapeutische Balintgruppenarbeit. Musikther. Umschau,* Band 9, Heft 4.

Petzold, H. G. (1993). *Integrative Therapie. Modelle, Theorien und Methoden für eine schulenübergreifende Psychotherapie.* Reihe Integrative Therapie. Schriften zu Theorie, Methodik und Praxis, 3 Bände. Paderborn: Junfermann.

Petzold, H. G. (1996). *Materialien zur Integrativen Supervision und Organisationsentwicklung—"Supervisorische Kultur," "Reflexives Management," "Konflux."* Europäische Akademie für Psychosoziale Gesundheit (EAG) (Fritz Perls Institut).

Petzold, H. G. (1998). *Integrative Supervision, Meta-Consulting & Organisationsentwicklung.* Junfermann, Paderborn.

Stern, D. (1990). *Diary of a Baby.* New York: Basic Books.

Smeijsters, H. (1991). *Kreative Therapie—Musziektherapie.* Hogeschool Nijmegen, Nijmegen.

Strauss , A. L. (1978). A social world perspective. In M. K. Denzin, *Studies in Symbolic Interaction.* Vol. 1, Greenwich: Jai Press, pp. 119–128.

Tüpker, R. (1998). *Reflexion seelischer Verhältnisse in der musikalischen Improvisation.* In M. Lenz and R. Tüpker (eds.), Wege zur musiktherapeutischen Improvisation. Materialien zur Musiktherapie. Universität Münster.

Wyss, D. (1987). *Der psychosomatisch Kranke-zwischen Krisen und Scheitern.* Neue Wege in der psychosomatischen Medizin Vol. 3, Vandenhoeck & Ruprecht.

Zuckerkandl, V. (1963). *Die Wirklichkeit der Musik. Der musikalische Begriff der Außenwelt,* Rhein Verlag, Zürich.

Appendix

In order to analyze the video I will briefly offer here some categories that can be considered (also see Frohne-Hagemann, 1999, p. 262f).

1. Resonances

1.1 General and spontaneous perception of atmospheres, scenes, emotions, feelings, actions, fantasies, metaphorical thoughts, imagery, associations, memories (countertransferences).

1.2 Corporeal resonances to the music and the scene. Is the resonance a widening (opening associations like joy, sun, light, openness, growth, etc.) or a narrowing (opening associations like anxiety, darkness, sadness, withdrawal, threat, etc.)? With accelerating (expectation, tension, hurry, etc.) or slowing down (exhaustion, coming to rest, losing hope, losing trust, etc.)? With increasing (growing, longing, tension) or diminishing (falling asleep, getting out of sight, becoming thinner, etc.)? With exploding (noise, bombs, fire, danger, bursting out, etc.) or cooling down and growing stiff (death, winter, calmness, silence, etc.)? Or others?

2. Musical phenomena:

In time, in space, in dynamics, in form, connections by pulse and rhythm; spectrum of timbre and sound, process of melody, phrase, variation, texture, timing, preferred intervals, etc.

3. Media, behavior, roles:

3.1 Playing behavior, personal expression of the patients (corporeal expression, muscle tension, color of face, coordination of hands, head–hands, eye contact, mimic, gesture, attitude, approach to the instrument, etc.

3.2. Choice, function, of instruments: are they carrier of symbols and projections, do they seem to have the function of transitional or intermediate objects?

3.3. What role configurations are developing in the improvising group? The victim and the aggressor, the insulter and the insulted person, the protecting mother and the naughty child, the alpha and the omega-type, harmonist and the chaos maker? Which roles are taken in by individual patients: the grumbler, the scapegoat, the director, the watcher, the action man, the judge, the angel, the "therapist," etc?

4. Forms of relationship:

Is the individual patient in: isolation, confluence, contact, encounter, bond, (negative: commitment)?

Examining pathological and salutogenetical forms of contact, attachment and autonomy: what does the individual patient play like? Avoiding, breaking off, burning his/her ships, blurring, dissolving, pretending to be dead (anesthesia), blocking, boycotting, splitting, becoming silent, playing with oneself, melting into one another, attacking, drowning a sound, sticking obstinately to something, harmonizing in any situation, playing perfectly, answering inadequately, feigning to be in contact, imitating, playing funny, playing in a give and take modus?

Archaic (immature), neurotic or mature forms?

Examine constructive interventions and stimulations: supporting, holding, framing, protecting, calming, reinforcing, confronting, provoking, listening, forming, varying, changing, etc. (too much, too little, adequate)? Homogeneous stimulation, inconstant stimulation, contradictory stimulation, overstimulation, understimulation?

5. Transference and countertransferences:

Concordant, complementary, reciprocal, projective identification, role configurations.

6. Pre-knowledge

Assumptions we have about the patients' social background concerning their familiar, social, political, cultural background, concerning their social world and identity (corporeality, social net, work, material resources, values)

Chapter 17

The Supervision of Clinical Improvisation in Aesthetic Music Therapy: A Music-Centered Approach

Colin Lee PhD, RMTh, MTA
Associate Professor and Director of Music Therapy
Wilfrid Laurier University, Waterloo, Canada
Kimberly Khare, MA, CMT, NRMT
Director of Music Therapy
Community Music Center of Boston, MA

Introduction

Music identifies who we are as living beings and therapists. Until we understand music itself we can never understand the effect it has to change people's lives. Evaluating clinical improvisation through a music-centered approach to supervision is a process that can help define a supervisee's clinical maturation as a student and/or developing music therapist. The connections between the strands of being human and being professional are multifaceted and many. Music is as intricate as the human condition with all its foibles and frailties. The relationship among music, people, and therapy is a natural phenomenon that must in essence originate from the forms and qualities of music itself. Taking this proviso into account, it would seem natural that a music therapist should first be able to accurately hear and describe the music being used within the therapeutic setting. This crucial belief contains the necessary boundaries for the supervisee to develop, learn, and grow.

A music-centered approach to supervision can be studied in isolation or in combination with other approaches. Music-centered supervision is not in and of itself a complete theory of supervision. Rather it should be perceived as a first and critical step in understanding the therapeutic process and relationship. The four stages of supervision discussed in this chapter are intended to be used not necessarily in isolation, but rather as a means to elucidate the ongoing musical understanding of clinical practice. Music therapy supervision as a discipline involves not only musical parameters but also the intra/personal aspects of words and all the complexities of the developing relationship. Rather than deny the universal evaluation of music therapy, music-centered supervision states that musical listening and description should be studied with precision before exploring the interpretation and balance between music and therapy. While the goal of musical understanding should be ongoing throughout a music therapist's life span, it can be used as a springboard to other theoretical frames that further highlight the intricacies of the music therapy process.

The supervisee must acknowledge and believe that the musical content of music therapy is fundamental to the process. Music-centered supervision also acknowledges and helps integrate past musical history, and the effect this may have on the supervisee's clinical/musical development. Musical inspiration and preference should be an important part of a therapist's resources. Learning how to use extracted idioms that are characteristic of the musical personality of the therapist will add a unique substance to the therapeutic process.

Why then is a music-centered approach to supervision important? As the profession of music therapy matures, the balance between the "art" and "science" of our practice becomes ever more complex. Until recently, the essence of music and its analysis has taken a secondary role to psychological, psychotherapeutic, educational, and medical research. Taking a music-centered approach to music therapy and supervision can help review the balance between music, meaning, and clinical purpose. The complex structures of music require complex clinical critiques and assessment; balancing musical illumination alongside clinical understanding. It is not enough to describe musical responses in simple terms. We should attempt to hear and describe chords and their inversions, modulations, melodic lines, rhythmic structures, textures, and intensities of playing, as they impact the therapeutic/musical dialogue. Developing the accuracy of our listening will illuminate our clinical awareness musically, verbally, and in silence. A music-centered approach to supervision then, is a challenge not only for music therapists undertaking supervision, but also for the profession as a whole. The recent evaluation and research on the use of music and words (Amir, 1999), psychotherapeutic influence and interpretation (Streeter, 1999), and physiological and emotional responses (Iwanaga and Moroki, 1999) continues to afford contemporary music therapy with ever more complex questions and demands. It is important that all future questions and challenges to music therapy be regarded with equal significance.

Background

The supervision of music in music therapy is only briefly addressed in the literature. Stephens (1987) describes, through the use of experiential music therapy, aspects of music listening that are essential to our understanding and learning of the process: "In order to learn the 'ways' of music in music therapy, the music therapist must experience in an intimate manner, not only the elements of music but also the therapy process that emerges through and with them" (p. 169). In describing the integration of verbal and musical work during supervision, Stephens states that in moving from music to music "the therapist works from the music and is encouraged to let the music lead to a possible solution" (p. 173). Learning to use clinical improvisation effectively is further discussed by Oldfield (1992). In considering the evaluation of musical choice she states that: "Even the most skilled musical improvisers worry at times about whether they should play in one key or another, whether they should use tonal or atonal improvisation or whether they should improvise around a given tune rather than inventing completely new material" (p. 14).

In considering Nordoff-Robbins music therapy supervision, Brown (1997) proposes five areas of concern: a) musical relationship in the therapy room; b) practical management in the therapy room and workplace; c) interpersonal dynamics in the therapy room; d) interpersonal dynamics in the workplace; and e) interpersonal dynamics in the supervision room (p. 5). Brown considers "a" to be the most important in terms of developing practice, while acknowledging that in her opinion the supervision process needs to encompass "a" to "e" to be fully balanced. In discussing and reflecting the weight between musical and personal analysis in supervision, Brown points out that nonmusical considerations of supervision and the emphasis of her writing do "not reflect the balance in my overall supervisory work, where enabling the supervisee to listen, to hear what is happening in the musical interaction from moment to moment, and to develop clinical perceptions about this, would be my major aim" (p. 10). If purely musical insights are incomplete in our understanding of music therapy as Brown suggests, is this then because to focus on solely musical structures in assessing the music therapy process is clinically unsound, or is it because of our ignorance of the complexities of music?

Nordoff-Robbins (1977) developed a passionate and perceptive music-centered focus to music therapy. Recent publications (Aigen, 1998; Ansdell, 1995; Lee, 1997; Pavlicevic, 1997; Robbins and Robbins, 1998) reveal that now, even more than ever, music remains at the epicenter of this work. Aesthetic Music Therapy (Lee, in press), an approach and philosophy I (Colin) recently developed, was inspired and profoundly influenced by the teachings of Paul Nordoff and Clive Robbins. It describes the foundation from which music-centered supervision originates. Aesthetic Music Therapy is defined here as a process that views the core of musical dialogue as its explicit theoretical base. Fundamental to Aesthetic Music Therapy is the consideration of the aesthetic qualities of the client, their disability and/or illness, in direct relation to their musical expression and therapeutic relationship with the therapist. In Aesthetic Music Therapy interpretations of the process come from the musical infrastructures. The form and architecture of the musical interplay and the clinical responses and understanding, are determined and reflected in and of itself through the music. As a composer and music therapist, Aesthetic Music Therapy speaks to my professional voice in combining the essence of musical creativity and personal growth. Neither is eliminated at the expense of the other. Clinical intent and aesthetic judgment survive as essential allies in the understanding of the music therapy relationship. Aesthetic Music Therapy is vital in shaping the backbone of a music-centered approach to supervision. Both writers of this chapter are therapists educated in the Nordoff-Robbins approach to music therapy.

The Supervisory Relationship

The supervision described in this chapter is based on work that is initiated outside the physical domain of the music therapy session. Supervision is not conducted during sessions themselves unless there is a clearly identified reason for doing so. That is not to say that supervisors could adopt the model of being present at every session. It is rather that music-centered supervision is a reflective process addressed through audio and/or video recordings and the supervisee's written reflections and assessments. Supervision sessions are normally held on a weekly basis and last on average between one and two hours. Supervisees come prepared, having listened intently beforehand to the improvisation under discussion, and have fully indexed the complete session.[1] Clarity of aims stemming from detailed ongoing assessment help inform the balance between the aesthetic and clinical both during supervision and in the ongoing music therapy sessions. It is critical to the supervision process that the supervisee come prepared to analytically listen, describe, and debate. The intensity and number of sessions vary depending on the supervisee's stage of development and level of experience. The single session is advised against, though this may, with careful guidance, provide the therapist with the necessary provocation and challenge to consider the music in their work in greater detail. The student in training, the therapist during formative years as a clinician, and the experienced therapist, will all work at different levels and intensities during music-centered supervision. Supervision, then, is unique to each supervisee's needs.

Stages of Supervision

The four stages of supervision described in this chapter—clinical listening, clinical evaluation, clinical interpretation, clinical judgment—do not move sequentially but accumulate, each adding and enriching as the supervisee's clinical experience and understanding of the relationship between music and therapy deepens. There are no limits to the amount of time spent on each stage, the process being ongoing, exacting, and enriching. The initial stage of clinical listening forms the backbone of this approach and can be returned to at any point. Indeed, to return to previous stages only adds to the understanding of a supervisee's philosophy and his or her continuing clinical practice. Unless otherwise stated supervision develops from detailed listening and analysis of audio- and/or videotapes. The fundamental task of intense listening forms the core and bias of work described in music-centered supervision.

Throughout the descriptions of each stage this text is highlighted with transcribed notational examples that illustrate the musical underpinnings discussed. Also central to the descriptions of each stage, Kimberly Khare, a recent supervisee, adds reflections that bring a sense of personal reality and searching to the dialogue. Kimberly worked in supervision with me for two years and has contributed her perspectives as a supervisee on each of the four stages. Kimberly works exclusively with children and had been practicing as a music therapist for two years before our supervision. The clarity of her musical and clinical questioning illustrates the potency of this music-centered approach to supervision.

---

[1] Indexing is a form of evaluation that describes, assesses, and interprets the music therapy dialogue. Listening back to the session the therapist will stop the tape or video at salient points (the tape counter number is noted) and transcribe through words and/or music the meaning and intent of the segment. Through evaluation and interpretation, index notes provide a detailed map of a session that can be used as assessment data, and also be referred to before the next session.

Clinical Listening

One of the main tenets of music-centered supervision is hearing objectively and precisely the musical constructs contained within the musical relationship. Music as a complex and multilayered phenomena in music therapy should be precisely evaluated, considered, and analyzed at all levels of its experience. Separating what we think we hear from the reality of sound, music and their interrelationships can provide a new basis and understanding for our work. Living in the knowing of music can dramatically transform our sense of the process. Music then is the starting point for our greater understanding; not words or exterior clinical theories but the pure phenomena of music itself.

Listening to audio recordings of sessions enable greater and more detailed study of the musical building blocks in improvisation. Clinical listening is the ability to determine the balance between the actuality of music and the potential therapeutic outcome. Clinical here is defined as the identification and understanding of musical constructs that constitute the musical/therapeutic dialogue. The supervisee must extend their aural skills to describe what they hear without bias—listening without interpretation or reflection to describe chord progressions, melodic lines, client's responses, and their musical combinations. This first stage of supervision is fundamental in providing the base from which the supervisee can then move into more interpretive assessments. In *clinical listening* there is re-examination of the boundaries of knowing and understanding. Knowing the musical exchange as pure data will give a greater sense of where the therapeutic relationship is beginning and the possible clinical pathways that lie ahead. The supervisee must learn to hear precisely and clinically before he or she makes choices that are truly balanced and therapeutically informed.

This stage of supervision is usually challenging, as supervisees will instinctively feel the need to interpret. Indeed, the education of a music therapist is built on postulates of observation, interpretation, and clinical orientation. Music therapy could not survive without the therapist's ability to critique, interpret, and proceed. Supervisees may wish therefore to select passages of improvisations for musical discussion that are therapeutically significant and that relay to the supervisor work that they feel is effective. As supervisor it is important that these assumptions are challenged.

Initially, the most important segments of a tape to explore are the beginning passages of the improvisation. The reasoning is that these beginning passages will normally contain simpler musical patterns. Here, therapist and client explore a musical groundwork from which the ongoing musical relationship may develop. By accurately describing these musical beginnings the supervisee will begin to understand the importance of clinical listening and responding. These opening moments also often contain musical seeds from which improvisations develop. If we explicitly hear these generative musical cells expressed from the client, therapist, and musical relationship, we may begin to unravel the complexities of the ensuing therapeutic and musical direction. As the supervisee develops his or her ability to clinically listen to these opening moments, so will this be transferred to the ongoing work.

Music can be broken down aurally into many components, from intervals, melodic lines, and rhythmic motives to harmonic sequences and structural themes. The starting point for clinical listening is the identification and qualities of the "tone" itself and its effect on the ensuing musical structure.[2] Once the opening tone is ascertained others can then be identified as the evolving intervals become apparent. Returning to the initial tone, however, is always the fundamental focus. A diatonic center may then be inferred or tones may continue to be freely placed as the dialogue develops. It is that sense of tone as the musical epicenter that holds both the answer to the supervisee's precision of musical identification and the potential understanding of the ensuing musical therapeutic relationship.

Case Material—Clinical Identification of Tones

This example comes from the opening of a piano, four-hand, improvisation. The client is playing in the treble register, and the therapist in the bass. Example One is divided into twelve musical segments, with time indicated in seconds.

The opening repeated B played by the client (Example 1, Segment 1), forms the core of the musical dialogue. In Segment 2 the therapist plays a major 7th, inferring a D tonal base. In Segment 3 the therapist adds musical color by playing a chord based on F sharp, the opening tones—B, D, and F sharp—therefore forming a B minor triad. The chord in Segment 3 is a combination of a perfect 5th on F sharp (left hand) and an inferred G major 7th (right hand). At Segment 4 the therapist plays a C major root position chord adding another possibility of a tonal base. The client responds with a B forming a 7th overlay. In Segment 5 the F sharp chord is reiterated, inferring F sharp minor with the added A natural. The client in Segment 7 moves away from the repeated B tone to move finally to an A, thus resolving the F sharp minor tonality. From Segments 8 to 9 the clients melodic placing of tones includes an 8va (A-A), downward 7th (B-C), augmented 4th (B-F), and a final resolution to an E, which matches the C major chord. The therapist at Segments 8 to 9 responds with a perfect cadence in C, with a flattened 6th on the first chord, to add dissonance. At Segment 10 the therapist plays a repeat of an open 5th on F sharp with an inferred C major overlay (G and C). The client plays repeated Bs and as in Segment 7 finally resolves to an A which again infers an F sharp minor tonality. At Segment 11 the client improvises a similar melodic development as at Segment 8 (A, G, B, C, A, and B). The therapist responds at Segment 11 with a repeat of the major 7th interval based on D, through to a short responding melodic line (A, A flat, G, and A). The quality of playing throughout this opening is dynamically quiet and texturally measured.

---

2 Tone is described here as a single pitch that may also be described in terms of its quality, character, timbre, color, and intensity of singing and/or playing.

Example 1

Moving from the specificity of the tone is the ability to ascertain the overall musical architecture of an improvisation. Once the supervision has moved past the identification of opening themes, whole musical infrastructures can be examined so that the minutia of specific moments can be placed within the context of the whole. Here random segments of the tape can be heard that will classify developing musical constructs which can then be related to the original thematic material. From this premise it is possible to gain a sense of overall musical architecture that is reliant on, yet disconnected from, the moment to moment responses of client(s) and therapist.

Case Material—The Architecture of Musical Form

Example 2 shows three further segments from the same improvisation and shows the relationship between the opening tones and their significance in the overall structure of the ensuing improvisation. How we hear the opening tones of a client's playing— the choice of pitch, the intensity of playing, the possible melodic and harmonic inferences and the texture of expression—should define our response to their musical articulation at its most finite level.

In Example 2, Segment 1 on the following page, the client plays displaced tones, the therapist responding with a repeat of the opening tones (D and C sharp). It is interesting to note that after the statement of this core interval, the client immediately imitates it; D in the left hand and the C sharp in the right hand. In Segment 2 a melodic motive (B flat, B, F sharp, F) is repeated by the client. The therapist responds again with the D/C sharp interval recapitulating the F sharp chord initially improvised in the opening example at Segment 3. Finally in Segment 3, which is the closing moments of the improvisation, the client plays repeated minor and major seconds. The therapist responds with punctuated chords, at times repeating the F sharp chord of the opening and ending on the inferred C sharp tonal base that was initiated at Segment 2 in the first example.

These examples show a clarity and musical consistency in the development of the tone and the developing harmonic structure. The understanding of the musical relationship evolves from both the detailed articulation of the tome, to the more complete musical picture of the whole improvisation. The sophistication of this musical dialogue has significant implications for our understanding of the therapeutic process and the potential for future directions and goals. We should never underestimate the importance of the tone and its ability to provide a rich tapestry of improvisation. The tone can lead to infinitesimal possibilities. It is fundamental therefore, that we hear, identify, meet, and reflect the client's unique and essential tone.

Transcribing the tape into notation, as shown in the above examples, can also help develop the musical ear. When moving from the initial pitch it is possible to transcribe simple melodic, harmonic, and rhythmic outlines. Inferred bar lines help give a sense of shape without implying a definite meter. Transcriptions can be outlined during supervision as the supervisee becomes more adept at identifying musical structures, or the supervisee can write it beforehand so that the musical intricacies can be more detailed in their classification. Moving into the concrete parameters of notation brings a reality to clinical listening, further challenging the supervisee's musical ear.

Example 2

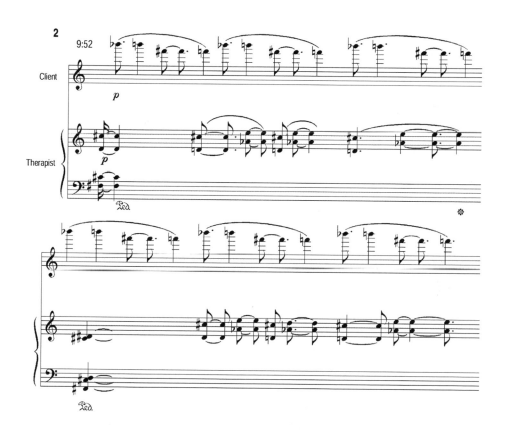

This initial stage of clinical listening is a precise and intense art. It can cause frustration if the supervisee is not prepared to challenge his or her musical capacity to listen and describe in musical terms. To hear on the level required for this stage of the work is not an easy task. This experience normally has a lasting effect on the supervisee's perceptions of his or her work. The supervisor must keep the direction on a purely musical theoretical basis. To detract from this path can invalidate the musical foundations necessary to work in a truly music-centered approach. The supervisor must be clear in his/her role to facilitate only that which is heard and described. This can mean repeated listenings of short extracts of music to ascertain both the explicit and implicit musical infrastructures. The meticulous nature of this stage can be illuminating as the supervisee begins to hear the complexities of the client's musical discourse, the connection with their own musical responses, and the musical unification of both.

The Supervisee Reflects—Kimberly Khare

Music, as emotions, is immediate. I never perceived these experiences as separate. It was during supervision that I first began to understand the clinical implications that my lack of conscious separation was creating. In "clinical listening" the "I feel. . ." and "I think. . ." are removed. The clinician's personal and musical biases are stripped away to reveal the musical intention and clinical direction. By directly dealing with the factual experience—what is actually happening musically, rather than one's own perception—the focus is shifted from *therapeutic presence* to *musical presence*.

Initially it is frightening to listen at this level. Feelings of self-doubt and inadequacy are shamelessly experienced. But that is not the purpose of listening in this capacity. To listen "clinically," not perceptually or even therapeutically, is shocking. We have rules and fundamental concepts of the inherent nature of the medium, that when disregarded can lead to a situation not unlike playing with fire. The aesthetic of music is a combined effort of profound emotions and fundamental clinical aptitude. Knowing the geography of one's instrument can only support knowing the geography of one's emotional landscape. And in supporting a client's growth toward self, we must know the precise application of the music that effects the emotions.

Clinical listening brings you to the basics. What is the timbre of the client's instrument/expression, the pitch, the duration of the tone? What is the attack, the phrasing of their rhythmic/melodic work? Here is where we separate from style. We do not ask the "feel" of the expression, but the precise measurement of it.

The next question for me was not "how can I match the sound," but rather "how can I meet the sound?" This concept is the key in that I believe it is what helps the clinician continue to separate clinical listening from perceptual listening. By "meeting" a client's sound we remain separate, presenting our own identity, our own voice, which ultimately supports the client but does not impede or step upon their individual voice. By "matching" we tend to "do the same" which neither indicates our intention as clinicians or provides direction for our clients. *Matching* can at times simply be repeating, whereas *meeting* is a conscious choice. Meeting supports co-creating, it motivates independent thinking and awareness of the present, immediate moment.

Clinical Evaluation

Moving from the rigor of clinical listening, the supervisee is then ready to assess and appraise the music therapy dialogue. During this stage two central areas are covered: the quality and intent of musical resources and the development of musical assessment skills. The supervisee's use of her musical dexterity in clinically reflecting the client's initiations and responses now becomes important as she looks to extend her musical palate. This further leads to the development of specific assessment procedures that will help illuminate the musical and therapeutic dialogue.

Music therapists who use improvisation will normally acquire musical resources from their specific education. Nordoff-Robbins (1977), in particular, has documented a system for gaining musical skills necessary to use improvisation in music therapy. The techniques learned and used should be considered as only the beginning in the supervisee's/therapist's ongoing involvement and expansion of musical resources. During supervision musical skills and responses can be analyzed for future therapeutic scenarios. By isolating critical sections of the improvisation, the music can be examined in detail to understand the client's musical expression, how the supervisee responded, and other possible musical answers. These musical crossroads can become multifaceted exercises that will help both the ongoing sessions and the supervisee's expansion of musical proficiency for future clinical situations.

Case Material—Expanding Harmonic Sequences
The following harmonic sequence was extracted from a good-bye song with a physically disabled child. The progression of 7ths added warmth and a sense of holding for the child. Based in A flat the sequence of 7ths move from I to V concluding with a plagal cadence (IV- I). This chord progression was used as a basis for developing further harmonic sequences in ensuing improvisations and acted as a musical thematic anchor for the child:

Example 3

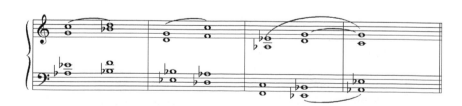

Finding an appropriate form of musical assessment can help the supervisee clarify the balance between musical and therapeutic responses. Bruscia's (1987) illuminating and detailed Improvisation Assessment Profiles (IAPs) provide a clear assessment theory that can be used as a base for a supervisee's initial musical evaluations in aesthetic music therapy supervision. There are three simultaneous steps: 1) clinical observation, 2) musical analysis, and 3) interpretation. The six profiles—integration, variability, tension, congruence, salience, and autonomy (p. 404)—each contain musical criteria that during musical analyses deal with:

- Rhythm—pulse, tempo, meter subdivision, and pattern
- Tonal—modality, tonality, harmony, and melody
- Texture—fabric, pitch registers, voicing configurations, musical roles of each part, and phrasing
- Volume—sound intensity, mass, and dynamics
- Timbre—sound quality, attack, resonance, and instrumentations
- Physical—motor action of playing and various other expressive uses of the body
- Programmatic—lyrics, stories, programmes, verbal reactions, or interpersonal relationships associated with the improvisation (p. 406).

These detailed analyses do not, however, include transcriptions into musical notation. Bruscia states that IAPs are "not designed to describe every single moment of an improvisation or to facilitate microanalyses of every musical detail" (p. 409). The question then becomes: How important is it that we have the actual hard data, the notes themselves to examine? To describe musical infrastructures through the written word can illuminate our perceptions of the qualities of improvisation. However, until we are able to study the notes themselves—to see the relation between exacting tones, harmonic sequences, and rhythmic forms—I believe there will be a link missing in our understanding of the process. Through the exacting study of musical transcriptions and the repeated listening to session recordings, we can fully deduce and analyze the complexities of the musical underpinnings and their influence on the therapeutic process. This question of importance of notation in supervision and assessment should be contested and debated at length during this stage of supervision. It holds the key in helping a supervisee formulate her own philosophy of music therapy and the balance between the artistic and clinical.

The supervisee should also be encouraged to begin finding her own unique musical assessments that best suit the needs of her clients, the continuing therapeutic process, and her own musical and clinical learning. My own formulated musical assessment (Lee, 1999) came from my research studies (Lee, 1992) and corresponding supervision. It is based on the relation between music analysis and clinical understanding. The stages—1) holistic listening, 2) reactions of therapist to music as process, 3) client listening, 4) consultant listening 5) transcription into notation 6) segmentation into musical components 7) verbal description 8) in-depth analysis and 9) synthesis—show the step-by-step possibilities of detailed musical inquiry and how these apply to the construction of improvisations and the balance between musical and clinical assessment.

The Supervisees Reflects - Kimberly Khare
In terms of developing resources my first resource was realizing I had more concrete concepts that could be applied, and that could guide me in my clinical interventions and choice making. Up until this point, my understanding was when faced with a client with whom I was going to improvise, my choices were either divine intervention or the key of D major! I always began a session by creating a *song* in a certain "style" or "feel." In essence, I was rushing beyond the client's expression with sound that made me feel certain and competent. By leading with an emotional edge I was supporting only my own emotional experience. Through supervision I began to give myself the option of "tone" versus "chord progression." I began to work more focusing on intervals, rather than improvising in a specific key. By challenging my thinking, my listening, to the level of reception versus response I began to develop the resource further, from clinical listening, to "meeting" versus "matching." Reception indicates a taking in and is a step toward integrating. We are to respond to our clients, but not haphazardly. Through my inexperience and naivete that was exactly what I was doing.

Clinical listening gave me the ability to develop clinical evaluation. I was no longer evaluating my personal responses to the ambiguities of relationship in music, but developing clinical strategies and awareness that led to clear, justified clinical evaluations. The relational connections between my music choices and the child's became clearer, more definite, more flexible, and more integrated in our developing relationship. The responsibility for that relationship and meeting was now more conscious for both client and therapist.

My supervisor's guidance was at times direct and then subtle, but always specific. There were times when we listened to the same three seconds over and over again until I began to move through the levels of listening and began grasping the explicit form created. My developing ability to listen had to be mine. Supervision could not just simply point out what I should be listening to because that would impede the development of my judgment. So, painfully and slowly we moved through entire sessions listening mainly "in-between" and "behind" obvious moments of expression and connection. By doing this I began to hear nuances, subtleties, possibilities, and potential. I began to hear "ahead" of the moment because I was directly aware of the music's intention—what the music was conceiving—and the clinical direction that was to come.

This resource, hearing "behind," "in-between," and "ahead," created a fuller spectrum of listening for me. I was now working in the "past," "present," and "future" of the clinical moment. I was in the *creative now* (Clive Robbins, personal communication, October 1994, see chapter 22 for further discussion) living in the immediacy of music within the therapeutic relationship. The emotional implications of this awareness were obvious, but the musical, not as simple. As therapists we often, I think, start the music and keep going. We don't breathe, pulse, fluidly move, or even stop—yet our clients do. We tend to create a chorus, or a refrain, or a style of song, or a theme that embodies these characteristics. But rarely do we use the architecture of music itself to actualize the moment.

My recognition of pitch, rhythmic expression, phrasing, and timbre dramatically changed. When I heard a cymbal I no longer played a long pedal tone but actually received and integrated the attack of the mallet, the physical force, the crispness or dullness of the sound. I had more to choose from. By having these choices I realized that the child had all these choices too. I could now begin to musically, and therefore clinically, assess their decision-making abilities, their processing, awareness, presence, and directedness.

Through the clinical evaluation of learning to separate I also learned to differentiate. Starting with a tone instead of a chord determines so much more. I could then distinguish other tones and tone colors that would effectively affect the clinical moment. This stage naturally led to clinical interpretation.

Clinical Interpretation

Analysis is now encouraged, while always retaining the link to the initial platform of musical clinical rigor. This remains constant and is always the focus. Exploring the supervisee's reactions to the client, the musical dialogue, the stage of the process, and the possible meanings in relation to the ongoing therapeutic process, now become the focus. While the whole spectrum of clinical intervention is now potentially available for investigation music still remains the focus. The supervisee may bring issues of musical and intrapersonal questioning:

- What was happening at the specific point in the improvisation?
- How would I interpret it musically?
- How would I interpret it therapeutically?
- What are the connections between the two?
- What were my musical reactions?
- What were my personal reactions?
- What was it about the client's music that made me respond?
- What was it about the physical presence of the client that made me respond?
- How do my personal reactions to the clinical situation, the client and the process influence my musical and therapeutic responses?

These questions and more provide the base from which more hermeneutic discussions may begin.

Interpreting and making sense of improvisations in music therapy is complex and multilayered. Music contains a labyrinth of patterns that are in, and of themselves, intricate. If we amalgamate these many structural and theoretical possibilities of music with the human condition, then the limits become even more enigmatic and infinite. To study music through analytical, psychological, and musicological designs are in themselves challenging. Adding the different theoretical structures of medicine and psychotherapy may potentially only add to the confusion in finding a theoretical foundation that adequately speaks to music therapy's own internal workings. Here is a contentious question that can be challenged and debated in supervision. In highlighting these questions and dilemmas, through supervision we can begin to help find individual pathways that will allow for differing balances of music therapy practice.

Case Material—Exploring Meaning in Music and Therapy

I would like to highlight this stage with an example of supervision from work with Susan, a music therapist I supervised for a period of three years. She explained that during a recent session with an eight-year-old autistic child there was a moment when the child's pathology appeared to evaporate as he became involved in an unfolding four-hand improvisation at the piano when the child was playing in the treble and the therapist in the bass (example 4 on the following page). She questioned the validity of this experience and speculated on the balance between musical intent and the potential music has to transcend his autistic state. For Susan this was a profound experience and she was eager to explore the possible meanings behind this musical opening. This allowed Susan the opportunity to examine, interpret, and then make deductions about the links between music, emotion, and creativity.

After a detailed musical examination and identification of specific musical segments, we turned to the relationship between this information and Susan's interpretations of the event. She described how the child's preoccupation with his playing, his physical relation to her and the intent with which he moved to the keys, was compelled by her music built on perfect fourths. This choice was made consciously. It clearly allowed the child the opportunity to find a simple melodic motif that he repeated and developed:

This was the first time the child had found his own improvised melody and the first time that there had been an authentic musical communication between them. Susan inquired as to the musical potential of perfect fourths and how the suspended intervals, with which she answered, may have facilitated his measured melodic response. What was the significance of the musical dialogue in terms of the ongoing work and the developing aims for this child?

Further interpretations confirmed that the use of perfect fourths were a significant musical element that facilitated emotional, aesthetic, and clinical responses from this child. From a psychological perspective the child concentrated for a period of approximately ten times greater in length than at any other time in the preceding sessions. Musically the composition developed in a precise and delicate manner demonstrating musical sensitivities that had not been heard before. Finally, the aesthetic content of this section was clearly shown through the control of his musical phrases, his piano playing and the relationship between players. Personally, Susan considered her sensitivities at this spontaneous flowering of his music. She described an intense emotional urgency and a physical response of shivers down her spine. Feelings of personal tenderness toward the child at this time were seen to be a natural feature of her response. Susan concluded that the finite combination of musical, clinical, and personal reactions contributed to this powerful therapeutic outcome, and that by identifying each in isolation and association, a clear assessment of this important part of the session had been explored.

Example 4

The Supervisee Reflects—Kimberly Khare
My value judgments were now musically no longer limited to major or minor keys, idioms, or chord structures, but were based on tonal relationships, melodic directions, the essence of intervals, cell formation, and the development of clinical themes. My activity level when it came to conscious creative thinking increased in this area. The responsibility to clinical music, and the analysis of my reactions to it, became foremost. I reconsidered *everything*. Is a hello song necessary? What in fact is a hello song and what does it mean to clinically sing hello? What is the transition needed to move into the music work? I also realized that I alone was not responsible for the music making. I had a partner, the client, and this changed the value of the work greatly. I needed to leave space for the child's ideas and expressions, and I needed to value the child's receptions of my expressions. I acknowledged to being "met" by the client. It was *our* work, not my work. Exploring my emotional reactions to this stage of the work was necessary and personally revealing.

I also began to play against and not always on every pulse of a child's musical expression. This was not abandonment but exchange and interchange. I was better able to value the emotional time of clinical music-making, not just the physical obvious time, and what this meant for my personal growth as a music therapist (Robbins and Forinash, 1991). I was developing judgment and ways to exercise that judgment clinically, emotionally, and musically.

Clinical Judgment

The importance of developing and defining goals is a central alliance between the many methods and models of music therapy. In Aesthetic Music Therapy aims and objectives stem initially from an understanding and assessment of the musical relationship and clinical foundations. Musical and nonmusical goals extend from an investigation of how the elements of music develop. Of equal weight, the therapist must recognize extra musical considerations, such as identified behaviors and desired outcomes that include specific desired goals. The clarity, balance, and understanding between musical and nonmusical intent ultimately allows clients a therapeutic process that is reflective of their needs. The therapist's evaluation and understanding of the developing relationship, their professional role in providing the needed musical and clinical skills, and the ability to reflect the client's personal complexities and reactions combine to provide a therapeutic and artistic essence that is needed for growth.

The identification of short-term and long-term aims is congruent to the four stages of supervision. To understand the entire picture we must explore, question, and analyze the countless components that come together to make up the whole. By defining what is essential for the moment we may begin to consider how this affects the complete design of the session and the overall music therapy design. Goals should be constantly questioned and challenged in supervision:

- How might changes in clinical direction affect the clients and your responses to the overall therapeutic musical substructure?
- What were the musical goals?

- What were the nonmusical goals?
- Why were each important?
- How can we integrate and balance the two?
- How do musical changes affect, contest, and transform overall goals?
- How important it is for you to contest and amend your short-term goals? Do these change your long-term goals?
- How does the ever-shifting balance between the musical and clinical affect the goals and objectives, as the music therapy process deepens?
- How do you define musical growth?
- How do you define therapeutic growth?

The Supervisee Reflects—Kimberly Khare
I now began to differentiate between emotionally forced beating and rhythmic skill development that enables creative freedom—and by discerning this, I could consciously choose which need, which aim to meet (Nordoff and Robbins, 1977). I was able to acknowledge when I'd gone in the wrong direction and change my aims in the session, not after. This allowed the child to do the same. I am now more able to clearly determine musical and nonmusical aims and can follow through in meeting these goals. The change in my perception when formulating goals is the difference of "being" in music versus "doing" in music. Activity does not necessarily determine the effects of the use of clinical music. Direct contact with an instrument comes in many forms, such as actively drumming or playing the piano or *actively listening*. Children who move away from direct contact and who appear to retreat into idiosyncratic behaviors or speech scripts provide a therapeutic and musical challenge. Here the use of skillfully and one might say surgically appropriate music is a challenge that demands a clear connection between listening, evaluation, interpretation, and judgment. Through exploring my own clinical listening, my understanding of the child's clinical listening changed. Listening for me has been the intellectual and emotional nucleus. Music therapists must listen on many levels and work on many listening levels.

Closing Thoughts and Reflections

Supervision is as complex and multifaceted as the therapeutic process itself. Defining a clinical epistemology and then relating it to the supervisory process is an association that requires finite examination and judgment. The supervisor's role is to contain, debate, question, and challenge. That the first stage of supervision described in this chapter is so exacting bears witness to the boundaries and clarity with which the supervisor must work. While the supervisor should always be open and sympathetic to the immediate needs of the supervisee, there is indeed a bigger picture, that of clinical challenge and exactness. That the four stages of supervision may uncover ever more musical and personal vulnerabilities requires both criticism and support. This should be finely balanced as the supervisor and supervisee strive to find the symmetry between clinical listening, learning, and maturation.

So what can music-centered supervision add to clinical practice and the future of music therapy? The direct challenge is that we must pay greater attention to, and strive to understand in ever greater detail, the music in music therapy. Listening is at the heart of our work:

- Listening to the client, their music, our music, and the musical relationship
- Listening behind and beyond the music
- Listening to silence
- Listening to the client as personhood and musichood
- Listening as musicians and therapists
- Listening as sound and community

Listening at ever deeper levels will help define who we are as clinicians and how we shape the future of our work. If we cannot hear accurately and clinically, then we will never understand the musical eloquence of our clients and the potential for growth.

Aesthetic Music Therapy is an exploration of both the dignity and elegance of music and people. This refers to not only the therapeutic relationship and outcome of treatment, but to every aspect and nuance of the balance between music, therapy, identity, and health. The aesthetic potential of therapeutic resistance and disturbance is equal to considering the rounded expression of the beautiful. Aesthetic here means both the offensive and the beautiful. The balance between personhood and musichood is central to Aesthetic Music Therapy and a music-centered approach to supervision. This means always returning to the central frame of music as the yardstick and core of understanding. Listening defines who we are as musicians and music defines who we are as clinicians. It is through music that we offer clients the chance for human transformation.

In supervision we challenge our supervisees to listen, respond, interpret, and advance. In music therapy we challenge ourselves to constantly and continually define and redefine what makes the bridge between epistemological and emotional thought. A music-centered approach to supervision can highlight the ever-changing framework of music versus clinical reality. This approach demands exactness and dedication, and the desire for musical self-examination and confrontation. Music-centered supervision should also be inspiring and enlightening. As we begin to appreciate the magnitude and dignity of music, our clinical creativity will radiate. Discovering the direct relation between music, people, and transformation is ultimately revealing. True meeting and listening in music is a profound experience. Supervision attempts to facilitate this understanding and the supervisee's path in finding that balance which will nurture individual growth and maturity.

References

Aigen, K. (1998). *Paths of Development in Nordoff-Robbins Music Therapy*. Gilsum, NH: Barcelona Publishers.

Amir, D. (1999). Musical and verbal interventions in music therapy: A qualitative study. *Journal of Music Therapy,* 36(2), 144–175.

Ansdell, G. (1995). *Music for Life.* London: Jessica Kingsley Publishers.

Bruscia, K. (1987). *Improvisational Models of Music Therapy.* Springfield, IL: Charles C Thomas.

Brown, S. (1997). Supervision in context: A balancing act. *British Journal of Music Therapy* 11(1) 4–12.

Iwanaga, M., and Moroki, Y. (1999). Subjective and physiological responses to music stimuli controlled over activity and preference. *Journal of Music Therapy,* 36(1), 26–38.

Lee, C. (1992). *The Analysis of Therapeutic Improvisatory Music with People with the Virus HIV and AIDS.* Unpublished PhD thesis. London: City University.

Lee, C. (1996). *Music at the Edge. The Music Therapy Experiences of a Musician with AIDS.* London and New York: Routledge.

Lee, C. (2000). A method of analysing improvisations in music therapy. *Journal of Music Therapy* 37(2).

Lee, C. (in press). *The Architecture of Aesthetic Music Therapy.* Gilsum, NH: Barcelona Publishers.

Nordoff, P., and Robbins, C., (1977) *Creative Music Therapy.* New York: John Day Company.

Oldfield, A. (1992). Teaching music therapy students on practical placements—some observations. *Journal of British Music Therapy,* 6(1), 13–17.

Pavlicevic, M. (1997). *Music Therapy in Context.* London: Jessica Kingsley Publishers.

Robbins, C., and Forinash, M., (1991). "Time as a multilevel phenomenon in Music Therapy. *Music Therapy,* 10(1) 46–57.

Robbins, C., and Robbins, C. (1998). *Healing Heritage.* Gilsum, NH: Barcelona Publishers.

Stephens, G. (1987). The experiential music therapy group as a method of training and supervision. In C. Maranto and K. Bruscia (eds.), *Perspectives on Music Therapy Education and Training.* Philadelphia, PA: Temple University, Esther College of Music.

Streeter, E. (1999). Finding a balance between psychological thinking and musical awareness in music therapy: A psychoanalytic perspective. *British Journal of Music Therapy,* 13(1), 5–20.

Acknowledgments

Colin Lee

To Dr. Michele Forinash for her enthusiasm when Aesthetic Music Therapy was first conceptualized and her continued support since. To Dr. Rosemary Fischer for being my constant critical companion during the writing of this chapter. To Carol and Clive Robbins for always contesting my music, and finally to Paul Nordoff for posthumously being a composer kindred spirit.

Kimberly Khare

I wish to thank the staff of the Nordoff-Robbins Music Therapy Center in New York for their guidance and encouragement during the beginning phases of my development; the Massachusetts music therapy community for taking me in with open arms and nurturing my warrior within; Colin Lee for his patient mentoring, friendship and music; and Carol Robbins, Michele Forinash, Karen Wacks, Caryl-Beth Thomas and Penny Khare for their insightful supervision and the many ways they inspire me.

Chapter 18

Psychodynamic Perspectives in Professional Supervision

Mechtild Jahn-Langenberg, PhD
Director of Music Therapy Department
University of the Arts, Berlin, Germany

Introduction

Supervision is the shared attempt of both the music therapist in the clinical field and the supervisor to better understand the case. The subject of treatment within that context comes first into focus within the working process of the supervision itself. Thus, treatment techniques, methodology, conflicts within the working field of the institution, and the way in which the therapist understands his/her own role and function within a team can all be considered "the case." When transference and countertransference constellations are taken into consideration, the work toward understanding becomes a joint composition created by the supervisor and the supervisee together. This basic tenor determines the working alliance; it is necessary to differentiate between the music therapist's own personality, which arises as a matter of course, and the personality of the patient. The music therapy treatment case determines the frame of reference within which the treatment takes place, and poses the challenge of dealing with the functions and goals of the therapist's own role as well as with psychodynamic problems in the relationship work of the treatment process. When conflicts within the institutional framework become a priority, the therapeutic work can become overburdened and even stagnate. Stagnation can occur before any clear assignment of functions among the therapists involved has had time to take place. And yet, dealing with ego-ideals, setting limits for the overblown fantasies of music therapists, reality checking, and the renewed establishment of goals can be a necessary but painful process. All of these contributing factors require definition, so that the psychodynamic of the patient's personality, restaged both in the scene of relationship activities with the music therapist and within the setting of supervision, can become the clear subject of treatment.

Within the therapy process, the patient projects his/her inner conflicts onto the treatment team, thus challenging the treatment team to continually redefine and clarify their positions and relationships to one another. The goal of supervision is to help the supervisee define reality and maintain a grip on it in the face of the shifting roles set into motion by the patient, who is using the therapeutic relationship to free him/herself of inner conflicts. The outward prospect of professional supervision serves as the regulator for all those involved with the treatment activities. For this work, the relationships between those involved should be clearly defined through precise separation into the roles of supervisor and supervisee. The rule of abstinence, which recommends that no other relationship be maintained for the duration of the working alliance, facilitates the understanding of transference relationships. According to Tüpker (1996) in some settings, such as a training situation, role conflicts which arise between the student and the institute can be worked on because the act of student supervision does not imply a professional responsibility on the patient.

The following chapter will focus on working out the conditions of a psychoanalytically justified treatment within psychotherapeutical medicine and psychosomatic within the framework of an integrated total treatment plan. The treatment as a whole plays a role within the functions of all those involved. This means that they are challenged to understand their role in the play which the patient, due to his/her inner conflicts, must set into motion. Only when the "treaters" understand this "play" together with the supervisor are they able to develop interventions for the patient. In the center is the patient, who through the diagnostic process is assessed as needing treatment. The patient confers permission to treat; the goals of the treatment will be developed together with him/her, and the specifics of his/her treatment plan will be established. With this, questions about the abilities of the treatment team, and indications for creative procedures such as music therapy as an accompanying or primary therapy, play an important role. From this, central questions about the characteristics of "therapist" as a profession are raised, not only those related to method and treatment techniques of the music therapist, but also those on an occupation related level of contracts and salary.

Experience with supervision within the professional framework has shown that the calling to consciousness, the processing, and the clarifying of these questions determines the successful content of music therapy work. Colleagues' dissatisfaction and distorted perspectives, which can result from poorly defined relationships, make an otherwise meaningful therapy work seem questionable.

Psychoanalytically-Oriented Music Therapy

The work toward meaning carried out within professional analytically-founded supervision can result in gains in knowledge through the experiencing of changes in perspective. In order to make this work clear, specifics of psychoanalytically-established music therapy will now be presented.

Music therapy as a psychoanalytically-oriented method is understood as a modification of analytical psychotherapy. It came about in the wake of institutional developments, for example, at the Clinic for Psychosomatic Medicine and Psychotherapy at the University of Dusseldorf (Heigl-Evers, Henneberg-Mönch, Odag, and Standke 1986; Heigl-Evers, Heigl, and Rüger 1997). The methods of treatment find their roots in the analytic music therapy of Mary Priestley and Johannes Eschen, as well as those involved in New Music who bring a new understanding of the role of music (Eschen, 1983; Karkoschka, 1966; Priestley 1983). Through increasing professionalism, further training and recognition in the clinical setting, psychoanalytically-established music therapy, within the framework of an integrated total treatment plan in a clinical setting, could take on the function of an independent psychotherapy procedure (Langenberg 1986, 1997). A specific characteristic of active music therapy is the active relationship between patient and therapist. Encounters in therapy take place within the scope of joint musical improvisation, and in conversations which take place before and after playing. Through this, an understanding occurs, a vocalisation of what is experienced during the process of playing and the intrapsychic and interpersonal phenomena that come up. In the triad Encounter–Produce–Integrate, the treatment process, understood as the interactive occurrence of improvisation as a reproduction of, in part, the earliest experiences of relationship, becomes complete. The therapist and patient play what comes into their heads, and shape a common musical product, which is understood as the treatment piece. The therapist plays the piano both on the keyboard as well as on the strings inside the piano; there is an array of percussion instruments, there is a second piano as well as string and melody instruments, thus offering a wide range of expression for the patient. The lively encounter between the therapist and patient and the relationship-forming process ignites feelings, fantasies, and pictures, which are indications of internalized relationship experiences and conflicts from earlier phases of development. A space is created where subconscious fantasies become audible and a psychodynamic understanding of the specific encounter is brought to awareness.

In the transference relationship of the therapeutic situation, a particular quality is created in that a direct resonance—a sympathetic vibration between the therapist and the patient established by the sounds and the playing—is perceptible. The way in which another is perceived, according to psychoanatically-oriented music psychotherapy, in the sense of a personal instrument of relating and understanding, was termed as the "resonator function" in an earlier work (Langenberg, 1988). Alongside the ability to resonate with, to become audible and palpable within the process of the therapeutic encounter, this term contains the idea of "instrument." Thus the difference in the quality of a transference relationship in *music* therapy becomes clear. Sound and relationship-forming within music occur at the time when the players encountering each other enter into a perceptible, audible, and palpable relationship. Within the security of the music room, bonding and separating can be experienced.

The resonator function as a treatment instrument implies physical and psychic answers in the treatment process. The therapist must be aware of his/her own inner associations and fantasies in order to derive meaning from what the patient expresses during the improvisation. This bringing the inner world into focus is facilitated by going back and forth between two poles, and significant clues could be discovered in an oscillation between primary and secondary processes during improvisation, setting interior and exterior into relationship, or looking at the movement of time in music, examining the material and the ideal. The specifics of psychoanalytically-oriented music therapy are, alongside the space for playing and speaking, techniques of working with the improvisation process, as well as working in the psychotherapeutic process. The method has received important stimulation from the psychoanalytic-interactive therapy developed by Heigl-Evers in the psychosomatic/psychotherapeutic context of patients with structural ego disturbances who, in the clinical context, required modifications in psychoanalytic technique (Heigl-Evers, et al., 1986).

Parallels to the position of the selectively authentic, felt, and active in the sense of "playing together" music therapist are found within the answer principle and the principle of the palpable opposite.

In these basic statements on methods of treatment, I have tried first to present in theory the specificity of the working methods and their appropriateness for patients with psychosomatic symptoms and experience deficits in earlier affective attunement processes.

Especially in work with patients who, because of structural ego disturbances, are trying to make their own inner incompatibility understandable through relationship disturbances, the sometimes vehement scenes which are staged within a therapy session can place a serious emotional burden on the therapist. The immediacy of the therapeutic space, which really invites one to play and experiment imaginatively again, brings earliest relationship experiences to expression in a way in which they can be physically sensed.

The musical material that is offered through the arrangement of the music therapy room with two pianos, xylophones, vibes, drums, chimes, cymbals, wood blocks, flutes, and several small percussion instruments and the instruction: "Play whatever comes to mind, determined by whatever needs to be expressed." leads to free, often atonal musical improvisation. The therapist's musical role is to give space for experiences with sounds, to let the patient find his own way and his own tones while developing one's own sound and form in this unique encounter. When establishing a structure that fits the theme of the improvisation, the therapist helps to create the work by supporting or contrasting the patient's musical ideas. The therapeutic role of the music is to find a way to the inner world of the patient. The joint musical improvisation and the conversation afterward (a verbalization of the experiences that came up within the active process), provoke feelings, fantasies, and images. These are indications of the staging of subjectively experienced, internalized interpersonal relational experiences and conflicts from earlier developmental phases.

In the transference relationship of the therapeutic situation a unique quality emerges from the fact that direct resonance, through the tones produced and through shared playing, becomes perceivable with the senses. An opportunity allowing unconscious fantasies and a psychodynamic understanding of the specific encounter situation to become *audible* is created. In the encounter each relationship partner remains continuously in close contact with the other and is a counterpart with whom times of togetherness and separation can be experienced in a secure space.

Supervision

The therapist under supervision brings his/her case to the supervision meeting, and restages the relationship dynamic from the therapy session in which they make themselves available as a living instrument of perception and answer. The work toward meaning occurs now through a countertransference analysis, which is the resonance work of psychoanalytically-oriented music therapy. This encourages a re-experiencing of the therapy situation, a renewed suffering through, a sympathizing with the problem. The supervisor is drawn into the common processing field, brought to life in the shared work of the improvisation with its accompanying associations. The inner work of the music therapist acquires space in the reproduced field of professional supervision.

When this work takes place within a supervision group, a variety of transference relationships within the interpersonal field of group members and the resulting group dynamic can be discovered. This special theme will not be handled within this chapter; instead, the way in which new perspectives for the supervisee result from a psychodynamic way of working within individual supervision will be demonstrated with an example. The analytic treatment technique forms the background of this method.

The treatment task for the supervision of therapist Ms. M is the processing of problems which arise within the stationary setting of a psychosomatic clinic. Here, music therapy assumes the function of a special procedure accompanying psychoanalytically-oriented, verbal individual and group therapy. The posing of indications for treatment takes place during trial meetings with a specialist colleague, as well as during discussions within an interdisciplinary team. In combination with additional therapy procedures, an integrated treatment plan toward processing their problems is placed at the disposal of the patient. The path of either individual or group music therapy is chosen. Colleague Ms. M continually brings new questions about her function and role within the institution into supervision. These are triggered on the one hand because the station where she works is brand new within the clinic, and on the other, by serious transference complications with patients who have structural ego disturbances. The patients' underlying insecurities, early traumas, and oral needs stimulate the narcissistic basic needs of the therapist; it is necessary to meet these face to face.

This prototypical example of a supervision is placed under the special aspect of the music therapist's own "psychohygiene." The theme must be "Remain with Yourself—Take Care of Yourself." The desired psychoanalytic perceptual attitude of balanced-floating attentiveness, an openness for the events of the inner world, is described as the optimal centering of the therapist on his/her own person. Coupled with this is the ability to perceive the outer world, and at the same time to be able to be reached by the inner world of the patient within the relationship activities. For the therapeutic process, in which we are ready to be used as living instruments of perception, this optimal attitude remains a posture to be continually reacquired and practiced. The resonance work of the attunement process, which has its own character within music therapy, is applied to a case in supervision. Improvisation, an instrument toward deriving meaning, is applied in order to center on transference occurrences and the position of the music therapist on the case, in that the supervisor offers him/herself as a play partner and answering opposite.

In this example, in the supervision meeting the colleague reports on a patient with whom she works in individual music therapy sessions for fifty minutes, twice a week. Within the surroundings of this case work, the clarification of function within the team, questions of competency, job-related legal problems, and the determination of realistic therapy goals for this treatment embracing both the possibilities and limitations of music therapy, first stand at the heart of the work. This establishes the face of reality, and thus serves to unburden the colleague in the sense of psychohygiene, which in turn makes possible a more efficient application of music therapy for the patient.

The breaks in dialogue (withdrawal from the treatment team) and other aggressive affects which occur frequently in therapy with patients who have structural ego disturbances are expressions of inconstant relationship-forming conditions in very early childhood, which inevitably manifest themselves as a lack of object constancy. The patient will, of necessity, revive these conditions of uncertainty and unreliability as he/she sets the relationship with the therapist in scene. On the real level of the working alliance and his/her own reliability, the therapist can offer a new opportunity to experience object constancy. The supportive, space-giving music therapist has special possibilities of meeting the patient on a preverbal level, to establish an anchor that was lacking, to bring security and structure, to heal the narcissistic wounds through the forming of a relationship where the patient is recognized as an individual. The music therapist supports the patient in the effort to make his/her own tone heard. The constantly reappearing break in dialogue (Heigl-Evers, et al., 1997) as a sign of the inability of the patient to reliably sense him/herself, requires a clearly present, palpable "opposite" for the further development from monadic existence to dialogue. In this process, the therapist is challenged to withstand phases of searching, finding, and losing, to bear boredom and monotony, in which he/she can rely only on his/her own ability to "Remain with Yourself."

Colleague Ms. M obviously has guilt feelings during the supervision meeting, as she tells how she is becoming more and more bored during the meetings with her patient, how her thoughts wander, how she calls the treatment into question because she seems to be losing herself and with this, possible goals within the relationship process. While Ms. M is speaking, the supervisor as well feels that she must make an effort to remain in the relationship, feels affected by a mood of monotony and meagreness. Both patient and therapist seem to disappear into vagueness. In the sense of psychoanalytical work, countertransference is held to be an indication of the problem in the therapist-patient relationship. The patient makes the therapist feel incompetent to remain within the dialogue. In turn, during the supervision session, the therapist under supervision makes the supervisor feel the type of countertransference entanglement he/she is involved in.

From her experience, the supervisor diagnoses this condition as a break in dialogue, in that, after a phase of going with the current without structure and empathizing, she perceives associations to similar cases of narcissistic wounding in her own inner work. Object constancy doesn't seem to be maintainable, and the retreat to a monadic condition is a necessary lifesaving shield against being overwhelmed. The music therapist treating the case is, due to the burden of countertransference by the patient, clearly overwhelmed by her own narcissistic needs for security, safety, and an attention which does not smother but instead supports, which allow her to center herself on her own existence. The regaining of one's own presence for the important condition of balanced-floating attentiveness requires methodical steps in supervision work which restore an affective getting in touch with one's own needs. Such a space is formed in a supervision session by the music therapy technique of improvisation.

The colleague is challenged to "Take Care of Yourself," to equip herself well with instruments, to find her own place, to look for her own tone, to find her own playing style, during which the supervisor plays with her, remaining a palpable opposite and providing space for her colleague's work. The goals of this intervention are, in basic therapy work and reexperienced in case supervision: classification, identification, and clarification of the affects stimulated through the treatment. The colleague can only be a palpably present opposite for the patient again, when, through the improvisations, her attunement with herself brings out new inspiration, and the ability to carry out attunement procedures within the therapy session is restored.

In this example, the supervisor and the supervisee both experience pressing impulses toward confrontation after a musical improvisation phase of searching. Out of rigidity and lack of structure arise new contours of steadiness and encouraging, dialogue-initiating elements which revive both players. Ms. M's ideas, found while playing with the supervisor, brought to a point in the conversation which followed, and understood as an indication of the relationship dynamic which had been set in scene by the patient, show that the break in dialogue was brought about by the aggressive affect of the patient. As one of the protective functions of the patient, this could be understood as a signal of defense against threat and overflooding. Touched by the instrument, its sound characteristics, and the intrapsychic reaction to it, the patient felt overwhelmed, went into regression, and took the music therapist with her.

Through her own regaining of affect in the supervision session, the music therapist comprehends that she can maintain a cautious but palpably lively posture for this patient who was disturbed in her early years, if she continues to constantly reinforce her own needs for self-definition and wishes for basic security, in order to not lose herself.

To start a relationship, to become more attached, above all in the emotional area, seems to be beset with ambivalent tension for the patient (Langenberg, 1999). The new, the unfamiliar, that which can't yet be classified, all create uncertainty, and thus the patient falls into a need for regulation in encounter situations. Indications for this understanding of the scene are to be found in countertransference, expressed in music therapy terms as the resonator function of the therapist. After the opening phase of joint improvisation, the careful accompaniment of the patient, a position of letting her find her tone undisturbed, in the authentically felt answer to being touched by the music, an unexpected vibratory process is set into motion.

The therapist experiences an affective prodding, a turning toward the offering of the patient, and applies the psychoanalytical interactional technique of the "answer"—the palpable opposite. Within the supervision meeting, the supervisor makes it possible for the supervisee to give an answer in relation to her own affect. This means making affective, personal resonance available to the patient. In our prototypical example, this resulted in a break in the dialogue, the patient appeared to experience a disturbance, changed instruments, and took up his former volatility again. Affective fear and tendencies toward flight from the development of this dialogue, both indications of aggressive affect, can be supposed.

The affect researcher, Krause, speaks about so-called affect rudiments, which, when mobilized within the patient, often trigger only vague feelings which cannot be clearly classified. It is a question of imparted experience (physical sensations) in watered-down form, neutralized and masked by another affect (Krause, 1988). This means that the affects of the patient currently being mobilized are only vaguely imparted through, for example, mimic-gestic microsignals. The patient experiences them in a deintensified form and the affects become neutralized and are partly masked through other affects. As an example, one psychosomatic patient from my own clinical practice attracted attention due to the fact that she always laughed when aggressive content arose. This connection became clear only over the course of the music therapy treatment.

The example of supervision with its reexperiencing of the therapist-patient relationship points out the inner state of feeling which patient and therapist share. Differentiated and complex affective attunement processes, within interpersonal orientation, basically need clarification. This becomes more difficult and can lead to a situation of regulation emergency for the therapist, visible then in symptoms such as breaking the dialogue, when competency and security in the identification and clarification of affects are not sufficiently experienced. Originally created by the imagination of the patient and taken up by the therapist, answered and implemented in their continuing relationship as a distinguishing characteristic, it challenged the necessary attunement of both patient and therapist to their needs and possibilities for coming closer and establishing borders, i.e., a situation-appropriate affect regulation. The measure of necessary openness, readiness to show oneself and get involved, and the need for retreat, security, and protection with one's own tone showed itself in the interaction. Regressive temptation means, in the case of patients with structural ego disturbances, the danger of the loss of structure, of getting lost. As mechanisms of coping with this, aggressive affect and physical cramping arise during therapy. Patients translate these into breaks in the dialogue, and in music they are experienced as volatility and lack of relationship. In the case of a strong inclination toward regression, within the scope of music therapy improvisation in interactional work, the contour-forming of the personality can be worked on.

The burden of such basic relationship work within music therapy requires differentiated affect perception in supervision as well, in order to unburden the therapist under supervision, to enable him or her to recapture a professional posture which places the necessary treatment techniques at his/her disposal as well as enlivening his/her creativity in dealing with the situation.

References

Eschen, J. Th. (1983). Assoziative improvisation *(Associative Improvisation)*. In: H. H. Decker-Voigt (ed). Handbuch der Musiktherapie *(Handbook of Music Therapy)*. Bremen: Eres, 41–43.

Heigl-Evers, A., Henneberg-Mönch, U., Odag, C., and Standke, G. (1986). Die Vierzigstundenwoche für Patienten: Konzept und Praxis teilstationärer Psychotherapie *(The Forty Hour Week for Patients: Concept and Practice of Partially-Stationary Psychotherapy)*. Göttingen: Vandenhoek & Ruprecht.

Heigl-Evers, A., Heigl, F., and Rüger, U. (1997). Lehrbuch der Psychotherapie *(Textbook of Psychotherapy)*. 3 überarbeitete Auflage. Stuttgart: Fischer.

Karkoschka, E. (1966). Das Schriftbild der Neuen Musik *(The Typeface of New Music)*. Celle: Moeck.

Krause, R. (1988). Eine Taxonomie der Affekte und ihre Anwendung auf das Verständnis der "frühen" Störungen *(A Taxonomy of Affects and their Application in the Understanding of "Early" Disturbances)*. PPmP 38, 77–86.

Langenberg, M. (1988). Vom Handeln zum Behandeln. Darstellung besonderer Merkmale der musiktherapeutischen Behandlungssituation im Zusammenhang mit der freien Improvisation *(From Acting to Treating. A Presentation of Special Characteristics of the Music-Therapeutical Treatment Situation in the Context of Free Improvisation)*. Stuttgart: Fischer.

Langenberg, M. (1986). Musiktherapie—Spielraum—Übergangsraum— Zwischenraum. Überlegungen zur Funktion einer künstlerischen Therapie *(Music Therapy—Space to Play—Temporary Space—Spacing)*. In: A Heigl-Evers, (ed.), Die Vierzigstundenwoche für Patienten. Göttingen: Vandenhoeck & Ruprecht, 176–192.

Langenberg, M. (1997). Musiktherapie *(Music Therapy)*. In: A. Heigl-Evers, (ed.), Lehrbuch der Psychotherapie. 3.überarbeitete Auflage. Stuttgart: Fischer.

Langenberg, M. (1999). Music therapy and the meaning of affect regulation for psychosomatic patients. In: T. Wigram, and J. De Backer (eds.), *Clinical Applications of Music Therapy in Psychiatry*. London: Jessica Kingsley Publishers.

Priestley, M. (1983). Analytische Musiktherapie *(Analytical Music Therapy)*. Stuttgart: Fischer.

Tüpker, R. (1996). Supervision als Unterrichtsfach in der musiktherapeutischen Ausbildung *(Supervision as a Teaching Subject in Music-Therapeutical Training)*. MU17, 242–251.

Chapter 19

A Model of Supervision
Derived from
Apprenticeship Training

Kenneth E. Bruscia, PhD, MT-BC
Professor of Music Therapy
Temple University, Philadelphia, PA

The purpose of this chapter is twofold: to describe an apprenticeship training program in supervision developed by the author at Temple University, and to present a model of supervision that emerged from the parallel processes encountered therein.

Design of the Apprenticeship

The apprenticeship was designed as an integral part of graduate study in music therapy. In the program, a clinically experienced music therapist enrolled in a graduate degree program serves as an apprentice to his/her major professor, and gradually learns to assume a full range of supervisory responsibilities in music therapy.

Rationale and Objectives

Because the apprenticeship was offered within an academic rather than clinical setting, a central concern was that the apprentice-supervisor would have an opportunity to learn about the full range of music therapy supervision. Music therapy supervision currently takes place in a wide variety of preprofessional and professional contexts. At the preprofessional level, supervision is provided on-site and in the classroom, by clinicians, educators, or both, as part of practicum and internship experiences, offered at undergraduate and graduate levels of certification studies. At the professional level, supervision may be provided on the job or privately, by more experienced music therapists or in peer groups.

This large range of supervisory practices poses fundamental questions about how to train supervisors. Should the learning objectives include all levels and contexts, and if so, how should they be taught differentially? Do differences in goal and method between these types of supervision require vastly different knowledge and skills on the part of the supervisor? Specifically, will an individual trained in supervision at the preprofessional level be adequately prepared to supervise at the professional level (or vice versa)? And, will an individual trained in supervision in an academic setting be adequately prepared to supervise in a clinical setting (or vice versa)?

In the present program, the apprentice serves as an academic supervisor for undergraduate music therapy interns. Thus, its primary and immediate focus is on preprofessional supervision from an academic perspective; however, in its approach to supervision, the apprenticeship has been designed to help the apprentice generalize his/her learning about supervision from preprofessional to professional levels, and from academic to clinical settings. This is accomplished in two ways.

First, supervision is conceptualized and taught in levels and stages. The levels of supervision are presented in direct relation to the depth of the apprentice's work with the intern, which in turn depends upon the depth of the intern's work with clients—with more advanced, comprehensive, and long-term work requiring deeper levels of supervision than early, focused, or short-term work. In this way, preprofessional and professional supervision are conceived together on the same continuum, according to the level of clinical work being supervised rather than according to the professional status of the supervisee. More will be said of these levels later.

Second, supervision is conceptualized as integrally related to teaching, according to a continuum of responsibility shared by both educators and clinical supervisors. This notion is a common one in those colleges and universities where supervision of practica and internships is a joint venture between the academic faculty and on-site music therapists. The main implication for training is helping the apprentice to understand and differentiate the roles and responsibilities of academic and clinical supervisors. For this reason, the apprentice is always asked to consider the intern's supervisory needs in a holistic way, identifying all the various kinds of supervisory supports that will help the intern to function and learn more effectively. Once this is done, the apprentice has to make clear distinctions between the roles and responsibilities of the academic and clinical supervisors, and then act accordingly. In this way, academic and clinical supervision are conceived together, on the same continuum, according to the supervisee's needs first, and then according to supervisory roles. Later, it will be seen that the actual techniques used by the academic supervisor are much the same as those used by the clinical supervisor.

Learning objectives for the apprenticeship can now be stated. They are: 1) understanding of the differential roles and responsibilities of academic and on-site supervisors; 2) understanding of the various approaches and levels of supervision and their appropriate application; 3) ability to observe and analyze clinical work in music therapy from a variety of perspectives; 4) ability to develop effective supervisory relationships; 5) ability to communicate clearly and effectively to supervisees and other supervisors; 6) ability to conduct individual supervisory conferences and group seminars; 7) understanding of the potential effects of one's own background and experience, personal and professional, on the supervisee, the supervisory process, and the clinical work of the supervisee.

Administrative Structure

An effective apprenticeship requires two layers of organization, one for the internship program being supervised by the apprentice and the other for the apprenticeship experience itself. At Temple University, the internship is an academic course required for the undergraduate degree and equivalency certification program at the postbaccalaureate level. The intern remains in academic residence during the entire internship experience, working under the direct supervision of both academic and clinical supervisors.

Upon beginning the internship, the intern receives a course syllabus and a comprehensive manual. The syllabus spells out the educational objectives, academic requirements, and grading policies for the internship. Academic requirements include attendance at a weekly seminar, keeping weekly logs, and making one case presentation per semester. The internship manual explains the roles and responsibilities of the intern, on-site clinical supervisor, and academic supervisor, along with expectations and rules governing all aspects of the internship. A manual is also given to the on-site clinical supervisor. It includes all the information from the intern's manual, and in addition provides pertinent information about the music therapy program at the university, along with student evaluation forms. These documents serve as continual sources of information for all parties concerned, and in many ways, are the standard parts of every internship contract.

At the second layer, the apprenticeship itself has to be well-organized. The professor has to provide clear guidelines on the apprentice's duties and responsibilities—both as an apprentice and as a supervisor (see below). In addition, the professor has to establish clear policies and procedures that the apprentice can follow in his/her interactions with interns and their cooperating clinical supervisors.

Considerable care must be taken in establishing lines of communication and protocols for interaction. Generally speaking:

- The intern communicates with the clinical supervisor and apprentice on all matters pertaining to the internship, and with the professor on all matters pertaining to his/her overall degree program;
- The clinical supervisor communicates with the apprentice on all matters pertaining to the intern, and with the professor on all matters pertaining to the relationship between the clinical agency and university; and
- The apprentice communicates with the professor on all matters pertaining to his/her supervision of the intern and interactions with clinical supervisors.

Of course, there will always be times and instances when, in the best interests of the intern, these lines of communication must be crossed, however when this occurs, it is essential that all parties involved be informed.

Basic Components of the Apprenticeship

The apprentice is given primary responsibility for supervising all aspects of the internship while under the continual guidance of the professor. This includes: developing internship placement sites and negotiating supervision contracts, placing students in an appropriate setting with an appropriate supervisor, maintaining telephone contact with clinical supervisors, observing the intern twice per semester, leading weekly group seminars for interns, holding individual supervisory conferences with the intern, and doing evaluations of the intern's work.

The professor supervises the apprentice in carrying out these responsibilities through:

- *Individual supervisory conferences*. The apprentice meets with the professor weekly for 1–2 hours. Most often, the apprentice sets the agenda for these meetings based on issues and questions that arise in carrying out his/her responsibilities; however, as necessary, the professor may also bring up matters of concern, or help the apprentice to recontextualize his/her original concerns and questions. Sometimes the discussion focuses on the interns and their supervisory needs; sometimes it focuses on the apprentice and his/her supervisory needs. Sometimes the discussion is very task-oriented, focusing on what the apprentice has to do, and how it is to be done; sometimes the discussion is very process-oriented, focusing on what the apprentice is experiencing as supervisor or supervisee. Sometimes the focus is the apprentice's relationship to the intern, sometimes it is the relationship with the professor. No hard and fast rules can be made for what will be discussed and how the various topics will be handled; however, what guides the professor's supervisory efforts is the stage and level of supervision of the apprentice and the intern.

- *Apprentice logs*. The apprentice is asked to write weekly logs which will be shared with the professor. The purpose of the logs is to help the apprentice explore his/her experiences and feelings both as a supervisor and supervisee. As such, they are meant to be reflective—opportunities for the apprentice to go inward and examine personal aspects of both sides of the supervisory process. They are different from the weekly conferences in that they are not meant to be a report on the internship program and the apprentice's activities. On the other hand, the logs do serve a communicative function. They often provide the apprentice with a more comfortable way of communicating deeper issues to the professor. Here again, the apprentice determines what the content and focus will be, and the professor responds according to the level and stage of supervision.

- *Ongoing contact*. The apprentice needs to have immediate access to the professor whenever serious problems or emergencies arise. Both telephone and e-mail are used for these purposes. Here it is important for the apprentice to learn how to identify when immediate action is necessary, as well as when consultation is warranted.

- *Observations*. The professor's main opportunity for observing the apprentice's group leadership style comes in the weekly group seminars for interns. At first, these seminars are co-led by the professor and apprentice, with each taking equal but different roles, and each dealing with different aspects of the internship. With time, the professor gradually gives more and more responsibility to the apprentice while still attending, observing, and afterward giving feedback to the apprentice. Eventually, when ready, the apprentice leads these seminars independently, without the professor even attending. An important criteria in determining when the observations can stop is the ability of the apprentice to accurately report what transpired in the seminar. When the professor can rely upon the apprentice's reports on the seminar, most problems can be resolved in the weekly supervisory conferences.

Parallel Designs

The intern and apprentice have much in common—after all, they are both doing apprenticeships. Both are learning in vivo under supervision; both face the myriad personal challenges of professional self-development; and both need very similar kinds of supervisory supports. To explore and utilize these parallels in the supervision process, the apprentice is given many of the same tasks as the intern, and asked to consider the similarities. They both work with others in individual and group settings; write personal logs of their experiences; work while being observed and monitored by a supervisor; observe the supervisor as a role model; have regular meetings with the supervisor before and/or after performing their assigned duties; and develop working relationships with the supervisor.

Because of these parallels in duties, the professor is able to supervise the apprentice using the same concepts and techniques that the apprentice will be using to supervise the intern. This provides myriad opportunities for the professor to serve as a role model, demonstrating various approaches, levels, and techniques of supervision directly to the apprentice. What makes this kind of modeling so effective is the added experiential component: the apprentice learns from direct experience about how each supervisory intervention feels to a supervisee, and more important, the apprentice is learning about the supervisee's perspective while being asked to use these interventions as a supervisor with the interns. Personalizing the modeling in this way not only deepens the apprentice's understanding of the supervisory intervention itself, but also deepens the parallel process considerably. Under these conditions, the supervisory relationship between professor and apprentice can serve as a mirror for the supervisory relationship between the apprentice and intern.

The key to implementing this parallel process is the use of a level/stage approach to supervision. In this approach, five levels of supervision are introduced during three stages of depth in each supervisee's work, with the apprentice being supervised at the same level as the intern, which in turn is determined by the depth of the intern's work with clients. Thus, as the intern's work with clients deepens, the apprentice is called upon to use deeper levels of supervision with the intern, and as the apprentice's work with interns deepens, the professor is called upon to use deeper levels of supervision with the apprentice.

A Level/Stage Model of Supervision

In the process of working through the parallel and complex layers of the apprenticeship, a model of supervision evolved. In this model, supervision is provided at five main levels of intervention, comprising three stages of readiness. To illustrate these levels, the same clinical problem will be addressed: the supervisee is having trouble with one elderly person in a group who continually gets out of his seat, and tries to walk out of the room.

- *Action-oriented*: What does the supervisee need to do? In the example, the supervisor suggests that the supervisee quietly remind the client where he is, and invite him to return.

- *Learning-oriented*: What knowledge, insight, or skill does the supervisee need to acquire? In the example, the supervisor asks the supervisee to examine whether there is a relationship between the pacing of the session, the transition time between activities, and the client's leaving.

- *Client-oriented*: What does the supervisee need to understand about the client? In the example, the supervisor asks the supervisee to read the chart on the client to determine what factors might contribute to such restlessness (e.g., medications, depression, status within the group, etc.).

- *Experience-oriented*: What must the supervisee be experiencing to operate as s/he does? In the example, the supervisor explores how the supervisee feels, or what the supervisee thinks about when the client gets up, and then when the client tries to leave. Once identified, the supervisor and supervisee try to work through and reframe the supervisee's experience. The purpose may be to help the supervisee be more accepting of and comfortable with the client's responses, or to help the supervisee develop an emotional tone with the client that might prevent or shift that restlessness.

- *Countertransference-oriented*: What personal issues of the supervisee are implicated in his/her work? At this level, the supervisor explores the supervisee's experience and responses to the client, and then tries to find parallels in the supervisee's past. In the example, the supervisor explores previous experiences of the supervisee with regard to being ignored, or abandoned, or not in control.

Once a level has been introduced, the supervisor may use it at any time thereafter, depending on the nature of the problem or issue presented by the supervisee. Thus, for example, even after the supervisee enters the client-oriented level, the supervisor may use action-oriented or learning-oriented interventions. Eventually, each level becomes part of a more complete supervisory intervention, which combines several levels. Thus, a supervisee may present an issue which calls for countertransference supervision, and the supervisor may begin at that level, and then depending upon the issue involved, follow up with client-oriented and action-oriented interventions. In the previous example, the supervisor might start with an exploration of the student's countertransference feelings (i.e., the client is abandoning the supervisee just as the supervisee's father did), and then deal with client-centered supervision (i.e., the client is not directing the behavior toward the supervisee, but is simply restless because of medication), and then move to action supervision (i.e., instead of inviting the client to return, the supervisee might ask the client what he needs at that moment). Eventually, the other two levels of supervision can also be brought to bear. In experience-oriented, the supervisor might revisit the supervisee's feelings of abandonment to help develop other feeling responses, such as empathy or understanding; in learning-oriented, the supervisor might help the supervisee understand the specific effects of the medication the client is taking, or which aspects of music therapy may exacerbate the client's restlessness.

The level of intervention depends greatly upon the supervisee's stage of readiness. These will be discussed later. In the sections below, more detail will be provided on each level of supervision, not only for when the apprentice supervises the intern, but also when the professor supervises the apprentice.

Five Levels of Intervention

Action-Oriented

The first level of supervision is action-oriented; the supervisor tells the supervisee what to do and/or how to do it. The aim is to help the supervisee develop the specific behaviors needed to perform basic tasks or duties at a functional level.

Within the context of the apprenticeship, this level might involve the professor giving the apprentice step-by-step instructions on what to do when making a field observation of the intern, or advise the apprentice how to respond to a particular pattern of events in the seminar.

Action-oriented supervision is warranted when: 1) the addition, modification, or elimination of a behavior is the most efficient and effective way of establishing or improving the supervisee's functionality; 2) when the supervisee understands the reason or need for the behavior; and 3) when implementing the behavior change will lead to further learning and insight. Most often these conditions occur during the earliest stages of supervision, and later whenever the supervisee begins any new task or responsibility.

At this level, a clear distinction should be made between the clinical responsibility and authority of the intern's clinical supervisor and the apprentice (or academic supervisor). The clinical supervisor has ultimate responsibility, authority, and liability for the safety and programming of clients under his/her care; the apprentice or academic supervisor does not. Thus, it is inappropriate for the apprentice (or academic supervisor) to tell the intern how to program for clients, or how to respond to specific clients clinically. This is the sole domain of the clinical supervisor. Instead, at this level, the apprentice (or academic supervisor) helps the intern to develop professional behaviors of a more general nature, not tied to the specific problems or needs of particular clients. Thus, for example, upon observing the intern lead a client session, the apprentice supervisor might suggest that the intern increase eye contact with clients, adjust the volume of his/her singing, or slow down the instructions; the clinical supervisor might advise the intern on how to program for a certain client, or how to respond to a particular client problem.

The apprentice and clinical supervisor also share many concerns at this level. Both help the intern to develop behaviors that are required of any professional, such as being on time, or calling in when sick. Another important role for both supervisors is to help the intern benefit from one another's supervision. At this level, this might involve telling the intern what to do before, during or after an observation or supervisory conference, or how to respond to a supervisor when suggestions are made, and so forth.

Learning-Oriented

The second level of supervision is learning-oriented; the supervisor helps the supervisee to gain the knowledge, insight, or skill needed to be more efficient or effective. Here the focus is not on what actions or behaviors will make the supervisee functional, but rather on what the supervisee still needs to learn—not only to become more functional, but also to move beyond mere functionality. In most cases, this level is a search for gaps in the supervisee's previous training, or blindspots and distortions in the supervisee's understanding. To identify these learning needs, the supervisor might ask: What must the supervisee not understand to work in such a way? Or, what does the supervisee still need to learn to work in ways that are more efficient and effective? The concern at this level is always what learning needs underlay the supervisee's level of performance, not only in the specific situation being supervised, but generally in the entire professional area of endeavor.

In the supervision of interns, the primary focus is not on session work as much as it is on the intern's understanding of music therapy in a more fundamental sense, or the intern's basic skills as a musician or therapist. And so the apprentice supervisor continually tries to determine what the intern needs to know or understand to be more effective as a entry-level clinician. Sometimes the intern does not really understand what the purpose of music therapy is with the client population; sometimes the intern has never been taught how to use a particular method or technique; sometimes the intern needs more skill on the piano; sometimes the intern does not understand the boundaries of a client-therapist relationship.

Similarly, in the supervision of the apprentice, the professor seeks to identify gaps in learning or understanding, not only about clinical practice therapy, but also about music therapy supervision and higher education. Here the questions are: What must the apprentice's understanding of music therapy be to supervise the intern in that way? What does the apprentice need to learn about the supervisory process to make his/her observations and supervisory conferences more relevant and helpful to the intern? What does the apprentice need to understand about group process to lead the intern seminar more effectively? What does the apprentice need to understand about the relationship between academic and clinical training in music therapy to improve relationships with the clinical supervisor?

Client-Centered

The third level of supervision is client-centered; the apprentice helps the intern to gain a deeper understanding of his/her clients, and the professor helps the apprentice to gain a deeper understanding of the interns. At this level, the understanding is based on time spent together, and repeated interactions; thus, it is deeper than at the beginning of the work, when the intern is just getting acquainted with clients, and the apprentice is just getting acquainted with the intern.

Several shifts take place at this level. First, in the internship, the focus of supervision shifts from the intern's needs as a supervisee to the clients being served, while in the apprenticeship the focus shifts from the apprentice's needs as a supervisee to the interns in training. Second, the focus shifts from specific areas of functioning to more global issues of identity. In the internship, supervision deals not with what the intern does or knows, but who the client is, and what the client needs to develop more fully. Similarly, in the apprenticeship, supervision deals not with what the apprentice does or knows, but who the intern is, and what the intern needs to develop more fully. And third, there is a shift from a treatment orientation, which emphasizes inducing change, to an assessment orientation, which emphasizes understanding.

Signs of readiness for this level of supervision include increased concern, empathy, and emotional investment in the other person. The intern becomes attached to or forms closer relationships with clients, and begins to empathize and understand the clients at a more deeply human level; and the same occurs for the apprentice with interns. With this comes a realization of how complex the other person is, and how many factors have contributed to who that person is, as well as their existing life circumstance.

The two main topics for supervision are the nature of the relationships developing in the work, and how these relationships induce change over time. The intern begins to take a closer look at the client-music-therapist relationships, and how they are contributing to the therapeutic process; the apprentice begins to look at the intern-client-supervisor relationships and how they are contributing to the learning process. Both interns and apprentices begin to explore what makes human beings change or learn, and the various steps that must be taken in helping them to do so.

Experience-Oriented

The fourth level of supervision is experience-oriented; the supervisor helps the supervisee to examine his/her personal perceptions and reactions to the work. The aim is to help the supervisee make connections between his/her own experiences and specific aspects of the work.

In the internship, the apprentice helps the intern to examine how s/he experiences the client, the client population, particular sessions or clinical events, the work setting, supervisors, and supervisory process. Sample questions might be: How does this client make you feel? What are your perceptions of the client population? How do you react personally when that happens? Through discussion of these questions, the apprentice helps the intern to make simple connections between how the intern feels at the time and its relation to what happens clinically or in supervision.

Similarly, in the apprenticeship, the professor helps the intern to examine personal perceptions and reactions to the intern, the intern's clinical setting, the clinical supervisor, the music therapy program at the university, and the professor. Sample questions might be: What feelings do you have when the interns are quiet in seminar? How do you perceive the intern feels about you? How does it feel when I ask you these kinds of questions?

At this level, the explorations of self are at the conscious or preconscious level rather than the unconscious, and no effort is made to delve into biographical material from the supervisee's past. In addition these self-explorations are always anchored to here-now or there-then reactions to a very specific individual, event, or aspect of the work.

Signs of readiness for this level of supervision may be a recognition of how unique each relationship is between the supervisee and other person (i.e., intern and client, or apprentice and intern), a realization of how the supervisee affects and is affected by the other person, and a heightened sense of responsibility and accountability for the various interactions that take place.

Countertransference-Oriented

The fifth level of supervision is countertransference-oriented; the supervisor helps the supervisee to recognize how interactions with the other person are replications of the past, either of relationship patterns in the supervisee's life or relationship patterns in the other person's life. Here the apprentice helps the intern to explore how his/her way of interacting with the client has been shaped by specific relationship patterns in his/her own life (usually parents and siblings), which in turn may be a replication of relationship patterns in the client's life. Or the apprentice may help the intern to explore how his/her way of interacting with the apprentice in supervision may be a replication of relationships in the intern's or the apprentice's life.

Similarly, the professor helps the apprentice to explore how the apprentice's way of interacting with an intern has been shaped by specific relationship patterns in his/her own life, which in turn may be a replication of relationship patterns in the intern's life. Or, the professor helps the apprentice to explore how the apprentice's way of interacting with the professor are replications of relationships in his/her life or the professor's life.

At this level, the explorations are aimed at unconscious motivations, and delve specifically into biographical material from the supervisee's past. The explorations may be triggered by a particular event or aspect of the work, however, these triggers are usually regarded as manifestations of larger issues or patterns from the supervisee's past. For a more complete discussion of the signs of countertransference, see Bruscia (1998).

Signs of readiness for this level of supervision is when the supervisee recognizes patterns and themes in his/her interactions and relationships with the other person. The previous level of supervision which explores the uniqueness of each relationship and situation now leads to a perception of sameness. The supervisee begins to recognize that the common denominator is him/herself, and that the repetition of these patterns and themes are somehow of his/her own doing.

This level of supervision is not appropriate for every supervisory situation. Much depends upon the theoretical orientation of the supervisor, the readiness of the supervisee for this level of self-exploration, and the nature of the supervisory contract. The supervisor has to be qualified to operate within a psychodynamic orientation; the supervisee has to be working with the other person at a deep enough level, using the relationship as a central vehicle in the therapeutic process; and the supervisor-supervisee contract must allow for this exploration of the private life of the supervisee. Ethically, the supervisee must give informed consent to enter into such a supervision contract, and thereby extend the boundaries of his/her relationship with the supervisor to include aspects of a therapist-client relationship.

Parallel Processes

A hallmark of this level/stage approach to supervision is a continual exploration of parallel process at the unconscious level. Once the various relationships have been solidly formed—intern with client, apprentice with intern, and professor with apprentice—and the work at all three levels has begun to deepen, parallel processes are usually operating with considerable clarity. For this reason, interactions between the professor and apprentice are often good reflectors of the other two relationships. Certainly, no hard and fast rules apply here, but in the author's experience, several parallels are worth exploring as appropriate. Keep in mind that these parallels are operating at an unconscious level, and therefore require careful exploration before any inferences or conclusions can be drawn for purposes of supervision.

- The level of supervision needed by the apprentice may reflect the level of supervision needed by the intern. For example, when the professor identifies a need for action-oriented supervision for the apprentice, the intern may also need to be told what to do with clients by the apprentice.
- The kind of problem encountered by the apprentice in working with the professor may reflect the kind of problem encountered by the intern in working with the apprentice. For example, when the apprentice needs continual praise and support from the professor to feel confident, it is worth exploring whether the apprentice is giving sufficient praise and support to the interns.
- The kind of problem encountered by the apprentice in working with the intern can reflect the kind of problem encountered by the intern when working with clients. For example, when an intern does not participate very openly or fully in the seminar led by the apprentice, the same intern may be having problems with clients participating in his/her groups. Or, when the apprentice feels superfluous or questions his/her role as a supervisor, the interns may also be questioning the significance of their role as music therapists.
- The feelings that the apprentice induces in the professor may reflect the feelings that interns are inducing in the apprentice. For example, when the professor begins to notice feelings of inadequacy in meeting the supervisory needs of the apprentice, the interns may be inducing feelings of inadequacy in the apprentice.

The significance of these parallels is that, when explored, the professor can gain a more thorough understanding of not only what is happening between the apprentice and intern, but also between the interns and their clients. The professor-apprentice relationship, and the interactions during each supervisory conference, can be a microcosm of the entire range of relationships and interactions contained in the internship and apprenticeship experiences.

The theoretical basis for these parallels lies in the mechanism of projective identification. Projective identification occurs when one person projects his/her own repressed feelings onto another person, and then treats the person in a way to induce those feelings in that person. In the above example, the intern has deep feelings of inadequacy, but rather than seeing them in him/herself, sees the apprentice as being inadequate, and then to justify this projection, treats the apprentice in a way that will make the apprentice actually feel or act inadequate. But in parallel process supervision of internship and apprenticeship, the dynamic does not stop there. When the apprentice begins to identify with these feelings of inadequacy induced by the intern, s/he in turn projects them onto the professor, and then treats the professor in a way to induce feelings of inadequacy in the professor. Thus, when the professor gets a certain feeling when working with the apprentice, it is worth exploring where along the entire supervisory chain such feelings are originating.

Three Stages of Readiness

The above five levels of intervention fall into three stages of development for both the intern and apprentice. The first stage is concerned with the development of technique. It includes both action-oriented and learning-oriented levels of supervision. During this stage, the intern learns how to lead client sessions effectively, and the apprentice learns how to use various methods of supervision effectively (e.g., observation, conference, group seminar). The stage ends when the supervisee demonstrates three main qualities: effectiveness, comfort, and self-confidence.

The second stage is concerned with the development of relationship. It includes both client-oriented and experience-oriented levels of supervision. With this stage, the supervisee's focus as intern or apprentice moves from the exterior aspects of the work to interior aspects of those doing the work. It is a shift from efficiency of action and interaction to depth of shared experiences. In addition, the intern begins to shift the focus from self as a therapist-in-training, to being aware of both client and self as persons interacting within a helping relationship. For the apprentice, the shift is from self as supervisor-in-training, to an awareness of the intern and self as persons interacting in a learning relationship. Of key importance in this stage is the development of empathy for the client (or student), awareness of self in relation to the client (or student), and clear boundaries between the two experiences. And these are the three hallmarks signaling completion of this stage.

The third and final stage is concerned with internalization. It consists entirely of the countertransference-oriented level of supervision. Here the various components of the previous stages become parts of the self that can be differentiated, fused, and/or integrated as needed. Specifically

- Knowledge, skill, and insight become integral counterparts of clinical action, so that upon self-reflection, the entire continuum between thought and action can be used effectively in either clinical or supervisory situations.
- The intern's experience within the relationship comes into relation to the client's experience; and similarly, the apprentice's experience within the relationship comes into relation to the intern's experience.
- The intern's experience as self comes into relation to the intern's experience as therapist, both of which come into relation to the client's experience; similarly, the apprentice's experience as self comes into relation to the apprentice's experience as a supervisor, both of which come into relation to the supervisee's experience.
- And finally, the supervisee begins to grasp the roles of helper and helped along a continuum which is configured differently in each relationship of client-therapist and supervisor-supervisee. More importantly, the supervisee has the sense of self and other to configure it in ways that will help the other.

Individual Differences

Conceiving of supervision in terms of the above levels, stages and parallel processes not only provides a theoretical framework for intervention, it also creates the foundation for identifying and responding to individual differences in supervisees and their needs. In fact, what makes a levels/stage approach to supervision most useful is its sensitivity to the different needs of each supervisee as they unfold developmentally in each unique clinical situation. Thus, rather than imposing the same approach to supervision on every supervisee, regardless of individual differences, the supervisor who uses levels and stages learns how to gear every intervention to the uniqueness of each supervisory and clinical situation, and in time, gradually evolves an equally unique approach to the supervision of each supervisee.

One of the most important areas of individual differences among supervisees is the ways in which they resist the supervisor and the supervision process. Resistance is commonly understood as any conscious or unconscious effort of the supervisee to reject, foil, contest, ignore, or devalue the supervisor's input. In a levels/stages approach, resistance is a multifaceted phenomenon—one that cannot be understood in terms of a single dynamic or a single theoretical orientation toward the phenomenon. In fact, the whole concept of resistance has to be reframed.

Within the present model of supervision, resistance is an outgrowth of four supervisory scenarios:

- *Intervention at an ineffectual level.* In this scenario, the supervisor intervenes at a level which does not address the supervisory problems and needs of the supervisee within the clinical situation at hand. For example, the supervisee is experiencing a clinical problem which calls for action supervision (e.g., how to keep the restless client in the room), but the supervisor provides countertransference supervision (e.g., how the client reminds the supervisee of his father). That is, instead of helping the supervisee figure out what to do, the supervisor jumps into how the problem is similar to the supervisee's past relationships with parents. When confronted with this level of intervention, the supervisee naturally (and justifiably) reacts by trying to redirect or neutralize the supervisor's efforts—and for good reason: a countertransference insight will not help the student in the concrete way that is needed at the time in that particular situation. In the example, examining abandonment issues with the supervisee's father does not address the supervisee's inability to handle the situation itself within the session. Note that intervening at an ineffectual level is a supervisory error in identifying the nature of the clinical situation, and that such an error can happen at any stage of supervision. Sometimes the clinical situation confronted by a beginning supervisee may call for experiential rather than action supervision (a more advanced level), and similarly, the problems of an advanced supervisee can call for action supervision instead of countertransference supervision (a less advanced level)—even though the level of supervision is not characteristic of the supervisee's stage of development.

- *Expectations at an inappropriate stage.* In this scenario, the supervisor intervenes without sufficient attention to the supervisee's developmental stage. For example, the supervisor may expect a supervisee at the "technique" or first stage to have highly developed "relationships" or a greater degree of "internalization" at the second or third stage; or conversely, the supervisor may not trust an advanced supervisee to work out technique when there is already high degree of internalization.

- *True resistance.* In this scenario, the supervisee has psychological issues which cause defensiveness toward the supervisor and the supervision process. For example, the supervisee may have problems with authority which lead to constant oppositionalism toward the supervisor, or low self-esteem which causes painful hypersensitivity to every supervisory comment. Within the present model, the supervisor intervenes at the appropriate level, has expectations at the appropriate stage, and is responsive to the supervisee's problems and needs, but the supervisee will not accept the level or stage of intervention. For example: the supervisee does not follow supervisory suggestions on what to do with the client, when the supervisee is not responding effectively and needs such direction; or the supervisee refuses to meet expectations at the technique stage when actually ready to do so; or the supervisee does not respond to any level or stage of intervention, regardless of how many methods or orientations to supervision that the supervisor takes.

- *Supervisor issues.* In this scenario, the supervisor has psychological issues and needs, or professional biases which have a detrimental effect on the supervisee and/or the supervision process. Here the supervisee may actually resist or only appear to the supervisor as resistant, but the origin of the problem is in the supervisor's own inability to be appropriately responsive to what the supervisee needs. The hallmarks of this scenario are myriad: inappropriate boundaries with the supervisee, defensiveness, authoritarianism, unwarranted reactions, insistence on supervising at only one level or only at one stage, rigidity of method or style of supervision, and so forth.

What is important to note about these four accounts of problems in supervision is that three of them implicate the supervisor, while only one implicates the supervisee.

Summary and Conclusions

A key discovery in establishing the Temple apprenticeship program was that supervising apprentice supervisors at the graduate level is a parallel process to supervising clinical interns at the undergraduate level. Both efforts require clear administrative structures, and both involve very similar learning experiences. The reason is that both the apprentice and the intern have much in common, yet there are significant differences in level of expertise and experience. These similarities and differences called for an approach to supervision which recognized the various levels and stages of supervisory needs in both the apprentice and the intern. Five levels of intervention were identified, oriented toward 1) action, 2) learning, 3) the client, 4) the supervisee's experience, and/or 5) countertransference issues. These levels fall roughly into three stages of development, concerned respectively with readiness for mastering 1) technique, 2) relationship, and 3) internalization. Upon implementation of this levels/stages approach, many parallel processes were discovered. The apprentice often manifests the same problems and supervisory needs with the professor that the intern is manifesting with the apprentice, while the intern often manifests the same problems and needs with the apprentice that the clients are manifesting with the intern. The most useful concept in understanding these phenomena is projective identification, when one person projects his/her own repressed feelings onto another person, and then treats the person in a way to induce those same feelings in that person.

One of the advantages of this levels/stages approach is the recognition of individual differences among supervisees and their work situations. This recognition necessitates a reframing of various phenomena usually identified as resistance. Four scenarios are given to account for such problems in supervision: intervention at an ineffectual level, expectations at an inappropriate stage, true resistance by the supervisee, and issues and biases of the supervisor. An important conclusion is that three of the four problems originate in the supervisor, while only one originates in the supervisee.

References

Bruscia, K. (ed.). (1998). *The Dynamics of Music Psychotherapy.* Gilsum NH: Barcelona Publishers.

Part Four

Institute Supervision

Chapter 20

Forming an Identity as a Music Psychotherapist through Analytical Music Therapy Supervision

Benedikte B. Scheiby, MA, MMEd, DPMtp, CMT
Music Therapy Supervisor, Beth Abraham Hospital
Adjunct Faculty, New York University, New York, NY

Analytical Music Therapy (AMT) is a music therapy model that incorporates an approach to supervision where musical and verbal processing of clinical material are essential components. AMT was developed in the 1970s over a two-year period by three pioneers in Great Britain: Mary Priestley, Peter Wright, and Marjorie Wardle. The model was developed through self-experimentation with the term "analytical music therapy" first used by Peter Wright as a description of the work. Because Mary Priestley took the leading role in describing the model extensively in her 1975 text, *Music Therapy in Action*, she is considered to be the founder of the model.

Priestley, the daughter of author J. B. Priestley, was originally a skilled performing violinist. She was educated as a music therapist in a one-year, postgraduate diploma course at the Guildhall School of Music and Drama in London and granted the title LGSM, a licentiateship granted by the school. Juliette Alvin, who founded the British Society for Music Therapy, directed the training. Priestley also undertook a full course of Kleinian analysis and worked for several years under psychotherapeutic supervision at Saint Bernhard's Hospital in London prior to developing AMT.

According to Priestley (1994), AMT is the "analytically-informed symbolic use of improvised music by the music therapist and client. It is used as a creative tool with which to explore the client's inner life so as to provide the way forward for growth and greater self-knowledge" (p. 3). The term "analytic" refers partly to the psychoanalytic thought behind the approach—incorporating influences such as Freud, Jung, Klein, Adler, and Lowen—and partly to the analysis of the musical and verbal content of the session undertaken jointly by therapist and client.

The approach is in use with a variety of populations and clinical work has been documented with the following types of individuals: psychiatric patients; neurological rehabilitation clients; geriatric clients; victims of sexual, physical, or emotional abuse; clients with eating disorders and substance abuse problems; developmentally-delayed individuals; and clients in forensic settings. Clients who are not able to understand or use language do not profit as much as those who can verbalize their experiences in the musical improvisations, but they can still benefit from the approach.

Priestley has trained over fifty music therapists from ten countries in AMT. Many of these practitioners have become trainers themselves, offering courses in AMT in academic settings and as private institute training.

In order to undertake training as an analytical music therapist one must first possess a master's degree in music therapy. The training consists of three sequential stages oriented to assisting the music therapist in learning how to integrate musical, verbal, relational, aesthetic, intellectual, emotional, psychological, and spiritual content into his/her music therapy being, and hence, into the clinical work. The first stage comprises self-experience in individual and group music therapy sessions offered by an Analytic Music Therapist. There is no specific number of sessions mandated. The second stage consists of a process called "Intertherapy" which comprises a minimum of twelve sessions in a which a dyad of training therapists alternate being each other's therapist and client with the entire process taking place under the direct supervision of the AMT trainer. The third stage incorporates individual and group supervision of the trainee's clinical work undertaken outside of the training dyad. The entire training can be completed in two years, but may take longer for students who do not have prior experiences in music psychotherapy or psychoanalysis. The present article will focus on stages two and three of the training process because the first stage does not incorporate a supervisory component as do the other two. This is not to minimize the importance of the first stage, as much of the material which emerges there will be of significant value to the supervisor during the subsequent stages.

Supervision in Inter Music Therapy (IMT):
Stage Two of AMT Training

Mary Priestley introduced Intertherapy in the early 1970s together with her two colleagues, Marjorie Wardel and Peter Wright. The process was first called "Intertherap," then IMT for Inter Music Therapy, and currently "intertherapy" (Priestley, 1994), although the terms are interchangeable. It started as an experiment, the purpose of which was to identify the uses of a variety of music therapy techniques on relatively well, normal, unmedicated human beings. Mary Priestley called it a learning and research enterprise. Each member was a therapist to one and client to another member: Mary was therapist to Peter and client to Marjorie who was client to Peter and therapist to Mary.

Figure 1
Relationships in Intertherap

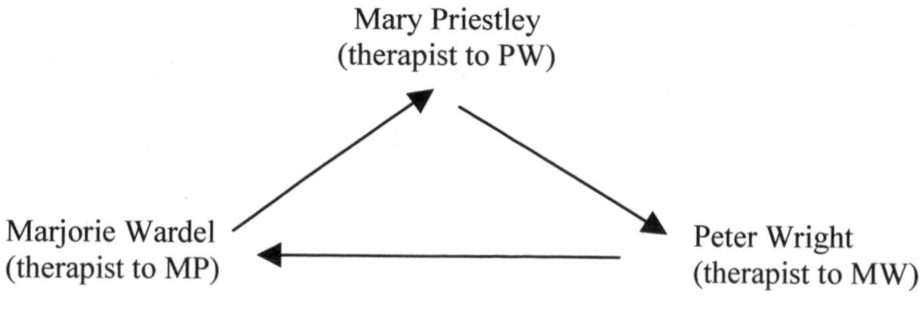

Mary Priestley
(therapist to PW)

Marjorie Wardel
(therapist to MP)

Peter Wright
(therapist to MW)

There was no observing supervisor, but occasionally the third member, who documented the process, upon completing the note-taking would make a comment afterward, thus behaving in an embryonic supervisory role. These situations are well described by Priestley (1975).

Priestley decided to offer Intertherapy as a supplementary training to music therapy students, when in the mid-1970s a student at the music therapy program at Guildhall School of Music and Drama, Johannes Eschen from Germany, asked if he could join the IMT (Inter Music Therapy) team. Instead of letting him join the team, she asked him to find a partner and asked both of them to take a number of individual music therapy sessions with her before she would allow them to experience the IMT under her direct supervision. She writes about the preparation for IMT: "Regarding the dialogue in the therapy, where a trainee has had no experience of longer-term analytical psychotherapy of once weekly or more, he may need anything from 20–120 AMT sessions before he feels ready to start Intertherapy" (Priestley, 1994, p. 298).

The format was such that the two students took turns being a therapist for each other, while at the same time Priestley would take notes. After the ending of the two "therapies" she would make comments to the one that had been the therapist first, then to the one who had been the therapist the second time. The duration of the whole session was two hours, divided as follows: A is a therapist for B for thirty minutes. B is a therapist for A for thirty minutes. Supervisory comments and theory last for sixty minutes and both A and B would be present during each other's supervisory comments.

By 1979, students from seven different countries completed what is now described as the first two stages of AMT training. Some of those students have become AMT trainers and have continued this training practice in their respective countries.

After Johannes Eschen returned to Germany, he incorporated the IMT supervision with students in the music therapy program at Hochschule fur Musik und Dastellende Kunst, and later integrated this type of training in music therapy training in Herdecke, Germany, in 1978. The IMT supervision of this time is discussed by Priestley (1994).

This author established a masters music therapy program at Aalborg University in Denmark, in 1980, together with Inge N. Pedersen and we integrated IMT as a part of the training program. We changed the design, so that during A's supervision, B leaves the room, and during B's supervision A leaves the room. The specifics of how this form of supervision is integrated in a university setting are discussed in Scheiby and Pedersen (1999). There are case examples and a description of evaluation procedures. Since 1990, I have been developing a private training program, where IMT is an essential part of the training. A minimum of twelve IMT sessions are offered to postgraduate music therapy students that have undergone AMT individual music therapy for at least one year. After the IMT training the students undergo a half to a whole year of individual AMT supervision sessions, and a half to a whole year with AMT group music therapy supervision, depending on the needs of the student.

The Format of IMT in Private Training

The AMT supervisor may help to establish the IMT team and the team meets once a week or once every second week for two hours. The format is as follows. A is a therapist for B for thirty minutes. B is a therapist for A for thirty minutes. Both sessions are audio taped. A receives individual supervision for thirty minutes while B is not in the room. B receives individual supervision for thirty minutes while A is not in the room. Both supervisions are audiotaped. During the session the supervisor takes notes in a corner of the room. The final IMT session will be one hour long so that the student experiences and understands the difference between the half-hour training sessions and the more typical sessions of one hour. In the beginning the supervisor may serve as a timekeeper and if needed make verbal suggestions.

It is important to emphasize that during IMT the trainees are not engaged in role-playing. They are not simulating issues that they want to work with. The process is authentic and they are bringing in material from their lives. The situations described are not imagined or hypothetical. It can be viewed as a natural next step of the student's individuation process and personal growth begun during the formal education and pursued in the individual and group music therapy sessions comprising the first stage of AMT training.

The importance of this type of genuine self-experience has recently received support in the music therapy literature: "A therapeutic training cannot only consist of an enumeration of skills and techniques. A student has to experience the process him/herself" (Wigram, De Backer, and Van Camp, 1999, p. 289). These authors advocate that students receive music psychotherapeutic self-experiential training during their education to become music therapists. Otherwise, they will not be able to deal with and understand the phenomenon of transference and how it presents itself to the music therapist in clinical situations. They learn from experiencing the presence of their music therapist in their own personal music therapy and how to take up a neutral position musically and verbally so that the client can use him/her for transferring feelings toward central persons and relationships in his/her life. They also learn when and how to help the client to gain insight regarding the content of the transference on the basis of musical content and interactions in the sessions.

My experience has shown that many students are able to continue their personal individuation process when they enter in the position of client in IMT. However, it has sometimes initially been difficult for the student to trust that a fellow student may be experienced enough and have enough authority to conduct the music therapy.

As part of the theoretical training the student therapist submits written notes to the supervisor where the session is described. The audio recording of the session facilitates this task. The following areas must be described in the notes: session number; objective description of session process, both musically and verbally; subjective description of the process, musically, verbally, and bodily; summary of musical/verbal interventions and issues that were addressed; problem areas for the therapist; potential goals and objectives for the next session.

After all the sessions have been completed, the student therapist is asked to write a paper where he/she

- Presents an overview of the process of the whole treatment and identification of goals and objectives,
- Identifies different phases in the process,
- Presents developmental steps expressed musically and verbally,
- Identifies strengths and weaknesses as a music therapist
- Discusses his/her roles as a music therapist in this course of therapy,
- Presents an overview of the developmental process of the music therapist.

The student is also asked to make an audiotape with clinical excerpts that demonstrate significant musical dialogues or solos from different phases of the process; significant changes in the client's musical/verbal presence; examples of musical interventions, techniques, and construction of playing themes.

Areas of Competency in Private IMT Training

In general this stage of the training is the beginning of integration of four areas of music therapy competency:

- *Personal* competency—ability to *be* therapeutically relevant (*being*)
- *Technical* competency—ability to *act* therapeutically relevant (*doing*)
- *Artistic* competency—ability to *create* therapeutically relevant (*creating*)
- *Theoretical* competency—ability to *think* therapeutically relevant (*thinking*)

In the following description all the categories are woven into each other as all levels are practiced at the same time in the session. The area of theoretical competency is particularly focused upon in the supervision session described in detail below, where in addition to the working through of personal issues, theoretical papers and texts are to be read. These papers and texts relate to the topics that emerge from the music therapeutic practice of the student. The addressing of the area on personal competency has been started in the individual AMT sessions of stage 1 that the student has undergone before beginning the IMT sessions in stage 2. When the student has undergone individual and group music therapy supervision, the material from all four content areas should have been learned and integrated. And if that has not happened after finishing training the music therapist is encouraged to receive weekly AMT supervision in order to continue growth in all areas.

Identifying and Developing a Personal Philosophy and Method

Prior to beginning the IMT stage, the trainee's identity as music therapist is not yet formed. The student often has not settled down to a certain way of working, has not clarified a particular methodological interest, and may not be conscious of a philosophy behind the work. Here, the student can have an opportunity to develop a personalized style of working within an analytical context and can become conscious about how philosophical and ethical issues affect clinical work. This also includes becoming conscious about preferences and avoidances in musical idiom and style, cultural differences with the clients, and the consequences of this in the choice of music. A music therapy professional must have a well grounded training in clinical improvisation and the use of composed music as well as in the field of psychotherapy, no matter what kind of clients one works with. In IMT these two fields are integrated. Wigram, De Backer, and Van Camp (1999) support this belief: "The development of the psychotherapeutic identity is as equally important a cornerstone as the development of the musical identity. The way in which music is handled in a therapeutic setting is embedded in a specific therapeutic background" (p. 288).

The fact that a student is being trained in AMT does not mean that one will be practicing as an AMT music therapist the rest of his or her life, and it does not mean exclusion of other forms of music therapy. Personally, I received training in the Nordoff-Robbins method as a part of the education curriculum in my training in Germany (Herdecke) and I have incorporated the skills that I was taught in clinical improvisation in my current practice. The AMT training will provide the student with a solid music psychotherapeutic foundation and consciousness, on top of which the student can add musical and therapeutic knowledge. In this setting one also can test the theoretical framework that one has learned from reading material on music therapy. The trainee learns if it is possible to transfer to the clinical reality particular ideas and practices from the music therapy literature.

In an informal survey of professional music therapists conducted by Inge Pedersen and the present author regarding how the IMT component of the AMT training had affected their present practice, one person wrote the following:

> When I, as a finished educated music therapist was entering the real therapy world, I was fumbling for finding an answer to the question: Who am I as a music therapist? Exactly in this development the IMT training has given me the best tools to get closer to my identity as a music therapist. In IMT there is peace and time to test oneself as a therapist, testing different methods and techniques – and not the least realizing that what one believed to be true in theory did not apply to one's practice, because one's client suddenly was a different place . . .. And what do I do now? (author's translation from Danish).

Permission to Make Mistakes and Experiment

It is important to offer a place for the student to make mistakes without being nervous about harming the client. As a supervisor with over twenty years of experience I have learned that one will mostly learn from one's mistakes. The fear of making mistakes is a well-known phenomenon among music therapists (performance anxiety), because their working medium is music, and because one traditionally has learned to avoid making mistakes in the music in order for the product to sound good. Through the supervision the student will be encouraged not to cover up if they make a mistake, and sometimes admit to the client that they indeed made a mistake. Nobody is perfect, not even a music therapist, and many clients who may feel like one big mistake themselves may feel a sense of relief when they realize that the music therapist also is struggling with making mistakes. When a situation arises with a client where the therapist just doesn't know what to do or say, this will not be a devastating experience because he/she can identify with it from the training process and learn how to use this in a positive way.

Flexibility Moving Between One's Inner Process and the Client's Process

It is important to offer an opportunity in training where one must quickly move between one's own "inner music" and inner reality as a therapist, and the client's inner and outer reality. The fact that the student has to switch so quickly from focusing on the client's needs to focusing on his/her own needs as a therapist (keeping track of process, overview, which technique to use) will automatically develop this ability and flexibility. One can compare it with the ability to oscillate between being strictly objective (observing the client) and being subjective (observing myself being a therapist).

In an article about the importance of the psychotherapist's authenticity and about the importance of training this skill, Olav Storm Jensen (1998) writes that "the fact that the therapist is experiencing and is in touch with the process of the client in the given moment it is happening, must be a definitive prerequisite for the fact that the theoretical understanding and the technical skills can be brought to relevant use. It can be described as available concentrated presence and attention in an empathic understanding of the process of the client" (1998, p. 275) [author's translation from Danish].

One professional music therapist who took the IMT training wrote the following about her learning experiences of IMT:

> *I think IMT is a good training method in terms of teaching the therapist to be empathetic with and understand the therapy from the client's point of view. The ability to be able to switch between being aware of oneself and the client. To train this sensitivity towards the client is a very essential part of this music therapeutic method.*
> (author's translation from Danish).

Another professional music therapist who took IMT wrote:

> *IMT has been training me in the ability to be 100% involved in the process of the client and at the same time keeping an overview— looking at the process from the outside. At the same time it has been teaching me the ability to protect myself and letting myself become involved without being too much pulled into the process of the client. I also have a feeling that IMT has sharpened my ability to adapt to quick changes in the therapy work. In the work with the triad of client, interpreter and therapist, it has helped me to maintain a clear consciousness about the different channels of*

communication and an ability to make quick changes between these. (author's translation from Danish).

These comments attest to the value of developing the ability to have therapeutic presence. As Arthur Robbins (1998) writes in his book on this topic: "I am being present, in the presence of my client. In so doing, I temporarily suspend my boundaries and let the full force of the client enter my inside. Yet at the same time, I am separating out my feelings and giving them shape and form" (p. 21).

The student is trained in identifying the flow and pattern of the rhythms that not only develop in the musical interactions with the client, but also those that develop outside the musical contact. This occurs in the movement for the therapist between a more interactive stance in identifying with the conflicts of the client, to a more cognitively separate one, structuring of the offered material. The student will be able to get in touch with the dissonances and resonances that are created when the client meets the therapist in and outside the music.

Transition Management

The fact that in training there is such a rapid change between being a client and being a therapist can help the student to better manage the transitions inside and outside the sessions in future work situations. This helps develop the ability to change focus quickly and the ability to stay as neutral as possible in the musical and verbal realms. This will help the music therapist working in an institution who must meet with many clients consecutively without breaks or a transition time in between.

In the beginning of the IMT process, some students complain about having difficulty in making such a quick change between being a client and being a therapist. In my own experience as an AMT trainee and later as a professional music therapist, it has been very helpful to develop my ability to put my own immediate needs aside and to be able to focus completely on the needs of the client.

Mary Priestley (1994) has commented on this aspect of the training: "It is not a bad idea for a student to realize that he is capable of this change of role, for as a working therapist he will be vulnerable to life's bruises outside therapy and will have to walk into the workroom and put his own troubles behind him until his working day is finished. Until he has tried it he will not realise his strength in focusing his mind firmly in one direction towards another human being in trouble" (p. 305).

Transitions from verbal to music or music to verbal interactions will be invented and explored. Particularly important will be discovering how silence can give space and honor the musical statements, and as such function as transition to and from musical interaction.

Time Management

The relative brevity of the sessions (thirty minutes for work of an individual and in-depth nature) forces the therapist not to waste time and to be economical with time management. Many verbal clients spend a large amount of session time talking and often end up playing music briefly. The short time frame makes it even more urgent to help the client to either identify the issue rather quickly, or find a way to initiate playing/singing, and get to create and process musically before the session is over. In many institutions there is only half an hour available for sessions, so the time limit is not that unrealistic.

The student therapist will also learn how to help the client to stop himself/herself inside and outside the music when the session has ended. Many clients will continue to play or talk even though there is no time left in the session. The student will learn how to prepare the client for the end, either musically or verbally.

Management of Key Phenomena in AMT

The student can become familiar with key concepts in AMT such as musical transference, musical countertransference, musical resistance, defenses, regression, symbiosis, separation, developmental stages in the music, and learn how to deal with such phenomena in music and words. The following are the types of questions to which students will develop their own answers: How do I determine if the music is transferential? How do I deal with musical resistance? Do I go with it or do I break it? Do I encourage playing mutually or do I encourage playing dialogical and separate? How do I pull a client out of a musical regression? Which aspects of the client's music are eliciting musical countertransference (intersubjective countertransference)? Is there any intrasubjective countertransference? What are the developmental aspects of the music? How can I facilitate or bring the client to the next stage?

Management of Musical Interventions
I define a musical intervention as a focused musically expressed action with the intentional purpose of making a change in the client's inner and outer music. The student will get an understanding of when to accompany and when not to accompany the client's playing or singing. Initially, students tend to automatically accompany the client, but there might not be a clinical rationale for this intervention in the particular situation. When the trainee can identify if the focus is on intrapersonal or interpersonal work, then the decision can be made as to whether the playing should be separately or together.

When is it appropriate to offer a musical structure through rhythm, melody, harmony, or in the form of a style such as blues, gospel, pentatonic, or the Middle Eastern? The student will learn by trial and error, and by getting to know the musical being of the student client. The students will be trained in creating clear musical beginnings and endings, and help the client learn phrasing. Some clients stop abruptly in their music and do not know how to create an organic musical phrase.

As the sessions will be audiotaped, the student will be able to use listening to the taped music as an intervention in sessions where the client cannot remember what he/she played/sang. The student therapist will also be asked to listen for and "vacuum clean" redundant tones in his/her music. In the beginning of one's training there seems to be a tendency to play more tones than needed. There are tones that seem to have no intention and direction and are there just there to fill up the space. They will be encouraged to make the music simple—it does not have to be very complicated in order to have an effect.

The student will be asked to become familiar with the musical identity of the client, and become able to reproduce the musical and vocal expression of the client. This is done in order to examine how it feels to have such a musical identity and in order to be able to mirror the person musically, when needed. The student will be helped to identify when improvisation, song writing, song singing, and composition is appropriate to use, and when not.

The student will receive training in transforming verbal questions into music. Students are often very verbal in the beginning of the training, and get trapped in a very verbal student client's "verbality." They will get exposed to musical interventions that can help the student therapist and the student client communicate more with each other through the music.

Consider this example of a very verbal student client. He began a session wanting to work with a dream. He told the content of the dream in lengthy details and reflected over the meaning of several symbols. The student therapist got drawn into the verbal process of working with the dream, and when the two of them had decided how to work with the dream in music the session was almost over, so they had to stop and break up the organic flow of the musical processing. In the following supervision session, the student therapist learned to ask the student therapist not to tell the dream first, but to communicate its content in music first, and then in the end there would be some time if needed to process verbally what was significant for the student client.

Because I consider silence to be an important part of the music and as such can be used as an intervention, the students are trained to endure the long pauses that there may be, where seemingly "nothing happens"—where one listens to one's own breathing and "inner music" or where one is re-centering oneself.

Students will receive training in trusting musical intuition, which means that they play spontaneously without filtering from the thought process.

The student will learn to get an overall consciousness of the session as viewing it and conducting it as a piece of music: tuning in—middle—closure.

He/she can for example try out different ways of being for each of these sections of the session: tuning in: listening to and staying with the silence or listen to and focusing on the rhythm of the breath of the student client and attuning himself/herself to that; middle: let happen what needs to happen in an organic flow; closure: musical guidance through slowing the tempo and toning down the dynamic and intensity.

The student will get used to experiencing musical interventions that turn out to have unknown, mysterious qualities that are unexplainable, and should remain like that. They will develop awareness that not everything can or should be explained or verbalized.

Amir (1999) interviewed six music therapists about their musical and verbal interventions and she concluded her article with actual words of one of the therapists interviewed: "I allow myself to 'not know,' to make mistakes, to learn. I never know that my interventions are right. Sometimes they are right, sometimes they are wrong, and sometimes they are proven to be unimportant" (p. 173).

Verbal Interventions and Interactions
I will define a verbal intervention as a focused verbally expressed action made with the intention of effecting a change in the client's inner and outer music. Students are

likely to be working with both verbal and nonverbal clients when they have finished their training. Therefore it is necessary to be trained in handling the possible verbal parts—verbal interventions and interactions—of the music therapy session. The IMT training is an ideal place to start practicing verbal skills because the client is verbal and one can get a direct response from the client if the verbal communication is not clear. The student will be trained in how to help the client to form an improvisation title that can serve as an entrance or invitation to the music-making. The title is often an essence of what the client has expressed verbally or bodily in the communication before the music.

Here are some examples of titles from my own IMT experiences as a student client:

- Improvisation a) I am manipulating
- Improvisation b) I am becoming manipulated

I was encouraged to express in music how it felt to be manipulated and how it felt to manipulate, in order to explore what the underlying emotions may be. In another session the verbal focal point was:

- Improvisation c) being surrounded by a wall
- Improvisation d) being without the wall

I arranged the instruments in c) so they surrounded me and explored what that felt like. In d) I played without having the instrumental wall and explored musically how that felt.

Mary Priestley writes about the role of the title: "This title may focus the therapy in a vital direction for the work, or it may turn away from this important aim and make the music into a defensive and vapid note-patting" (1994, p. 301).

Students will also gain knowledge in how to handle the verbal parts of the session that occur before and after the improvisation(s). For example:

- to ask non-leading and non-manipulative questions,
- to avoid asking questions that tend to put the client in a defensive position,
- not to give advice,
- to sometimes repeat essential words mentioned by the student client.

Another area that will be explored is how to integrate the verbal part with the musical part. Words do not always have to be used before or after an improvisation. Only in those situations where material needs to be brought into the conscious are verbal communications needed and the words can function as a bridge between the unconscious and the conscious.

Student therapists will learn to listen to the music of the voice and the music of the words used by the client. He/she will also learn to listen to the body language of the client while he/she is speaking. Is the client saying one thing with the body and another with the words, for example? How does the client make me feel in my body, when I work with him/her? How can I reflect that back in the music?

The reason body awareness is part of the training is that as music therapist one will often be working with populations of non-verbal individuals and together with the music the reading of body communication can be an effective diagnostic tool. I studied as a bioenergetic body psychotherapist when I worked with schizophrenic adults, psychotic adolescents and autistic children. At the beginning of treatment, these patients often are afraid of touching the instruments for a long period of time. It can be difficult to understand what is going on in the client without these bodily skills. The IMT offers a particularly ideal situation in terms of identifying body language, because the supervisor is present and is observing both partners' bodily communications. It may be a little difficult later on in the AMT individual and group supervision for the student therapist to reflect to the supervisor exactly what the body communication was.

Often, it takes some time before the student therapist is able to relax and allow images and symbols to emerge in the consciousness driven from the verbal and nonverbal presence of the client. These images and symbols may be appropriate for the student therapist to share or not.

The student will learn how to distinguish between when words are needed and when not. In terms of music and meaning the student will be taught how to help the client to develop his/her own interpretive world unique to each person.

Instrumental Vocal and Body Language
In AMT it is the understanding that instruments can function as a vehicle of meaning in terms of symbolic representation and a vehicle for imagination of objects or situations. Therefore the student must be trained in having awareness about the following: Which instruments is the client picking in relation to which theme? How does the client arrange the instruments? How does the client play the instruments? How does the client sit with or hold the instruments during the verbal part of the session? Which ones are preferred and which ones are avoided? Which instruments does the student therapist tend to choose? When should the student therapist choose instruments that are like the ones the student client chooses and when should the instruments be contrasting?

Vocal techniques will be explored and examined, and in case the student therapist has problems using his/her voice as an instrument in a dynamic way, that will be taken up and worked with in supervision. The student will also be trained in observing the body language of the client while he/she is playing/singing.

The Contract
The students will learn to adhere to the rule of analytical confidentiality. The students are not supposed to discuss the content of their sessions outside the sessions. The audiotaped sessions are not supposed to be played in other contexts except if the client and the therapist have given permission. They will also get an understanding of the function of having a contract. For example, as a rule the time and day in the week of the session is always kept the same, and the student therapist cancels only when ill. It creates stability in the relationship and a trust in the fact that the relationship has an inner rhythm that is maintained.

Tuning In to Communication through the Unconscious or Subconscious

In AMT one makes use of the fact that music can open up contact with the unconscious. Sometimes the spontaneous improvisations are direct communications of what is going on in the unconscious, taking on somewhat the same function as our nightly dreams. Sometimes music is functioning for the client as a bridge or a channel to contact the unconscious. Consequently, one of the tasks of the student therapist in IMT is to learn to make him/herself available for connecting with the unconscious of the client. This can be taught by helping the student therapist to tune himself/herself as an instrument and resonator either just before the session has to be conducted or in the beginning of the session. The student therapist focuses on his/her breathing, grounding, centering, and hearing. He/she starts listening to the sounds of the client, the rhythm of the breath of himself/herself, the body feeling and movements and the overall psychological tempo or pace of both the client and himself/herself. Sometimes when one is working with a client a certain song may be coming up in the therapist's mind, and this song may either be an unconscious communication from the client, or be containing essential material that is related to the client's issues in the here and now. This type of openness is also trained in IMT.

Model for Analysis of the Musical Material

The student is encouraged to develop his/her own model of analysis of the musical material that emerges in the sessions. In addition, I offer a basic model that can be a helpful starting point for catching the essence or the significance of the music.

Figure 2 represents a variety of categories that are involved in and have to be taken into consideration when one analyzes improvisations.

Figure 2
Categories in the Analysis of Improvisations

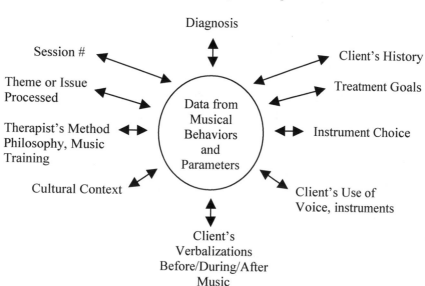

Figure 3 describes a variety of listening categories that one has to be aware of.

Figure 3
Listening Categories

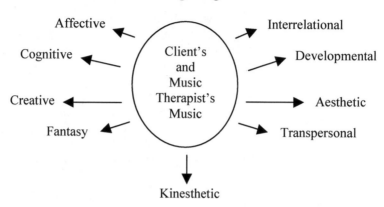

Table 1 describes a variety of types of information that one may gain through making use of the different listening categories. As all the sessions are audio taped, the student can use the taped version of the music to analyze from in case the student cannot remember the music.

Table 1
Examples of Information Leading to Clinical Data

Affective Information: Emotional qualities, musical transference, musical countertransference
Interrelational Information: Style of connecting
Cognitive Information: Level of organization, structural components
Developmental Information: Ego-function, drives, defenses, differentiation between self and others, authenticity, level of integration/chaos/dissociation
Released Fantasies and Images Information: Images, gestalts, mirroring significant experience in past and present
Transpersonal Information: Spiritual quality, meditative quality altered state of consciousness
Aesthetic Information: Quality of Beauty
Kinesthetic Information: Body expressions/sensations released by the music
Creativity Information: Absence/presence of ideas that develop, playfulness

I developed this model of analyzing on the basis of the following considerations:

- Mary Priestley's referential position: music can refer to something else; for example, emotions and unconscious content. It may not always be sufficient with the musical experience per se.
- My experiences working with AMT with a variety of verbal populations. When asked what the meaning of the music was for them, they would refer to at least one of the categories in the figure.
- My experiences in my private supervision, where supervisees and my supervisor would listen to tapes from my sessions with patients, and would interpret what the significance of the music might be.
- My own experiences as a client in individual and group music therapy.
- My IMT training with Mary Priestley, where the student client's music was analyzed by Mary and me as the student therapist. Mary Priestley was doing direct supervision on the work.

Containment, Timing, and Pacing

The student will be trained in the ability musically to contain emotional states that are unmanageable or unbearable for the client in the moment. The student learns to hold the emotions for the client until he/she is ready to own them. Perhaps the therapist needs to develop a musical form for the stressful material that is modified and seems more manageable to the client. By trial and error the student will also learn about musical and verbal timing. For example, when do I musically reflect this feeling of tremendous frustration or anger? When is the client ready to reflect upon this feeling? How can one "de-poison" the music of the client, so it doesn't seem so toxic to the client? When do I address certain phenomena that I hear in the client's music, and when not?

The student will learn about the importance of pacing the session, so that, for example, the tempo does not become hectic or unbearably slow. He/she will learn to observe the pace of the client and how that affects the pace of the student therapist.

Supervisor's Function while Observing the Dyad

When one looks upon supervision, one can focus on client-oriented or therapist-oriented supervision. In the following I am occupied with the part that is focused on the therapist.

I see my function as a helper for the student therapist with anything that creates problems in the therapy process. Every person has a unique way of expressing him/herself musically, verbally, and bodily and of being in the world. Does the therapeutic presence stand in the way of the clinical work? We have to identify areas together that have to be worked on and changed. Every student has a different pace in his or her individuation process as a music therapist and that has to be respected by the supervisor.

During the observation, the supervisor takes notes while sitting quietly in the background not interrupting the session. The presence of the supervisor should be as neutral as possible in order for the student therapist to be allowed to find his/her own way to make contact with the student client and to develop his/her own relational music together. Mary Priestley writes about the presence of the supervisor: "The supervisor empathically feels himself into the inner music of the therapeutic couple, and remains observant and silent for as long as he can. While the therapy is moving, even stammering, silent or raging, he can leave them to themselves, and take up any points afterwards" (1994, p. 299).

Often, timekeeping may be a problem for the student therapist and it can be helpful in the beginning for the supervisor to indicate when there are five minutes remaining in the session. Mary Priestley suggests that the supervisor also may want to make a suggestion if the student therapist has trouble deciding upon a title for the improvisation. I personally do not do that, but if the title seemed not to be effective, I will address this in supervision. The long-term goal is for the couple to get rid of the supervisor, so it is important to create as little dependency as possible. One can compare the position of the observing supervisor as a receptive and empathic container, and a radar that records the strengths and weaknesses of the student therapist in terms of being, doing, creating, and thinking.

I pay particularly close attention to the following questions during my observation. Is the student able to give space inside and outside the music to the client? Can he/she be nondirective and directive inside and outside the music at appropriate times? Is the student handling the verbal part in an appropriate way? Is the student clear in her verbal part? Were the musical interventions working? Is the student presenting him/herself in an emotionally neutral position so that the student client can use him/her for transference? How is the pace of the student therapist compared to the student client? Is the student able to contain musically and verbally? Is the music of the student therapist creative and flowing naturally, or is it stiff and nonorganic? Does the student project her voice in the music? Is there intentionality in the musical interventions of the student therapist? How does the student handle silences? Does the verbal, bodily, and musical language complement or contradict each other? Are the musical parameters used appropriately? Does the student tend to get stuck in the use of a certain parameter, such as displaying little flexibility in tempo or rhythm? Is the student physically as well as mentally grounded in his/her presence? Is the student operating from a centered place, or does the student speak/play from an overly intellectualized position?

As a supervisor I use my own feelings in two different ways during the observation. I tend to oscillate between empathizing with the student client and the student therapist in order to detect possible transference and countertransference that is going on inside and outside the music. Am I getting bored? If I am, there will be a high likelihood that the process is stuck or moving in circles. Is the student merging with the client in the music, or can the student keep a separate musical identity? Does the student give a clear message about his/her role before the music (for example: reinforcer, companion, mirror, a certain defined role in a musical psychodrama, supporter)? Does the student make sure that it is clear what the verbal starting point is or the rules for the improvisation are? Did the student notice what went on in the first five minutes of the session? That is important, because the first five minutes often reflect the issues that the client is struggling with in a condensed form. Was there any obvious musical or extra musical countertransference?

What kind of presence is the client calling for in the therapist? What does that indicate diagnostically about the client? It can sometimes be a difficult job for the supervisor being a third excluded part of a triangle. Mary Priestley writes about this subject: "First of all this can stir up feelings from earlier periods in his life when he was an excluded third party, possibly in a trio of mother and father against him, or mother and sister against him. This may arouse in him an impulse to interject at all costs, or it may cause his interest in the intimate scene revealed before him to die mysteriously away. If he understands these possibilities he will be able to withstand the feelings better and to act from this understanding rather than from blind impulse" (1994, p. 303).

Individual Supervision in the IMT Context

The individual supervision that follows immediately after the therapies can be viewed as a condensed form of what the student will receive in the third stage of the training where the individual supervision session lasts one hour. In general, it is the student's responsibility to bring up areas of concern and to discern where help is needed. However, I will bring up things that I noticed if I believe it is important to the learning process of the student. Because this may represent the first opportunity that the student has to experience the offer of assistance in relation to her clinical expertise, I pay close attention to see if the student can allow himself/herself to receive help or has difficulty in requesting assistance.

Usually, the supervision follows five steps within one session:

- Identification of musical/verbal phenomena that the student therapist was not able to handle
- Identification of the issue(s) that the student want to work with
- Working through the issue(s) in music if possible.
- Verbal integration and clarification
- Identification of possible parallel process (aspects of what happened in the discussed session are reflected in the supervision session.)

The Role of the Supervisor

First and foremost the supervisor must be able to function as a container for the student therapist in the sense that Bion uses the term: "It is the creation of a psychic space in which each and every communication, however confused and painful, is received by the therapist, retained and mentally digested with the aim of removing any unbearable qualities from the client's feelings" (1962, p. 306).

The student therapist will often be overwhelmed by feelings of incompetence, inner critiques, impotence, failure, feelings of having to rescue the client, feelings of not knowing enough or not being good enough, feeling stuck, and mixed emotions released by the previous session. The supervisor has to be able to receive, retain, and sit with these feelings, and eventually help the student to express them in music, accompany and give shape to the expressions, so that the student does not feel alone with this, and feels accepted. After the musical expression he/she can help the supervisee to gain insight from the music.

The second role of the supervisor is to help the student to develop a personal musical identity. In case this already has been formed, one's role may be to challenge and to encourage the student to learn new ways of musical expression, such as how to incorporate atonal language in the improvisations, or to incorporate particular songs or musical styles that may relate to the issues that are brought up by the client.

The third important role of the supervisor is to help the student to develop a personal interpretation universe, to help the student to see that there are no recipes and that the client is the one with the knowledge of the meaning of the music. The student can develop an ability to help the client discover his/her unique interpretation universe.

In the following I will mention areas that I often bring to the attention of the student therapist.

It is important to look at the student's verbal skills. Often, students feel responsible for giving answers to client questions. They need to learn to help the client to find his/her own answers. Advice giving and too much questioning are not helpful for the client. It seems hard for the student therapist to stay neutral in the first IMT sessions, and often I will suggest that the student therapist make an improvisation where the person explores where the tendency to give advice and questioning is coming from.

It is important to clarify with the client what the improvisation theme is, and in cases where a particular intervention calls for more than one title, deciding which improvisation title is played first. It is also important to clarify the role of the student therapist in the music before the music starts. It is important to try to remember to create connections, if there are any, between the previous sessions and the present one. A musical/verbal/emotional theme may recur or a dream may be connected to what was processed in a former session.

Sometimes I find a missing resonance on the part of the student therapist. Sometimes the student is not able to co-respond to the client's reality or to let himself/herself become touched by the client's being.

At times I find that authenticity is missing from the student therapist. In the beginning the student therapist may be copying the style of previous therapists or supervisors and not daring to be himself/herself.

The supervisor is charged with the responsibility for uncovering unconscious material inside and outside the music of the student therapist and the student client. This includes becoming aware of phenomena such as transference, countertransference, repressed material or resistance, and bringing these to the attention of the student therapist.

The overly represented "doing" mode of the student therapist may also be a focus. Often in the beginning of the therapy course, the student is doing too much and almost taking away from the client the responsibility to work.

The presence of artistic creativity may be missing. Sometimes the creativity of the student seems to be dead or missing. In this case we will identify if the student therapist is allowing himself/herself to be stimulated creatively outside the therapy room. Is he/she playing or singing in any other context? Is she receiving instruction or musical nurturing and inspiration on her instrument? Is he/she listening to music or going to concerts? If not, that may be the reason for the stuckness or the deadness of the music.

The awareness about the process in the session as such and in the whole course of sessions may be missing. In the beginning of training the student may not be aware of what process means, so I will often ask the student to describe the process that just unfolded in the previous session. How does this process relate to the rest of the sessions, and where are we in the overall course of the treatment—beginning, middle, or at the end? How can one start a music therapy process and how can one terminate a music therapy process?

Supervisory Techniques and Common Student Problems

Depending on what has to be accomplished, one can develop a repertoire of techniques that can be helpful to give the student therapist personal and technical insight.

- *Musical role-playing.* The student therapist plays the client in music. The supervisor takes the role of the student therapist. This technique will help the therapist to be able to better resonate with the client.
- *Musical release.* Sometimes the student therapist has been building up tension during the earlier session, but the student cannot localize the source(s) of it. The student is supported to experience and express the tension on a musically symbolic level. Verbalization of such a release can lead to insights about which conflicts are evoking the tensions.
- *Theme-identification.* If it is obvious that the student therapist is identifying with his/her client, one can suggest the student therapist to improvise over the same theme as he/she had asked his/her client to improvise over. This will reveal some of the identification pitfalls that the student therapist may have.
- *Closure solutions.* If the student has problems finding a natural closure, I sometimes suggest improvising over titles like: "Important Good-byes," "Endings," "Boundaries," and "Separation" to detect the more unconscious reasons for this difficulty.
- *Doing/being problems.* In cases of the student therapist being too much in the doing mode, I suggest improvising over titles such as: "Playing as little as possible," "Improv. A: Doing, Improv B: Being," "Improvise over a situation, where you just 'are' (could be lying in the sun on a beach or meditating or other images that facilitates this state of being), "being out of control" or "being in control." Unconscious reasons and traumas may come up to the surface and cause the student to have the urgency to act.
- *Authenticity problems.* As performing therapy is dealing with our relational reality, issues of ability or lacking the ability to be authentic in stressed situations are activated. If the student therapist has trouble being authentic inside and outside the music, I suggest improvisation titles as "accepting the

needs of my inner child" or I may suggest that the student thinks about the earliest situation in his/her life where he/she was not allowed to be authentic or be themselves, and then improvise on that situation.

- *Controlled musical regression.* There may be several reasons, often unconscious, that hinder the student therapist in listening and empathizing with the client. Depending on what was the issue in the former session that the student therapist conducted, the starting point of an improvisation could be "The first time I remember being accepted for who I am."

- *Dream exploration.* Often, the student therapist has dreams that are related to the sessions that one conducts. If these dreams are brought in, they can be musically explored in a variety of ways. Symbols from the dream can be the focus of improvisations. One can play the dream through chronologically, one can play the emotions that the dreamer had during the dream, and one can play the emotions that the dream evoked after waking up. This work with dreams can also give the student guidance in his/her work with the client's dreams.

- *Listening attitudes.* As the IMT sessions are audio recorded the supervisor and the student therapist can listen to the musical and verbal parts of the session together. The supervisor can help the student to develop a way of listening that is reverent and uses intuition. During listening to the music together, the student can relax the usual superego function, and let the music resonate inside without having to focus on anything specific. Every preconception and personal interpretation can be put aside so that anything that is being played and/or sung can be fully taken in by the student therapist. It may be compared with the situation of a parent holding a child so that it can be able to take in the sounds around it in a safe atmosphere. This listening attitude may then be transferred to when the student therapist is working with the client.

- *Facilitation of musical self-acceptance.* In the beginning stages of becoming a practicing music therapist, students often experience performance anxiety or discomfort with his or her own musical expressive language. There may be an academic or formal quality to the musical language. When I notice this phenomena, I often have the student play music with me right after the session. My role in the music is a holding and dialogical attitude, just like the mother or father vocalizing and holding a baby in his/her arms. This may facilitate development of the student's own musicality, musical identity, and growth. This is of importance, because the client will sense, consciously or unconsciously, if the music therapist is unhappy with his/her own music. It will be hard for the client to find his/her musical self if this is the case.

- *Dialogical playing/singing.* In the beginning of the IMT training, I often encounter students who have a preference for playing simultaneously with the client. When one plays dialogical, one is more exposed and cannot hide or merge with the music of the client. Perhaps there is a natural fear of being too exposed in one's actions in the beginning of the training. When I notice this avoidance, I offer myself as a musical partner in the supervision. In this dialogical playing, one can train functions of organizing and timing the switch from one player to another, and developing skills in musical timing which include when to pause and the appropriate duration of musical statements.

- *Types of accompaniment.* Sometimes a student therapist is not aware when to accompany in unison, harmonizing, mirroring, reinforcing or opposing. If it is not clear to the student when to do what, I improvise with the student therapist, letting him or her be in the client position and notice how the different accompaniment relations feel. A musical unison can be experienced by clients as being held in a symbiotic or merging state. When the therapist is accompanying with harmonies to the client's music, it can be experienced as being held, but at the same time as having independence or freedom to separate (the client can make dissonance when he/she wants distance). Mirroring can be experienced by clients as encouraging, strengthening of the self, recognizing and validating. In cases where a client has difficulties sensing his/her emotions or is defended in his/her expression, reinforcement of the client's sounds can help the person to acknowledge or identify the emotional or defended content of the expression. For clients that need to have something or somebody to go up against or to rebel against, it can be helpful to accompany in an opposing style, for example tonal versus atonal, major versus minor.

Evaluation

When the whole course of the IMT sessions have been completed (the clinical part, the theoretical part, the audiotaped excerpts) the students will be asked to do a self-evaluation and the trainer will evaluate them. The evaluation covers the four areas of music therapy competency: personal, technical, artistic, and theoretical competency. If the student is missing skills in any of the areas, recommendations are made depending on which areas are not fulfilled. If the student has obtained the necessary skills, he/she will be recommended to receive half to a whole year of weekly individual AMT supervision and after that or at the same time half to a whole year of weekly group AMT supervision depending on the growth and needs of the student. These supervision sessions last for one hour each.

Individual and Group Supervision: Stage Three of AMT Training

Description and Requirements of Individual Supervision

The student will be asked to work with a minimum of two individual patients and two groups weekly, on which they will receive weekly individual supervision. The student can either make his or her own arrangements to get clients or the supervisor will provide them with clients. It can be any client population depending on the interests of the student and the availability of clients. As the AMT model can be adapted to most populations, even clients without verbal skills or with moderate degrees of developmental delay, it is up to the student to choose which population they want to be supervised with. The student will need an entire year of individual supervision and possibly more depending upon the level of the student at the beginning of the training.

Because the supervision sessions in this part of the training last one hour, there will be more time to focus on various needs and issues the student brings up. What has been previously discussed regarding skills that are taught in the IMT can also be said about the individual and group supervision. We fine-tune and continue to grow in areas that have been addressed in the IMT.

The role of the supervisor is multifaceted and less active than in the IMT supervision, and I experience myself as fluctuating between using my skills as a music therapist and using my skills as a teacher.

The student is expected to take more responsibility for what is happening or not happening in the supervision sessions. I make it clear that it is a shared responsibility that we finish on time.

In this form of supervision, there will be sessions that straddle the gray area between clinical music therapy and clinical supervision because countertransference, among other phenomena, related to the clinical material will be processed inside and outside the music in order to facilitate insight and professional growth. It is the job of the supervisor to stop at the point of realization or recognition of possible countertransference issues. The supervisor does not encourage further exploration of the relational experiences in the past that may have led to the behavior of the supervisee. One may suggest that the issues are brought to personal therapy for further exploration.

Dvorkin writes about her experiences in this area: "The boundary between supervision and therapy can be very thin, due to the similarity in techniques and the enormous effect the therapist's own unresolved issues can have on the clinical work" (1999, p. 278).

Arthur Robbins, an experienced therapist, trainer, teacher, and supervisor in the creative arts therapies, writes about the importance of training creative arts therapist students in processing transference and countertransference communications: "The study of transference and countertransference cannot be put aside until the student enters a later stage of professional development. The fundamentals of treatment technique are often compromised by highly charged emotional reactions on the part of the therapist. When opportunities are presented for processing these reactions through artwork, blocks towards learning are often lifted, leading the artist/therapist to a deeper comprehension of therapeutic process" (1994, p. xii).

The countertransference reactions from the music therapist are processed in music as well as verbally in the supervision, if the countertransference stands in the way of the treatment of the client.

In the supervision sessions we are entering a process that is characterized by a constant oscillation between primary and secondary process thinking. Primary process thinking is handled by the right hemisphere of the brain, and governed by the laws of the preconscious; this happens mostly in the musical parts of the session. Secondary process thinking is handled by the left hemisphere and governed by more rational and conscious thinking; this happens mostly in the verbal parts of the session.

The goal is to achieve an integration of both sides of the brain. This also reflects the process that we go through with our clients in the sessions.

The steps of the supervision often take the following form:

- Identification of the issue(s) that the supervisee wants to work with. This can be verbalized or expressed in music. If the supervisee is unprepared or has no idea where to start, I suggest that the supervisee improvise alone or together with me and see what comes up. If the supervisee is prepared, he/she will be presenting audiotaped or videotaped material in this part of the supervision. Certain demographic information may be communicated to me, such as diagnosis of client, age, history, goals, objectives, number of session, and number of clients. In this part it is clarified if the focus is on the client or on the supervisee or on both. We may start verbally, if the focus is on the client(s), to identify which approach may be appropriate according to the needs and the goals of the client. Questions may come up such as: Will there be a need to focus on the self (mirroring, self-affirmation), or on the drives (control/out of control), or on behavioral modification, or on a spiritual dimension, or on an actual physical skill (speech, movement), or will an object relations approach be more appropriate? Which developmental stage or which physical/psychological need does the client have right now?
- Musical facilitation and exploration of issues/techniques, that was brought up in the previous step.
- Verbal integration and clarification of what was brought up in the previous step.
- Identification of possible parallel process inside and outside the music in the session (the client's behavior with the music therapist is often reenacted in the music therapist's behavior with the supervisor).

The Role of the Music

The music can play a variety of roles in the individual supervision. First and foremost the music can be used as a tool of clarification and insight in aspects of the presented issue.

- It can be used to clarify musical countertransference, defenses, resistance, projective identification, musical transference, if the supervisee is able to reproduce musically, what the client(s) sang/played in the presented session.
- It can be used to mirror how a supervisee connects with himself/herself in the interaction with the client.
- It can be used to improve the musical repertoire or improvisational reservoir of the supervisee.
- It can be used to help the supervisee to connect with his/her creativity.
- It can be used for the purpose of stress reduction in situations where the supervisee is in danger of burning out.
- It can be used to establish connection between supervisee and supervisor, if the communication for some reason is blocked or unclear.

- It can be used to identify parallel process that is occurring in the session.
- It can be used in general to bring unconscious associations to a conscious level, when there is a need for that. (This way of using the music can be very helpful when there is resistance on the client's or the music therapist's part, for example resistance toward playing/singing.)

Stages in the Process of Individual Supervision

A supervision process can be compared, in a condensed form, with the individuation process of a child growing up.

Stage I: "Tuning in and getting to know each other."
The supervisor and supervisee are starting to form a relationship through verbal and musical relating, getting to know each other and getting to know the content of the contract. Assessment of the student's strengths and weaknesses musically, verbally, and theoretically is done here and goals and objectives are set for the future. The supervisee gets into a routine, learning to receive supervision and to present material. The role of the supervisor often seems to be like a parent or authority, and the need for structure and direction surfaces often. Didactic instruction and support are key words. The supervisee often experiences and expects a certain degree of dependency on the supervisor. The supervisor often carries a function of being a holding container while the supervisee is learning about basic concepts of AMT.

Stage II: "Working on improvement of skills and personal growth."
The supervisee works on musical and verbal skills. Often the verbal skills are in great need of improvement because many music therapy students have not been trained in verbal skills related to musical communication and interaction. Work is also being done on integrating musical, verbal, and theoretical skills. Relationship issues between supervisor and supervisee may surface and may be processed musically and verbally. This indicates the beginning of work and knowledge achievement in the area of transference, countertransference, resistance, projection, and resonance. The stance of the supervisee is less dependent than in Stage I. Often the supervisee has fluctuating needs moving between polarities of being active and passive. The seeds are getting laid for a beginning music therapeutic AMT identity and style. The supervisor is "giving permission" to make mistakes and learn from these.

Stage III: "Establishing AMT identity and personal style: Beginning separation."
An identity and style will now emerge in bits and pieces and the supervisor will facilitate growth and confidence for the supervisee. The supervisor is letting go more of the supervisee and he/she is often at this stage working on issues of integrating his/her own authority in the work. The relationship between supervisor and supervisee may be tested, conflicts may arise, and transference and countertransference between each other may be identified and worked on. The supervisee's work is starting to demonstrate the fundamental basics of AMT practice. Goals of skill development and personal development are reevaluated. The supervisor is constantly evaluating the progress or areas of need at this point. The supervisor ensures that the supervisee is

exposed to a variety of musical and verbal techniques in the supervision sessions. The supervisor is taking a more challenging stance in the supervision.

Stage IV: "Consolidating AMT identity and style: Termination."
In this stage the supervisee may often reject the ideas and values of the supervisor (like the teenager, that is challenging the parent), and power struggles may occur in the sessions. The supervisor supports the supervisee's autonomy and feels moments of being peers instead of being in a purely supervisor/supervisee relationship. A thorough termination process is being worked through musically, verbally, and emotionally. A theoretical case study on an individual client and on a group is being produced with appropriate video- and audiotaped material. At the end of this stage the supervisee will have reached a grounded and centered sense of professional music therapeutic identity and the goals of technical skills and personal growth have been met. The supervisor and supervisee will evaluate the whole supervision process. The quality of the relationship will be more like peers and of a collegial nature. The supervisee has developed his/her own "internal supervisor."

Clinical Supervisory Example:
"Sometimes I Feel Like a Motherless Child"

Background of Supervisee
A supervisee, S, twenty-nine year old, was working with developmentally delayed blind children, ages three to seven, within a school context, and had been doing this for one and a half years. Before the session subsequently described, she was dealing with the recurring problem of feeling stuck in the approach to her clients. We role-played being the blind children through music and came up with a variety of techniques that could be applied.

Another theme involved feelings of insecurity in terms of musical efficacy when S was being observed by others (teachers, interns, helpers, and parents) which we also dealt with musically. Meanwhile, this did not prevent her from having some episodes of feeling stuck so I suspected that some deeper underlying professional and personal issues might have been at the root of the recurring phenomena. At the same time I was puzzled by the fact that in positive moments the supervisee reported that the children were improving, the school psychologist was very impressed with the work of the supervisee, and the school that provided the internship to the supervisee was more than satisfied. When the issue of feeling stuck came up in the following session, I suggested that we explore more directly the emotional underlying issues connected to this complex issue.

She started the session by saying that she had fallen into her old pattern of depression and she related it to feeling *frustrated* in her music therapy work with the children. She had very little help in the classroom and felt that her techniques did not work or that she was *stuck* when it came to improvisation skills and management of the children who were *out of control*. She had had a very chaotic session where nothing seemed to work. She stated that "the session was horrible." She felt very alone on the institution, was the only music therapist there, and received little support from the staff, who were mostly teachers. Nobody *listened* to her. It made her feel that she was at an entry level and not a *skilled* master's level clinician. She said, "Perhaps I am just a little stuck."

She also felt stuck in her marriage. I suggested that she improvise over the title "Being stuck together" and I would be reinforcing and supportive when needed in the music. I encouraged her to stay as long as she could in the stuckness and not try to consciously find a way out. I also encouraged her to use her voice. She said: "I feel that the defenses are up—it's going to be hard for me!"

The Music

S chooses to play the piano. The tonality moves between tonal and atonal language. The tones do not seem to be very related to each other; it is as if they are not listening to each other. She used the whole register of tones. The rhythm is the structural component that holds the music together in a march-like 1-2-walking-rhythm. It sounds as if it is marching robot-like on the spot with no specific direction. She looks like a child playing on a piano with pleasure in making the tones clash. The tempo is rather quick and there is not much variation in the dynamic, which is medium loud.

I underline the rhythm playing on a high-hat cymbal (mirroring). While I am playing, I get in touch with feeling like marching in an army, not knowing the direction that I am going. I feel restricted and stuck in this position.

After a while S moves down in the bass register and stays there for a long time, still keeping the monotone rhythm. I sing to S: "Where are you now?" (checking in). She sings back: "I feel so alone. I feel like I don't have peers to talk to. I feel so alone." I sing back in the same tonality and melody: "I feel so alone" (mirroring).

She makes an explosive atonal and arhythmical dramatic outbreak in a loud volume (anger?). I support her volume and intensity. Then it slowly quiets down in tempo and dynamics and she stops playing. There is a five-minute long pause.

In the pause I get the sense of sitting with a little girl who is angry, lost, and stuck. I ask her what she would do when she was a little girl and was alone and stuck (verbal intervention). S answers: "Take a doll."

I then asked: "Is there any way you can hold and comfort yourself in music?" (musical intervention). After a little pause S walks over to the client chair, sits down and starts to hum by herself pianissimo, playing with little melody pieces in a minor mode.

I take the guitar and start accompanying her with playing on single strings, one at a time, fitting the tones into the tonality of the melodic fragments (musical intervention). S sings in a blueslike fashion and a sad blues song grows out of our music. S sings: "I feel so alone." Her voice slides down in glissandi several times. Out of this grows a line which she sings half crying: "Sometimes I feel like a motherless child, sometimes I feel like a motherless child, alone, alone, alone, away from home." She sings a variation of the well-known song: "Sometimes I feel like a motherless child," adding some of her own text. I am accompanying her gently with minor accords on the guitar until she stops singing.

In the verbal processing of the music S talks about the loneliness in her work situation, the transference of loneliness and anger of the children, which reinforces her own loneliness and anger. She mentions feelings of loneliness in her relationship, and feelings of not being understood by her family. Her feelings of being insecure and not skilled enough are being dismissed and even I, as a supervisor, do it sometimes (parallel process), which we talk about. I am happy that she finally expresses some negative feelings toward me, because I sense that she has been hiding her anger from me in previous sessions. In the improvisation there was a short passage with explosive material and perhaps this part of the music gave her permission to let some steam out. S also started talking about feelings of being disconnected that were released during the improvisation. These feelings were well known in relation to her family.

I pointed out to her that maybe these feelings of being stuck and depressed were released every time she felt *disconnected* from the children. Then she would be reminded of her areas of disconnection in her past and present life, and that may make her feel stuck.

She realized in the end that she needed to nurture and stimulate herself musically, perhaps taking a summer course in improvisation, and make her needs be heard and listened to better by her husband and by me. She also talked about feeling underpaid compared to other work contexts. She seemed relieved when she left.

Reflection on the Musical Process

In the next supervision session S made comments about how amazing it was that that song ("Sometimes I feel like a motherless child") just came flowing out of her mouth from the unconscious. She seemed to be in a more flowing process during that session. She mentioned that she had asked for a raise at her work and if they would not agree to that, she would ask to have less hours per day for the same amount of money that they were paying her, thereby improving her work conditions.

So the music helped in the supervision to "de-mask" what was behind or underneath the feelings of being stuck. We sat in the stuckness (the intra- and intersubjective countertransferencial reaction to the clients) together until the "motherless child" theme emerged from the unconscious. It has to be added that this supervisee mentioned in earlier sessions that her mother did not seem to be able to give her a good mothering experience while she grew up.

Concerning the choice of the music instruments and the accompaniment of the supervisor: I chose to accompany S in the first improvisation on the high-hat cymbal, underlining the rhythm, the volume, and the energy level in order to reflect and mirror that back to the supervisee. The music did seem to be stuck, but not completely without movement, which was important to reflect to her. There was an underlying quality of repressed anger that may have had the potential to surface, which it did in the end for a short while.

In the second improvisation, I chose to accompany her on the guitar, which is S's main instrument, one that she uses primarily with her voice in her clinical work. I thought that might make her feel heard and held, but not intruded upon. I made the accompaniment simple, on open strings, so that there would be offered enough space for S to explore vocally.

We may have come to the insights through talking, but my experience is that the music facilitates the process of gaining insight in a creative way, which touches and sometimes surprises oneself, and it seems as if it is easier to take in the knowledge when it emerges from an artistic process that is not guided in a purely cerebral way.

Indirectly, the supervisee is being taught music therapeutic techniques through the supervisor's musical and verbal interventions as illustrated in this session.

Description and Format of Group Supervision

The group supervision session consists of four to five supervisees and lasts for one hour. The group is lead by an experienced AMT group supervisor. The student receives group supervision for at least one year. At the end of the year, the student will be evaluated by the group supervisor, the group members, and by self-evaluation.

It is up to each individual group member to decide what they want to work with and how they want to work with the presented material musically. The supervisor may decide to play or not to play during the musical part of the sessions. There is no rule about who has to present at any given time. The group senses who has the biggest need if there is not clearly a person who has brought in clinical material. Sometimes the group or a group member starts playing without any verbal contact. The verbal processing then takes place after the improvisation. The model describing the different phases in the actual session in individual supervision is the same for the group supervision.

One of the purposes of the group supervision is to explore, exchange, and investigate a variety of theoretical and affective issues, approaches and methods that each group member represents. Each person may handle a problem differently and use music therapeutic techniques that the other members do not know about. An important part of the process is the emotional and cognitive feedback from the group.

The training is, in general, focused on training of the supervisee's professional, personal, and social competence. Training of the musical (for example, improvisational flexibility, meaning within the music) and the verbal skills of the music therapist takes up much space in supervision.

The Role of the Supervisor

The supervisor has a variety of roles in this work:

- To promote a warm, nonjudgmental, accepting atmosphere where the supervisees can learn from each other and the supervisor, grow and improve. Key areas in this supervisional growth matrix are varied and include the following: empathy; emotional support; a place to try out new techniques; realization of insight and meaning; connectedness; resonance; training of listening skills and observational skills; reloading of the creative batteries; consolidation of one's own music therapeutic identity; networking; experiencing allies; experiencing strengths and limitations; emotional expressivity; inspiration to read, practice, and write; a place to hear a variety of types of music; support of self-promotion; support of wellbeing (to avoid burnout); training of openness to preconscious as well as conscious presented material.

- To be the group leader and facilitator of the group process. Among others, to assess what is going on with the group process, and relate this to the actual presented material.
- To be responsible for the time management.
- To pick up upon possible resistance toward learning and address it.
- To facilitate that the presented material is processed in music in one way or another. This may include help with formulation of improvisation theme or rule.
- To facilitate integration between musical and verbal processing.
- To provide support with identification of what the issue(s) is, if this is unclear to the group members.
- To help to maintain the goal of supervision rather than treatment or therapy for the supervisees.
- To be a musical facilitator in the improvisations.
- To help out analyzing the music that is being played and examined (audiotape/videotape improvised music in the session).

The role of such a group is basically a container or holding environment, where material can be presented and explored creatively through musical, bodily, and verbal interactions.

Arthur Robbins (1988) writes about supervision groups of mixed creative arts therapists. He articulates a concept of the group as container which is congruent with how it is used in AMT supervision: "The *group* becomes a 'container,' as members support the presenter's attempts to expand his ability to project, externalize, and investigate the myriad of affects that arise in transference/countertransference reactions. This 'holding' helps neutralize the anxiety associated with the enormous strain under which a therapist works in grappling with client's primitive emotional states" (p. 17). It is often experienced in such groups that over time the group members develop strong bonds to each other.

The Role of the Music

In addition to the roles of music described earlier, we can add the following:

- It can help each supervisee to experience a wide variety of types of musical expressivity and improvisational flexibility in terms of listening to the music of the supervisees and to the music of the clients of the supervisees. This can help the supervisee not to become stuck in his/her musical language and expressivity.
- Listening to the analysis of music of the clients and the other supervisees can help the supervisee to expand his/her understanding of multiple or specific meanings of the music. The music is contextualized and interpreted in relation to the informed musical analysis.
- By listening to the musical presentations the supervisee can acquire a reservoir of techniques for responding to client's music.

- Through the other supervisee's responses to the music played in a session of one supervisee he/she can receive feedback from them about what he/she is carrying as unconscious musical luggage, both instrumentally and vocally.
- In cases where pre-composed music is presented or used, the supervisee can extend his/her musical repertoire.
- The fact that the group members are playing music together as a processing tool creates cohesiveness, authenticity, and a deep level of intimacy among the group members.
- If there are problems between the group members, the music can be used to facilitate problem solution.

Techniques

Besides training in employing the AMT techniques mentioned previously, the supervisee will indirectly experience group music improvisation techniques that will be helpful in facilitating knowledge and insight about presented issues.

After one person has presented an issue or a problem, it will be discussed how the group can help through music. There are many techniques that can be used depending upon the need:

- The presenter plays a musical portrait of a client with whom the presenter has difficulties. The rest of the group members take turns trying to act as music therapists.
- The presenter explores his/her countertransference musically and the group musically supports the expression and exploration.
- The presenter plays a tape with the music of a client. After having listened to the tape, the group responds in music to the client's music either individually or together.
- A group member presents a problem, theme, or issue with a client. The rest of the group members may be able to identify the same problem, theme or issue in their own clinical reality. The group starts out in an improvisation together, and when everybody is ready, each member improvises a solo piece over their specific problem, theme, or issue thinking about a particular client with whom it arises. In this way the presenter does not feel alone with the problematic situation and can experience different ways of relating to the same problem, theme, or issue.
- The group starts playing music without verbalizing beforehand and sees what material comes to the surface from the improvisation.

Clinical Supervisory Example:

Group Description
The group to be discussed consisted of four supervisees, one male, A, and three females, B, C, and D, of varying levels of clinical experience. The group had been together for half a year, seeing each other weekly. All the group members were highly

intellectual and the group frequently spent much time verbalizing before they started playing.

Supervisee A was presenting about not knowing how to approach an issue brought up by a client who he was working with. The client was a twenty-one-year-old shooting victim, who was paralyzed in both legs. In the session, the client was bringing up this issue: How can I be a sexually attractive man when I am paralyzed and not able to please a woman? This issue had come to the surface at a point when the client was about to end the relationship with his girlfriend. The supervisee felt the trauma of the client inside, but chose to comfort the client by telling him that his legs were just a vehicle to transport him around but there was more to him than his legs. It did not seem to be a satisfying answer to either the supervisee or to the client.

Another supervisee, B, who was from Japan, empathized by starting to talk about a male Asiatic client of hers who also had a physical trauma. The client kept asking the supervisee if she thought he would get back to normal again and if she would go back with him to his home country. She did not know how to react to the client, particularly also because in this Asiatic culture it was not appropriate to talk about feelings or show them directly. A couple of group members said to B that perhaps her client expressed to her that he was in love with her. She said, "No! No! No! No!" and it was obvious that she did not feel comfortable talking about that subject.

A third supervisee, C, who frequently took on the role of therapist in the group, asked B what she felt about being asked such a question by the client. She couldn't answer and she seemed even more uncomfortable.

As supervisor, I sensed three things at this point. First, that the group could go on at an intellectual level and spend a long time discussing approaches, as it had a habit of doing if not interrupted by an intervention that would allow them to get into the music. Second, that some of the group members had a need to explore feelings evoked when they were working with physically traumatized clients. Third, that it was important to relieve the pressure on B of having to talk about feelings.

Therefore I suggested that each group member, after a common musical entrance, expressed and explored in solo instrumentally and vocally what feelings, images, and music were evoked in them when they thought about a particular physically traumatized client in their work. In this way they may be able to detect possible countertransference and also possible ways to empathize.

The group found this suggestion a good idea. Each person identified a client that they would improvise on. I defined my role as a musical supporter, if needed.

The Music

The male supervisee, A, chose a drum set and a jimbe drum, B chose a violin, C chose a frame drum and a horn, and D chose the piano. I chose a cymbal and an accordion.

Beginning phase: Each person seemed to experiment with musical expressions, as if they were finding their way to the variety of feeling qualities. A was dominating the sound picture rather quickly with heavy drumming which forced the rest of the group members to become louder so they could hear themselves better. I choose to play in the background in a very soft and quiet way with melody on the accordion to harmonize with the energy and dynamic of B's developing violin melody. I indicated my connection with the rest of the group by bashing the cymbal in the rhythm of A's and C's music.

The participants seemed to find a communal ending rather quickly. There was a small pause. Then B started a violin solo that sounded like a structured eastern folk song in a major tonality in a rather slow tempo. The emotional quality seemed to be hopeful and reaching out. The music had a high degree of aesthetic beauty.

A followed after B with loud outbreaks on jimbe and drum set, first at a slow tempo but quickly accelerating in tempo and loudness. There was a clear sense of rhythmical structure in the beginning of the solo, which changed in the end where the rhythm seemed more chaotic.

Supervisee D followed with a solo on the piano with one hand in F major. The music seemed a little stiff and arrhythmic but communicated a sense of a strong and sturdy identity through medium loud volume, the particular chosen harmonic progressions, and clear direction and intentionality in the music.

Supervisee C followed after with blowing and vocalizing on a horn in a way that sounded like musical sighs and resignation. This was followed by an outbreak of loud uncontrollable drumming. She ended with swinging a rattle, which gave off a wrenching noise like an old wagon wheel that is almost falling apart. All the music of C was musically arhythmical, and was carried by a strong expressive quality in the melody, dynamic and timbre.

All the solos seemed rather condensed and short. After the end of C's music there was a short pause. Supervisee D initiated the verbal process by talking about what she had come in touch with through playing like her client, who could only use one hand. She talked about what she had in common with this client—among other things that they both played by ear, the pros and cons about that ability, and they had both taught themselves how to play. She also got in touch with this client's assertiveness and need to be independent by playing with firm tonal direction, F major, the client's preferred tonality and style of playing. She was surprised that she found a freedom in this type of playing, and not the frustration she had suspected expected. This corresponded to her client's character, which seemed to deal with his physical trauma in a positive "survivor" way: How can I get the best out of the situation that I am in?

Supervisee B took over and asked if she could just play a Japanese song on her violin. It seemed to resemble what she played in her solo in the former improvisation, but there seemed to be a longing emotional quality to the tune. After the playing she said that she felt very nervous playing this song, but she did not know why. I asked her what this song symbolized for her, and she said that it was a song that came from the town that both she and her client came from. She then talked about her strong empathy with her client being from such a different Eastern culture and the trauma she and he had in common having to face adapting to a Western culture. She also got in touch with missing her country, just like he did.

Supervisee A spoke about getting in touch through playing the drums with a deep frustration and anger that he could feel by imagining being in his client's situation. The group talked about the therapeutic value of the music therapist being able to empathize with this feeling and communicate that to the client, who indeed did have a problem with anger management, which had to be addressed by A in future sessions.

Supervisee C said that she was empathizing with a client who had multiple sclerosis in the end stage, that she currently felt stuck with. She got in touch through the playing with a variety of feelings: the endlessness and hopelessness expressed on the horn, anger and stubbornness expressed on the drum, and the weakness and feeling of almost giving up and abandonment by playing the rattle the way she did. The group identified together with C these feelings as partly possible transference from the client, partly countertransference from C. The supervisee felt helpless because she was not getting any direct verbal or nonverbal response from the client. By identifying the musical transference and countertransference dynamic together as a group, it seemed to help C in not feeling so stuck and alone with the client. She got some ideas about how to possibly reflect back musically some of the possible transferential feelings through playing and singing songs and improvisations containing those emotional qualities to the client in the future. She also realized how her countertransference, being stuck, could be partly a source of information about what the client may go through being in her particular physical condition (being abandoned by the body functions and feeling angry about the illness). Time had run out and we ended the session at that place.

Reflection on the Musical Process
The role of the music seemed to help each group member empathize with their physically traumatized clients, each in their own way. Aspects of musical transference and countertransference were identified and shared for one group member.

The main role of the supervisor in this session was to help the group to get into the musical processing. I chose to suggest that each group member think about a physically traumatized client, which seemed to be the theme for two of the group members. This was done in order to spread the work out to all group members, so A and B would not feel so much in the spotlight.

I chose the timing of suggesting the improvisation, when one group member asked B how she felt about her client asking her these difficult and intimate questions. B had in former sessions expressed discomfort in expressing feelings verbally to group members, which indeed is inappropriate following a Japanese cultural code. I thought that getting into the music might make B feel more comfortable and facilitate expression of her emotions and her connection with her client. I also wanted to prevent it from happening that some group members could feel tempted to play therapist for another group member. I consider this phenomena to promote a resistance toward learning.

My role in the verbal part was minimal in this session. This often seems to be the case, because the music opens up to experiences at an emotional and cognitive level as well. The group process flowed naturally both verbally and musically. The level of intensity was high due to the theme of physical and psychological trauma.

My role in the musical part seemed to be minimal except from showing my support to B through harmonizing with her violin playing. I took the musical backseat as I could hear in the music that everybody was fully engaged in his or her process internally and externally. At this point in the group process I had other reasons for not being very active and directive: I was indirectly encouraging the group members to take leadership so that they could start to become less dependent on me and enter a more autonomous state of functioning.

Completing AMT Training

If the student finishes all the training modules of the AMT training including individual music therapy, group music therapy, IMT, individual supervision, and group music therapy supervision, he/she receives a certificate that indicates that he/she is a trained AMT music therapist who is granted permission to practice AMT.

Each student is doing the training at his/her own pace, and some students may need more training in each of the areas, dependent on their level of skills in the four areas mentioned earlier in this chapter: personal competency, technical competency, artistic competency, and theoretical competency.

After having received an AMT certificate, the AMT music therapist is expected to continue to receive weekly music therapy supervision. The character of this type of supervision is more focused on process according to the need of the moment, oscillating between the concrete content of the session and taking wider factors in consideration. Audiotaped or videotaped material from cases is also presented.

Coda: Final Words on Supervisory Presence

From my own experience as a supervisee for twenty-one years I would like to sum up some essential qualities that an AMT music therapy supervisor who trains supervisees must present as a professional:

- to show respect to the supervisee's own learning process,
- to be able to adapt style and focus to the musical/verbal style and developmental stage of the supervisee,
- to be consistent,
- to have clear boundaries,
- to exert disciplined subjectivity in analysis of the musical/verbal presented material,
- to be able to listen clinically and to listen to his/her own inner and outer music,
- to be willing to receive professional supervision and to being taught himself/herself,
- to trust the process of the student and not push,
- to be able to serve as a musical and verbal container,
- to be able to empathize musically and verbally,
- to be able to admit mistakes,
- to avoid idealization and omnipotence,
- to love his/her work,

- to be committed,
- to be nonjudgmental,
- to have a broad experience working with a variety of populations.

Let me end this article repeating what my own supervisor through the last nine years has said on many occasions: "Do not forget: A supervisor is not God."

References

Amir, D. (1999). Musical and verbal interventions in music therapy: A qualitative study. *Journal of Music Therapy.* 36 (2), 144–175.

Bion, W. R. (1962). A theory of thinking. *International Journal of Psychoanalysis,* 43. 306–310.

Dvorkin, J. (1999). Psychoanalytically oriented music therapy supervision. In T. Wigram and J. De Backer (eds.), *Clinical Applications of Music Therapy in Developmental Disability, Paediatrics and Neurology.* London: Jessica Kingsley Publishers.

Frohne-Hagemann, I. (1999). Integrative supervision for music therapists. In T. Wigram and J. De Backer (eds.), *Clinical Applications of Music Therapy in Developmental Disability, Paediatrics and Neurology.* London: Jessica Kingsley Publishers.

Jensen, O. S. (1998). Psykoterapeutens autencitet—terapiens afgoerende led. *Psyke & Logos,* 19(1), 271–286.

Priestley, M. (1975). *Music Therapy in Action.* London: Constable.

Priestley, M. (1994). *Essays on Analytical Music Therapy.* Gilsum, NH: Barcelona Publishers.

Robbins, A. (1988). *Between Therapists.* New York: Human Sciences Press.

Robbins, A. (1994). *A Multi-Modal Approach to Creative Art Therapy.* London: Jessica Kingsley Publishers.

Robbins, A. (1998). *Therapeutic Presence.* London: Jessica Kingsley Publishers.

Scheiby, B. B. and Pedersen, I. N. (1999). Intermusic therapy in the training music therapy students. *Nordic Journal of Music Therapy,* 8(1), 59–72.

Wigram, T., De Backer, J., and Van Camp, J. (1999). Music therapy training. In T. Wigram, and J. De Backer, (eds.), *Clinical Applications of Music Therapy in Developmental Disability, Paediatrics and Neurology.* London: Jessica Kingsley Publishers.

Chapter 21

Supervision in the Bonny Method of Guided Imagery and Music

Madelaine Ventre, MS, MT-BC, FAMI
Director of the Creative Therapies Institute
Forestburgh, NY

Overview

The Bonny Method of Guided Imagery and Music (GIM) is a model of music therapy developed by Helen Bonny in 1972 while working as a music therapist and research fellow at the Maryland Psychiatric Research Center (Bonny, 1980). Since that time, Bonny has been active in practicing and disseminating the work. In her article in *Music Therapy Perspectives* (1994) she wrote, "Our orientation is humanistic and transpersonal; interpretation is client-centered; music is the generating stimulus and, with the guide, serves as therapist and healer" (p. 70).

The Association for Music and Imagery (AMI) sets the minimum GIM training standards and endorses GIM training programs (AMI, 1999). AMI recommends that a master's degree or equivalent be attained by the completion of advanced training. Presently there are twenty-four AMI endorsed primary trainers and thirteen endorsed training programs (AMI, 2000). Fellows, those who have completed AMI-endorsed training, live in the U.S., Australia, Canada, Denmark, Germany, Ireland, Italy, Mexico, New Zealand, Sweden, and the United Kingdom and training has been conducted in all of these countries.

Introduction

What are the first words that come to you when you hear or read the word "supervision"? Grueling? Scary? Anxiety provoking? Annoying? How about: Challenging! Supportive! Growth provoking! Fun! Some would say it might depend on what side of the supervision you are on, who the supervisor is, or how new you are to the clinical setting or population. Having been on both sides of supervision, I have come to have an enormous respect for what a supervisor can offer me and a great sense of responsibility to the student when I am the supervisor. Above all, in both instances, I consider supervision challenging, supportive, growth provoking, and fun. This has been especially true in Guided Imagery and Music supervision.

Perhaps this is because GIM is my specialty area and I love the work. Perhaps it is because GIM students are already accomplished clinicians. Perhaps it is because we are primary therapists and have the joy and responsibility of working with our clients on any and all of their issues. Perhaps it is because as GIM therapists we are challenged and privileged to travel with clients as far and deep into their internal worlds as they need to go to rebalance and reenergize their lives. Perhaps it is because GIM students, therapists, and supervisors explore their own internal worlds and know from experience how that feels. Probably it is all of the above, and more. Certainly, supervision is a vital, crucial part of GIM training and professional clinical work. The following pages describe the GIM supervision process as practiced at the Creative Therapies Institute. While every training program must meet the minimum guidelines set by AMI, each program has the freedom to emphasize different specialty areas in accordance with the trainer's philosophy of therapy and training.   To support the philosophy of therapy and training as practiced at the Creative Therapies Institute, requirements at CTI exceed the minimum AMI standards.[1]

Overview of Guided Imagery and Music (GIM) Training at the Creative Therapies Institute (CTI)

GIM training is done at the Center for Creative Therapies and the Arts, a thirty-acre retreat center in the lower Catskill Mountains of New York State. The atmosphere is relaxed and classes are held in a comfortable room with music, audio, and video equipment available. While the format is flexible to suit student and faculty schedules, most often training is conducted in weekend or four to five day modules. Room and board is provided at the center. Many students and faculty find that with the intensity of the classes, breaks are essential to maintaining energy and focus. A swim in the lake, a game of tennis, a walk in the woods, or a nap in a comfortable bed helps in recharging the energy for a long day's work.

Introductory classes are offered at the center as well as at nearby universities. Group supervisions are done at the center and individual supervision is done at the student's office. The training at CTI is based on the philosophy that GIM is a depth-oriented, reconstructive, and transpersonal form of therapy. Because it is a holistic process, it may involve exploration of the client's unique physical, psychological, cognitive, social, and/or spiritual realms. These may be expressed and explored in the context of intrapersonal, interpersonal, and transpersonal relationships. In addition, GIM is often used as the client's primary therapy and is conducted in a private practice setting. For this reason, the training program in GIM involves a serious commitment to the student's own personal and professional growth. Applicants must come to the training with prior clinical and musical training and experience.

The three-year training includes course work in GIM, psychodynamic and transpersonal theory and practice, research, and GIM-related adjunctive techniques. These fall within three broad categories: processing techniques, bodywork, and specialty areas. The student is required to engage in ongoing GIM personal work. GIM clinical work and supervision are integral to the training. What follows is a detailed description of the CTI training program in GIM. It might be helpful to see the overall program requirements and the place that supervision has in the training. In

---

[1] For more information contact AMI at P.O. Box 4281, Blaine, WA 98231-4286.

addition to course descriptions I have included comments about the purpose of that course or requirement.

The pre-requisites are as follows:

- *Master's degree in a clinical discipline and two years' post master's clinical experience.* These ensure that a prospective student will have had some advanced clinical theory and some clinical experience after this theoretical work. Many of the students coming in at this level have been practicing therapy at a reeducative level and now desire to work at a reconstructive and/or transpersonal level. However, some students have worked with populations or in settings (i.e., physically handicapped children) that do not necessarily prepare them for in-depth psychodynamic and transpersonal primary therapy work with adults. For those students I strongly recommend, and in some cases require, that appropriate clinical work be done. This can be on a paid or volunteer basis. I also make exceptions for those students who have a bachelor's degree and many years of clinical work with an appropriate population, provided that they agree to complete a clinical master's degree before attaining fellowship in AMI.
- *Music experience*: formal or informal training in music history, music theory, and music therapy. If the student is not a music therapist, independent study and readings are required. Music and music therapy skills will be necessary to engage in the CTI training.
- *Introduction to GIM*: a thirty-hour course done at a university or any of the approved AMI training programs. I consider this only an introduction. In thirty hours a student can get a flavor of GIM. The main objectives I have for the course are to enable a student to be able to define GIM, get a sense of whether GIM is the therapy of choice for his own personal work, and whether GIM is something he may want to pursue professionally.
- *Recommendation letter from the previous trainer (Introduction to GIM).*
- *Five personal GIM sessions.* This is so that the student will have a taste of the GIM process from the client's point of view, and to help achieve the Introduction to GIM course objectives.
- *Professional liability insurance.* It is professionally responsible to have insurance. Many incoming students have been covered by their facilities. Now these GIM students will be working clinically, in private practice, under supervision, and all must be covered for liability.
- *Application form and interview.* This is a chance for me to get to know the students: the personal, educational, professional backgrounds; prior GIM experience; why they want to study GIM and why they have chosen this program; their special skills, strengths, and needs in relationship to GIM work and what they are hoping to do with GIM professionally. It is also a chance for the students to get to know me. This is a very important part of the screening process. The training is an intense three-year commitment and if the fit of student/training program/faculty is not good, everyone suffers. GIM training is not for everyone, even if they want it, and this training program is not appropriate for everyone who is right for GIM.

Year One

The first year of training concentrates on the dynamics of a first session including analysis of all session components for educational, screening, diagnostic, and evaluation purposes. In much the same way as the screening process is crucial to the prospective student, the screening process is crucial to the client. If the therapist does not quickly (within one or two sessions) gain enough and/or appropriate information on the client's history, background, needs, strengths, and purpose for therapy, the ensuing therapy process may lack focus or at worst be completely inappropriate for the client. The GIM process is an open growth exploration, but this should not translate into a situation where anything goes or one in which the therapist has no idea of where the process is going or what might be needed or helpful in getting there.

Throughout the training there is an emphasis on blending theory with clinical experience. In year one students are expected to complete coursework which addresses the following areas. This coursework can be completed at the CTI, at nearby graduate programs in music therapy, private institutes, or through independent study with an accomplished practitioner.

- A detailed exploration of each of the GIM session's components: intake, screening and diagnostic work, prelude, induction, music, and postlude.
- A detailed examination and presentation of the dynamics of initial sessions with particular emphasis on the function of the music and the case material.
- Intensive study of the music used in GIM including: a background sketch of the composer with personal and historical information about the life and times of the composer, especially at the time the piece was composed; information about the performer's and conductor's attitudes, knowledge, and feelings about the piece; a full score musical analysis; imagery/clinical analysis (taken from client sessions) and an overall discussion of the music: observations, generalizations, possibilities for use in GIM.
- Studies of theories of psychotherapy and their relationships to music therapy.
- Development of a personal theory of music psychotherapy.
- Study in a GIM related adjunctive technique. There are three such courses that are required throughout the training and they address supplementary and complementary processing techniques such as mandala work, journaling, dream work, etc.; body work (i.e., Reiki, Shiatsu, Therapeutic Touch, massage, etc.) and population/setting specialty and adaptation work (hospice, in-patient, intensive retreat, abuse, physical illness, research, teaching, and supervision, etc.).
- Study of the practical components of private practice including: ethics and professional responsibility, marketing, how to conduct introductory workshops, how to build a private practice, and how to design and set up a professional, secure office.

In addition to the above coursework, students are expected to take co-requisites.

- Fifteen personal GIM sessions.
- Twenty-five (intake or initial) client sessions with no more than one or two per client.
- Eight individual on-site supervisions.
- Ten group supervisions.
- Present one case study.

Sixty-five personal sessions are required during the three-year training. This ensures that a student will be actively (approximately bimonthly) pursuing GIM as his primary therapeutic modality. This year's clinical work (twenty-five client sessions) allows students to practice their beginning GIM skills. Students do not begin long-term therapeutic relationships until the supervisor, the student, and I agree that they are ready. These are practice sessions, but frequently many future clients later come from this initial pool.

The ratio of approximately one on-site supervision to three client sessions allows students to correct "beginner errors" quickly so that these mistakes don't become ingrained. This also helps students feel supported when their skills are still shaky. Some examples of these beginner's mistakes involve positioning of the client, therapist, and equipment. A simple shift in chair or equipment can facilitate eye contact, comfort level of the client, and accessibility of materials for the therapist. It is hard enough for the beginning therapist to listen to the client, choose the music, and take the transcript without having the client or the equipment inaccessible. The group supervisions at this level set the stage for peer supervision as well as support the beginning efforts of the students in verbally presenting case material. The students have the opportunity to bring general questions to the group that may arise from confusion in translating theory to practice, or "how to" questions that apply to both individual sessions and general practice. These group supervisions can be supportive and often fun.

As each of us shares our horror stories of beginning sessions, we remember that we are not only therapists but we are human too. Silly mistakes such as forgetting to put the CDs near the CD player, hitting the pause button instead of the play button thus having to deal with silence instead of the expected music, forgetting body parts or whole body sections in a progressive relaxation are considered grist for the mill. These beginner's mistakes are easily corrected and help us to keep our sense of humor as we go on to more serious work.

A total of eighteen supervisions on twenty-five sessions might seem like a lot, but to beginning students, these supervisions serve as a safety net, a chance to get the introductory issues taken care of quickly, so that they may move on to depth-level GIM work. These supervision sessions also provide a solid support base where students can bring any question, problem or success story.

Year Two

In order to enter the second year, students must demonstrate satisfactory completion of prior coursework and co-requisites and submit letters of recommendation in support of further training from primary trainers, supervisors, and therapists. An interview with the student addresses any specific needs or questions related to this stage of training. Again, the learning model that is used is the presentation of theory followed by clinical and musical applications. However, since the students are working at deeper levels and with more complex theory, the theory is introduced in the second year and the applications courses are offered in the third year.

This year's theoretical coursework centers on the dynamics of the therapeutic relationship and process. Jungian and transpersonal theories are discussed as they relate to the GIM process. Relevance to myth, archetype, culture, religion, spirituality, and stages of development and awareness are explored. Students examine how they and their clients relate to fairy tales, myths, gods and goddesses, symbols, archetypes, religious holidays and customs, and personality types. GIM ethics and standards of practice are covered.

While most of the students have covered the basic concepts of psychotherapy and music psychotherapy in their master's or doctoral training, it is through this coursework that concepts are related specifically to GIM with a focus on how they manifest and how they are worked through. Required courses in the second year address the following areas.

- An exploration of the dynamics and issues of the therapy process (i.e., defense mechanisms, transference, countertransference, etc., as they relate to GIM work).
- Study in specialty areas and adaptations of the GIM process to specific problems, issues, populations, and settings.
- Study in clinical analysis and application of the music used in GIM. GIM casework is presented with particular attention paid to the relationship of the music and the process to the theoretical coursework.
- Study in a GIM-related adjunctive technique as in year one.

The students have a great deal of input into the course content. It is structured around not only the basic problems and issues found in any population but in the populations and settings in which these particular students want to specialize. Again, whenever possible, GIM practitioners who specialize in these areas are brought in to teach these courses.

The clinical and personal co-requisites include the following

- Twenty-five personal GIM sessions.
- fifty client sessions.
- sixteen individual supervisions/consultations.
- eight group supervisions.
- one music paper.
- one case study.

Year Three

At this point students are actively engaged in their clinical practice of GIM. As before, satisfactory completion of preceding coursework and co-requisites and letters of recommendation are required. The interview at this level concentrates on final requirements and direction for professional work. Areas of study include the following:

- In-depth study of the GIM process, especially as it relates to the applications of the GIM process to various populations and settings,
- Ethical considerations of GIM private practice.
- Research techniques.
- Further musical analysis of music used in GIM work.
- Study of a third GIM-related adjunctive technique. This is usually done in a related specialty area either population/setting centered or related to furthering teaching, supervision or research techniques and skills.

Co-requisites for year three are:

- Twenty-five personal GIM sessions.
- sixteen individual supervisions.
- eight group supervisions.
- seventy-five client sessions.
- one music paper.
- one research paper.

As you can see, supervision is integrated into every phase of training at a ratio of approximately one supervision to two to three sessions.

The Role of Supervision

The role of supervision in this GIM training program is crucial. Supervision of clinical work allows the student to forge the critical link between theory and practice and to clarify professional and personal issues. Professional issues can then be addressed in further individual or group supervision and consultation. Personal issues can be worked on in the student's personal GIM sessions. A unique feature of GIM supervision involves the fact that students who are training in GIM are already professional clinicians. Many are music therapists, but students are accepted from other clinical disciplines. Therefore, all of the students have an accomplished repertoire of clinical skills. While these skills may have been sufficient to meet the needs of the student's prior clinical work, they may not necessarily be appropriate to the GIM clientele, the private practice setting, or GIM therapeutic style and methodology.

An extreme example might be a GIM student who is a social worker with experience working with in-patient physically handicapped children. The role of the training, and especially the supervision, would be to hone the existing skills, while filling the possible gaps in understanding and methodology of adult out-patient populations, private practice, and the role of music in GIM therapy.

The Supervisor

In order to better understand GIM supervision, it is necessary to discuss briefly the requirements of the supervisor. Supervisors must be recognized as Fellows by the professional organization, the Association for Music and Imagery, which ensures that they have met the minimum requirements for entry-level GIM clinical work. In addition CTI supervisors are required to have conducted a minimum of 150 GIM sessions after completion of GIM training as well as a minimum of two years of experience as a clinical supervisor. Supervisors must attend supervision meetings, or must be in ongoing GIM supervision and be in regular contact with primary trainers.

GIM Fellows who want to begin supervising at CTI must have a minimum of fifty GIM sessions after completion of training and they must attend supervision meetings. The meetings have become a very important part of maintaining the quality and enthusiasm of the trainers and the supervisors. The content of the supervision meetings varies depending on the skills and needs of the supervisors and the issues they raise. This is a time when the supervisors can explore general issues or specific problems in supervision, generate new ideas, gain practical information about the theory and practice of supervision and receive peer support.

Typical areas of discussion in supervision meetings are: problems encountered in a specific supervision or with a particular supervisee; style of supervision; skills needed to supervise; expectations of skills and competencies for students at each level of training; confidentiality; transference and countertransference as the impact on supervision; matching the skills and style of the supervisor to the needs and style of the student; mechanics of supervision including travel, scheduling, fees, and peer supervision of the supervisor's clinical work.

Most students are nervous about supervision. One way to help alleviate that anxiety is to carefully pair student and supervisor, taking into account such things as communication and therapy styles, respective skills in the student's client population, special theoretical skills (music analysis, diagnostics, etc.), possible areas of transference and countertransference, scheduling, and location. One of the most frustrating supervision problems is knowing that a student needs help in a particular area and having a supervisor who has those skills, but either "talks a different language" or can't fit that student into his schedule. Creative problem solving beforehand can save many months of aggravation after.

Types of Supervision

Students are required to have forty on-site and twenty-six group supervision sessions regularly spaced over the required 150 client sessions. Therefore, the ratio is usually one supervision session for every two or three GIM sessions. In this way, students feel supported throughout their clinical work, and have the opportunity to discuss therapeutic options and possible problems as they arise. Most students use the first few on-site supervisions to determine who they want to work with for the major portion of their clinical work. If a specific need arises, we (the student, supervisor, and primary trainer) discuss options for consults or supervisions with another supervisor who has expertise in that area. As the students progress in their clinical work, many opt to have an occasional consult instead of an on-site supervision. Consults may be done in person or by phone and usually address general therapeutic questions or issues.

On-site supervision

On-site supervision usually concentrates on the client–music–therapist relationship and therapeutic process within the session observed by the supervisor. Skill areas for discussion include the student's general behavior; the mechanics of the session; interviewing techniques; techniques used to facilitate an altered state of consciousness; the use of the music; guiding skills; skills used to facilitate the transition of the client back to a normal state; processing techniques and closure.

Transference, countertransference, transcripts and interpretation of the session, including self-evaluation as well as client evaluation, goals, objectives, and options for future work are covered as well. Depending on the level of training and expertise of the student, a supervisor may concentrate on one area or discuss choices and possibilities in a number of areas. After the on-site supervision discussion, the supervisor gives a written report to the student and the primary trainer.

It is an important part of this training to emphasize the value of on-site supervisions, in the student's office with the student's actual clientele. In order for the student to "graduate" to depth-level practice, the supervisor must have an accurate picture of what that level of practice is and on what level the student is working in his or her own clinical environment. Clinical work is as much an art as a science and it is in the "in the moment" nuances of a live session that fine-tuned clinical work can be identified and encouraged.

On-site supervisors have access to the context and feel of the moment in which an image is given. They are present to each musical moment and the way in which the client and therapist react. These therapeutic nuances are hard to teach in the abstract, even with clinical examples. A supervisor who is "in the moment" with the student and client has access to immediate, personally relevant teaching material.

We will now look at supervision at various stages of the GIM training. This will include typical problems and issues encountered at each stage along with how a supervisor might work with these.

The first supervision session is the one fraught with the most anxiety on the part of the student. Although I do attempt to have an introductory meeting at which students can meet and feel out potential supervisors and therapists, the supervisor is usually an "unknown quantity." The logistics of scheduling and traveling to the site often require a number of phone calls and there may be a question on both sides as to whether the supervisor will arrive on time.

Most often, the student has not established his own private GIM office space or it is still relatively new. Positioning and layout are barely secure for the student-therapist and the client and now there is a third party to accommodate. The student's GIM skills are brand new and this may be the student's first or second session. I sometimes wonder how the student survives this at all.

Naturally the supervision topics are pretty introductory. Can the student establish rapport? Can the student create an environment in which the client feels comfortable and at ease? Is the layout of the office conducive to effective work? Are the equipment and supplies appropriate, professional, and accessible? Can the student explain GIM and the session format to a new client? Is the intake interview complete and are the techniques for eliciting information relaxed and client directed? Can the student facilitate the transitions from the prelude to the induction, from the induction into the music, and from the music into the postlude? Is the student able to manipulate the equipment and transcript while staying focused on the client and the music? Are the induction skills basically on target? Is the music appropriate? Are the interventions in sync with the client and music? Was facilitation out of the music to the postlude effective? Was processing appropriate to a first session and the material elicited? Was the student able to conduct the business of the session such as determining the next appointment and/or any follow-up? I do remind the supervisor to be gentle and remember his or her own first session. Although we haven't even gotten to the "meat" of GIM, I don't want the students or supervisor to choke on the "appetizer."

Early supervision sessions usually coincide with the work done in the first year of training, and concentrate on the student's general behavior, the mechanics of first sessions, and intake skills. For students who have never had the joy and responsibility of creating a therapeutic environment, early sessions may be fraught with problems caused by the physical environment or setup of the environment, equipment, and materials. Creating a safe, comfortable space in which both the therapist and client can work goes a long way in establishing trust and rapport.

In a first session that I supervised, a student had set up the music area (a mat for the client, music equipment and therapist's chair) and felt ready for this first session. However there were some obvious problems. The client's head was close to the therapy room door and the CD player and speakers were on a bookshelf across the room. The client stated she felt insecure because she could hear sounds from the hallway and felt that at any minute someone might knock on the door or enter the room. The therapist could not actively monitor the music without getting up and going to the equipment, thus leaving the therapeutic space she had created. In the supervision following the client's session I was able to quickly help the student reposition the mat and equipment so that future sessions would proceed more smoothly and securely.

Initial sessions include the necessity of explaining GIM and the session format. Many clients are new to two-hour sessions, altered states work, imaging to music, and the GIM session format. The therapist must be able to explain these and answer any questions while putting the client at ease. A student can get tongue-tied in these descriptions and may need to think through the presentation. Role-playing with the supervisor is sometimes very helpful. Supervising interviewing techniques is especially crucial to students who have previously not been trained in verbal counseling and interviewing skills. On-site supervisors are invaluable in helping the student hone the skills of interviewing as well as interpreting all of the information received. The supervisor can be especially helpful in clarifying how the student can get the information needed in a style that is comfortable to both the student and the client.

The following example of a supervision session involved the student's general timing and pacing of the session. The student had been a social worker for many years and this was apparent in her therapeutic presence, her body language, eye contact, voice quality, and interviewing skills. However, adjusting to a two-hour time frame for a session that necessitates adequate time to enter and leave an altered state of consciousness (ASC) was new for her. She spent too much time in verbal counseling (a skill she was strong in) and found that the time left for therapeutic exploration in the music was insufficient. Being aware of this she did adjust the time frame for the music so that the client would not have to abruptly leave an ASC. After the session, the supervisor worked with the student to pinpoint places in the session where music could have been introduced earlier and to good advantage.

Facilitation of a client entering and leaving an ASC is not usually taught to therapists unless they are specifically trained in altered states work, and a really fined-tuned choice of induction and music is too advanced for a first supervision. In very early supervisions, if the student can provide some semblance of a transition to an internally oriented state and choose music that is both known to him and broadly appropriate to a client's presented issues in this first session, it is usually considered successful.

Let me clarify that I do not give recipes for inductions or for choices of music. Students are expected to hear the client's cues, build an induction from the prelude and choose music that fits both the client and the induction. Much time is spent on learning this, and I know that this is much harder than going with a rehearsed induction and designated "beginner's music program." I instruct supervisors to support this approach and help the students learn to hear and respond to a client and make therapeutic choices accordingly.

Even the best of circumstances can be interrupted by mechanical problems. What does one do when the induction is so good that the client is well and truly altered and then the CD just doesn't start when the play button is pressed, or the audiotape starts spitting out of the cassette deck all over the floor? It's easy to say, "Stay calm, explain the situation succinctly and deal with the problem," but having seen the look of surprise, panic and pleading in a student's eyes reminds me how helpful it is to have a friendly, experienced supervisor nearby. The value of being familiar with the equipment, having back-up equipment available and secondary choices of music cannot be underestimated. Facilitating transitions from an ASC, which is an internally focused state, to a more externally focused state are taught in GIM classes, but again, observing the student and client in this important part of the session can help a student recognize and attend to the individuality of the process.

Helping a student choose and facilitate an appropriate processing medium such as verbal work, art work (mandala, clay, etc.), or writing, and provide closure for a session is also a part of these early supervisions.

In advanced supervision the student is now expected to be able to conduct intake, initial and educational GIM sessions. The basic bugs should have been eliminated and the supervisor and student can concentrate on the relationship and process issues that arise in long-term therapy. Courses have introduced fairy tales, myths, symbols, archetypes, religious archetypes and customs, cultural customs, spirituality, and Jungian and transpersonal theory.

Principles and dynamics of music psychotherapy as they manifest in GIM specifically GIM have been introduced. Adaptations for different populations have been discussed. A great deal of music has been analyzed and explored for its potential uses in GIM.

The following is a supervision example that focuses on countertransference issues which, if ignored, can lead to confused and ineffective therapy sessions. A student whose mother was dying of cancer was working on this sensitive issue in her private GIM therapy sessions. A client was referred to her who also had terminal cancer. The student contacted her therapist as well as her supervisor. In consults with both her supervisor and therapist it was decided that she was clear enough in her own process to accept the client, provided that she continued to work on this in her own therapy sessions and have regular, consistent consults and on-site supervision of this client. The student had access to the professional support she needed.

The "meat" of a GIM session is the work with the music. Music choices and the timing and type of interventions are what facilitate the client's process. A supervisor can help the student identify the many choice points in a session. These are moments when the client is at a crossroads and the therapist's choice of music, verbal, and/or nonverbal interventions will enhance or impede the therapeutic process. In this supervision example a client was working with feelings of anger, jealousy, and resistance, and lack of trust. She wanted to push away these painful feelings. At the outset of the music she was feeling weak in the face of these strong emotions and was trying to maintain control. The student chose music that was supportive and allowed for some emotional expression. The first choice point occurred when the client identified a big eagle that came beside her. The music was supportive and so was the student. The client resisted any help from the eagle (or the student or the music), but the eagle persisted. Unfortunately at this juncture, the student suggested that the music might help, but the music was too gentle, too noncommittal, and not very persistent. This was the moment when the student could have changed to music that would match the strength and persistence of the eagle. Instead, the student did not change the music and the client languished in the netherworld of wanting but resisting the strength offered by the eagle. No permanent damage was done, but a moment of change was missed.

Another example of the importance of sensitivity in the music-client relationship occurred when a young male client came to a session shortly after attending his grandfather's funeral. The client held the position of head of the family and immediate and extended family members looked to him for support and guidance. The man was tired but also extremely angry that rather than having the opportunity to grieve his loss, he was required to take care of his family's grief. The student picked up on the client's anger and centered the induction and choice of music around providing an opportunity for him to express the anger. He chose an induction involving raging water, and began the session with the Brahms Piano Concerto No. 2, allegro non troppo. The induction matched the music but not the client. The student was unaware of just how tired the client was and for over seventeen minutes the client tried to survive the raging water. He gave the student many cues such as "The water is moving too fast, I can't keep up. I'm trying to get out of the water but I can't grab hold of anything. There are whirlpools everywhere and I am getting sucked into them. I just need to find a place to rest and be safe." Just as the piece was ending, the student changed to the Haydn Cello Concerto in C, adagio. This was certainly a relief for the client and he was able to settle down into a quieter space where he could have his needs tended to and his grief expressed. In actuality, the piece that follows the piano concerto in the original taped program is Part I of the Brahms Requiem and this would have been perfect! The chorus sings, "Blessed, blessed are they that mourn, for they shall have comfort." When the client left, the student and I had a detailed discussion about hearing all of the client cues, verbal and nonverbal, how to interpret the information received, and translate the information into music choices. We then discussed the clinical impact of the Brahms Piano Concerto and the Haydn Cello Concerto on this client in this session. Finally, we looked at the differences, both musical and clinical between the Haydn Cello Concerto and the Brahms Requiem.

A supervisor can also help the student identify the different levels of work in which a client may be engaging. A GIM therapist must respond with music and interventions that meet the client on the level of work that is most productive for that moment. Recognizing when a client is working on a literal, symbolic, archetypal, or deeply transpersonal level facilitates therapeutic progress. If a client needs very supportive and/or practical work geared to his relationships and place in his everyday world, the work done is quite different from work done in a more open, symbolic, and/or transpersonal mode. The issues may be, and often are related but the choice of induction, music, and interventions would be quite different.

In this example a client had been working on issues related to having had a non-nurturing, demanding, self-absorbed mother. The work had been steady and the client was on the verge of accepting the painful fact that her mother never gave her what she needed, nor would her mother ever be capable of such love. This session had the potential of helping the client achieve some healing and closure on this issue. The student's choice of the level on which to work was crucial. In past sessions the prelude, induction, music, interventions, and processing were appropriate to work with the client's literal mother. In the prelude, the student chose to help focus the client on the pain of the loss of nurturance. Her induction continued this focus, and also introduced feminine symbols (the moon and night sky).

Thus the night sky replete with moon and stars became the place in which the client expressed her pain. The music chosen was more open. Some of the selections included solo soprano and choral music (Brahms, Requiem, Part V; Mozart, Laudate Dominum; Vivaldi, Et in Terra Pax). This allowed for interaction with a feminine source that was received as receptive to the client's grief and unconditionally nurturing. Verbal interventions were gentle, supportive, and respectful of the deep space the client was exploring, and thus supported the music interventions. The client moved through the grief and was able to stand in and share the moonlight with her mother. The pacing, voice quality and content for the transition to an externally oriented state and the processing were reflective of the expanded space the client was in. The student had integrated theory into practice and the client was the beneficiary of this integration.

Supervision in this case was one of those experiences where the work is easy and reaffirming. And yes, supervisions can be positive and joyful affirmations of work well done!

Consultations

Consults are another aspect of supervision. They are conversations between the student and supervisor that may or may not be done at the student's clinical site. They often are used to discuss issues or questions that arise within the course of a series of sessions. These are most helpful for students who are engaged in long-term or depth-level work with their clients. Some examples of consult topics are: When and how do I deepen the work? How do I deal with resistance? How can I effect a smooth termination process? In addition, a student who is considering work with a new client who has issues in an area in which the student does not have much experience, may opt to have a consult with a supervisor who has expertise in that area.

Group Supervision

Supervision in a group setting can also be an effective. In group supervision, students learn how to present case studies. They raise questions about therapeutic techniques, choices, and problems. They have the opportunity to discuss personal issues that may affect their clinical work. They use group supervision to clarify and/or explore deeper philosophical, ethical, and therapeutic questions related to casework. The environment of group supervision is supportive and constructive and provides for different perspectives and therapeutic styles. The participation and camaraderie of peers in group supervision can be a most valuable asset. Learning to share one's therapeutic strengths and foibles, problems and solutions can set the model for future professional growth. Students have used beginning group supervisions to get feedback on their professional advertising materials (cards, flyers, letters of introduction), when to start charging for sessions and how much to charge, workshop content and format, networking and referrals to each other when friends, colleagues, and family want to sample or start GIM work, case presentations and honing of diagnostic skills. Later discussions may revolve around innovative successful and unsuccessful choices of music, how to continue working effectively when personal problems or difficult life situations are present, getting feedback on a particularly difficult client or case material, adjusting case presentations to different audiences, subtle nuances of therapeutic choices in long term primary therapy.

Conclusion

GIM supervision serves the purpose of connecting theory and practice; identifying small mistakes and large problems in clinical work; alleviating stress and anxiety that can accompany clinical insecurity; providing a fresh, objective alternative to clinical decisions and styles; establishing a solid clinical support system and encouraging and acknowledging good work. All forms of supervision are used as models for continued professional work.

It is stressed that for quality professional clinical work to continue after fellowship, supervision must play an important role. This is especially necessary because GIM is most often conducted in private practice. Regular contact with other GIM therapists, or indeed, any other therapists, is not automatic and a conscious effort must be made not to become isolated. Therefore, it is incumbent on the training program director to create a supervisory environment that is nurturing, supportive and constructive. My experience of GIM supervision, as supervisor and supervisee, is that it is often a lifesaver, it is supportive and it is even fun.

References

Association for Music and Imagery. (1999). *Standards and Procedures for Endorsement of GIM Training Programs*. Blaine, WA: Author,

Association for Music and Imagery. (2000). *Fellows Registry*. Blaine, WA: Author.

Bonny, H. (1980). *GIM Therapy: Past, Present and Future Implications. GIM Monograph #3*. Baltimore: ICM Books.

Bonny, H. (1994). Twenty-one years later: A GIM update. *Music Therapy Perspectives*, 12, 70–74.

Chapter 22

Supervision in the Nordoff-Robbins
Music Therapy Training Program

Alan Turry, MA, MT-BC, NRMT
Co-director of Nordoff Robbins Center for Music Therapy
New York University, NY

Overview

Nordoff-Robbins music therapy is based on the work of Paul Nordoff, an accomplished composer/improviser, and Clive Robbins, who began the work as a special educator with a musical background. Both therapists are acknowledged as pioneers in the model of live, interactive music-making with clients that has come to be known as Creative Music Therapy. Still a practicing clinician, Robbins has spent nearly his entire professional life teaching and researching the creative process in music therapy—what he and Nordoff called the art of music as therapy. The approach is music-centered in that musical processes are viewed as the primary vehicles of change. It is a form of music psychotherapy in that relationship factors are considered, and there is recognition that music affects the psyche. It is a transpersonal discipline in that the approach utilizes music to harness the client's will and recognizes that musical peak experiences can help clients transcend behavioral or dynamic patterns that impede self-enhancement. Training in this approach is musically advanced, its primary goals being the development of *clinical musicianship* and the release of creativity in the therapist. Instructional resources include much of the original Nordoff-Robbins clinical research, supplemented by the expanding field of exploration by therapists skilled in this approach. Recording and comprehensive documentation of every therapy session is standard practice, and provides trainees with a resource for supervision and self-evaluation. Supervision frequently utilizes the recordings of therapy sessions. An advanced (post-master's) training, it is open to credentialed music therapists who have already utilized improvisation in their clinical work. This chapter will describe the training program and the supervision process during the training.

Foundations of Nordoff-Robbins Supervision

The graphic representation on page 355 was created by Clive Robbins to display and interrelate the various skills and capacities that are recognized in developing *clinical musicianship* in the Nordoff-Robbins trainee. It indicates each area of creative potential as it relates to its mode of clinical application. Drawing on his considerable experience as a clinician and teacher, and influenced by a transpersonal worldview that incorporates elements common to many spiritual approaches, Robbins created this model to identify and differentiate the components of creative endeavor and their polarities. The upper part of the model encompasses the artistic qualities needed in the training of the therapist; the lower part references the craft or practical tools—the nuts and bolts skills and methods necessary to conduct the therapy. Each category serves as a balance for another; the freedom needed to create musically must be balanced with the clinical responsibility of applying that improvised music as therapy. The top half can be looked at as the transpersonal meeting ground of the client and therapist and considers the inner aspects of creative musical processes. The bottom half of the diagram contains the application of these aspects. By addressing the inner aspects of creative music therapy with trainees, the creative process becomes more understandable and reachable for them. They are thus able to participate in their own development of creative capability with more insight. This approach to training serves to integrate the intrinsic and extrinsic aspects of their training experiences. The gestalt of the model itself emphasizes the integrative, holistic approach inherent to the Nordoff-Robbins practice of music therapy. There is a dynamic, interactive relationship between the categories. There is an art to the understanding of behavior, a science to the construction of chords and progressions; musical and psychological processes are not seen as separate but as synthesizing: all the subjects that make up the model connect and coordinate.

Just as each quality represented in the diagram has implications for the process of therapy, so too each quality represented has implications for the process of supervision. In many ways, these two processes are parallel, and a full understanding of the terms in the diagram on the following page illuminates them both.

The *Creative Now* refers to the potential of the creative moment in which the therapist is open to receive and respond to what the client is presenting—either in active playing or merely in presenting him/herself in the room—as music. The idea of the *Creative Now* has some similarities to the more common phrase used to describe the therapeutic space conducive for change, the "here and now." The therapist is described as being *Poised in the Creative Now*—this refers to a state of balanced, receptive alertness on the part of the therapist. In this state of readiness, listening is a creative, musical act. There is no script, no game plan, but a willingness on the part of the therapist to act, respond, and enter into a mutual musical relationship with the client.

The *Creative Now* is a place for both therapist and client. Creating music, "creative musicing"[1]—in a mutual fashion with freedom and clinical intention—is potentially in and of itself an agent of change, a transforming experience for both client and therapist. By entering into an active musical relationship both client and therapist have the possibilities of realizing untapped potentials. In the immediacy of the moment, the musical relationship is in a constant state of forming. The *Creative*

---

[1] Musicing, as described by Elliot (1995), denotes the importance of perceiving music as a living, human activity and not merely as a cultural artifact or object.

Now is a space where resources within the client can begin to be activated, come to expression, and in the process initiate changes that are self-enhancing. The therapist has the responsibility—and opportunity—to create this space, observe the process, and undertake to serve its continuing development.

Figure 1
Poised in the Creative Now

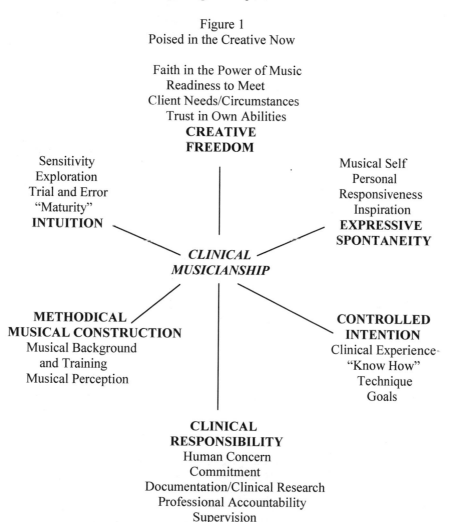

Faith in the Power of Music
Readiness to Meet
Client Needs/Circumstances
Trust in Own Abilities
CREATIVE
FREEDOM

Sensitivity
Exploration
Trial and Error
"Maturity"
INTUITION

Musical Self
Personal
Responsiveness
Inspiration
EXPRESSIVE
SPONTANEITY

CLINICAL
MUSICIANSHIP

METHODICAL
MUSICAL CONSTRUCTION
Musical Background
and Training
Musical Perception

CONTROLLED
INTENTION
Clinical Experience
"Know How"
Technique
Goals

CLINICAL
RESPONSIBILITY
Human Concern
Commitment
Documentation/Clinical Research
Professional Accountability
Supervision

Creative freedom/Clinical responsibility

In order to have *creative freedom*, the trainee must inevitably develop faith in the power of music, a readiness to meet the client's needs or circumstances, and trust in his/her own abilities. Belief that music has capabilities to effect change is the underlying motivation for the therapist in creating music. As trainees develop creative freedom they are increasingly able to improvise responsively and with variety so that the music is uniquely suited for their client. Rachel Verney (personal communication, April, 1999) feels it is important for supervisors to help trainees become more aware of what brought them into music therapy in the first place. By rekindling his or her "personal flame" to music, she feels each trainee may become a more effective therapist, trusting in music in a genuine way.

A supervisor must recognize that creative freedom in music therapy takes courage. The supervisor is a role model in trusting music. Also, the importance in supervision of respecting individual choices, and respecting the uniqueness of each trainee is paramount in developing creative freedom in the trainee. Supervisors communicate that they are learning from trainees, valuing different perspectives, and discovering with them. This helps to cultivate each trainee's trust in his or her own music. It is essential that the supervisor creates a safe space for the trainee and respects his/her own individual growth time, helping the trainee find his/her creative voice.

Creative freedom is balanced by *clinical responsibility*. In order to balance the creative freedom needed in the development of clinical musicianship, the trainee must learn to be professionally accountable for his or her actions. In describing the processes inherent to the Nordoff-Robbins approach in another publication (Turry, 1998) I stated that "becoming too inwardly focused in an effort to be creative can be a defense against problematic dynamics and threatening feelings" (p. 164). A major task for the supervisor is to help the trainee understand musical/clinical processes in order to move the process forward. The supervisor also helps the trainee to speak with clarity about their clinical work. The supervisor works with the trainee to cultivate a genuine human concern for the client, a commitment to stay in a challenging process, and an ability to document and research the work so that new understandings can feed back into the creative process. The trainee has an obligation to monitor the therapy process and adjust his/her approach to benefit the client.

Expressive spontaneity/Methodical musical construction

Expressive spontaneity allows for genuine, energy-producing interaction. It allows for flexible, dramatic musical interventions that can motivate and engage clients. In order to be personally responsive with expressive spontaneity, the trainee needs to develop a musical identity, a firm musical self from which to draw musical ideas without hesitation.

Expressive spontaneity allows the trainee to act on a musical inspiration with immediacy. This quality allows for moment-to-moment freedom and energy—an ability to shift flexibly and interact with mutuality. The ability to be playful with a client can help to facilitate this kind of spontaneity. Jean Eisler (personal communication, April 1999) suggests to trainees to find time to play with infants and toddlers in order to cultivate this playful interactive spontaneity.

Another way to cultivate expressive spontaneity in trainees is to provide a space where they don't need to know or explain; they can simply *be* in music, and express themselves freely. Ongoing participation in their own music therapy can be an important part of the training process. This process allows trainees to explore themselves, their relationship to music, and their relationship to others through musical interaction. It is also important for supervisors to bring experiences to trainees that reinforce their love of music. This will allow trainees to utilize music with authentic expression, not merely as a technique.

One cannot be spontaneous without the building blocks of musical thinking, the musical know-how. That is why expressive spontaneity must be directly dependent on the trainee's capacity for methodical musical construction.

Methodical musical construction—the craft of musicing—is vital for the development of clinical musicianship. In order to have the ability to express oneself musically with spontaneity, the trainee must have the musical foundations, the musical background, to tap into. Technical musical training is also important in developing the skills of musical perception. This allows the therapist to listen musically to what is occurring in the session and create with coherent fluidity and form. Trainees need to have the technical control over their musical ideas in order to shape them aesthetically. This allows for expressive spontaneity; musical inspirations can be realized.

During the training, new musical resources are introduced which may be unfamiliar to the trainee. These extrinsic experiences become intrinsic when the trainee develops a personal relationship to them. It is only after these new musical structures become meaningful that they are useful; often this discovery can come in the experience of musicing with the client. Therefore trainees are encouraged to try out newly learned musical forms in sessions—not in a haphazard sense, but tuned in to what is happening. Musicing is not prescriptive, and as therapy is a mutual process, the meaning only comes after the client and therapist share in the experience.

Intuition/Controlled intention

Intuition is an immediate perception of reality—a way of knowing that transcends rationalization and also bypasses the usual sensory processes. Developing intuition will allow the trainee to improvise music with a sense of purpose. The trainee must be willing to explore, to try out ideas. Trying out ideas in sessions brings musical experiences to the trainee which help develop clinical maturity. This maturity feeds back into the intuitive processes. Rather than developing theories or prescriptive strategies about music, the trainee learns principally by doing, by living in the experience of interactive musicing with his/her client. For the trainee, an intuition often originates with an insight into the client, and a completely new musical idea may occur in the moment. There needs to be a willingness to live in uncertainty, mystery, and doubt without anxiously searching for a logical conclusion to the situation. The very fact that the clinical situation is in essence unrehearsed and unprescribed can force trainees to experience living in the creative now. As they continue to enter into this enhancing situation, they grow more confident in coping with its challenges. Their increasing ability to rely on their capacities for intuition and inspiration results in a natural development of clinical perception. This is strongly supported by the close analysis of session recordings.

How can supervision help to develop intuition in the trainee? The supervisor cultivates *sensitivity* in the trainee as well as the *courage* to develop and trust intuition. This can be a highly individualized potential within each trainee. Some are ready to tap into their intuitive faculties without hesitation. Others may struggle. Often when trainees begin working they have blocks that prevent them from developing and trusting intuition. The supervisor needs to discern if the inability to trust intuition is due to the trainee's low self-esteem, or some other personal dynamic. Or could it be that he/she simply does not have sufficient technical ability yet? Has he/she internalized parental or other authority figures that have discouraged nonrational explorations? Is he/she afraid he/she will not be able to explain why they did something? Is he/she afraid of making a mistake? Talking about these possibilities in supervision may help the trainee to enter more fully into the clinical situation. Exploring the fear of failure by exploring the worst possible scenario of what might happen helps to alleviate anxiety. This search is done to help expand the trainee's awareness and ability to be more fully present in the session, without fear. The less psychic energy that is dedicated to inner concerns, the more receptive the trainee can be to the client, picking up on subtle communications which feed into the intuitive process.

Many factors contribute to the intuitive process. Consider a clinical example from the early Nordoff-Robbins work that led to the creation of a song that has subsequently been used with other clients. When Paul Nordoff improvised the phrase "Oh when you feel like crying, just cry," to help a crying boy in a group feel supported and accepted, he was reacting to a situation about which he personally felt impatience; the classroom teacher was, in Nordoff's view, mocking the boy, not taking his feelings seriously enough.[2] Nordoff impulsively acted to change a situation he felt was unjust. He allowed his personal reaction to trigger his intuitive response that immediately took the form of a song. In his clinical practice, he often approached the clinical situation with a kind of impatience toward the restrictions of pathology, an urgent readiness to do something to move the client forward, to release him or her into new levels of awareness and capability. The challenge in the training is to help trainees to take this kind of interventional stance without being too demanding or insensitive to the client.

Assessing the condition of the client, and how the restrictions imposed by the condition affect the client's overall functioning, can help provide an orientation in therapy that facilitates the intuitive-creative direction taken by the therapist. Nordoff was particularly adept at perceiving what kind of musical stance to take based on a client's condition. He seems to have wondered—Is the client somehow imprisoned within the confines of the condition? Or is he or she withdrawing into the protection of the condition? How can the client's will be activated? Did Nordoff need to work *through* the condition, for instance, through matching a perseverative behavior with music? Or could he build upon the potentials not currently displayed? Adopting this stance of perception fed directly into his intuitive process. His approach, not just in improvising, but in *perceiving*, was an active one. The concept and diagram of the

---

[2] "The Crying Song" by Nordoff and Robbins is in *The Second Book of Children's Play Songs* (1968). New York: Presser.

"music child" and the "condition child"[3] was developed in part to help trainees acquire this kind of perception.

The development of intuition cannot be directly taught to the trainee in supervision. It needs to be nurtured, like cultivating a plant. By creating an understanding, resonating space for the trainee, the supervisor can create the conditions for him/her to become more intuitive. Gaining experience and expanding awareness by entering into the creative situation with the client is the ultimate source of developing intuition. The supervisor can help the trainee to reflect on the events that took place in the clinical situation, and these reflections feed back into the intuitive process.

There are times when trainees are so focused on their own feelings that they cannot act. Brown (1997) finds that it can be helpful to remind trainees to stay focused on their clients when feeling uninspired. By guiding trainees to keep their thoughts and focus on the client, the supervisor is reminding them that they do not have to provide everything in the session—clients are giving input all the time, even if they are not active. Gentle reminders to listen to the client, feel the client, and find the music that is motivated by that feeling and hearing can help the trainee create music in the session.

In applying intuition through *controlled intention* the trainee progressively gains a sense of how to proceed. With clinical experience, the trainee begins to develop the "know how," or technique, and formulates fluid, flexible goals that can change adaptively from moment to moment. Having controlled intention provides direction—in the musicing, and for the client. Studying archival material and integrating the feedback they receive in supervision build upon the trainee's ability to develop controlled intention.

Understandably, there are times when a trainee has the personal need to gain an overt response from the client, or needs a sign that he/she is liked or is an effective therapist. Acting on this need may lead to ineffective musical interventions—and may result in working to be responded to personally rather than letting the contact come through musical interaction. Awareness of this need, which is natural in all of us, can help trainees maintain controlled intention in their sessions.

It can be helpful for trainees to recognize their personal need for musical expression and to be heard as musicians. For this reason it can be important for trainees to provide for themselves opportunities outside of their clinical sessions in which they can find release from the demands of controlled intention in the service of their own musical expression. This is another reason why being involved in personal music therapy can be valuable to a trainee.

---

[3] Originally developed by Nordoff and Robbins, first published in an article by Clive and Carol Robbins entitled "Self Communications in Music Therapy" in Bruscia's *Case Studies in Music Therapy* (1991), Gilsum, NH: Barcelona Publishers.

The Supervisory Relationship

The Creative Music Therapy approach recognizes that people make music. Music played between people creates interpersonal, intrapersonal, as well as transpersonal experiences. Therefore it is important to look at intrapsychic processes, the musical relationship, and what it reveals about the therapy process. The supervisory relationship is the microcosm in which these experiences can be addressed. The trainee entering into such a relationship must be prepared to ask, "How will I have to change, what will I need to learn, how will I develop, in order to do effective therapy?"

Supervision has traditionally been a place to help trainees move past emotional blocks, expand awareness of unconscious processes, and gain insight into their own personal dynamics and how those dynamics influence the therapy situation. It is imperative for trainees to become aware of and more fully understand their motivations, assumptions, and needs in order for them to become more effective therapists. Discovering previously unknown personal qualities can help them to gain insight into the therapy situation. Looking at their own music played in the therapeutic relationship can help trainees to gain further insight into themselves and their client.

In the same way that a therapist becomes sensitive to a client's presence, mood, and potential areas of need and strengths, the supervisor gathers this same information from the trainee. In order to feel empathy for the client, the therapist puts himself or herself into a vulnerable state. In the therapeutic relationship, the therapist does not approach the situation with the assumption that he/she has all the answers or that everything will run smoothly. The therapist understands that it is essentially a musically facilitated adventure in human encounter in which both client and therapist are human and possess human frailties and vulnerabilities. Kornfield (1993), a psychologist who has integrated eastern spiritual teachings into his psychotherapy practice, writes that "when we let ourselves become vulnerable, new things can be born in us" (p. 49). This approach and process is similar in supervision—supervisors need to allow themselves to be humble in their relationships with trainees. They do not have all the answers for their trainees in exactly the same way that therapists do not have all the answers for their clients. As supervisors, we are entering into a creative situation, and we cannot know or anticipate the extent of our abilities to help. We are approaching this situation with vulnerability, openness, and a willingness to learn from the trainee. In these important ways, the relationship between a trainee and supervisor is similar to the relationship between a client and therapist.

In Nordoff-Robbins Music Therapy, important practices for the trainee to implement include the ability to be spontaneous, to trust the unknown, and to move away from repertoire and improvise in sessions. The supervisor can encourage the trainee's integration of these concepts by approaching supervision in a spontaneous way. Rather than setting up an agenda, the supervisor can be poised in the creative now with the trainee. This way the supervisor and trainee are mutually responding to each other, as coactive partners who are growing together, as the client and therapist do. The development of creative freedom, expressive spontaneity, and intuition often blossoms in the trainee when the relationship with the supervisor becomes a trusting one through time and experience. When the trainee has a genuine sense that the supervisor is not a judge, but an invested mentor who genuinely wants the trainee to succeed, creativity within the trainee can flourish.

By being poised to respond to what happens *in* the moment, rather than focusing on and planning for the next moment, the supervisor responds to the trainee as a unique individual and does not use the same method or expect the same responses from all trainees. Rather than teaching, the supervisor listens with intention and focus to the trainee, sensing how to move him/her forward in his/her development. The trainee's skills and temperament will affect how supervision proceeds. The supervisor must be open to the trainee's individual mixture of talent and personality.

Barbara Hesser (personal communication, September 1991) has developed a method of supervision that distinguishes between what is a technical skill and learning issue for the trainee, and what is a personal/insight-oriented issue to work on in supervision. This distinction helps to guide the direction of the supervisory session. The amount of experience of the trainee may determine what aspects of the session may be focused on. Is the focus to be insight oriented, or to provide a practical account of what took place in the session? The supervisor needs to take into account the length of the supervisor-trainee relationship and the capacity of the trainee for insight and self-exploration. The focus of the supervision will change as the trainee gains experience.

The timing of these new discoveries for the trainee is important, in that insights can create self-consciousness, which can trigger inhibition. It is important in the supervisory relationship to set a tone of acceptance and help trainees to embrace previously unknown parts of themselves so that they do not come to fear the unknown. They must trust in their unconscious as that is where intuition begins and triggers musical action. Carl Rogers (1995) has pointed out that only after people accept themselves can they make changes and grow.

Supervision is a developmental process. Susan Feiner (see Chapter 7) has described various stages the trainee goes through during the training process. Moving from a dependent position, trainees learn to be independent, forming their own identity as therapists. There may be a stage when it is important for trainees to disagree, to develop their own way of thinking and working. At a certain point in trainees' development there can often be a need for challenge and it can be expected that crisis situations will develop that require resolution in ways that cannot be anticipated. At such a time, the supervisor may need to become more directly interventional in guiding trainees.

Finally, trainees must separate from their supervisor, feeling they can do the work on their own. They have taken in the ideas they believe and discarded the ones they feel are not right for them. This is an important and natural step for trainees. As part of the separation process, they begin to integrate and take away what they have learned from the experience. At the end of the supervisory process, the supervisor and the trainee are on a more equal level, relating more as peers.

The Supervision Process

A supervisor's role is multifaceted. He/she can function as a coach, enthusiastically supporting trainees' gains; a counselor, sorting out the trainees' feelings that may be impeding their development; a role model, acting in a way they would like the trainee to act; or a teacher, imparting practical techniques. Yet, supervision is different from all of these. At some point, coaching must lessen and the confidence the supervisor has tried to instill must be internalized in the trainee. Supervision is not therapy and personal issues may need to be explored further in that context. As the relationship changes, the trainee develops the ability to relate to the supervisor as more of a peer rather than as a role model. The process is different from teaching in that it is important to ask trainees what *they* think or feel about the session rather than to just tell them ideas or impart values.

Supervision can arouse feelings of vulnerability in the trainee. It is an experience that the supervisor must treat with sensitivity. The trainee has his or her own feelings and reactions to the process. It is important for the supervisor to try to understand the trainee's style, perspective, and approach, which helps the trainee to develop his/her own theoretical understanding of their work. The supervisor can build on a trainee's individual potential in the same way that the trainee does with his or her clients.

When listening to trainees, the focus is not on advice-giving but, rather, trying to understand what they need in order to take the next step as aspiring therapists. Is there a particular reason why trainees bring certain sessions to supervision? How can their developing beliefs in themselves be cultivated and nurtured? How can the supervisor help them to trust their intuition, their own creativity? As supervisors, we try to understand the essential themes presented through the trainee's choice of *what* to present in the session and *how* they describe it.

In body language, facial expressions, and responsive comments, the supervisor can convey an authentic belief in the trainee, and respect for his/her willingness to share and be vulnerable. It is crucial that the supervisor have patience and the faith that with time this trainee can be an effective music therapist. Ultimately, the supervisor must attempt to convey a genuine caring about the trainee as a person and the conviction that by allowing who they truly are to blossom they will develop as clinicians.

As we begin to listen to tapes of the trainee's work, we do not seek to find what is *wrong*, but rather, what is *right* in the work, striving to build on that strength or ability. Usually the objective of the supervisor's first comment is to point out and acknowledge a particularly effective intervention. This gesture creates the atmosphere for the ensuing supervision session and can determine the tone of the meeting. However, this kind of praise must be genuine as a trainee can sense when the supervisor is giving false praise. After the trainee has begun to internalize a positive self-image, the supervisor can build on that by asking what could be done further. Instead of pointing out what is lacking in a session, ask what can be added to something that is already present.

It is important for supervisors to become aware of their own personal motivations and attitudes and how they affect the supervisory process. When a supervisor is not conscious of these attitudes or prejudices, it can be detrimental to the supervisory relationship and process. Supervisors sometimes make the mistake of looking for problems in the trainee's work in order to feel that they (the supervisor) are smart, are experts, and have all the answers. To feel superior to the trainee might be a way for supervisors to feel good about themselves and their own clinical work. As a supervisor, be aware of the possibility, even if very subtle, of personal motivations to point out mistakes in the trainee's work in order to feel like a competent supervisor. This creates an unhealthy, competitive atmosphere in the supervisory relationship.

The trainee may possess personal characteristics and dynamics that make supervision more difficult for the supervisor. It is important for the supervisor to explore his/her personal feelings toward the trainee. Does the trainee possess certain qualities that remind the supervisor of him or herself and what kind of response do these similarities arouse in the supervisor? For example, the supervisor may find that he/she is unusually harsh when a trainee does not leave enough space for the client. With some personal reflection, they realize that this is a personal issue that they themselves had to work on in the past in order to correct this tendency. So when confronted with a trainee who is struggling with the same issue, the supervisor may have little patience and respond in a harsh or insensitive manner. Once the supervisor becomes aware of this dynamic, the supervision can progress in a healthier and more effective way.

Sometimes, events in the supervision session can reveal previously hidden dynamics that are simultaneously occurring in the therapy session. For example, the supervisor may notice that the trainee talks endlessly in the supervision session and the supervisor begins to feel there is not enough space for him/her to respond. It could be that the trainee's client might be experiencing the same feeling—that there is not enough space for him or her. In order to help trainees with this problem, it may be important to have them reflect on how they are feeling in the supervisory session. They may feel anxious, which causes them to talk without reflecting or pausing. That same feeling of anxiety may be present in trainees in both supervision and the therapy session. By addressing the issue in supervision and helping to alleviate the anxiety, the supervisor can help them feel less anxious and be more sensitive to leaving space for his/her client.

One of the most difficult challenges for supervisors is to refrain from immediately reacting when they see the trainee do something that needs to be changed. It is important to not give advice in an impulsive fashion, but to reflect and consider how to most effectively communicate so that the trainee is able hear what the supervisor is saying. Instead of telling the trainee *what* to do, the supervisor can suggest possibilities by asking, "What if you tried . . . " It is possible to encourage the trainee to reflect more deeply on the client by asking guiding questions such as "What prevents the client from joining in life in a way that is fulfilling? What limitations does the client experience due to the disability? How can you address this in music?" However, there *are* times in supervision when a supervisor needs to give suggestions or teach a concept. So, when a trainee does something that needs to be changed, it is helpful for the supervisor to view it as a positive opportunity to teach something new and develop alternative approaches.

It is important to learn the way the trainee thinks. Can the trainee explain *why* he/she is doing/playing what he/she is doing/playing? Sometimes trainees can focus on the details of a session and lose sight of the big picture. When this happens, the supervisor can ask broad questions aimed to help the trainee reflect on the larger meaning of therapy. For instance, a supervisor might ask, "Why work in a group? What are the benefits of working in a group situation for the clients? Why use music? What are the qualities of music that are important for this client? How can you make the musical interaction meaningful? How can you connect the outer activity of music-making to the inner experience of thought and feeling for the client?"

The supervisor can start the supervision by asking trainees what it is they want from supervision. It is helpful to ask them to articulate what they would like the supervisor to focus on and to identify aspects of the session that they are particularly interested in getting feedback on. The supervisor considers how they can raise their awareness. Another approach is to ask about trainees' relationships with the clients. Is there anyone they feel particularly close to or someone with whom they feel a special connection? The supervisor can learn about the trainee through their relationships with various clients. This also helps the trainee to reflect on the qualities of his/her client and what the client needs.

It is helpful to ask trainees what they thought was positive about their session. One task of the supervisor is to help trainees to think in a more accepting and less judgmental way about their work. Asking the trainee to think about it him or herself can help the trainee more fully integrate the positive aspects of the session. Through the trainee's own process and insight, his/her awareness of personal strength and ability becomes more solid and he/she can more fully internalize the gained knowledge. Therapists who embrace the object relations approach talk about the child who internalizes "the good mother" who provides positive feedback. This is a basic developmental task. As the mother provides consistent positive feedback, the child eventually internalizes this praise and positive self-image and becomes able to provide positive feedback to him or herself. The supervisor-trainee relationship has similar characteristics. Our aim is that the trainee is eventually able to trust in the unknown, in their abilities as a clinical improviser and internalize a professional, positive self-image as a music therapist.

Musical Supervision

In another publication (Turry, 1998), I wrote that despite new insights into a situation, a trainee may not be able to make the musical changes necessary for effective therapy to take place as he/she may not have the skills necessary to play in a new way. More important, they have not had the opportunity to experience a new way of playing. Therefore it is an important part of the supervisory process in the Nordoff-Robbins approach to bring musical experiences to the trainee—to actively play and teach musical ideas to move the therapy process forward for their clients.

Challenges that often arise for trainees when improvising clinically include a difficulty in developing flexibility in tempo, dynamics and articulation, awareness of the importance of silence, remembering musical ideas and repeating them to create form, and the ability to enhance, rather than merely imitate a client's music in order to lead to new developments. Because trainees are struggling to create form in their improvisations, their improvisations are often so complete in and of themselves that the client is not motivated to respond. Often a trainee is trying to activate a client without a clear purpose. He/she may follow every discrete action of the client and the music thus becomes scattered and unclear. All of these struggles may be due to an underlying sense of not knowing what to do in the session. As the trainee gains experience, development is made naturally. The music becomes more individualized, more uniquely suited to the client. Clients, in the way they respond to the trainee's music, are the best teachers of these skills. Listening closely with their supervisor and playing music together can help trainees develop a wider and more flexible musical response to their clients.

A general guide for the supervisor is the competencies needed for successful completion of the Nordoff Robbins training.

Certification in Nordoff-Robbins Music Therapy Competency Goals

Music
Able to:
- play and sing flexibly and responsively
- play in a range of idioms, modes, and styles and capture their essential characters
- create a wide variety of moods
- play with expressive, communicative musicianship—this includes:
  - tempo freedom
  - a variety of articulations/touches
  - varied and mobile dynamics
  - freedom in using the range of the keyboard; playing a variety of registers,
  - hands close together or separated
  - awareness of and sensitivity to tone, intervals, modes, scales, chord voicings, and piano sonorities
  - a variety of rhythms and meters
  - awareness of phrasing
  - harmonic variety—simplicity as well as complexity
  - playing with pulse and without pulse
  - utilizing consonance and dissonance
  - utilizing a wide range of accompaniment patterns
  - creating and shaping tensions and resolutions
  - playing with compositional awareness and intention

Clinical Applications of Music
Able to:
- actively listen: "Poised" to "listen musically"
- trust in music and in the "Creative Now"
- create a dependable space in which a client's potential may be realized
- maintain a focus on the "musical between"[4] through:
  - listening while playing
  - adjusting the music accordingly, in the level of its energy, particularly with regard to its tempo and dynamics
  - being responsive to the client musically
  - improvising with mutuality
  - forming the improvisation with the client aesthetically creating musical energy and momentum without abandoning the moment-to-moment focus on the client's process
  - using silences with clinical intention
  - improvising with clinical focus
  - evoking through music making the client's responses vital to the musical-clinical flow
  - developing a sense of what to play, how to play, when to play
  - supporting, enhancing, and leading with music
  - gaining a sense of how musically direct or indirect to be
  - producing music that calls for response
  - recognizing and utilizing important musical events
  - creating and potentiating "clinical themes"—musical themes that embody clinical goals—and working with them from session to session
  - identifying and working at the "developmental threshold" of the client
  - knowing when to offer an experience for the client rather than pressing for co-activity

Clinical Process
Be aware of:
- qualities and tendencies of clients in how they play/respond to the music
- personal musical qualities and tendencies of the therapist

Able to understand and articulate:
- the music therapeutic process
- therapeutic process/evolution over an extended period of time
- goals—development and implementation for each client
- important moments in the therapy
- client-therapist relationship dynamics

---

[4] Ansdell (1995) considers this to be the potentially therapeutic, shared auditory area; the interactive space created by music makers. It is where "a creative sharing of musical thought" occurs (p. 221), and where the relationship develops between client and therapist. The client "hears himself being heard and responds to his being responded to" (p. 69).

- the contribution/impact of self-exploration in the examination of the therapy process
- Nordoff-Robbins concepts, theory and philosophy and their contribution to each case
- scales of assessment and their application
- formal presentation of a case study

Learning to Listen

Including music in supervision, either by listening or playing, can be an immediate and effective way of working with a trainee. It provides for an experience that parallels that of therapist and client and provides an opportunity for the trainee to develop sensitivity for their client. In addition to talking about the process, it is important to have the experience of relating through music and feeling the freedom to improvise. In her theories of music therapy, Pavlicevic (1997) distinguishes actual experience from description; what we say about an experience is essentially different from the experience itself. Music-making in supervision encourages trainees to continue to develop their relationship to music and improvisation and to relate to another through shared music making. It helps the trainee internalize and integrate an experience of music as a potential agent of change. Rather than having an intellectual theory about musicing, they have an intrinsic knowing of it.

Musicing affects how we think and how we feel, and how we think and feel affects how we music. Musicing is not merely a physical skill. Elliot (1995) describes musicing as an act that is thoughtful, that entails acting with intention. In that sense musicing is a psychological phenomenon: by examining musical events we can also examine psychological events. One of the paramount tasks of the supervisor is to help the student to integrate psychological and musical understanding. Through careful listening to the session music in supervision, the supervisor guides the trainee in sharpening his/her listening skills in order to discern the more subtle aspects of musical interactions. These dynamics can subsequently be explored by playing in supervision. It can help trainees to discover how they feel about the client, and how these feelings are affecting the specific ways in which they are responding to the client musically. Focusing on the trainee's musical response to the client may give the trainee insight into the client. Is the client evoking a musical response from the trainee that reveals something of the client's inner makeup? While these kinds of psychological issues are appreciated, the primary focus is how these dynamics manifest in the music, and how music can be utilized to help the client and the relationship between client and trainee move forward.

The ambiguity inherent in the musical experience may initially arouse a natural sense of anxiety for the trainee and provoke him or her to utilize psychological models and jargon in an effort to understand the process and establish a sense of inner control and mastery. The trainee understandably may be trying out how to communicate "like a therapist" by adopting psychological theories. External psychological interpretations can alleviate a trainee's anxiety by providing a context for the therapy process and concretizing specific dynamics by labeling them. However, doing this can also provide a way to avoid the ambiguity and abstract nature of musical interaction. Labeling a musical event in psychological terms may be a way to avoid examining the more fundamental, albeit threatening, components of the music therapy situation: the music, the trainee, and the client. Trying to understand events primarily in psychological terms can devalue the importance of the trainee's playing or the client's music and distract from listening to the events in the session in more *musical* terms. By labeling a musical event in psychological terminology, the trainee may inadvertently be adapting a reductionist stance about musicing, and this is antithetical to how its potentials are seen in this approach.

The supervisor can be a role model for the trainee facing this challenge by letting the discoveries emerge from the music, ensuring that psychological understanding is based on genuine musical events. The art of supervision is to assess what the trainee needs—verbal insight that triggers a more complete understanding, or musical experience that creates new musical paths in the session. At times one experience leads to the other, at others they happen in concert. It may be important to point out to the trainee that it is not truly possible to know exactly what the experience means for a client. The supervisor helps the trainee to make attempts at understanding by describing musical events, by exploring music, and then coming to a hypothesis about what it may mean.

Session Listening

A unique aspect to the supervision in the Nordoff-Robbins approach is that the supervisor and trainee can listen closely to the session together, since every session is either audio- or videotaped. When trainees feel insecure about their music, they might talk over the recording that they are playing for the supervisor. The supervisor sets the tone that when the session is being played all auditory focus is on the session.

During the listening sessions, Sandra Brown (personal communication, April 1999) likes to listen quietly and let the tape of the session play for a while in order to get a feeling for the session. She pays attention to who controls what is heard in the supervisory session. Is the trainee holding the controls to the recorder? Does this help them to feel in control of the session and is that important for them? Is this a reflection of the therapy session itself, a parallel process—do they fear losing control in their session?

When she hears that something significant has happened in the music she asks her trainees why they played what they did. To further this examination, she asks trainees to describe the music. In the beginning of the student's training, this description can often be challenging so Brown sometimes asks what the music *isn't*. The aim of this strategy is to help the trainee begin to identify and describe the music that occurred. She asks the trainee to describe the client's music, and then explores with the trainee what they were feeling in the session as well as in that particular moment. She might ask, "Where was the connection made? Where was the connection lost? What might help?"

Brown feels that questions are preferable to statements or suggestions by the supervisor. Through questions, a supervisor encourages a trainee to explore different perspectives within a given event rather than trying to find the "correct answer." Instead of telling a trainee what to do, the supervisor can help the trainee to reach his/her own insights or generate alternative options to a situation. In addition, the questions asked can guide the trainee to consider areas that the supervisor feels are important and bring greater awareness of what is going on in the session. This process encourages trainees to begin to trust their own perceptions and develop their own identity as therapists.

Rachel Verney (personal communication, April 1999) also emphasizes the need to develop rigorous and precise music-listening skills. Her approach to Nordoff-Robbins supervision is designed to help trainees develop musical intention and begin to formulate their own model about music and music therapy. Like Brown, Verney also asks the trainee questions—"Who can this client be in music? How can you play to facilitate that?"—and closely explores the trainee's musical responses to the client in order to determine their intention in the moment. She affirms that every note is important and helps the trainee to examine their musical responses to the client in a given moment—the musical dynamic, an energy level, or a subtle response from the client. Through these explorations, the trainee can develop a sense of how direct, reflective, supportive, or challenging the music needs to be in order to optimize a client's developmental potential.

In supervision, trainees bring a tape of a session that has already been indexed (analyzed in close detail and documented). In the supervision session, Verney assigns three tasks for the trainee:

- To summarize or characterize the session—to give a musical portrait of the client
- To identify the significant events in the session, particularly in the music
- To articulate why those events were significant

Through the trainee's answers and descriptions, Verney is able to understand more fully their perceptions of the session, how closely they listen to the music, what they hear and don't hear, and how aware they are of the musical subtleties. This process gives the supervisor a sense of the areas of further focus for the trainee.

After the above questions are answered, the tape of the session is played. In this approach, the supervisor stops the tape when the session music does not match the trainee's description. Helping trainees to become aware of the disparity between their a priori description and what they hear while listening in supervision can trigger new directions for them to take in the sessions.

However, Verney assures the trainee that it is a common and normal occurrence to hear things differently during subsequent listening sessions. The context of where and when one listens to a session affects one's perceptions. For example, the trainee can be influenced by how the supervisor listens and begins to hear the music with more objectivity and clarity than previously. On the other hand, supervisory transference issues may interfere with a trainee's ability to objectively listen to the music in the presence of the supervisor, or authority. They may become overly critical of the music and base their listening on distortions they project onto the supervisor. Or the trainee may conclude that their initial description of what they heard in the session was based on how they felt in the session rather than on what actually occurred. This may or may not be true, and the supervisor needs to help sort this out for the trainee.

This careful kind of listening to moment to moment musical interactions can help the trainee develop more clarity. The trainee begins to listen more closely as the supervisor helps them to focus and notice subtle events with greater detail and understanding. This takes time, and is often exhausting for a trainee. Endurance and a willingness to expand his/her listening awareness are required at this juncture. While it is important for the supervisor to challenge and support, it is equally important to maintain a constant belief in the potential of the trainee. It must be understood that the trainee is in the therapy room and has perceptions that cannot be accounted for on the tape.

Live Music in Supervision

As trainees begin to work, because they are unsure of where to lead the client, their music may contain the necessary warmth, comfort, and nurturance, but lack vitality, direction, and drive. As they learn that music can be supportive and challenging, indirect yet leading, they begin to create music with a wider emotional and structural framework. Having the experience of this by playing music in supervision can help the trainee trust in music's qualities to both support and challenge, follow and lead.

It is important to meet each week in a room with a piano, even if there is no foreseen agenda to play. The trainee has been playing everywhere else and may feel vulnerable playing in supervision. They may need time to acclimate and develop trust in order to feel safe. Therefore, the supervisor might suggest playing without any agenda to "break the ice."

Playing music in the supervision session can be an effective way to help the trainee achieve new insights and expressive musical capacities. The experience can help the trainee to feel more empathy for the client, gain more awareness about the client's experience during the sessions, and develop new ways of musically responding to the client. To increase a trainee's musical awareness, Brown often asks the trainee to play the opposite of what they played in the session. At other times, she plays the opposite and asks the trainee to describe the experience.

Often, a struggle with musical technique is connected to an emotional block. One trainee struggled in using the full range of the piano in order to play more dynamically powerful music for a client's drumming. Despite her awareness of and agreement with its importance, she found herself unable to spread her hands at the piano to use both the lower and upper registers. Through supervision, she had the opportunity to explore this experience. As she sat at the piano and played she had an insight into her fear of spreading her arms apart. The supervisor accepted and acknowledged the trainee's fears as legitimate, though she did not explore the underlying reasons behind this fear as this was supervision and not therapy. After this supervisory session, the trainee was able to play with more freedom.

Jacqueline Birnbaum (personal communication, September 1999) worked with a trainee who had difficulty staying musically connected to her client when the musical interaction became more energetic. She recognized this dynamic in other areas of the trainee's professional development, and encouraged the trainee to reflect on the issue.

Only after seeing the connection between her musical tendencies and how they were similar to her personal dynamics in relating to others did her music in sessions begin to change. This change occurred when the trainee gained insight into the issue.

Musical role-playing is common in supervision and can be structured in several ways. One method is to have the trainee role-play the client and play music as the client did in the therapy session. The supervisor role-plays the trainee and plays in a musically similar way to the trainee. The trainee will often gain insight into the experience and new possibilities in creating music in the session simply by trying this exercise. As the supervisory partners continue to role-play in this configuration, the supervisor might make changes in the music to provide a different experience for the trainee. The supervisor may exaggerate a specific component of the music or play in a way that might lead to new potentials for the client. Through this modeling, the supervisor offers new possibilities for the trainee and through role-playing the trainee has the opportunity to experience the various options that the supervisor feels are possible.

Another configuration is for the trainee to maintain his/her role as the primary therapist and the supervisor to role-play the client. The supervisor may emphasize specific qualities of the client's music that will help the trainee gain insight into their client's playing. Or, through his or her playing, the supervisor may try to evoke potential qualities within the trainee that have previously remained dormant. For instance, when working with a trainee who plays in a perpetually timid and quiet style, the supervisor might introduce a gradual crescendo or accelerando while role-playing the client on the drum. Through the musical experience, the supervisor leads the trainee into new ways of being with the client, rather than simply talking about the issue or offering the trainee a suggestion to play more loudly.

In general, the supervisor seeks to identify areas in the trainee's playing that are fixed or rigid and tries to develop more fluid mobility in these areas. The more flexible the trainee is with his or her music, the more he or she will be able to be musically responsive and sensitive in sessions.

Another goal of using live music in supervision is to help trainees to increase awareness of their attitudes toward a client by addressing their feelings in the moment as they play in the session. In a previous publication (Turry, 1998), the use of music in a supervisory session was described in which the trainee became aware of feelings that were keeping her from connecting more fully to her client. Through the supervisor's use of musically expressive components that were not present in the trainee's music, i.e., rubato, rounded phrasing, a wider use of register, the trainee became aware of previously blocked emotions toward the client. This insight allowed the trainee to become more open and responsive to her client in subsequent sessions.

To begin this kind of exploration, the supervisor may ask the trainee to play their impression of the client or ask the trainee to play how the client makes them feel—their reaction to the client. All of these musicing situations can lead to new ideas for the trainee. Psychological considerations are made by the supervisor in order to unleash the musical power of the trainee. The goal is not necessarily for intellectual insight or emotional catharsis for the trainee, but for new musical paths that can ultimately lead to gains for the client.

One way for the trainee to understand a client's experience might be to adopt the body posture of the client, moving and playing as similarly as possible. It is helpful to ask the trainee to close their eyes to enhance the auditory experience of the moment. This helps the trainee to experience how the music may affect their client. Important questions might include, "What is the music telling me to do? How does the music influence me? What do I want the music to do? How do I feel now that it is over?"

During certification training, a supervisor may assign the trainee music to listen to and review a case from the Nordoff-Robbins archives that has relevance for their current work. During one course of supervision, Michele Ritholz (personal communication, May 1998) had made several suggestions to her trainee about the music in his sessions. Since this approach failed to help the trainee, Ritholz spontaneously brought in a piece of music that contained qualities she felt were important for the client and that were lacking in the trainee's music. The trainee played the piece in a metronomic fashion. Ritholz then played it with rubato. The trainee then played the piece again, and felt differently about the piece. He had a new awareness of the kind of musical experience that might benefit his client. The quality of the music—its character and expressive nature—touched a part of the trainee. Later in the course of therapy the trainee was indeed able to play in a more effective way in the sessions.

Developing Musical Resources

Trainees often have a difficult time breaking out of their familiar musical styles and habits. Rachel Verney (personal communication, April 1999) has developed an exercise in order to develop the ability to improvise in a variety of aesthetic forms. The first four measures of a composition are given to trainees. They sight-read it in order to get a sense of the style. In addition, they are asked to identify its qualities: the melodic sequence, articulation, harmonic style, etc. Verney then asks trainees to continue to play, improvising in the style of the piece. This exercise is done with a variety of composers and styles over time and helps to expand the trainee's musical resources. They begin to develop the ability to improvise in a wider variety of musical forms.

Church modes, and a wide variety of scales and idioms, are introduced to the trainee as a springboard for improvisation. I have created an exercise that helps the trainee become more fluent in a variety of tonal structures. Using one tone as a tonal home base, the trainee moves through various structures from Chinese pentatonic to Japanese pentatonic to middle eastern, etc., by making an adjustment of one tone—either adding one or altering one. This helps the trainee understand the qualities of each tonal structure, contrast them, and transition from one to the other.

It is important to help the trainee understand what makes each particular scale or mode unique. Particularly with modes, there is a tendency to play them without bringing out the tones that help to identify them. Pointing out the unique tones in comparison to a major or minor scale can be helpful. This kind of exercise can help the trainee to develop fluidity and direction in their improvisations.

It can be difficult for beginning trainees to play in a wide range of tempos and they often play with a fixed tempo and pulse. This can be due to a feeling of anxiety

and an urgency to create something, stemming from a need for some sense of security. Trainees also demonstrate limited dynamic flexibility and are concerned more with the specific notes they are playing rather than *how* they are playing. The supervisor can try to address this through musicing with the trainee, perhaps leading with a melodic instrument and playing with variety. If the issue continues to challenge the trainee, it may be an indication of an emotional block and insight into the issue may help the trainee to change his/her playing. One trainee was able to play with significantly wider tempo flexibility after realizing she was playing in a fast tempo in order to "run away from being judged."

The trainee may not be aware of all of the adjustments that can be made to their music. They may not have control over how they play. Verney has devised an exercise in which the trainee improvises a simple phrase and is directed to repeat it, attempting to play it exactly the same way each time. The trainee is then asked to change one aspect of the music—articulation shift from legato to staccato, for example—while keeping everything else exactly the same. This exercise encourages the differentiation of musical elements and a more focused awareness on the part of the trainee. In general it has been observed that trainees tend to play softer when getting slower and louder when playing faster. This kind of exercise can help to create mobility and differentiation.

Developing a sensitivity to tones, intervals, chord voicings, and inversions, and an awareness of the natural directions that melodies take and the creative leaps that are possible are important areas to develop in the trainee. Studying the natural directions that tones take, including intervallically to create melodies, and how chords connect to create progressions can help the student to hear in "chunks"—to hear the potential of an entire musical phrase from one musical action. This is an important skill in developing direction and form while improvising. Paul Nordoff's lectures on the power of tones as dynamic forces, recently published in *Healing Heritage* (1998) are a vital resource to base understandings in this area. The idea is not to memorize, but to be able to hear internally where tones can move—to think musically. By practicing progressions, inversions, various voicings, and scale structures, the fingers begin to acquire a kind of memory. Often the hand moves to a tonal direction before the mind is conscious of where it is going.

Hearing the music of the client as a question, or posing a question in their own music by creating an ascending melody or an unresolved harmony, can be a way of approaching the musical interaction that helps the trainee to extend and enhance the client's music. Rather than play musical ideas that are complete in and of themselves, the music is mutual and builds upon each person's contributions.

In order to help trainees remember their improvisations, it is suggested to begin with melodies that span a small range, and fit within the span of the hand. This simplifies and limits the choices that can be daunting to a beginner. The small movement helps the player to retain what was played.

Creating intentional silences in the service of the musical relationship can be a challenge for the trainee. In some ways this is more challenging for the trainee as they feel responsible for the session and feel compelled to *do* something. The supervisor can help the trainee to live in silence and appreciate the value in it. Silences are active and there are different types of silences. The quality of the silence will be influenced

by what precedes it. Through silence, the therapist can communicate that the client's music is most important.

From a technical perspective, the trainee's ability to generate a variety of musical moods can be expanded in a variety of ways. After an exploration in a mode, ask the trainee to play in an opposing way. Suggesting shapes (i.e., angular) or landscapes (i.e., a desert) can also be a source of inspiration for the trainee when creating a type of musical mood. Suzanne Nowikas (personal communication, September 1998) asks trainees to choose a card which has an emotion written on it. The other trainees do not know what the card says, and the trainee at the piano tries to play in a way that portrays the emotion. The group subsequently discusses the music and identifies what worked in the improvisation and what could have been different. This exercise helps trainees to develop musical ideas as well as to expand their appreciation of how different the experience can be for each person.

Kana Okazaki (personal communication, September 1999) asks trainees to try and create imagery while listening to improvisations. After sharing the image with the group, the trainees together try to identify the specific qualities in the music that helped to create the imagery. This exercise helps to expand awareness to the musical elements and their role in evoking imagery and an emotional response. Sharing these ideas builds trust among the trainees.

In cultures that cultivate musical improvisation such as India and Africa, improvisation is taught by the teacher playing phrases in turn with the trainee, bringing out the character of the music rather than looking at written notation. Reading notation is seen as a potential impediment to the progress toward creative expression and aesthetic musicality. Written notation is used in the training as a starting point rather than an end product. Intrinsic learning of the essential qualities of the music is what is valued.

Supervision as Part of the Overall Training Process

Because the Nordoff-Robbins certification is an advanced training in music therapy, the candidate already understands the basic concepts of being a therapist. They already have the ability to talk about therapy processes; now there needs to be a willingness to live in the musical moment without the distancing provided by theorizing. There are a variety of components to the training program to address these needs. Classes are given that contain new information and practical workshop experience about music. Lectures are offered that give the trainee an opportunity to closely analyze archival work that illustrates the effectiveness of clinical improvisation. Improvisation classes that work on developing resources, enhancing clinical awareness, and developing awareness of personal musical characteristics are offered. Methods of analysis—indexing,[5] the relationship scale,[6] and the tempo

---

[5] Indexing is the method of analyzing therapy sessions in the Nordoff-Robbins model. It consists of two major aspects: a brief written description of events in the sessions which are catalogued in real time, and a transcription of the significant musical events in the session for possible use in subsequent sessions. Each session is indexed before the client's next session.

dynamic schema[7]—are learned in a group setting. The study of archival material, practical musical technique, self-awareness, and sharing contemporary clinical experience are all important components of the classes in the training. Because the classes take place concurrently with clinical work, the experience of the trainee is integrated, and what is discussed in classes is related to what is happening in sessions. Trainees then follow up on these teachings in individual supervision.

Kaoru Robbins (personal communication, July 1999) has compiled excerpts to create an instructional video that she utilizes in her supervision sessions. After choosing themes that she feels are challenges in general for trainees, such as the importance of silence or the ability to create musical consistency when a client's playing is fragmented, she shows a variety of therapists to illustrate learning points. This also helps to emphasize that there are many ways of working and that each therapist will find his/her unique way of utilizing effective musical resources.

At the Nordoff-Robbins Center for Music Therapy, the supervisor has input into what kind of client the trainee will work with, choosing clients that will help the trainee as well as the client grow. It is also important to assess who will best work together as teams. Each trainee will work as both therapist and co-therapist, and work with a peer as well as a staff member. Each experience allows the trainee to try out a different role. Some trainees are ready to begin with peers; others need the guidance of a senior staff member. A potential hazard when a trainee works with a senior staff member is that he/she might abdicate authority in the session, accompanying the action with their music rather than taking leadership in their music. Though this is natural in the beginning of the work, it can become a problem if this reliance on the supervisor continues and is not addressed.

Trainees learn how to be co-therapists as well as primary therapists in the training. Co-therapists need to learn how interventional to be, how to facilitate the musical relationship between primary therapist and client, and how to work with an understanding of where the primary therapist wants to take the client with their music. The co-therapist is constantly assessing "How close do I need to be to the client? How much direction do they need? What will help the client to live in the music more deeply?" The experience of being a co-therapist contributes to trainees' developing abilities as primary therapists, as insights gained while being close to clients and listening to music can be internalized and utilized when they are playing in a session.

The supervision of teams is relevant in this approach. It is important for the supervisor to look at the team dynamics, and give feedback that does not split the team. At times it may be necessary to meet with the team together. Nowikas (1994) has studied the dynamics of working as a team, and this study is presented to the trainees during the training. This can help to bring awareness of team dynamics, and lead to a more supportive and understanding team. This in turn leads to more creative freedom on the part of the trainee.

During the training, trainees are placed together and share their work in a class designed to give trainees feedback on their work. In this situation, two trainees can work together by playing under the supervisor's guidance. While they role-play the

---

[6] In *Creative Music Therapy* (1977) Part Four: Evaluation (pp. 175–189).
[7] In *Creative Music Therapy* (1977) (pp. 158–159).

client-therapist situation, the supervisor can conduct the pianist, helping them to adjust their music in "Now time."[8]

Indexing is a way to develop perception of what is important in the sessions and to define subsequent directions in the therapy. In this way the trainee learns how to identify and work with the client's unique musical responses while asking important questions. Is establishing a basic beat important? What is the next musical development that this client may be able to make? Can the client beat the melodic rhythm? Can they hear the punctuation inherent in the phrase? Are they drawn into playing music in the tempo and on the beat? Are they responding to tempo or dynamic changes? What is the quality of the client's playing? Are they moving in a physically free way? Would a different instrument, mallet, or position of the instrument enhance the experience? Would a stick rather than a mallet help for rhythmic clarity? What would happen if the music were comprised of a clear melodic idea in octaves rather than a continuous harmonic support? Did the client respond to the change from legato to staccato? Why is it important for the client to be active? Is it more relevant to work on musical mood and match the emotional quality of the client? What motivated the client to play? What triggered the vocalizations? How would one describe the sound being created? Since these are all areas that every trainee needs to understand, they can be discussed as a group. The trainee can choose to share a particular session, handing out their index notes to the group. As part of the indexing process, manuscript paper is used to write down important musical ideas that are brought back in subsequent sessions. As team members, one trainee can write the index, describing the events and qualities of the client's responses and noting their significance, while the other can summarize more broadly what is happening in therapy specifically and the therapy process in general. As the session is played, the supervisor may suggest what can be included in the index and what can be excluded.

In these group learning situations, various group dynamics are activated and at times will need to be addressed in supervision. Issues of belonging, comparison, and competition can be aroused. It is important that the supervisor be alert to these dynamics and allow for the trainee to discuss them in supervision. There is a distinct group process that exists which includes stages of growth as a group as well as individual growth. It is important to remind trainees that each person learns at his/her own pace and that each therapist will play something differently; there is not one right musical intervention. Each trainee has the opportunity to learn from the others. As the trainees realize that there is room for all of them, that each one is unique and valued, they can begin to trust each other and share in an honest fashion. This sharing builds deeper levels of trust and can enhance the learning process for everyone involved. When anxiety is high, which is often the case in the beginning of the training, feelings of competition surface. By the end of the training, an understanding of how hard each person has worked in their own individual fashion allows for support, camaraderie, and recognition. It is important for supervisors at our Center to communicate to each other about the group process and discuss how to facilitate healthy development for

---

[8] From "Time as a multilevel phenomenon in music therapy" by Robbins and Forinash (1991). Now time, also called Creative time, is "the moment of intuition, of perception, of sudden insight or understanding. It takes place in the creative instant" (p. 53).

the group as a whole. The more trainees feel that their true selves can be revealed and integrated into their identity as therapists, the more successful their training will be.

Working with their supervisor can stimulate in trainees feelings of being judged, fears of making mistakes, and the need to be perfect. These are all natural reactions that need to be discussed in supervision. One way to counter the supervisor being experienced in this way is to have the trainee work with the supervisor as co-therapist. All the supervisors at the Center are active clinicians. The trainee is able to see the supervisor with the same challenges that they have. The supervisor, rather than holding on to an authority position, is in a vulnerable position similar to the trainee. After allowing trainees to have their initial phase of idealizing the supervisor and the situation, the supervisor can share his/her own struggles, difficulties, and uncertainties when it is appropriate. This encourages the trainee to assume a more genuine and realistic attitude toward the supervisor.

Nordoff-Robbins Training as a Spiritual Discipline

Although trainees usually complete their certification process within two years, the continued development of the competencies is a lifelong process. The training is a discipline that demands commitment and focus. And through supervising, supervisors continue to work on these competencies within themselves. The devotion to mastering a discipline such as Creative Music Therapy is, if looked at in the context of spiritual practices, a type of yoga that leads to raised consciousness and an expanded capacity to love, just as do meditation and prayer.

Traditionally, supervision has been based on developmental or psychological concepts. These are important in the cultivation of clinical awareness, creativity, and musicality. The act of being a music therapist brings artistic discipline and sensitivity to the forefront. As supervisors, we are helping trainees become *arts* therapists, to utilize their art to transform. Artists in the heat of creation produce a state of absorption similar to the mystic rapture described in both Hindu and Buddhist literature. Murphy (1993) states that spiritual practices depend upon a certain amount of trial and error, the love of adventure, and improvisation. Kornfield (1993) mentions the importance of "risking the unknown," in order to "gain a sense of life itself" (p. 52). These are all qualities that are cultivated in the training. Aigen (1998) suggests that Nordoff-Robbins training include some kind of personal process aimed to expand awareness, including personal therapy or a spiritual practice. It is my contention that the demands inherent in the Nordoff-Robbins training—the expansion of awareness, the application of the will, the focus on creativity, the challenge to live freely in the moment, and the development of a loving attitude—inevitably introduce the trainee to the elements inherent in a spiritual practice.

In trying to cultivate genuine human concern for the client within the trainee, the supervisor is really helping the trainee develop a certain quality of perception. This perception, that nourishes the attitude of the trainee, is one of love—not in the romantic sense of the word, but as an active thinking and doing. In his teachings,

Robbins often quotes Herbert Geuter,[9] stating that "love is not just a warm happy feeling, love is perception." This is a way of saying that how we perceive an event or a person is colored by our present underlying attitudes. Practicing love as perception means trying to understand the client, gain insight into the client's needs, and develop a sense of the client's potentials. The trainee may not experience love as the familiar feeling of fondness and protectiveness. In fact, the client can teach the trainee to give up the need to express love in that way. We are trying to teach unconditional love, a love that may be challenging. The trainee may experience this as unsettling, yet it sets the tone for new developments. It is a love that is not possessive or dependent. As aspiring professionals, trainees try not to invest in their clients in order to feel better about themselves, yet it may be from this that they need to start. As they gain clinical maturity, their capacity to love becomes more perceptive and more resourceful. In reality, they are following a path of spiritual learning.

Also to be considered is the unique nature of music itself. This approach recognizes the transpersonal powers of musicing. It considers the living dynamics of musical archetypes. Utilizing the aesthetic energies of musical creation is at the heart of the trainee's task. Musical peak experiences cannot be explained solely by psychoanalytic interpretations such as regression in the service of the ego. They are more than behavioral rewards or stimuli; they are holistic, integrative, often transcending issues of personality.

In this way then, the commitment to the supervisory process by the trainee and the supervisor can be recognized as a contemporary form of spiritual training. Robbins himself has called Creative Music Therapy a transpersonal discipline (1991). This challenges us to see the integration of applied spirituality into the professional practice as a natural consequence of inherently creative work. It requires that we ground our research in the study and comprehensive documentation of clinical phenomena and process.

Conclusion

Supervision in the Nordoff-Robbins training program is multifaceted. Its foundations lie in the philosophy inherent in the approach, which includes the cultivation of musical creativity and awareness, personal growth, and technical understanding. The supervisory relationship contains the same elements as the client-therapist relationship, as supervisor and trainee enter the *creative now* with a willingness to learn from each other and develop together. The supervisor has the responsibility to observe the process and discern what steps to take to enhance the trainee's development. Musical supervision is paramount in sharpening listening skills, increasing musical awareness and sensitivity, and deepening insight into the musical relationship. The supervisor helps to enhance the trainee's musical facility by

---

[9] Dr. Herbert Geuter was the director of research at Sunfield Children's homes, where Nordoff and Robbins began their teamwork, and was a guiding influence on their early development. Geuter was well versed in anthroposophy and was invested in updating and extending Rudolf Steiner's teaching, particularly in the areas of ego psychology and therapy practice and process.

developing their musical resources and helping them become more musically responsive. The trainee gains confidence in supporting and leading the client while improvising with mutuality. The training program builds cohesion and support among the trainees; this helps them to trust their development, gain a sense of belonging, and establish a professional identity. Ideally, the trainee takes steps that enhance their personal, social, and transpersonal development.

References

Aigen, K. (1998). *Paths of Development in Nordoff Robbins Music Therapy.* Gilsum, NH: Barcelona Publishers.

Ansdell, G. (1995). *Music for Life.* London: Jessica Kingsley Publishers.

Brown, S. (1997). Supervision in context: A balancing act. *British Journal of Music Therapy,* 11(1).

Elliot, D. (1995). *Music Matters.* New York: Oxford University Press.

Kornfield, J. (1993). *A Path with Heart.* New York: Bantam Books.

Murphy, M. (1993). *The Future of the Body; Explorations into the Further Evolution of Human Nature.* New York: The Putnam Publishing Group.

Nordoff, P. and Robbins, C. (1977). *Creative Music Therapy.* New York: John Day Company.

Nowikas, S. (1994). *A Qualitative Investigation of Teamwork in Nordoff Robbins Music Therapy,* Unpublished master's thesis. New York: New York University.

Pavlicevic. M. (1997). *Music Therapy in Context.* London: Jessica Kingsley Publishers.

Robbins, C. and Forinash, M. (1991). Time as a multilevel phenomenon in music therapy. *Music Therapy,* 10(1) 46–57.

Robbins, C. and Robbins, C. (1991). Self communications in Creative Music Therapy in K. Bruscia (ed.). *Case Studies in Music Therapy* Gilsum, NH: Barcelona Publishers.

Robbins, C., and Robbins, C. (eds.). (1998). *Healing Heritage: Paul Nordoff Exploring the Tonal Language of Music.* Gilsum NH: Barcelona Publishers.

Rogers, C. (1995). *On Becoming a Person.* New York: Houghton Mifflin Company.

Turry, A. (1998). Transference and countertransference in Nordoff Robbins Music Therapy. In K. Bruscia (ed.), *The Dynamics of Music Psychotherapy.* Gilsum, NH: Barcelona Publishers.

Acknowledgments

I would like to thank Clive Robbins for his everyday enthusiasm, countless moments of inspiration, and unceasing support; David Marcus for once again sharing his clarity and wisdom; Ken Aigen and Barbara Hesser for their overall counsel and guidance; Rachel Verney, Sandra Brown, and the staff of the Nordoff-Robbins Music Therapy

Centre in England for sharing their ideas; Michele Ritholz, Jacqueline Birnbaum and the staff of the Nordoff-Robbins Center for Music Therapy in New York for their feedback and Ann Turry for her patience.